Wicket in Action

Wicket in Action

MARTIJN DASHORST
EELCO HILLENIUS

MANNING

Greenwich
(74° w. long.)

For online information and ordering of this and other Manning books, please visit
www.manning.com. The publisher offers discounts on this book when ordered in quantity.
For more information, please contact:

Special Sales Department
Manning Publications Co.
Sound View Court 3B   Fax: (609) 877-8256
Greenwich, CT 06830   Email: orders@manning.com

Manning Publications Co.
Sound View Court 3B
Greenwich, CT 06830

Development Editor: Cynthia Kane
Copyeditor: Tiffany Taylor
Typesetter: Denis Dalinnik
Cover designer: Leslie Haimes

ISBN 1-932394-98-2
Printed in the United States of America
1 2 3 4 5 6 7 8 9 10 – MAL – 12 11 10 09 08

*In memory of Maurice Marrink—a friend of ours
and a friend of Wicket, right from the start*

brief contents

contents

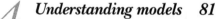

foreword

In the spring of 2004, I was working on a startup idea with Miko Matsumura, whom I met in 1997 when he was Sun's Chief Java Evangelist. This particular idea was called Voicetribe (a name I have since used for another startup) and involved VOIP and cell phone technologies (and might still one day make a good startup). Unfortunately, even in the earliest stages of prototyping this system, I found myself extremely frustrated by then-existing Java web-tier technologies. This brought my attention to a technically interesting infrastructure problem that nobody had yet solved to my full satisfaction: web frameworks.

Several 60-hour weeks later, the first version of Wicket was born. (In case you're wondering, *Wicket* was the first fun and unique-sounding short word that Miko also liked and that wasn't being used for a major software project. It also appears in some dictionaries as a cricket term for "a small framework at which the bowler aims the ball.") I'm happy to say that after more than four years and the input of many man-years of effort from the open source community, Wicket now meets most if not all of my criteria for a web framework.

Although Wicket has grown into a sophisticated piece of technology that has extended my original vision in every direction, I feel the community that has formed around Wicket is even more impressive. That community began when I made Wicket open source under the Apache license on Codehaus. A group of programmers from the Dutch consulting firm Topicus, led by Eelco Hillenius, Martijn Dashorst, and Johan Compagner, saw the potential in Wicket and were inspired to join Juergen Donnerstag and Chris Turner in forming the core team that would propel the project forward.

This core team has now been extended to include a dozen other top-notch engineers and scores of individual contributors, but there was an intense period in those first months in which the Wicket vision and the Wicket team gelled into something special. To this day, the core development team, the wicket-user mailing list, and the Wicket IRC channel (##wicket) are a reflection of the energy and enthusiasm of this original group. Today, Nabble.com shows wicket-user as one of the most actively trafficked mailing lists in the Java space (third only to Java.net and Netbeans) and the single most actively trafficked web-framework mailing list in the Java space (even more than Ruby on Rails, by a wide margin). This traffic is a reflection of countless hours of helpful support, brainstorming, negotiation, and open design work. I'm thankful to the global community that has invested so much in Wicket.

This growing Wicket community is now in the process of bursting out all over the web—and blog posts, download statistics, new projects, user groups, and articles in the press reflect that. Startups like Thoof, Joost, Sell@Market, GenieTown, and B-Side; midsized companies like Vegas.com, LeapFrog, TeachScape, Servoy, and Hippo; and large companies like IBM, Tom-Tom, Nikon, VeriSign, Amazon, and SAS are all joining the Wicket community, whether for large, scalable front-end websites or internal projects with a high degree of UI complexity.

Although Wicket was born once in my study and again in the open source community (and in particular in its migration to Apache), it's now being born one final time, because a framework without an authoritative book somehow isn't quite "real." I've been watching from the sidelines for over a year as Martijn and Eelco have slavishly devoted long nights and weekends to write the book you're now reading. *Wicket in Action* is the complete and authoritative guide to Wicket, written and reviewed by the core members of the Apache Wicket team. If there's anything you want to know about Wicket, you are sure to find it in this book, described completely and accurately—and with the sense of humor and play that the Dutch seem to bring to everything.

Enjoy!

JONATHAN LOCKE
Founder of Apache Wicket

preface

In 2004, we had a good idea what was wrong with the web frameworks we'd been using (Struts and Maverick) at Topicus for a number of our projects. They didn't scale for development, they made refactoring hard, and they inhibited reuse, to name a few of our complaints. Just about everyone in our company agreed that developing web applications with Java wasn't a lot of fun, particularly when it came to the web part; and those with experience in programming desktop applications wondered about the huge gap between the programming models of, say, Swing and Struts.

After a long search, one of our colleagues, Johan Compagner, stumbled across Wicket, which had been made publicly available by Jonathan Locke a few weeks earlier. Although it was still an alpha version and far from being ready to be used in our projects, everyone involved in the framework quest recognized its potential. We decided to start a prototype with it, and unless the prototype turned out to be hugely disappointing, this would be the framework for future projects.

Our personal involvement in Wicket came about suddenly when, a few weeks after our discovery, Jonathan announced that he planned to drop the project and accept a new position at Microsoft; he felt that continuing to work on Wicket might be a conflict of interest. We quickly got a group of people together—Johan Compagner, Juergen Donnerstag, Chris Turner, and the two of us—and took over the project. As it turned out, Jonathan's job was short lived due to other conflicting interests (regarding a startup he co-owns), and he was soon back on the Wicket project.

We spent our evenings over the next few months ramping up for the first Wicket version; during the day, we used Wicket for a first real project. The fact that Topicus allowed us to do that has made all the difference for Wicket; it wouldn't otherwise have become so good so quickly. We believe the investment has paid back tenfold.

Soon after the 1.0 version was released, we started to promote Wicket on Java community sites like The Server Side and JavaLobby. After all, the more users an open source project has, the more testing hours it gets, and the greater the chance that corner cases will be well-covered; and, in the long run, projects need enough people to continue when the interests or priorities of older members shift.

The feedback we got from those first promotions wasn't always positive. Most people liked the programming model, but some had objections: that we should have been supportive of the proposed standard web framework for Java (JSF), that a stateful programming model wouldn't scale, and—last but not least—that we were lacking documentation.

With a few notable exceptions, most open source projects are poorly documented. These projects are worked on by software engineers, not copy writers, and most of them (including us) prefer to write code instead of manuals, especially when doing it in their spare time.

Wicket has had pretty good API docs from the start, and the code is well organized, but the documentation was sparse at that time. And even though the community has contributed enormously to our wiki, and most of the questions you'll ever have about Wicket can be found in the mailing-list archives, Wicket still lacks a well-written online tutorial (although you can find several on the internet, focused on specific topics).

We launched several initiatives for writing a good tutorial. We tried to write one ourselves, but improving the code always felt more important. We tried to get writers to join us. Alas! Although we had a few candidates, their endeavors turned out to be short lived. We realized that the only way there would ever be authoritative documentation on Wicket would be for us to write a book. Yep, that's the book you're reading right now!

acknowledgments

First of all, we're immensely grateful to everyone who has helped make Wicket a success. Jonathan Locke for envisioning and architecting the framework, and for being our mentor in the first stages of the project. The initial team for getting Wicket 1.0 realized. Later members Gwyn Evans, Igor Vaynberg, Matej Knopp, Al Maw, Janne Hietamäki, Frank Bille Jensen, Ate Douma, Gerolf Seitz, Timo Rantalaiho, Jean-Baptiste Quenot, and Maurice Marrink, for putting in monstrous amounts of energy to make Wicket into the kick-ass framework it is today. Supportive decision-makers like Kees Mastenbroek, Harry Romkema, Leo Essing, and Henk Jan Knol of Topicus; Jan Blok of Servoy; and Evan Eustace of Teachscape for providing us with the opportunity to use Wicket in serious projects at an early stage. Wouter de Jong and Vincent van den Noort for designing the logo and look and feel of the website. Klaasjan Brand for being our toughest critic and making us think hard about our weaknesses compared to JSF. Geertjan Wielenga, R.J. Lorimer, Kent Tong, Karthik Gurumurthy, Nick Heudecker, Peter Thomas, Timothy M. O'Brien, Erik van Oosten, Justin Lee, Romain Guy, Tim Boudreau, Miko Matsumura, Daniel Spiewak, Nathan Hamblen, Jan Kriesten, Nino Saturnino Martinez Vazquez Wael, Cemal Bayramoglu, James Carman, and many others for writing blogs, articles, and books about Wicket, giving presentations on it, and promoting the framework in other ways. Niclas Hedhman, Bertrand Delacretaz, Sylvain Wallez, Upayavira, Arjé Cahn, Alex Karasulu, and Timothy Bennet, who supported us in our journey to become a top-level Apache project. Ari Zilka, Orion Letizi, and others from Terracotta for giving Wicket a viable scaling strategy. The folks from NetBeans for building in basic Wicket support in their IDE and using Wicket for examples and talks.

And then there are the hundreds of people who have contributed to the wiki, created Wicket support projects or spin-offs, helped out on the mailing list and the IRC channel, and submitted patches for bugs and feature requests. We believe Wicket is the poster child of a successful open source community, and Wicket would not be one of the leading web frameworks it is today without all those people participating in the project.

We wouldn't have been able to pull it off without the support of our home front. Diana, Kay, and Veronique, thank you so much for being supportive and pressing us to go on writing when we were on the brink of giving up.

We'd also like to thank those who were directly involved in the creation of this book. Publisher Marjan Bace of Manning Publications for his trust in us. Cynthia Kane, our editor, for the excellent suggestions and relentless criticism: we truly believe you made a huge impact on the quality of this book! Thanks also to Peter Thomas, our technical editor, and to Karen Tegtmeyer, Tiffany Taylor, and Elizabeth Martin of our production team at Manning.

Finally, we'd like to thank Jonathan Locke for reviewing our manuscript and writing the foreword as well as our peer reviewers for taking the time to read our manuscript in various stages of development and to provide invaluable feedback. You contributed greatly to making this the best book we could write: Jeff Cunningham, Evan Eustace, Bill Fly, Nathan Hamblen, Phil Hanna, Chris Johnston, Matthew Payne, George Peter, Michiel Schipper, Chris Turner, Erik van Oosten, and Chris Wilkes.

about this book

Wicket is a framework that makes building web applications easier and more fun. It boasts an object-oriented programming model that encourages you to write maintainable code and helps you scale your development effort with its facilities for reusable components and separation of concerns.

This book will show you how Wicket works and how you can use it effectively to write web applications, and it will point out the occasional gotcha. It covers a broad range of topics relevant to programmers who are in the business of building web applications.

Roadmap

The book is organized in four parts:

- *Part 1*—Getting started with Wicket
- *Part 2*—Ingredients for your Wicket applications
- *Part 3*—Going beyond Wicket basics
- *Part 4*—Preparing for the real world

If you're new to Wicket, you're probably best off following the sections (and chapters) in order.

Chapters 1 and 2 give you a high-level overview of what Wicket is and what kind of problems it tries to solve. If you're already experienced with Wicket, you should still read the first two chapters, because they explain the framework from our perspective. Chapter 3 gives you a quick example of how to develop an application with Wicket. After reading this chapter, you'll have a good idea of what developing with Wicket looks like, and although the chapter doesn't explain all the code in detail, you'll pick up a few things intuitively.

Part 2 covers you all you need to know to develop straightforward web applications with Wicket. Chapter 4 starts out with an in-depth explanation of models, which is something many people struggle with when they begin using Wicket. Chapters 5 and 6 talk about the components you'll use no matter what kind of application you're building: labels, links, repeaters, forms, and form components. Chapter 7 discusses effective strategies to build your pages from smaller parts, and how to apply a consistent layout.

Parts 3 and 4 go into specific areas that can be relevant when you develop non-trivial web applications, like localization and component-level security. This is where you'll learn how to take Wicket to the next level. Chapter 8 explains the advantages of organizing your Wicket-based projects around reusable components. Chapters 9–12 explore additional techniques that you can use to develop sophisticated Wicket applications: shared resources, Ajax, security, and localization. These techniques are explained by themselves and also in the context of reusable components, using a gradually evolving example. Chapters 13 and 14 talk about the practical matters of how to fit your Wicket code in with the rest of your architecture, how to test pages and components, how to map URLs for bookmarkability and search engines, and how to tweak and monitor your Wicket configuration for the best performance.

In addition to these chapters we also provided a free bonus chapter titled "Setting up a Wicket project." In this chapter you'll learn how a Wicket application is structured and how you can build your Wicket application using the open source build tools Ant or Maven. You can obtain this chapter from the publisher's website at http://manning.com/dashorst.

Who should read this book?

If you're considering using Wicket to write web applications, or you're already doing so but would like to have a better understanding of the framework and how to best utilize it, this is the book for you. This book can be a good read for tech-savvy managers and architects who are in the process of selecting a web framework, and for anyone who is interested in web application frameworks. Finally, we invite our moms to read along.

Code

Most of the source code in this book is part of a Google Code project you can find at http://code.google.com/p/wicketinaction/, and which is ASF 2.0 licensed.

We aimed for a smooth narrative by employing an evolving example throughout the chapters. We hope the examples, which talk about a cheese store, aren't too far fetched; we tried to make the book fun for you to read while addressing the technical nuances we had in mind.

The downloadable source code is structured in packages that reflect the chapters so that you can easily play with the code while reading the book. Trying things for yourself is a great way to learn technology.

The code in this book is pretty much printed as is, with the exception of the imports that are needed to compile the code. You can find those imports in the Google Code project, although in most cases asking your IDE to autocomplete them for you should work fine.

You can also download the source code from the publisher's website at www.manning.com/WicketinAction or www.manning.com/dashorst.

Author Online

Purchase of *Wicket in Action* includes free access to a private web forum run by Manning Publications where you can make comments about the book, ask technical questions, and receive help from the lead author and from other users. To access the forum and subscribe to it, point your web browser to www.manning.com/WicketinAction or www.manning.com/dashorst. This page provides information on how to get on the forum once you're registered, what kind of help is available, and the rules of conduct on the forum.

Manning's commitment to our readers is to provide a venue where a meaningful dialog between individual readers and between readers and the authors can take place. It's not a commitment to any specific amount of participation on the part of the authors, whose contribution to the AO remains voluntary (and unpaid). We suggest you try asking the authors some challenging questions lest their interest stray!

The Author Online forum and the archives of previous discussions will be accessible from the publisher's website as long as the book is in print.

About the authors

MARTIJN DASHORST is a software engineer with more than 10 years of experience in software development. He has been actively involved in the Wicket project since it was open-sourced and has presented Wicket as a speaker at numerous conferences, including JavaOne and JavaPolis.

EELCO HILLENIUS is an experienced software developer who has been part of Wicket's core team almost from the start. He works for Teachscape, where he is helping to build the next e-learning platform. A Dutch native, he currently lives in Seattle.

About the title

By combining introductions, overviews, and how-to examples, the *In Action* books are designed to help learning and remembering. According to research in cognitive science the things people remember are things they discover during self-motivated exploration.

Although no one at Manning is a cognitive scientist, we are convinced that for learning to become permanent it must pass through stages of exploration, play, and, interestingly, retelling of what is being learned. People understand and remember new things, which is to say they master them, only after actively exploring them. Humans learn in action. An essential part of an *In Action* book is that it's example-driven. It encourages the reader to try things out, to play with new code, and explore new ideas.

There is another, more mundane, reason for the title of this book: our readers are busy. They use books to do a job or solve a problem. They need books that allow them to jump in and jump out easily and learn just what they want just when they want it. They need books that aid them in action. The books in this series are designed for such readers.

About the cover illustration

The figure on the cover of *Wicket in Action* is taken from the 1805 edition of Sylvain Maréchal's four-volume compendium of regional dress customs. This book was first published in Paris in 1788, one year before the French Revolution. Each illustration is finely drawn and colored by hand.

The colorful variety of Maréchal's collection reminds us vividly of how culturally apart the world's towns and regions were just 200 years ago. Isolated from each other, people spoke different dialects and languages. In the streets or the countryside, they were easy to place—sometimes with an error of no more than a dozen miles–just by their dress.

Dress codes have changed everywhere with time and the diversity by region, so rich at the time, has faded away. It is now hard to tell apart the inhabitants of different continents, let alone different towns or regions. Perhaps we have traded cultural diversity for a more varied personal life–certainly for a more varied and fast-paced technological life.

At a time when it is hard to tell one computer book from another, Manning celebrates the inventiveness and initiative of the computer business with book covers based on the rich diversity of regional life of two centuries ago, brought back to life by Maréchal's pictures.

Part 1

Getting started with Wicket

This part of the book prepares you to build Wicket applications quickly. After reading part 1, you should be able to start playing with Wicket using the examples as a guide. Chapter 1 introduces the Wicket framework and explains the principles at Wicket's core. It ends with examples showcasing the basic usage of Wicket components. Wicket's fundamentals and how they fit together are discussed in chapter 2—how Wicket processes a request, and which classes play a central role in handling requests. In chapter 3, you'll build an online cheese store. In the process, you'll learn about Wicket's components, apply Ajax, and build your first custom component.

What is Wicket?

The title of this chapter poses a question that a billion people would be happy to answer—and would get wrong! Due to the popularity of the game of cricket throughout the world, most of those people would say that a wicket is part of the equipment used in the sport (see figure 1.1 to see what a wicket is in the cricket sense). Cricket is a bat-and-ball sport much like baseball, but more complicated to the untrained eye. The game is popular in the United Kingdom and South Asia; it's by far the most popular sport in several countries, including India and Pakistan.

Keen *Star Wars* fans would say that Wicket is a furry creature called an Ewok from the forest moon

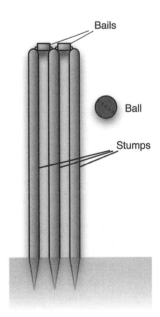

Figure 1.1 A cricket wicket: a set of three stumps topped by bails. This isn't the topic of this book.

3

Figure 1.2   Google search results for *wicket*. The number one result has nothing to do with cricket or with the furry and highly dangerous inhabitants of Endor.

Endor. True *Star Wars* fans would also say that Ewoks were invented for merchandising purposes and that the movie could do well without them, thank you very much. However, *Star Wars* fans would also be proved wrong by their favorite search engine (see figure 1.2, showing a search for *wicket* on Google).

What Google and other search engines list as their top result for the term *wicket* isn't related to 22 people in white suits running on a green field after a red ball, nor to a furry alien creature capable of slaying elite commandos of the Empire with sticks and stones. Instead, they list a website dedicated to a popular open source web-application framework for the Java platform.

1.1   How we got here

Don't get us wrong. Many people think cricket is a great sport, once you understand the rules. But in this book we'll stick to something easier to grasp and talk about—the software framework that appears as the first search result: Apache Wicket.

Before going into the details of what Wicket is, we'd like to share the story of how we got involved with it.

1.1.1   A developer's tale

It was one of those projects.

The analysts on our development team entered the meeting room in a cheerful mood. We'd been working for months on a web application, and the analysts had demoed a development version to clients the day before. The demo had gone well, and the clients were satisfied with our progress—to a degree.

Watching the application in action for the first time, the clients wanted a wizard instead of a single form there. An extra row of tabs in that place, and a filter function there, there, and *there*.

The developers weren't amused. "Why didn't you think about a wizard earlier?" "Do you have any idea how much work it will take to implement that extra row of tabs?" They were angry with the analysts for agreeing so easily to change the requirements, and the analysts were upset with the developers for making such a big deal of it.

The analysts didn't realize the technical implications of these change requests; and frankly, the requests didn't seem outrageous on the surface. Things, of course, aren't always as simple as they seem. To meet the new requirements, we would have to rewire and/or rewrite the actions and navigations for our Struts-like framework and come up with new hacks to get the hard parts done. Introducing an extra row of tabs would mean rewriting about a quarter of our templates, and our Java IDE (integrated development environment) wouldn't help much with that. Implementing the changes was going to take weeks and would generate a lot of frustration, not to mention bugs. Just as we'd experienced in previous web projects, we had arrived in maintenance hell— well before ever reaching version 1.0.

In order to have any hope of developing web applications in a more productive and maintainable fashion, we would need to do things differently. We spent the next year looking into almost every framework we came across. Some, like Echo, JavaServer Faces (JSF), and Tapestry, came close to what we wanted, but they never clicked with us. Then, one afternoon, Johan Compagner stormed into our office with the message that he had found the framework we'd been looking for; he pointed us to the Wicket website.

And that's how we found Wicket.

Let's first look at what issues Wicket tries to solve.

1.1.2 What problems does Wicket solve?

Wicket bridges the impedance mismatch between the stateless HTTP and stateful server-side programming in Java.

When you program in Java, you never have to think about how the Java Virtual Machine (JVM) manages object instances and member variables. In contrast, when you create websites on top of HTTP, you need to manage all of your user interface or session state manually.

Until we started using Wicket, we didn't know exactly what was wrong with the way we developed web applications. We followed what is commonly called the *Model 2* or *web MVC* approach, of which Apache Struts is probably the most famous example. With frameworks like Spring MVC, WebWork, and Stripes competing for the Struts crowd, this approach remains prevalent.

Model 2 frameworks map URLs to controller objects that decide what to do with the input and what to display to the user. Conceptually, if you don't use Model 2 and

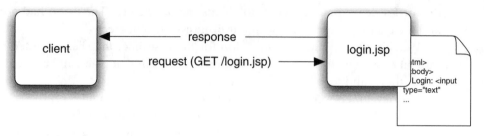

Figure 1.3   A request/response pair for a JSP-based application

instead use plain JavaServer Pages (JSP), a request/response pair looks like what you see in figure 1.3.

A client sends a request directly to a JSP, which then directly returns a response.

When you use a Model 2 framework, the request/response cycle looks roughly like figure 1.4.

Here, requests are caught by the framework, which dispatches them to the appropriate controllers (like LoginAction in figure 1.4). Controllers in turn decide which of the possible views should be shown to the client (typically, a view is nothing but a JSP).

The main feature of Model 2 frameworks is the decoupling of application flow from presentation. Other than that, Model 2 frameworks closely follow HTTP's request/response cycles. And these HTTP request/response cycles are crude. They stem from what the World Wide Web was originally designed for: serving HTML documents and other resources that can refer to each other using hyperlinks. When you

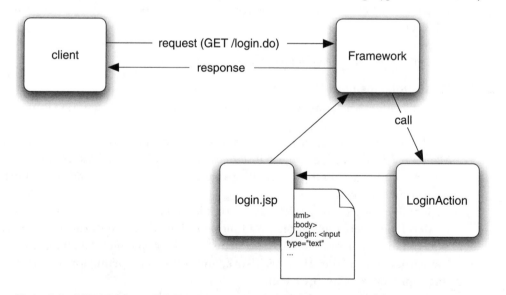

Figure 1.4   A Model 2 framework lets the controllers decide what views to render.

click a hyperlink, you request another document/resource. The state of what is being requested from the server is irrelevant.

As it turns out, what works well for documents doesn't work well for applications.

WEB APPLICATIONS

Many websites host *web applications*: full-fledged applications that differ from desktop applications only in that they run in a browser. For example, figure 1.5 shows the web application Eelco is currently working on.

If you look at this figure, you should easily be able to identify user interface (UI) elements like tabs, panels, and buttons. The screen is highly dynamic and interactive, and it hardly resembles a static document, as you can imagine.

If you used this application, you'd expect it to work like a desktop application. If you clicked the Components Available to Members tab, you'd expect the selections and navigation you'd performed so far (in the figure, choosing Manage Workspaces > Groups > Members) to stay the same and not be lost, as you can see in figure 1.6.

Those selected tabs are part of the application's *state*, which should be available over the course of multiple requests: it wouldn't be nice for the selected tabs to change when, for example, the user removes a comment.

A natural way of implementing such screens involves breaking them into panels with tabs, where each panel knows which one of its tabs is selected. Such an approach could look like this code fragment:

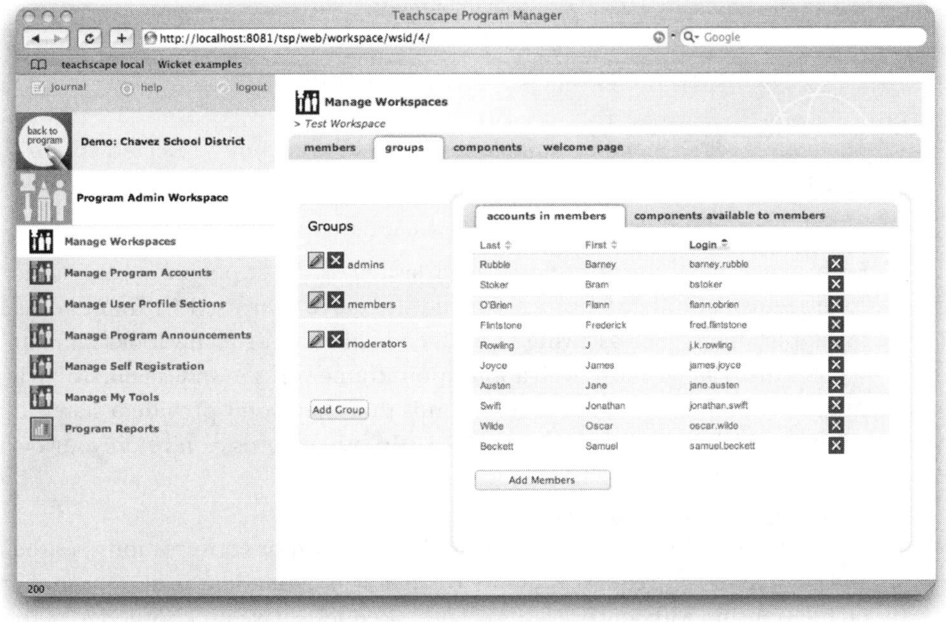

Figure 1.5 An example of a web application. This figure shows a screen from Teachscape, a learning-management application used by school districts throughout the United States.

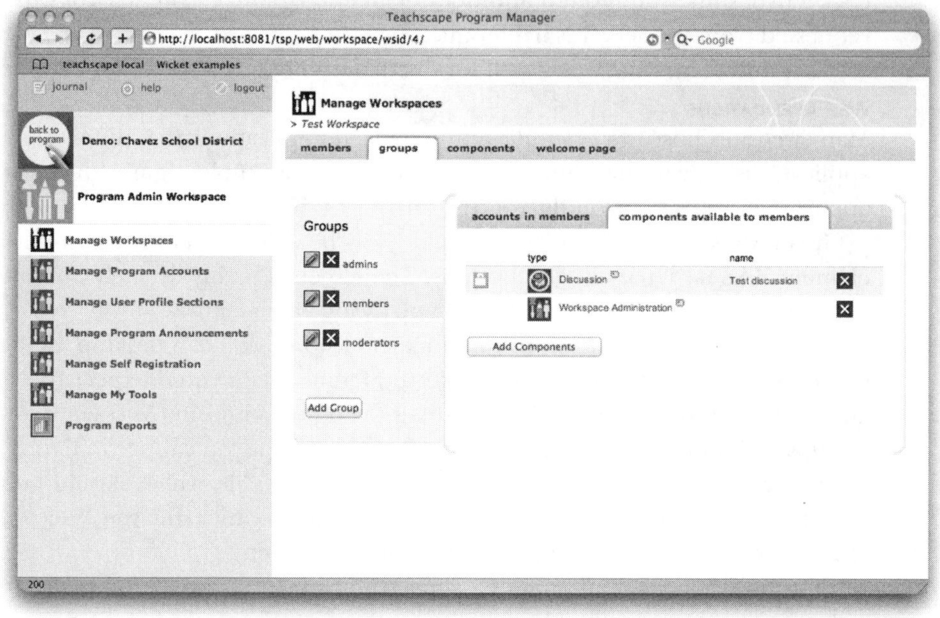

Figure 1.6   The web application after the Components Available to Members tab is clicked

```
public class GroupPanel extends Panel {
    private Tab selectedTab;
    ...
    public void select(Tab tab) { this.selectedTab = tab; }
}
```

The `selectedTab` member variable represents the currently selected tab for the panel. Switching to another tab could look like this:

```
groupPanel.select(new AccountsInGroupTab("tab"));
```

Each panel or tab is represented by a Java class. Most people would agree that this code seems natural and object-oriented. If you've ever used UI frameworks for desktop applications, such as Swing or SWT, code like this probably looks familiar.

Unfortunately, most web-application frameworks don't facilitate writing such straightforward code. The main reason is that they don't provide a stateful programming model on top of the stateless HTTP. In other words, you're on your own when it comes to managing state in your web application.

HTTP: THE STATELESS PROTOCOL

HTTP provides no support for extended interaction or conversations between a client and a server. Each request is always treated as independent in the sense that there is no relationship with any previous request. Requests have no knowledge of the application state on the server.

The obvious reason for designing the protocol like this is that it scales well. Because servers don't need to keep track of previous requests, any server can handle requests as long as it has the resources the client asks for. That means it's easy to use clusters of servers to handle these requests. Growing and shrinking such clusters is as easy as plugging in and unplugging machines, and distributing load over the cluster nodes (an activity called *load balancing*) can be performed based on how busy each node is.

But when it comes to web applications, we have to care about conversations and the state that gets accumulated when users interact with the application. Think about the tabs shown in the previous example, wizards, pageable lists, sortable tables, shopping carts, and so on.

One common approach to implementing conversational websites is to encode state in URLs.

ENCODING STATE WITHIN URLs

When you can't keep state on the server, you have to get it from the client. This is typically achieved by encoding that state within the URLs as request parameters. For example, a link to activate the Components Available to Members tab, where the link encodes the information of which other tabs are selected, could look like this:

```
'/tsp/web?lefttab=mngworkspaces&ctab=groups&ltab=members&rtab=comps'
```

This URL carries all the information needed to display the selected tabs by identifying which tabs are selected on the left, center, right, and so on. Encoding state in URLs follows the recommended pattern of web development as described, for instance, in Roy T. Fielding's seminal dissertation on Representational State Transfer (REST).[1] It makes sense from a scalability point of view; but when you're in the business of building web applications, encoding state in your URLs has some significant disadvantages, which we'll look at next.

For starters, encoding state in your URLs can be a security concern. Because you don't have complete control over the clients, you can't assume that all requests are genuine and nonmalicious. What if the application has an Authorization tab that should be available only for administrators? What is to stop users or programs from trying to guess the URL for that function? Encoding state in URLs makes your applications unsafe by default, and securing them has to be a deliberate, ongoing activity.

This approach of carrying all state in URLs limits the way you can modularize your software. Every link and every form on a page must know the state of everything else on the page in order for you to build URLs that carry the state. This means you can't move a panel to another page and expect it to work, and you can't break your pages into independent parts. You have fewer options to partition your work, which inhibits reuse and maintainability.

Finally, when you hold state within URLs, that state has to be encoded as strings and decoded from strings back to objects. Even if you're interested in, for instance, a member or workspace object, you must still create a string representation of the object. Doing so can require a lot of work and isn't always practical.

---

[1] See http://www.ics.uci.edu/~fielding/pubs/dissertation/rest_arch_style.htm.

Fortunately, it's widely acknowledged that transferring state via URLs isn't always the best way to go, which is why all mature web technologies support the concept of sessions.

SESSION SUPPORT

A *session* is a conversation that (typically) starts when a user first accesses a site and ends either explicitly (such as when the user clicks a Logout link) or through a time-out. Java's session support for web applications is implemented through the Servlet API's HttpSession objects. Servlet containers are responsible for keeping track of each user session and the corresponding session objects, and this is normally done using nothing but hash maps on the server.

Can you set the current tab selections in the session and be done with it? You could, but it's not an approach we recommend. Apart from minor caveats such as possible key collisions, the main problem with putting all your state in the session in an ad hoc fashion is that you can never predict exactly how a user will navigate through your website. Browsers support back and forward buttons, and users can go directly to URLs via bookmarks or the location bar. You don't know at what points you can clean up variables in your session, and that makes server-side memory usage hard to manage. Putting all your state in a shared hash map isn't exactly what can be considered elegant programming.

If you use Wicket, deciding how to pass state is a worry of the past. Wicket will manage your state transparently.

ENTER WICKET

Much like Object Relational Mapping (ORM) technologies such as Hibernate and TopLink try to address the impedance mismatch between relational databases and object-oriented (OO) Java programming, Wicket aims to solve the impedance mismatch between the stateless HTTP protocol and OO Java programming. This is an ambitious goal, and it's not the path of least resistance. Traditional approaches to building applications against a protocol designed for documents and other static resources rather than for applications is such a waste of development resources, and leads to such brittle and hard-to-maintain software, that we feel it needs fixing.

Wicket's solution to the impedance mismatch problem is to provide a programming model that hides the fact that you're working on a stateless protocol. Building a web application with Wicket for the most part feels like regular Java programming. In the next section, we'll look at Wicket's programming model.

1.2 *Wicket in a nutshell*

Wicket lets you develop web applications using regular OO Java programming. Because objects are stateful by default (remember: objects = state + behavior), one of Wicket's main features is *state management.* You want this to be transparent so you don't need to worry about managing state all the time. Wicket aims to provide a programming model that shields you from the underlying technology (HTTP) as far as possible so you can concentrate on solving business problems rather than writing plumbing code.

With Wicket, you program in just Java and just HTML using meaningful abstractions.

That sentence pretty much sums up the programming model. We can break it into three parts: *just Java, just HTML,* and *meaningful abstractions.* Let's look at these parts separately in the next few sections.

1.2.1 *Just Java*

Wicket lets you program your components and pages using regular Java constructs. You create components using the new keyword, create hierarchies by adding child components to parents, and use the extend keyword to inherit the functionality of other components.

Wicket isn't trying to offer a development experience that reduces or eliminates regular programming. On the contrary, it tries to leverage Java programming to the max. That enables you to take full advantage of the language's strengths and the numerous IDEs available for it. You can use OO constructs and rely on static typing, and you can use IDE facilities for things like refactoring, auto-complete, and code navigation.

The fact that you can decide how your components are created gives you an unmatched level of flexibility. For instance, you can code your pages and components in such a fashion that they require certain arguments to be passed in. Here's an example:

```java
public class EditPersonLink extends Link {

    private final Person person;

    public EditPersonLink(String id, Person person) {
        super(id);
        this.person = person;
    }

    public void onClick() {
        setResponsePage(new EditPersonPage(person));
    }
}
```

This code fragment defines a Wicket component that forces its users to create it with a Person instance passed in the constructor. As a writer of that component, you don't have to care about the context it's used in, because you know you'll have a Person object available when you need it.

Also notice that the onClick method, which will be called in a different request than when the link was constructed, uses the same Person object provided in the link's constructor. Wicket makes this kind of straightforward programming possible. You don't have to think about the fact that behind the scenes, state between requests is managed by Wicket. It just works.

Although Java is great for implementing the behavior of web applications, it isn't perfect for maintaining things like layout. In the next section, we'll look at how Wicket uses plain old HTML to maintain the presentation code.

1.2.2   *Just HTML*

When you're coding with Wicket, the presentation part of your web application is defined in HTML templates. Here we arrive at another thing that sets Wicket apart from most frameworks: it forces its users to use *clean templates*. Wicket enforces the requirement that the HTML templates you use contain only static presentation code (markup) and some placeholders where Wicket components are hooked in.

Other frameworks may have best practices documented that discourage the use of scripts or logic within templates. But Wicket doesn't just reduce the likelihood of logic creeping into the presentation templates—it eliminates the possibility altogether.

For instance, with Wicket you'll never code anything like the following (JSP) fragment:

```
<table>
  <tr>
    <c:forEach var="item" items="${sessionScope.list}">
      <td>
        <c:out value="item.name" />
      </td>
    </c:forEach>
  </tr>
</table>
```

Nor will you see code like the following Apache Velocity fragment:

```
<table>
  <tr>
    #foreach ($item in $sessionScope.list)
      <td>
        ${item.name}
      </td>
    #end
  </tr>
</table>
```

Nor will it look like the following JSF fragment:

```
<h:dataTable value="#{list}" var="item">
  <h:column>
    <h:outputText value="#{item.name}"/>
  </h:column>
</h:dataTable>
```

With Wicket, the code looks like this:

```
<table>
  <tr>
    <td wicket:id="list">
      <span wicket:id="name" />
    </td>
  </tr>
</table>
```

If you're used to one of the first three fragments, the way you code with Wicket may appear quite different at first. With JSPs, you have to make sure the context (page, request, and session attributes) is populated with the objects you need in your page. You can add loops, conditional parts, and so on to your JSP without ever going back to the Java code.

In contrast, with Wicket you have to know the structure of your page up front. In the previous markup example, a list view component would have to be added to the page with the identifier list; and for every row of the list view, you must have a child component with an identifier name.

The way you code JSPs looks easier, doesn't it? Why did Wicket choose that rigid separation between presentation and logic?

After using the JSP style of development (including WebMacro and Apache Velocity) for many commercial projects, we believe mixing logic and presentation in templates has the following problems:

- Scripting in templates can result in spaghetti code. The previous example looks fine, but often you want to do much more complex things in real-life web applications. The code can get incredibly verbose, and it can be hard to distinguish between pieces of logic and pieces of normal HTML; the whole template may become hard to read (and thus hard to maintain).

- If you code logic with scripts, the compiler won't help you with refactoring, stepping through and navigating the logic, and avoiding stupid things like syntax errors.

- It's harder to work with designers. If you work with separate web designers (like we do), they'll have a difficult time figuring out JSP-like templates. Rather than staying focused on their job—the presentation and look and feel of the application—they have to understand at least the basics of the scripting language that the templating engine supports, including tag libraries, magical objects (like Velocity Tools, if you use that), and so on. Designers often can't use their tools of choice, and there is a difference between the mockups they would normally deliver and templates containing logic.

These problems aren't always urgent, and, for some projects, mixing logic in templates may work fine. But we feel it's beneficial to the users of Wicket to make a clear choice and stick to it for the sake of consistency and simplicity. So, with Wicket, you use just Java for implementing the dynamic behavior and just HTML for specifying the layout.

To round out our initial exploration of Wicket's programming model, here is an explanation about how Wicket provides meaningful abstractions and encourages you to come up with your own.

1.2.3 The right abstractions

Wicket lets you write UIs that run in web browsers. As such, it has abstractions for all the widgets you can see in a typical web page, like links, drop-down lists, text fields, and buttons. The framework also provides abstractions that aren't directly visible but that makes sense in the context of web applications: applications, sessions, pages, validators, converters, and so on. Having these abstractions will help you find your way around Wicket smoothly and will encourage you to put together your application in a similar intuitive and elegant way.

Writing custom components is an excellent way to provide meaningful abstractions for your domain. `SearchProductPanel`, `UserSelector`, and `CustomerNameLabel` could be abstractions that work for your projects and such objects can have methods such as `setNumberOfRows` and `setSortOrder`, and factory methods like `newSearchBar`. Remember that one of the benefits of object orientation is that it lets you create abstractions from real-world objects and model them with data and behavior.

This concludes the first part of the chapter. You've learned that Wicket aims to bridge the gap between object-oriented programming and the fact that the web is built on a stateless protocol (HTTP). Wicket manages state transparently so you can utilize regular Java programming for implementing the logic in your pages and components. For the layout, you use regular HTML templates that are void of logic; they contain placeholders where the components hook in.

NOTE Wicket is specifically written for Java, which is an imperative programming language in which mutable state is a core concept. If it had been written for a functional programming language (where immutability is a core assumption), Wicket would have looked entirely different.

That was Wicket at a high level. In the second half of this chapter, we'll look at coding with Wicket.

1.3   *Have a quick bite of Wicket*

There's nothing like seeing code when you want to get an idea about a framework. We won't get into much detail in this chapter, because we'll have ample opportunity to do that later. If the code is unclear here, don't worry. We'll discuss everything in more depth in the rest of the book.

In the examples in this section, and throughout this book, you'll encounter Java features you may not be familiar with: for instance, you'll see a lot of *anonymous subclassing*. It's a way to quickly extend a class and provide it with your specific behavior. We'll use this idiom frequently, because it makes the examples more concise.

We also use one particular Java 5 annotation a lot: `@Override`. This annotation exists to help you and the Java compiler: it gives the compiler a signal that you intend to override that specific method. If there is no such overridable method in the superclass hierarchy, the compiler generates an error. This is much more preferable than having to figure out why your program doesn't call your method (depending on the amount of coffee you have available, this could take hours).

We need a starting point for showing off Wicket, and the obligatory Hello World! example seems like a good way to begin—how can there be a book on programming without it?

Hello, World!

Figure 1.7
The Hello World! example as
rendered in a browser window

1.3.1 Hello, uhm … World!

The first example introduces you to the foundations of every Wicket application: HTML markup and Java classes. In this example, we'll display the famous text "Hello, World!" in a browser and have the text delivered to us by Wicket. Figure 1.7 shows a browser window displaying the message.

In a Wicket application, each page consists of an HTML markup file and an associated Java class. Both files should reside in the same package folder (how you can customize this is explained in chapter 9):

```
src/wicket/in/action/chapter01/HelloWorld.java
src/wicket/in/action/chapter01/HelloWorld.html
```

Creating a `HelloWorld` page in static HTML would look like the following markup file:

```
<html>
<body>
<h1>[text goes here]</h1>
</body>
</html>
```
Dynamic part ←

If you look closely at the markup, the part that we want to make dynamic is enclosed between the open and closing h1 tags. But first things first. We need to create a class for the page: the `HelloWorld` class (in HelloWorld.java):

```
package wicket.in.action.chapter01;

import org.apache.wicket.markup.html.WebPage;

public class HelloWorld extends WebPage {
    public HelloWorld() {
    }
}
```

This is the most basic web page you can build using Wicket: only markup, with no components on the page. When you're building web applications, this is usually a good starting point.

> ### Imports and package names
> This example shows imports and package names. These typically aren't an interesting read in programming books, so we'll omit them in future examples. Use your IDE's auto-import features to get the desired import for your Wicket class.
>
> If you use the PDF version of this book and want to copy-paste the example code, you can use the "organize import" facilities of your IDE to fix the imports in one go.

> Make sure you pick the Wicket components, because an overlap exists between the component names available from Swing and AWT. For example, `java.awt.Label` wouldn't work in a Wicket page.

How should we proceed with making the text between the h1 tags change from within the Java program? To achieve this goal, we'll add a label component (`org.apache.wicket.markup.html.basic.Label`) to the page to display the dynamic text. This is done in the constructor of the `HelloWorld` page:

```
public class HelloWorld extends WebPage {
    public HelloWorld() {
        add(new Label("message", "Hello, World!"));
    }
}
```
               identifier   model

In the constructor, we create a new `Label` instance and give it two parameters: the component identifier and the text to display (the model data). The component identifier needs to be identical to the identifier in the markup file, in this case `message`. The text we provide as the model for the component will replace any text enclosed within the tags in the markup. To learn more about the `Label` component, see chapter 5.

When we add a child component to the Java class, we supply the component with an identifier. In the markup file, we need to identify the markup tag where we want to bind the component. In this case, we need to tell Wicket to use the h1 tag and have the contents replaced:

```
                                            gets replaced
<html>
<body>
    <h1 wicket:id="message">[text goes here]</h1>
</body>
</html>                    identifier
```

The component identifiers in the HTML and the Java file need to be identical (case sensitive). (The rules regarding component identifiers are explained in the next chapter.) Figure 1.8 shows how the two parts line up.

If we created a Wicket application and directed our browser to the server running the application, Wicket would render the following markup and send it to the web client:

```
<html>
<body>
<h1 wicket:id="message">Hello, World!</h1>
</body>
</html>
```

```
<html>
<body>
<h1 wicket:id="message">Hello, World!</h1>
</body>
</html>
```

component identified by wicket:id

```
public class HelloWorld extends WebPage {
    public HelloWorld() {
        add(new Label("message", "Hello, Wicket!"));
    }
}
```

Figure 1.8 Lining up the component in the markup file and Java class

This example provides the label with a static string, but we could retrieve the text from a database or a resource bundle, allowing for a localized greeting: "Hallo, Wereld!" "Bonjour, Monde!" or "Gutentag, Welt!" More information on localizing your applications is available in chapter 12.

Let's say goodbye to the Hello World! example and look at something more dynamic: links.

1.3.2 Having fun with links

One of the most basic forms of user input in web applications is the act of clicking a link. Most links take you to another page or another website. Some show the details page of an item in a list; others may even delete the record they belong to. This example uses a link to increment a counter and uses a label to display the number of clicks. Figure 1.9 shows the result in a browser window.

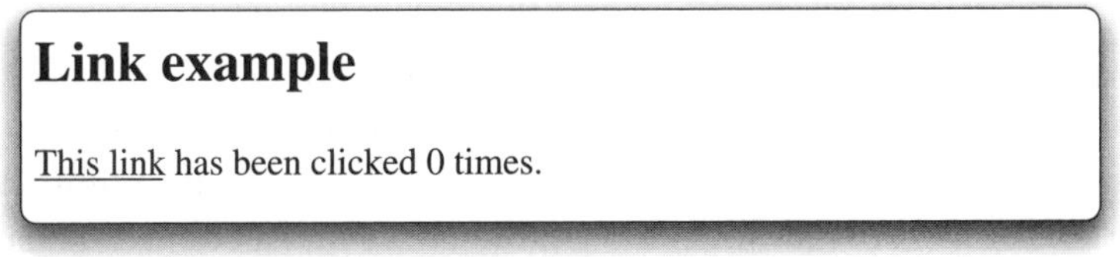

Link example

This link has been clicked 0 times.

Figure 1.9 The link example shows a link that increases the value of a counter with each click.

If we were to handcraft the markup for this page, it would look something like this:

```
<html>
<body>
<h1>Link example</h1>
<a href="#">This link</a> has been clicked 123 times.
</body>
</html>        Link component          Label component
```

As you can see, there are two places where we need to add dynamic behavior to this page: the link and the number. This markup can serve us well. Let's make this file a Wicket markup file by adding the component identifiers:

```html
<html>
<body>
<a href="#" wicket:id="link">This link</a> has been clicked
<span wicket:id="label">123</span> times.
</body>
</html>
```

Link component

Label component

In this markup file (LinkCounter.html), we add a Wicket identifier (`link`) to the link and surround the number with a span, using the Wicket identifier `label`. This enables us to replace the contents of the span with the actual value of the counter at runtime. Now that we have the markup prepared, we can focus on the Java class for this page.

CREATING THE LINKCOUNTER PAGE

We need a place to store our counter value, which is incremented every time the link is clicked; and we need a label to display the value of the counter. Let's see how this looks in the next example:

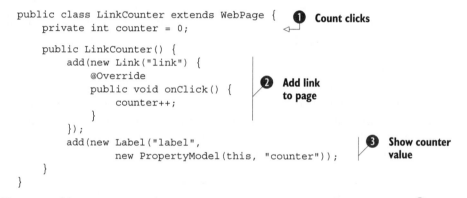

```java
public class LinkCounter extends WebPage {
    private int counter = 0;

    public LinkCounter() {
        add(new Link("link") {
            @Override
            public void onClick() {
                counter++;
            }
        });
        add(new Label("label",
                new PropertyModel(this, "counter")));
    }
}
```

❶ **Count clicks**

❷ **Add link to page**

❸ **Show counter value**

First, we add a property to the page so we can count the number of clicks ❶. Next, we add the `Link` component to the page ❷. We can't simply instantiate this particular `Link` component, because the `Link` class is abstract and requires us to implement the behavior for clicking the link in the method `onClick`. Using an anonymous subclass of the `Link` class, we provide the link with the desired behavior: we increase the value of the counter in the `onClick` method.

Finally, we add the label showing the value of the counter ❸. Instead of querying the value of the counter ourselves, converting it to a `String`, and setting the value on the label, we provide the label with a `PropertyModel`. We'll explain how property models work in more detail in chapter 4, where we discuss models. For now, it's sufficient to say that this enables the `Label` component to read the counter value (using the expression `"counter"`) from the page (the `this` parameter) every time the page is refreshed. If you run the `LinkCounter` and click the link, you should see the counter's value increase with each click.

Although this example might have been sufficient for a book written in 2004, no book on web applications today is complete without Ajax.

PUTTING AJAX INTO THE MIX

If you haven't heard of Ajax yet—and we don't mean the Dutch soccer club or the housecleaning agent—then it's best to think of it as the technology that lets websites such as Google Maps, Google Mail, and Microsoft Live provide a rich user experience. This user experience is typically achieved by updating only part of a page instead of reloading the whole document in the browser. In chapter 10, we'll discuss Ajax in much greater detail. For now, let's make the example link update only the label and not the whole page.

With this new Ajax technology, we can update only part of a page as opposed to having to reload the whole page on each request. To implement this Ajax behavior, we have to add an extra identifier to our markup. We also need to enhance the link so it knows how to answer these special Ajax requests.

First, let's look at the markup: when Wicket updates a component in the page using Ajax, it tries to find the tags of the target component in the browser's document object model (DOM). The component's HTML tags make up a DOM element. All DOM elements have a markup identifier (the `id` attribute of HTML tags), and it's used to query the DOM to find the specific element.

Note that the markup identifier (`id`) isn't the same as the Wicket identifier (`wicket:id`). Although they can have the same value (and often do), the Wicket identifier serves a different purpose and has different constraints for allowed values. You can read more about these subjects in chapters 2, 3, and 10. For now, just follow along. Remember the LinkCounter.html markup file? There is no need to make any extra changes to it; as you'll see, all the Ajax magic is driven through plain Java code. Here it is again, unmodified:

```
<html>
<body>
<a href="#" wicket:id="link">This link</a> has been clicked
<span wicket:id="label">123</span> times.
</body>
</html>
```

Let's now look at the Java side of the matter. The non-Ajax example used a normal link, answering to normal, non-Ajax requests. When the link is clicked, it updates the whole page. In the Ajax example, we'll ensure that this link behaves in both Web 1.0 and Web 2.0 surroundings by utilizing the `AjaxFallbackLink`.

`AjaxFallbackLink` is a Wicket component that works in browsers with and without JavaScript support. When JavaScript is available, the `AjaxFallbackLink` uses Ajax to update the specified components on the page. If JavaScript is unavailable, it uses an ordinary web request just like a normal link, updating the whole page.

This fallback behavior is handy if you have to comply with government regulations regarding accessibility (for example, section 508 of the Rehabilitation Act, U.S. federal law).

Accessibility (also known as section 508)

In 1973, the U.S. government instituted the Rehabilitation Act. Section 508 of this law requires federal agencies to make their electronic and information systems usable by people with disabilities in a way that is comparable for use by individuals who don't have disabilities. Since then, many companies that have external websites have also adopted this policy.

For example, the HTML standard provides several useful tools to improve usability for people who depend on screen readers. Each markup tag supports the `title` and `lang` attributes. The title can be read aloud by a screen reader. For instance, an image of a kitten could have the title "Photo of a kitten." Creating standards-compliant markup helps a lot in achieving compliance with section 508.

Although in recent years support for client-side technologies such as JavaScript has improved in screen readers, many government agencies disallow the use of JavaScript, limiting the possibilities to create rich internet applications. Wicket's fallback Ajax components provide the means to cater to users with and without JavaScript using a single code base.

Let's see how this looks in the next snippet:

```java
public class LinkCounter extends WebPage {
    private int counter;
    private Label label;        ◁─❶  Add reference

    public LinkCounter() {
        add(new AjaxFallbackLink("link") {    ◁─❷  Change class
            @Override
            public void onClick(AjaxRequestTarget target) {    ◁┐  New
                counter++;                                      ❸  parameter
                if(target != null) {
                    target.addComponent(label);
                }
            }
        });
        label = new Label("label", new PropertyModel(this, "counter"));
        label.setOutputMarkupId(true);    ◁┐  Generate id
        add(label);                        ❹  attribute
    }
}
```

In this class, we add a reference to the label in our page ❶ as a private variable, so we can reference it when we need to update the label in our Ajax request. We change the link to an `AjaxFallbackLink` ❷ and add a new parameter to the `onClick` implementation: an `AjaxRequestTarget` ❸. This target requires some explanation: it's used to identify the components that need to be updated in the Ajax request. It's specifically used for Ajax requests. You can add components and optionally some JavaScript to it, which will be executed on the client. In this case, we add the `Label` component to the target, which means Wicket will take care of updating it within the browser every time an Ajax request occurs.

Because the link is an `AjaxFallbackLink`, it also responds to non-Ajax requests. When a normal request comes in (that is, when JavaScript isn't available or has been disabled in the browser), the `AjaxRequestTarget` is `null`. We have to check for that condition when we try to update the `Label` component.

Finally, we have to tell Wicket to generate a markup identifier for the label ❹. To be able to update the markup DOM in the browser, the label needs to have a markup identifier. This is the `id` attribute of a HTML tag, as in this simple example:

```
<span id="foo"></span>
```

During Ajax processing, Wicket generates the new markup for the label and replaces only part of the HTML document, using the markup identifier (`id` attribute) to locate the specific markup in the page to replace.

As you can see, we don't have to create a single line of JavaScript. All it takes is adding a markup identifier to the label component and making the link Ajax aware. To learn more about creating rich internet applications, refer to chapter 10. If you want to learn more about links and linking between pages, please read chapter 5.

> **NOTE** With Wicket, you get the benefits of Ajax even when you're using just Java and just HTML. When you use other frameworks, you may need to do a lot more—for example, if you're using Spring MVC along with an Ajax JavaScript library such as Prototype or Dojo, you may have to use a mixture of HTML, JSP, JSP EL, tag libraries such as JSTL, some JavaScript, and then Java (MVC) code to achieve what you want. Obviously, the more layers and disparate technologies your stack contains, the more difficult it will be to debug and maintain your application.

In this example, we performed an action in response to a user clicking a link. Of course, this isn't the only way to interact with your users. Using a form and input fields is another way.

1.3.3 The Wicket echo application

Another fun example is a page with a simple form for collecting a line from a user, and a label that displays the last input submitted. Figure 1.10 shows a screenshot of a possible implementation.

Figure 1.10
This example echoes the text in the input field on the page.

If we just focus on the markup, it looks something like the following:

```html
<html>
<head><title>Echo Application</title></head>
<body>
    <h1>Echo example</h1>
    <form>
        <input type="text" />                            ❶ Input
        <input type="submit" value="Set text" />            form
    </form>
    <p>Fun Fun Fun</p>        ◁-❷ Message
</body>
</html>
```

The input for the echo application is submitted using a form ❶. The form contains a text field where we type in the message, and a submit button. The echoed message is shown below the form ❷. The following markup file shows the result of assigning Wicket identifiers to the components in the markup:

```html
<html>
<head><title>Echo Application</title></head>
<body>
    <h1>Echo example</h1>
    <form wicket:id="form">
        <input wicket:id="field" type="text" />
        <input wicket:id="button" type="submit" value="Set text" />
    </form>
    <p wicket:id="message">Fun Fun Fun</p>
</body>
</html>
```

We add Wicket component identifiers to all markup tags identified in the previous example: the form, the text field, the button, and the message. Now we have to create a corresponding Java class that echoes the message sent using the form in the message container. Look at the next class:

```java
public class EchoPage extends WebPage {
    private Label label;                        ❶ For later
    private TextField field;                       reference

    public EchoPage() {
        Form form = new Form("form");
        field = new TextField("field", new Model(""));    ❷ Add field
        form.add(field);                                     to form
        form.add(new Button("button") {
            @Override
            public void onSubmit() {
                String value = (String)field.getModelObject();    ❸ Add
                label.setModelObject(value);                         button
                field.setModelObject("");                            to form
            }
        };
        add(form);
        add(label = new Label("message", new Model("")));
    }
}
```

The EchoPage keeps references ❶ to two components: the label and the field. We'll use these references to modify the components' model values when the form is submitted.

We introduce three new components for this page: Form, TextField, and Button. The Form component ❷ is necessary for listening to submit events: it parses the incoming request and populates the fields that are part of the form. We'll discuss forms and how submitting them works in much greater detail in chapter 6.

The TextField ❸ is used to receive the user's input. In this case, we add a new model with an empty string to store the input. This sets the contents of the text field to be empty, so it's rendered as an empty field.

The Button component is used to submit the form. The button requires us to create a subclass and implement the onSubmit event. In the onSubmit handler, we retrieve the value of the field and set it on the label. Finally, we clear the contents of the text field so it's ready for new input when the form is shown to the user again.

This example shows how a component framework works. Using Wicket gives you just HTML and Java. The way we developed this page is similar to how many of Wicket's core contributors work in their day jobs: create markup, identify components, assign Wicket identifiers, and write Java code.

1.4 Summary

You've read in this chapter that Apache Wicket is a Java software framework that aims to bridge the gap between object-oriented programming and the fact that the web is built on HTTP, which is a stateless protocol. Wicket provides a stateful programming model based on just Java and just HTML. After sharing the story of how we found Wicket and introducing the motivations behind the programming model, we showed examples of what coding with Apache Wicket looks like.

We hope you've liked our story so far! The next chapter will provide a high-level view of the most important concepts of Wicket. Feel free to skip that chapter for now if you're more interested in getting straight to writing code.

The architecture of Wicket

Wicket is easy to use, once you grasp the core concepts, and you can be productive without needing to know the inner details of the framework. After you read this chapter, you'll know where to turn if you run into problems or when you need to customize the framework. Also, by lifting the veil on the magical Wicket box, we hope to make you eager to start using the framework.

First, we'll introduce the subject of many of the examples you'll encounter throughout this book. When I (Eelco) lived in Deventer, The Netherlands, I frequented a fantastic cheese store. Like many Dutch, I'm crazy about cheese, and this award-winning store sells an amazing selection. Now that I live in the United States, more specifically Seattle, Washington, (where I moved about the same time we started writing this book), I miss a good and affordable selection of Dutch cheeses. Seattle provides more than enough options to make up for this (like the city's impressive selection of sushi bars and Thai restaurants), but every once in a while I crave a piece of well-ripened Dutch farmer's cheese.

Yes, it's available but you pay sky-high prices and the selection isn't great. I tried my luck on the internet, but the Deventer store doesn't sell online; and although I came across some stores that cater to Dutch immigrants and sell Dutch cheese, their selection and pricing weren't to my liking.

Just when I was making peace with the idea of a drastic cut in cheese intake, I remembered I'm a programmer! I could build my own online store! If only I had a bit more time…(maybe it's something to pick up after I'm done writing this book). Until then, to keep the idea fresh, it serves as a good subject for a recurring example in this book.

Skip this chapter if you prefer to start coding immediately, rather than reading about the bigger picture. You can always return to the chapter.

We'll look at Wicket's architecture from several angles in this chapter. We'll begin by discussing how requests are processed—what objects Wicket uses and what steps it executes during processing. After that, we'll get to the meat of what Wicket is all about for end users: components, markup, models, and behaviors.

Let's start by examining request processing.

2.1 How Wicket handles requests

In this section, we'll look at how requests are processed. First we'll examine what objects play a role in request processing, then we'll discuss the steps Wicket executes during the handling of a request.

2.1.1 Request-handling objects

When you think about the concepts that play a role in an online cheese store—or any web application, for that matter—three immediately come to mind: application, session, and request. The cheese store, which is an *application*, handles *requests* from users, who want to do things like browsing through the catalog and placing orders. These requests in turn are part of a *session* (or *conversation*): a user browses a catalog, puts items in a shopping basket, and ends the conversation by placing the order for those items.

Figure 2.1 shows that Mary and John are using the cheese-store application. John did a search for *leerdammer*, browsed the *goat cheeses* section, and placed an order.

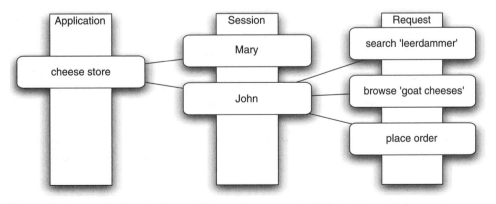

Figure 2.1 One application handles multiple sessions, each of which handles multiple requests over its lifetime.

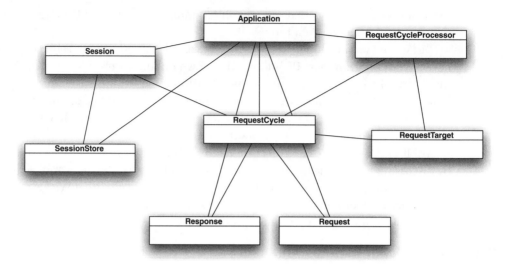

Figure 2.2   Important classes for handling requests. The `Application` class is responsible for the instantiation of most objects.

When you follow an object-oriented design approach, you typically translate concepts to classes. In Wicket, the `Application`, `Session`, and `Request` classes—or rather, their object instances—play a central role in request processing. Figure 2.2 shows these classes together with others that are directly related.

Let's take a closer look at each class.

APPLICATION

Conceptually, the `Application` object is the top-level container that bundles all components, markup and properties files, and configuration. It's typically named after the main function it performs, which in our example is a cheese store. (We call it `Cheesr-Application` in our examples, but we could have named it `CheeseStoreApplication` or something similar.)

Each web application has exactly one `Application` instance. Practically, the `Application` object is used for configuring how Wicket behaves in the service of your application, and it's the main entry point for plugging in customizations. The `Application` object provides a couple of factory methods to enable you to provide custom sessions and request cycles, and so on. Most of the application-wide parameters are grouped in settings objects—for instance, parameters that tell Wicket whether templates should be monitored for changes or whether to strip `wicket:id` attributes from the rendered HTML. If you use a framework like Spring to manage your service layer or data access objects (DAOs), you can set up integration with Wicket in the `Application` object.

SESSION

A session holds the state of one user during the time the user is active on the site. There is typically one session instance for one user. Sessions either are explicitly terminated (when a user logs off) or timed out when no activity has occurred for a certain time.

A nice feature of Wicket is the ability to use custom sessions—for instance, to keep track of the current user. Listing 2.1 shows a custom session that does this.

Listing 2.1 Custom session that holds a reference to a user

```
public class WiaSession extends WebSession {

  public static WiaSession get() {
    return (WiaSession) Session.get();
  }

  private User user;

  public WiaSession(Request request) {
    super(request);
    setLocale(Locale.ENGLISH);
  }

  public synchronized User getUser() {
    return user;
  }

  public synchronized boolean isAuthenticated() {
    return (user != null);
  }

  public synchronized void setUser(User user) {
    this.user = user;
    dirty();
  }
}
```

Unlike the key-value maps people typically employ when they use the Servlet API's HttpSession object, this code takes advantage of static typing. It's immediately clear what information can be stored in the session at any given time.

Note in this example, the methods are synchronized, because sessions aren't thread-safe (more on that later this chapter). setUser calls dirty so that any clustering is properly performed, and the static get method uses Java's covariance feature so users can get the current session instance without casting (you can do WiaSession s = WiaSession.get() instead of WiaSession s = (WiaSession)WiaSession.get()). When using Wicket, you typically never need to deal with the raw HttpServletRequest or Response objects; this holds true even when you're dealing with custom sessions.

SESSIONSTORE

The session store is responsible for where, when, and how long session data is kept. A typical implementation stores the current page in the HttpSession object (from the javax.servlet API) and stores older pages to a temporary store (by default a temporary directory) for Back button support. Each application has one store.

In addition to the user Session objects, the session store is also responsible for keeping track of the browsing history of clients in the application. Keeping track of this history supports calls to the current page and also supports the Back button.

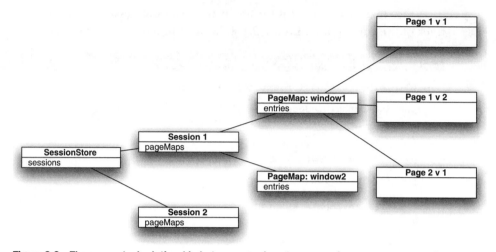

Figure 2.3   The conceptual relationship between session stores, sessions, page maps, and pages

As figure 2.3 shows, the request history is stored as pages in page maps, which in turn are linked to sessions.

Page instances are grouped in page maps. Typically, a single page map per session is sufficient to store the history of pages the user has accessed. But you may need multiple page maps to support the use of multiple browser windows (including popups and browser tabs) for the same logged-in user.

REQUEST

A Request object encapsulates the notion of a user request and contains things like the request's URL and the request parameters. A unique instance is used for every request.

RESPONSE

Responses encapsulate the write operations needed to generate answers for client requests, such as setting the content type and length, encoding, and writing to the output stream. A unique instance is used for every request.

REQUESTCYCLE

The request cycle is in charge of processing a request, for which it uses the Request and Response instances. Its primary responsibilities are delegating the appropriate steps in the processing to the RequestCycleProcessor and keeping a reference to the Request-Target that is to be executed. Each request is handled by a unique request cycle.

When you get to be a more advanced Wicket user, you'll probably use the request cycle a lot. It provides functionality for generating Wicket URLs, and it can expose some of the bare metal—like the HttpServletRequest—if you need that.

REQUESTCYCLEPROCESSOR

RequestCycleProcessor is a delegate class that implements the steps that make up the processing of a request. In particular, it implements how a request target is determined, how events are passed through the appropriate event handlers, and how the response is delegated. An instance is shared by all requests.

REQUESTTARGET

A request target encapsulates the kind of processing Wicket should execute. For instance, a request can be to a bookmarkable page (a public accessible page that is constructed when the request is executed), or the target can be a page that was previously rendered. It can be to a shared resource, or it may represent an AjaxRequest. The request target ultimately decides how a response is created. Multiple request targets may be created in a request; but in the end, only one is used to handle the response to the client.

Listing 2.2 shows a simple implementation of a request target.

Listing 2.2 Simple request target that redirects to the provided URL

```
public class RedirectRequestTarget implements IRequestTarget {

  private final String redirectUrl;

  public RedirectRequestTarget(String redirectUrl) {
    this.redirectUrl = redirectUrl;
  }

  public void detach(RequestCycle requestCycle) {
  }

  public void respond(RequestCycle requestCycle) {
    Response response = requestCycle.getResponse();
    response.reset();
    response.redirect(redirectUrl);
  }
}
```

When Wicket handles the request target, it calls the respond method, which in turn issues a redirect. Behind the scenes, the Wicket Response object delegates to the Servlet API to perform the redirect.

In this section, we looked at what objects play a role in request processing. You saw that the Application object holds settings and acts like an object factory. The session represents a user and helps you relate multiple requests. The request cycle is in charge of processing separate requests. In the next section, we'll look at the steps Wicket follows during processing.

2.1.2 *The processing steps involved in request handling*

When Wicket determines that it should handle a request, it delegates the processing to a request-cycle object. The processing is done in four consecutive steps, shown in figure 2.4.

Wicket's URL handling is flexible, and sometimes the same kind of request can be encoded in multiple ways. For instance, depending on your settings, the URL fragments foo=bar, foo/bar, and x773s=09is7 can mean the same thing. In the first step of the request handling, Wicket decodes (unpacks the values encoded in) the URL of the request so that no matter what the URL looks like, it's interpreted just one way. The decoding result is stored in a RequestParameters object.

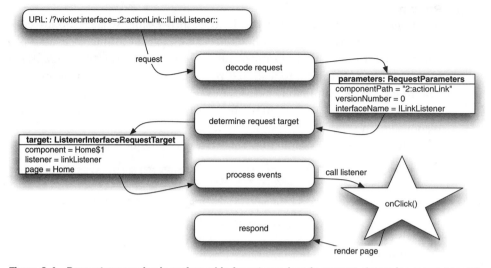

Figure 2.4   Request processing is performed in four steps: decode request, determine request target, process events, and respond.

If you look at the decoded values in the RequestParameters object in figure 2.4, you can guess what this request will do. The component path 2:actionLink refers to the component with path actionLink, found on the page that Wicket knows by identifier 2. Wicket assigns version numbers when structural changes occur to page instances (for instance, when you replace, hide, or unhide components). In this case, the page version derived after decoding the URL is 0, which means we're after the first (unchanged) instance of the page.

In the next step, Wicket determines the request target. Wicket can handle many different kinds of requests—for instance, to bookmarkable pages, shared resources, and Ajax requests. In figure 2.4, the request target is an instance of class Listener-InterfaceRequestTarget, and it encapsulates the call to a link (ILinkListener interface) on a previously rendered page. In this case, the previously rendered page is retrieved using identifier 2 and version 0, as you've already seen.

The third step, event processing, is optional. It's used for things like calling links or Ajax behaviors, but not for processing requests for bookmarkable pages or shared resources. During event processing, the request target may change. For example, this happens when you call setResponsePage in a form's onSubmit method, in which case a PageRequestTarget instance is used for the remainder of the request processing. Calling setResponsePage is how you can easily navigate from one page to another when handling events such as onClick or onSubmit.

The final step is responding to the client. As mentioned earlier, the processing of this step is delegated to the request target, because that target has the best knowledge of how the response should be created.

NOTE When runtime exceptions occur, a special variant of the response step is executed.

A page-request target takes care of rendering a page and sending it to the client, a resource-request target locates a resource (an image, for instance) and streams it to the client, and an Ajax request target renders individual components and generates an XML response that the client Ajax library understands.

2.1.3 *Thread-safety*

Much in Wicket centers around providing a natural programming model. Having to worry about thread-safety can be a pain, so Wicket tries to provide a single-threaded programming model wherever possible.

Pages and components are synchronized on the page map they're in. Every page is a member of only one page map; in effect pages can never be used by multiple threads concurrently.

You never have to worry about thread-safety as long as you keep two rules in mind:

- Never share component object instances, models, and behaviors between pages that are in several page maps. Although the chance that a user will trigger two pages in different page maps at the same time is slight, it's possible, especially with pages that take a while to render.
- Application objects, session objects, and session stores aren't thread-safe.

So far in this chapter, we've looked at Wicket from the perspective of request processing. It's good to understand what goes on in the background, but you're unlikely to deal with this often. Starting in the next section, we'll be more practical and look at classes you *will* use on a daily basis. Components, models, markup, and behaviors are all important concepts; take a break, drink some coffee, and get ready for components!

2.2 *Introducing Wicket components*

There are a million ways to build a house, but most people wouldn't consider building toilets, bathtubs, and glass windows from scratch. Why build a toilet yourself when you can buy one for less money than it would cost you to construct it, and when it's unlikely you'll produce a better one than you can get in a shop?

In the same fashion, most software engineers try to reuse software modules. "Make or buy" decisions encompass more than whether a module is available; generally, reusing software modules is cheaper and leads to more robust systems. Reusing software also means you don't have to code the same functionality over and over again.

Components, like objects, are reusable software modules. The distinction between components and objects is blurry, and as yet there is no general consensus on how to tell the two apart.

A workable explanation is that in addition to data, components encapsulate processes and can be thought of as end-user functionality; objects are primarily data-oriented and typically finer grained than components. Components are like prefab modules that merely require configuration and assembly to start doing their job; objects are building blocks that don't do much by themselves. Along this line of thought, examples of components are a weather forecast reporting service and a credit-card validation module, and examples of objects are a user and bank account.

One special class of components is specialized to function in UIs. Such components are often called *widgets;* we'll use the terms *components* and *widgets* interchangeably in this book. Technically, Wicket is concerned with markup manipulation, but because that markup is mostly used for rendering UIs, we can call Wicket a widget framework.

Here are a few key observations about Wicket's widgets/components:

- *They're self-contained and don't leak scope.* When you want to use a certain component, it's enough to place it in a container (like a `Page`); other components don't have to know about it.
- *They're reusable.* If you develop a cheese browser once, and you need it in another page or another application, you can use it there without having to rewrite half of it.
- *You build them using plain Java.* Java is an expressive language that is statically typed and has excellent tool support (for things like refactoring and debugging). You don't have to learn another domain-specific language (DSL) to work with Wicket.
- *You use them through plain Java programming.* If the cheese browser component has an option for setting the number of categories it displays on a page, you can find that option by using your IDE or by looking up the Javadoc. When you use that setting, and the API changes (for instance, if it's deprecated), the compiler and IDE will tell you.

When we zoom in on Wicket components, we can see that they consist of three parts that closely work together. We'll call this the *component triad.*

2.2.1 The component triad

Making up the component triad are the (Java) component, the model, and the markup. Each has a distinct responsibility. For plain vanilla web pages, the markup defines the static parts of the pages. The Java components fill in the dynamic parts of that markup, and models are used by components to get the data for those dynamic parts.

In figure 2.5, you can see the following:

- The markup (which formally is metadata that describes text, but in our example is HTML) that contains the bulk of what is displayed to a user. Wicket matches `wicket:id` attributes and attaches Java components to the tags in which these attributes are defined. Here, the `span` tag contains a `wicket:id` attribute.
- Java components `Page` and `Label`. *Pages* are special top-level components that we'll talk about a bit later, and *labels* are components that replace their bodies

with dynamic content. The label in figure 2.5 has message as its identifier, which matches with the wicket:id attribute of the span tag in the markup.

- The Label component, which uses a model that produces the string "Hello". The label replaces the body of the HTML tag it's attached to with the model value, so the browser receives Hello! as part of the page.

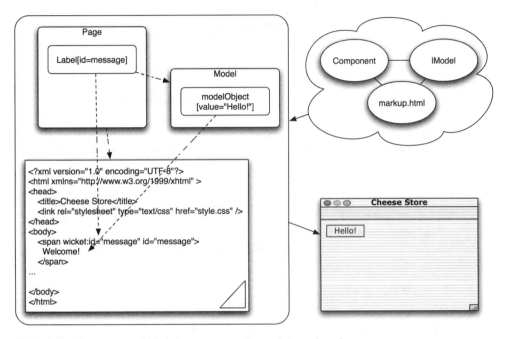

Figure 2.5   The component triad: Java components, models, and markup

As you saw in chapter 1, markup files in Wicket never contain real processing logic. You'll never find loops, conditionals, and the like in Wicket templates; they're only concerned with presentation. The UI logic, such as when to display a button and what to do when it's clicked, is encoded in the Java components. The Java components also function as state holders—for instance, to remember what page of a pageable list you're on.

Models are optional and are an indirection for how to get the data that drives the Java components. Models hide *what* data to get and *from where* to get it, and Java components hide *when* and *how* that data is displayed. We'll look at models later in this chapter.

Next, we'll look at Java components, markup, and models separately, starting with the Java components.

2.2.2   *Wicket's Java components*

Every Wicket Java component must extend from the Component base class somewhere down the line. The Component class encapsulates the minimal behavior and

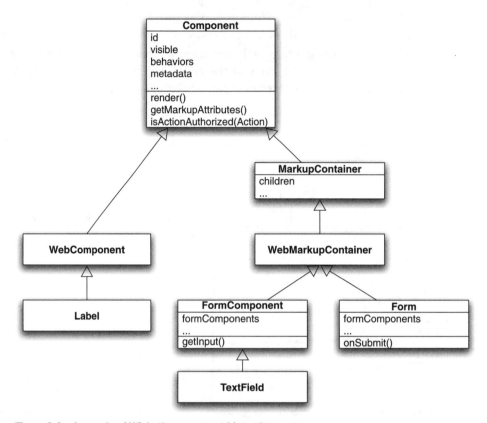

Figure 2.6   A sample of Wicket's component hierarchy

characteristics of Wicket widgets, such as how they're rendered, how models are managed, how authorization is enforced, and whether a component should be displayed for a given context. Figure 2.6 shows the hierarchy of a few commonly used components.

There are many kinds of components, ranging from generic to specific. Most non-abstract components are specialized for a certain task; for example, TextFields receive and display textual user input, and Labels replace their tag bodies.

We'll get into the details of many specific components later. At this point, we'll examine one special component: Page.

2.2.3   *Page: one component to rule them all*

Pages are special components that function as the root for your component trees. When you're using Ajax or a testing framework, individual components can be rendered independently; but as a rule, components are ultimately embedded in a tree structure with a Page as the root in order for users to see them.

Think of a Page as the equivalent of a browser window. Common names for the same concept in other widget frameworks are Window, Frame, and ViewRoot.

Figure 2.7 shows a component tree with a page that has a panel and a form as its direct children. The panel nests a label and a link; the form nests a text field and a button. A page and its nested components render recursively. When Wicket asks the page to render itself, the page asks its children to render, and they in turn ask any children to render.

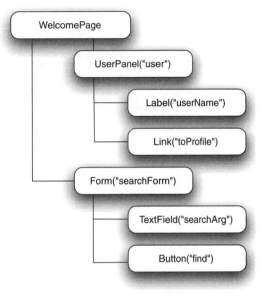

Component paths reflect the components' position in the component tree. Examples of component paths based on the tree in figure 2.7 are `user:userName` and `searchForm:find`, where the colon (`:`) functions as a separator between path elements.

The page isn't part of the path, because only one is rendered at any

Figure 2.7 A page with nested components

given time (you can't nest pages); that one is also always the root. That's why pages don't need to have a `wicket:id` like other components.

If you look again at the example from section 2.1.2, a request to the link in figure 2.7 could look like this

```
/?wicket:interface=:1:user:toProfile::ILinkListener::
```

where 1 is the page's identifier.

Pages have special responsibilities that are related to rendering and the way page maps are managed. They hold versioning information, and they have special abilities that make serializing the component trees as efficient as possible.

Pages also have associated markup files. A page's associated markup file functions as the starting point where that tree's markup is read. Markup is parsed into a tree structure in Wicket: you've probably guessed how Wicket matches the Java component tree and the associated markup tree, taking into account the hierarchy of parents/ children and the way Wicket identifiers are used to match siblings. In the next section, we'll look at how components and their associated markup work together.

2.2.4 *Components and markup*

In chapter 1, we introduced Wicket as a framework that bridges the impedance mismatch between the stateless nature of the web and Java code on the server-side. Wicket makes this possible by what we like to call component-oriented programmatic manipulation of markup. Components may do things like adding, removing, and changing HTML tag attributes, replacing the body of their associated tags, and in some cases generating more components and markup on the fly.

To illustrate how components and markup fit together, let's look at another Hello World! example. Listing 2.3 shows the Java part of the page.

Listing 2.3   Java code for the Hello web page (Hello.java)

```java
public class Hello extends WebPage {
  public Hello() {
    add(new Label("message", "Hello Earth"));
  }
}
```

Listing 2.4 shows the page's markup.

Listing 2.4   HTML code for the Hello web page (Hello.html)

```html
<html>
  <head>
    <title>
      Some example page
    </title>
  </head>
  <body>
    <span wicket:id="message">
      [message here]
    </span>
  </body>
</html>
```

The `Hello` class, as defined in Hello.java, is the Wicket `Page` component. The Hello.html file holds the markup for the `Hello` page. As you've seen before, Wicket automatically matches the Java page instance and the markup file if they have the same name (minus the extension) and reside in the same Java package. The `Hello` page instance has Hello.html as its associated markup.

The `Label` component doesn't have its own associated markup file. Only a few component classes—mainly pages, panels, and borders—work with associated markup files. Components that aren't associated with markup files are assigned a markup fragment of one of their parents. Wicket locates the markup fragment by matching the hierarchy of the Java component tree with the markup tree. Here, the label's associated markup is the `<span>` fragment that has the `wicket:id` attribute with the value `"message"`. That attribute is part of the markup as defined in Hello.html, which as we saw is the markup file associated with the Hello page—the label's direct parent.

In listing 2.5, a label is added to a link, which in turn is added to a page.

Listing 2.5   `HelloSun` Java code

```java
public class HelloSun extends WebPage {

    public HelloSun() {
        String url = "http://java.sun.com";
        ExternalLink link = new ExternalLink("link", url);
        add(link);
```

```
        link.add(new Label("label",
            "goto the java web site"));
    }
}
```

Listing 2.6 shows the markup for the page.

Listing 2.6 HelloSun HTML code

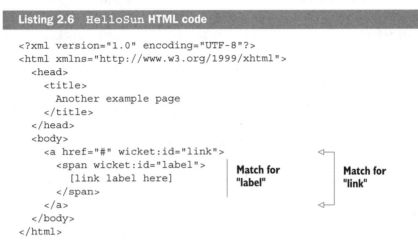

```
<?xml version="1.0" encoding="UTF-8"?>
<html xmlns="http://www.w3.org/1999/xhtml">
  <head>
    <title>
      Another example page
    </title>
  </head>
  <body>
    <a href="#" wicket:id="link">
      <span wicket:id="label">
        [link label here]
      </span>
    </a>
  </body>
</html>
```

The HelloSun page is linked to the HelloSun.html markup file, the external link encompasses the <a> tag and the tags nested in that, and the label is attached to the span tag. To illustrate further how the matching works, look at listing 2.7: the nesting doesn't match.

Listing 2.7 HelloSun HTML with incorrect nesting

```
<?xml version="1.0" encoding="UTF-8"?>
<html xmlns="http://www.w3.org/1999/xhtml">
  <head>
    <title>
      Another example page
    </title>
  </head>
  <body>
    <a href="#" wicket:id="link">
    </a>
    <span wicket:id="label">          Link isn't
      [link label here]               parent
    </span>
  </body>
</html>
```

Wicket would complain loudly about this page. The component tree doesn't match the wicket:id markings in the markup tree. In the Java code, the label is nested in the link; but in the markup, it isn't. If you want Wicket to do its job, the hierarchies have to match.

2.2.5 *Separation of presentation and logic: a good thing?*

Being required to synchronize the component tree with your markup has a disadvantage: you can't shuffle tags around and expect everything to work. Most other frameworks let you do this, which enables you to work quickly when you're in prototype mode. In such frameworks, you can get a lot done without writing any Java code, which may speed up your development even more.

But as is often the case, what is nice in the short term can be a pain in the long term. The fact that you *can* code logic in your templates means that more often than not, you'll code logic in your templates. Or if you don't, one of your colleagues will. Mixing logic code with presentation code should be avoided, because it poses these problems:

- UI logic is scattered over multiple locations, making it harder to determine how an application will behave at runtime.
- Any logic you put in your templates is plain text until it's executed. You don't have any static typing. And without static typing, simple typos can go undetected until you run the code. Changes can then be easily overlooked when you're refactoring.
- A problem that typically surfaces when projects become larger stems from the fact that frameworks that support scripting typically support only a limited subset of what you can do with a language like Java. Any DSL covers a subset of general-purpose languages. JSPs, for instance, have many different tag libraries with their own scope handling (meaning you can't easily mix them) and their own way of expressing things.

If you limit your templates to contain just the presentation code, which is something that Wicket enforces, it's a lot easier to keep your designs and prototypes synchronized. The designs are focused on presentation, and so are Wicket's templates. You can hire web designers to mock up the pages and panels, for which they can use their favorite HTML editors; you'll never have to explain to them how JSP tags or Velocity directives work. In the worst case, they may break the hierarchy, and you'll have to fix it. But they will never introduce bugs related to business logic (which can be hard to track) because they're completely isolated from all that.

Let's look at what we believe is good about Wicket's insistence on separating presentation from logic.

EASY-TO-FIND LOGIC

Wicket's strict separation of concerns means it's always straightforward to find the logic (in the Java code). And you have a good overview of what your pages and panels will look like when they're rendered—you can even preview them in your web browser or HTML editor.

CONVENTION OVER CONFIGURATION

The way Wicket matches component trees and markup trees is an example of convention over configuration. You don't need explicit configuration to get things accomplished; instead, you adhere to a few simple rules. The convention of the Java file having the same name as the associated markup file is a good example where Wicket uses the well-known Don't Repeat Yourself (DRY) principle.

COMPONENT NESTING

Component hierarchies are trees. It is easy to traverse the tree structure, navigating from parent to child and vice versa and collecting whatever information you wish—using, for example, the visitor pattern. You can even perform updates across a tree of components in this manner and reuse this kind of code across pages. Models can rely on the models of siblings, children, and parents of the components they're attached to, which can be a great help when you're creating composite components. And the order of processing (like rendering and model updating) is always predictable and natural.

PLAIN OLD JAVA OBJECTS

The acronym POJO, which stands for Plain Old Java Object, was for a while part of the battle cry in the struggle against inflexible, heavyweight, XML-centric programming models promoted by the industry as part of the first few releases of the Java Enterprise Edition (JEE). Hibernate, Spring, and a few other frameworks (and their loyal bands of passionate users) turned the tide, and now *lightweight* or *agile* approaches are increasingly being favored.

Lately, it's starting to fall out of fashion to talk about POJO programming. It no longer sounds fresh, and some argue that the fight is over and we should abandon the acronym.

But we believe the battle isn't over, and Wicket is at the front for the web tier. Even though JSF is probably an improvement over Struts (still regarded by many as the de facto standard) and other Model 2 frameworks, the web tier of JEE still has remarkably little to do with POJO. One of Wicket's main goals is providing a POJO programming model, and matching Java component and markup hierarchies is a key part of Wicket's strategy to achieve this.

In this chapter so far, you've seen that Wicket components consist of three parts: the Java class, the associated markup, and models. It's time to discuss this last part of the component triad.

2.2.6 *The component's data brokers: models*

Models provide components with an interface to data. What components do with that data is up to them. Labels use models to replace their tag bodies, list views to get the rows to render, text fields to render their `value` attribute and write user input to, and so forth.

The concept of models comes from the Model View Controller (MVC) pattern, first described by Steve Burbeck in the context of a user-interface framework of Smalltalk. Since then, it's been applied in many variations. Although the implementation of the pattern differs widely across those variations, the one thing they all have in common is that they talk about the MVC triad. There is much discussion about the pattern's degree of purity as it's applied, but for the purpose of this book we'll examine how MVC is implemented in Wicket. Figure 2.8 is a diagram that shows how the tree elements interact.

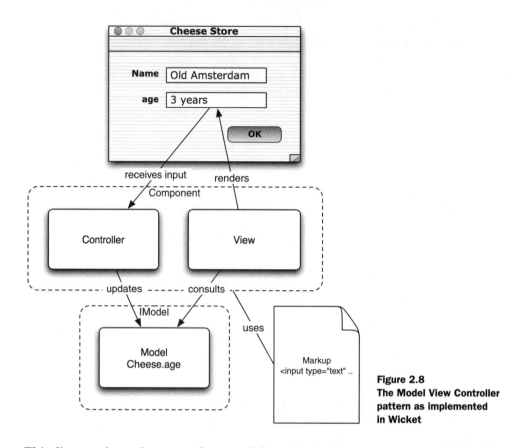

Figure 2.8
The Model View Controller
pattern as implemented
in Wicket

This diagram shows that every element of the MVC triad has its own responsibility. The elements represent different parts of a whole:

- The *model* represents the domain model and the interaction with it. A domain model includes objects like users, orders, cheeses, and spaceships. The domain model contains the abstractions of the outside world for which the system is built.
- The *view* renders UI elements. It takes care of how a component is displayed, and it queries the model for any dynamic parts.
- The *controller* receives user input. This can range from the value of a text field or a check-box selection to the user clicking a link or a button. The controller uses the user input to update the model, and it typically handles things like page navigation and sending events to other components.

In desktop application frameworks, the controller is typically responsible for sending messages to the view when it either detects model changes or receives input. But as in web applications, the view is rendered on a user request rather than when the component thinks it needs repainting; you don't need to let the controller notify the view. It's enough to update any model data that is used by the view so that the next time a component is rendered, the view will use the up-to-date data.

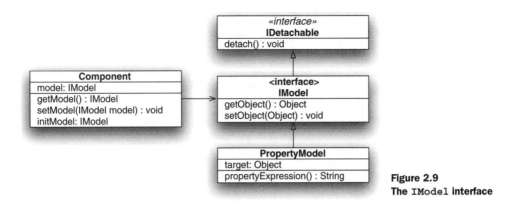

Figure 2.9
The `IModel` interface

Figure 2.8 shows a box labeled Component drawn around the controller and view parts. This illustrates that those two elements are combined in one class in Wicket. Much as in frameworks like Swing, components in Wicket are responsible for both their rendering and the handling of input.

The `IModel` model interface is fairly simple. It consists of two methods, `getObject` and `setObject`—or three, if you count the `detach` method that `IModel` inherits from the `IDetachable` interface. Figure 2.9 shows the `IModel` interface with some of its related hierarchy.

Components hold a reference to a model. It's possible to let a component use more than one model, but typically it uses one model or none (models are optional).

The term *model* can be confusing, because many people understand the model to be the data the component is interested in. But the concept of a model in Wicket is more like an indirection to the data than the data itself. We could have called models *model proxies* or *model locators*. Models provide only a means of locating the actual `Model` object. Figure 2.10 illustrates.

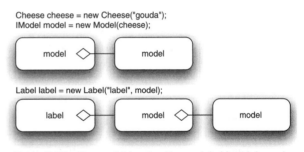

Figure 2.10   The model locates the model object (cheese).

Figure 2.11 shows the same concepts drawn another way.

In this example, the model holds a reference to the actual data you're interested in. How models locate their data is implementation specific. In this case, we used the

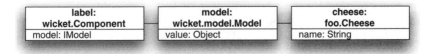

Figure 2.11   The model contains the logic for looking up the data you're interested in.

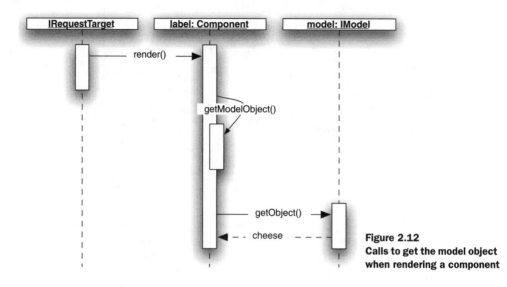

**Figure 2.12
Calls to get the model object
when rendering a component**

simplest model that ships with Wicket: `org.apache.wicket.model.Model`, which wraps the model value.

When the label from this example renders, it calls `getModelObject` on itself, which calls `getObject` on the model. This is illustrated in figure 2.12.

This diagram is simplified—in reality, an extra processing step occurs for type conversion when components render. But basically, this is what happens.

We haven't been entirely fair to one class in Wicket when we've talked about the component triad. There is a conceptually simple utility for extending components that is so powerful, it deserves a place in this chapter: behaviors.

2.2.7 *Extending components with behaviors*

The intuitive way to customize components—beyond instantiating and configuring them, if that satisfies your use case—is to extend them using inheritance. This isn't always the most flexible approach, though—certainly not when you take into account that Java is limited to single inheritance. *Behaviors* are a way around this inflexibility. They provide the means to extend components using composition, which is more flexible than extending them using inheritance.

Typically, components are meant for one purpose. Labels render text. Text fields handle text input. Repeaters repeat elements, and so forth. But in many cases, you want to use a certain component but add functionality that isn't related to its core function. For instance, when you provide a link that lets the user remove an item from a list, you may want to pop up a confirmation dialog. You could write a specialized link for this purpose, but by using behaviors you can add such a dialog without writing a special link class. As another example, wouldn't it be nice to attach a date picker to a text field without having to create a special class?

Behaviors must be attached to components to do something useful, and each component can have several behaviors attached. Some components use behaviors for their internal workings, but you can also add behaviors to components from the outside by calling Component's add(IBehavior) method.

Figure 2.13 shows the behavior interface.

All the methods in figure 2.13 except isTemporary share a common feature: they have a Component argument. This way, behaviors can be *stateless* (they don't have to keep the reference to the components they're attached to), and they can be shared among components.

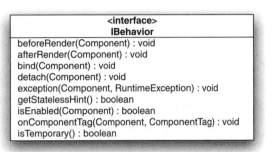

Figure 2.13 The base interface for behaviors

Behaviors are mainly used for—but aren't limited to—these two cases:

- Modifying attributes of HTML tags
- Responding to events or calls to the components they're bound to (their host components)

For the first case, two classes are available: AttributeModifier and SimpleAttribute-Modifier. An example is the quickest way to show what they do. Take this code

```
TextField myText = new TextField("myText", new Model("foo"));
myText.add(new SimpleAttributeModifier("class", "error"));
```

with the following markup fragment:

```
<input type="text" wicket:id="myText" />
```

This is rendered as:

```
<input type="text" wicket:id="myText" name="myText"
    class="error" value="foo" />
```

The class attribute is added to the tag the component is bound to. The text field first handles its own tag, where it sets the name and value attributes to the appropriate values. Then, it iterates through the bound behaviors and executes them. The relevant part of SimpleAttributeModifier is as follows:

```
@Override
public void onComponentTag(Component component, ComponentTag tag) {
    if (isEnabled(component)) {
        tag.getAttributes().put(attribute, value);
    }
}
```

This sets the attribute to the passed-in value when the bound component calls onComponentTag. As you'd expect, attribute modifiers are commonly used to dynamically change the look and feel of rendered components by tweaking the HTML `style` attribute or CSS class.

Behaviors that want to receive calls through their host components must implement an extra interface (`IBehaviorListener`). Behaviors that do this can receive the same kind of call that, for instance, links can receive, but they're always passed through their host components. Typically, such behaviors modify certain attributes, such as `onclick`, to trigger the call to themselves. Behavior listeners are mainly used to implement Ajax behaviors, which will be explained in chapter 10.

You'll have plenty of opportunities to see behaviors in action throughout this book.

2.3 Summary

This chapter provided an architectural overview of Wicket. We started by looking at the classes that play a role in request processing and the steps Wicket executes when it handles a request. You saw that the application object holds settings and function as object factories, that sessions represent users and can connect multiple requests, and that request cycles handle separate requests.

After that, we discussed components. The component triad consists of the Java component, associated markup, and the (optional) model. Components are nested in tree structures, and special-purpose components called `Pages` serve as root containers. Wicket uses convention over configuration to match component trees with markup trees. Models are used as an indirection to locate the data for components.

You also learned that behaviors form a special class that helps you configure and extend components using composition rather than inheritance. The two common forms of behaviors are attribute modifiers and Ajax behaviors.

Now that you understand the core concepts of Wicket, it's time to become active! In the next chapter we'll build the cheese store we just introduced.

Building a cheesy
Wicket application

Reading about components, pages, and models is interesting, but getting your hands dirty is more fun. To get a better understanding of working with Wicket, in this chapter we'll start building the cheese store we discussed in chapter 2. The store's functionality will be limited to the sales front end: the shop with our prime collection of cheeses and a checkout page so customers can buy our product.

This is a long chapter, so we'll cover a lot of ground. Even so, a lot is left as an exercise for you. We won't be designing a database and using JDBC, Hibernate, or any other database technology to create this application, but we'll look at user input, validating the input, using premade components in a panel, and creating your own custom component.

We assume you're familiar with setting up a project in your IDE of choice using Ant or Maven. If not, you should download the free bonus chapter "Setting up a

Wicket project" from this book's website: http://manning.com/dashorst. It explains in detail how to set up a Wicket project using Ant and Maven. A quick-start project template is available as a download from the Wicket project. The template provides all the items described in the bonus chapter and will enable you to develop and run the cheese-store application while you read.

Building the web shop will put to the test the knowledge you gained from chapter 2. In building our shop, we'll use the concepts of application, session, component, page, and model. Fortunately, we won't go into much detail about these concepts, so you don't need to be able to pass a lie-detector test on this subject (yet). If you find it difficult to place these elements, chapter 2 will provide the necessary foundation. Let's first introduce the Cheesr online cheese shop.

3.1   Introducing Cheesr

The online cheese shop will be called Cheesr. We'll create the two most important pages for any web store: the store front, displaying our collection of cheeses and a shopping cart; and a checkout page where the customer can fill in her address data and order the selected products. In this section, we'll introduce the application and the requirements, and then we'll show you how to build the pages one by one.

3.1.1   Setting up shop

The cheese store needs to show the details of our cheese products: the name, a description, and the list price. When a customer wants to order a cheese product, the product needs to be added to the order. When the customer is ready to check out, she needs to fill in her address data for shipping. Like any Web 2.0 website, our web shop doesn't care about profitability; so, for now, we won't add credit-card validation and processing to the checkout form. Making the shop profitable is one of those exercises left for you.

As a database for our collection of cheeses, we'll create a central, read-only list that is shared among all customers. As outlined in chapter 2, all Wicket applications need at least two classes: an application class and a home page. The `Application` class is used for configuration and to hold information in a single place that is shared among all users of your application. This makes it a perfect place for us to store the list of all cheeses. Our application class will be called `CheesrApplication`.

NOTE   Java web applications are inherently multithreaded. Therefore, be careful with the things you expose in your `Application` object. In this simple application, the list of cheeses doesn't change, nor do the contents of the objects, making it safe to share them between threads. If we want to provide a way to update the cheeses, or remove and add cheeses to our collection, we need to properly synchronize access to these resources or use a proper database abstraction instead of this solution.

Because each customer needs his own shopping cart, we'll store the cart functionality in the session: the session is specific to each user and can store data across requests. We'll create our own session class to store the user's shopping cart. The session class will have the surprisingly creative name `CheesrSession`.

The quick-start template defines a common base page for all pages in the application. As you'll discover, having a common base page class is convenient for reusing functionality and markup. In this chapter, we'll create the `CheesrPage` base page and subclass it for the two pages: `Index` and `CheckOut`.

Using `Cheese`, `Address`, and `Cart`, we've drawn a diagram showing the classes and their attributes. Figure 3.1 shows the class diagram for the application.

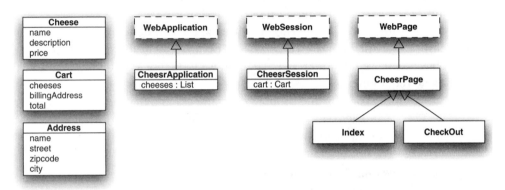

Figure 3.1   The class diagram for the cheese store showing the domain objects and custom `Application` and `Session` classes. The application consists of two pages: the shop front (`Index`) and the checkout page (`CheckOut`).

Now that we've identified the key domain objects and the necessary UI classes, it's time to begin. We'll start by implementing the `Cart` class. The `Cart` class is a simple Java object with a couple of properties and a method to calculate the total value of the contents; see listing 3.1.

Listing 3.1   Cart.java: Implementing a simple shopping cart

```java
public class Cart implements java.io.Serializable {          Must be
    private List<Cheese> cheeses = new ArrayList<Cheese>();   serializable
    private Address billingAddress = new Address();

    public List<Cheese> getCheeses() {
        return cheeses;
    }
    public void setCheeses(List<Cheese> other) {
        cheeses = other;
    }
    public Address getBillingAddress() {
        return billingAddress;
    }
    public void setBillingAddress(Address other) {
        billingAddress = other;
```

```
        }
    public double getTotal() {
        double total = 0;
        for(Cheese cheese : cheeses) {          Calculate
            total += cheese.getPrice();         total value
        }
        return total;
    }
}
```

This class has one notable aspect: it implements the `java.io.Serializable` interface. The session can be stored to disk by your servlet container or even transferred across the network to another node in a cluster to support fail over or load balancing. Java serialization is used when the session is persisted or sent across the wire like this. Because we store the shopping cart and its contents in our session, we need to ensure that they too are serializable. For now, we'll take a shortcut and make the objects serializable; in the next chapter, we'll discuss ways that circumvent the serializable requirement.

Given the code for the shopping cart, we assume that you'll be able to implement the `Cheese` and `Address` classes. Just remember to implement the `Serializable` interface. With our domain objects in place, we can now lay the groundwork for the shop starting with the `Application` class.

IMPLEMENTING THE CHEESRAPPLICATION CLASS

Each Wicket application requires its own `Application` class. In this case, it's the `CheesrApplication` class. The `Application` class is used to initialize the application and to configure Wicket (and possibly to set up integration with other frameworks, such as Spring). You can also use it to hold data that is shared among all your users—for instance, a cache for objects. In this simple web shop, we'll use it as a data store that stores all the cheeses in our collection.

Listing 3.2 shows how this class is implemented for the shop. We've abbreviated the descriptions of the cheeses to save space.

Listing 3.2 CheesrApplication.java: `Application` class

```
public class CheesrApplication extends WebApplication {
    private List<Cheese> cheeses = Arrays.asList(
        new Cheese("Gouda", "Gouda is a yellowish Dutch[...]", 1.65),
        new Cheese("Edam", "Edam (Dutch Edammer) is a D[...]", 1.05),
        new Cheese("Maasdam", "Maasdam cheese is a Dutc[...]", 2.35),
        new Cheese("Brie", "Brie is a soft cows' milk c[...]", 3.15),
        new Cheese("Buxton Blue", "Buxton Blue cheese i[...]", 0.99),
        new Cheese("Parmesan", "Parmesan is a grana, a [...]", 1.99),
        new Cheese("Cheddar", "Cheddar cheese is a hard[...]", 2.95),
        new Cheese("Roquefort", "Roquefort is a ewe's-m[...]", 1.67),
        new Cheese("Boursin", "Boursin Cheese is a soft[...]", 1.33),
        new Cheese("Camembert", "Camembert is a soft, c[...]", 1.69),
        new Cheese("Emmental", "Emmental is a yellow, m[...]", 2.39),
        new Cheese("Reblochon", "Reblochon is a French [...]", 2.99));
```

```
/**
 * Constructor
 */
public CheesrApplication() {
}

@Override
protected void init() {              ❶ Initialize
}                                      application

public static CheesrApplication get() {          Get application
    return (CheesrApplication) Application.get();
}

@Override
public Class<? extends Page> getHomePage() {      Set home page
    return Index.class;
}

public List<Cheese> getCheeses() {                Get all cheeses
    return Collections.unmodifiableList(cheeses);
}
}
```

In this example, we first create the grand collection of available cheeses in our store and put it in a list. The basic application doesn't have many configuration needs, so the initialization method is empty ❶. If you need to set a configuration parameter, you can do so in this method. Wicket calls this method just before the application is ready to start.

The next method sets the home page for our shop. The home page is served when a user hits the Wicket servlet or filter mapping for the application (as configured in the web.xml deployment descriptor) without any parameters. It's also used in the default Wicket Page Expired page for generating the Return to Home link, which is shown to users when their session has timed out. In this case, the Wicket filter is mapped to /*; if the context-path of the web-app is /cheesr, a user sees the home page when browsing to the URL /cheesr.

Finally, we create the accessor method to the cheese database. In more complex applications than the Cheesr shop, you'd typically use a service layer to get this information from a database. In chapter 13, you'll learn to use Wicket with a database in applications. For now, we'll use this in-memory list (you can consider this a poor person's cache solution). Let's continue building the infrastructure by implementing a custom session object.

IMPLEMENTING A CUSTOM CHEESRSESSION

When a customer wants to order cheese, we need a place to store the order. Because a shopping cart is unique for each user session, we can store the cart in a custom session class. As discussed in chapter 2, creating a type-safe session enables you to track what is stored in the session. Using the HttpSession directly is possible, but we wouldn't recommend that practice for pure Wicket applications (you should use it only when you need to interface with legacy applications or other frameworks).

Our custom session contains a field that holds the shopping cart, and it provides a getter for access to the shopping cart. Listing 3.3 shows our custom session.

Listing 3.3   CheesrSession.java: Custom session holding the shopping cart

```
public class CheesrSession extends WebSession {
    private Cart cart = new Cart();

    protected CheesrSession(Request request) {
        super(request);
    }

    public Cart getCart() {
        return cart;
    }
}
```

We have to tell our application that a new session of this type needs to be created instead of the default Wicket session. We can configure this by overriding a factory method—which is responsible for creating Wicket sessions—with one that returns our custom session in our application object, as shown in the next snippet:

```
public class CheesrApplication extends WebApplication {
    /** ... */
    @Override
    public Session newSession(Request request, Response response) {
        return new CheesrSession(request);
    }
    /** ... */
}
```

In this example, we don't use the request and response parameters. These can be used to query for cookies in the request or set cookies in the response—for example, to implement a remember-me functionality where a user's identity is retained across multiple sessions by setting a cookie.

Now that we're able to store the contents of our customers' shopping carts, let's look at implementing pages.

IMPLEMENTING THE CHEESRPAGE BASE CLASS

The CheesrPage base class helps provide common functionality for all the pages in our application. You can create base pages for each module of an application—for instance, an administration base page that requires administrator privileges (see chapter 11 for more information about security), or a ShopPage where you get instant access to a customer's shopping cart. Because it's all pure Java, you can easily achieve anything you want.

For our cheese shop, we'll create a single common base page. Listing 3.4 shows the Java code for CheesrPage.

Listing 3.4   CheesrPage.java: Base class for all pages in our application

```
public abstract class CheesrPage extends WebPage {
    public CheesrSession getCheesrSession() {      ❶ Get
        return (CheesrSession) getSession();            session
    }
```

```
public Cart getCart() {
    return getCheesrSession().getCart();
}
```
❷ **Get shopping cart**

```
public List<Cheese> getCheeses() {
    return CheesrApplication.get().getCheeses();
}
}
```
❸ **Get all cheeses**

The base page doesn't provide much functionality—just a convenience method to get at our custom session implementation ❶ without having to add type casts throughout our application code. We also implement convenience methods to directly access the shopping cart stored in our custom session ❷ and to retrieve all our cheeses ❸.

With these foundations in place, we're ready to work on the parts of our application that customers see and interact with: the UI.

3.1.2 *Designing the user interface*

The Cheesr online cheese store is created using web standards such as (valid) HTML and *cascading style sheets* (CSS). Respecting Wicket's philosophy of strict separation of concerns, we'll use CSS to decouple the way things look in the browser from the structure of the document. This approach has the benefit that people who know design can focus on that; programmers can focus on creating code. In this section, we'll design a common page layout that will be used for the store's two pages.

COMMON LAYOUT

For the pages that make up our shop, we'll adopt the popular two-column design with the main content in the left column and the shopping-cart contents in the right column. The two columns will be crowned with a full-width header showing our shop logo. The general layout and a standard markup template are shown in figure 3.2. In chapter 7, you'll learn how to use markup inheritance to apply the general layout consistently to all your pages. For now, each page will duplicate the markup.

We use div elements to line up the columns and the header. Using CSS, we can instruct the browser to format and even lay out the content the way we want. In this

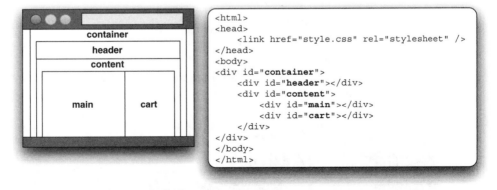

Figure 3.2 The general layout of the pages. All content areas are contained in div tags.

example, we'll keep things a bit dull. Listing 3.5 shows the contents of our CSS file. You can put the file in the src/main/webapp folder of the Cheesr project. The `link` tag shown in figure 3.2 makes sure the stylesheet is included in all our pages.

Listing 3.5 style.css: The shop's stylesheet

```
body {
    margin : 0; padding : 0;
    font-family : georgia, times, serif;          Cheesy
    font-size : 15px;                              font
}
div {
    margin : 0; padding : 0;                   Remove space
}                                              between elements
#container {
    margin-left : auto; margin-right:auto;        Center content
    width:720px;                                   in window
}
#content {
    width : 100%;
    padding-left : 10px; padding-right : 10px;
}
#main {
    width : 480px;        Main content
    float : left;         goes here
}
#cart {
    width : 220px;        Shopping
    float : right;        cart column
}

#header {
    width : 100%;
    height : 150px;
    background : url(logo.png) center no-repeat;   ❶ Replace hl
}                                                     with logo
#header h1 {
    display : none;
}
```

In this example, we highlight the header section ❶. This is a trick to replace some text with a graphic element. In our case, we replace `<h1>Cheesr</h1>` with the company logo shown in figure 3.3.

The benefit of this trick is that search engines will see the name of our shop and assume it's an important keyword for our website (because it's enclosed in `h1` tags).

Figure 3.3
The Cheesr company
logo, ready for Web 2.0

This technique also helps with accessibility: screen readers typically can't read images (only the `alt` and `title` tags), so embedding the logo using CSS enables such readers to ignore the image and use just the available text. It's even possible to implement a specific stylesheet for screen readers, but that is a topic for a different book.

Separation of concerns: designers like HTML, coders like Java

Wicket gives you complete control over your HTML markup, which means you have a lot of flexibility in terms of the layout of elements on screen. Your web designers will be happy that they can apply and preview CSS techniques on top of standard HTML without scripts or strange tags getting in the way. Some web frameworks like Echo and GWT take the approach of having the Java developer control the layout in Java code (similar to Swing). We prefer the Wicket way because of the true separation of concerns it provides; this allows the designer and the Java programmer to work without stepping on each other's toes. Getting layout and look and feel to work consistently across different browsers is a tricky business; even if things have improved over the last few years, you need all the flexibility you can get—and good web-design skills, of course.

We've covered the basics for our application: we have an application object, a session with a shopping cart, and a basic layout for the application's pages. Now we can start building on these foundations and creating the parts where users will interact with our application. First up is the store front, shown to all our visitors.

3.2　Creating the store front

In this section, we'll build the page that customers first see when they arrive at our shop. This is the store front. Our front page is where most users will interact with our store. It lists the available cheeses and lets users add them to their shopping carts. A mockup of the front page is shown in figure 3.4.

Figure 3.4
A mockup of the front page. It consists of a two-column layout: the left column features the main content, and the right column shows the contents of the shopping cart.

In this figure, you can see the two parts of our application: the main area that presents our collection of cheeses, and the shopping cart. If many cheeses are available, users need to be able to browse through the collection using a pagination widget, as shown at the bottom of the mockup. When a customer is ready to check out, he clicks the Check Out button. Doing so takes him to the checkout page.

We'll first concentrate on the main area that displays the list of cheeses. Next, we'll take a shot at implementing the shopping-cart part of our web page.

3.2.1   Cutting to the cheese

Figure 3.5 shows the part we'll focus on in this section, together with the corresponding markup we'll transform into a Wicket page.

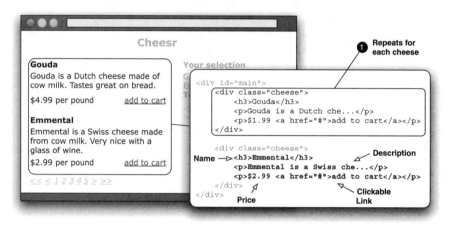

Figure 3.5   The main area and its markup for the front page. The `div`s with class `cheese` are repeated to show the entire collection.

Taking a closer look at the markup (figure 3.5), you can spot the repeating bits: the `div`s with `class="cheese"` ❶ have the same structure. For every displayed cheese, we generate this structure, only with different contents: a heading containing the name, a section with the description, and the price. In addition, each item receives a clickable link that adds the cheese to the customer's shopping cart.

Having identified the components to add, let's dive into some markup. We'll add Wicket identifiers to the tags to which we want to attach components. Listing 3.6 shows the markup of our front page, but now with strategically placed `wicket:id` attributes.

Listing 3.6   Index.html: Front page markup

```
<html>
<head>
    <title>Cheesr - Making cheese taste beta</title>
    <link href="style.css" rel="stylesheet" />
```

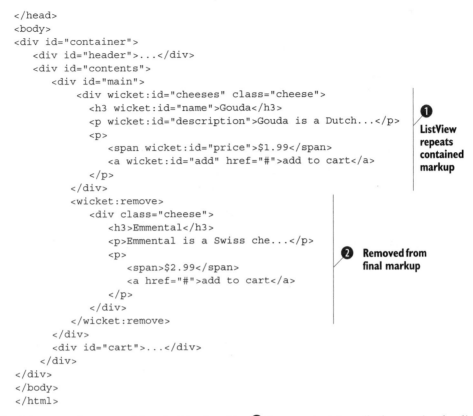

```
</head>
<body>
<div id="container">
    <div id="header">...</div>
    <div id="contents">
        <div id="main">
            <div wicket:id="cheeses" class="cheese">
                <h3 wicket:id="name">Gouda</h3>
                <p wicket:id="description">Gouda is a Dutch...</p>
                <p>
                    <span wicket:id="price">$1.99</span>
                    <a wicket:id="add" href="#">add to cart</a>
                </p>
            </div>
            <wicket:remove>
                <div class="cheese">
                    <h3>Emmental</h3>
                    <p>Emmental is a Swiss che...</p>
                    <p>
                        <span>$2.99</span>
                        <a href="#">add to cart</a>
                    </p>
                </div>
            </wicket:remove>
        </div>
        <div id="cart">...</div>
    </div>
</div>
</body>
</html>
```

❶ ListView repeats contained markup

❷ Removed from final markup

In this example, everything inside the div ❶ is repeated for all cheeses in the list, including the div tag itself. Inside the div, we add Wicket identifiers to the h3 tag, the p tag, and the span tag. The span tag is introduced into the markup as a placeholder for a Label component for displaying the price of the cheese. We also add a Wicket identifier to the hyperlink (anchor) tag. Because the markup needs to be repeated, we use a ListView component. A ListView takes a list of objects and repeats its markup for each item in the list. More about that when we delve into the Java code.

You probably noticed the special wicket:remove tags in the markup ❷. Those tags will remove the enclosed markup from the final rendered page . We have this section of markup in the page purely to add a second cheese to the list, so that when the page is previewed, it looks more like it would in real life. Note that previewing the page in our browser is as simple as loading it from the file system.

Having placed our component identifiers in the right places in our markup, we can now progress to the Java code.

IMPLEMENTING THE JAVA CODE

As you already know from chapters 1 and 2, each Wicket page consists of both a markup file and a Java file. Their names must be the same, except for the extension. Name the files Index.html and Index.java, and put both files in the same directory on the classpath: Wicket will automatically find the HTML file when the page needs to be constructed.

NOTE   Some IDEs need to be told to copy the HTML files to the generated class's directory. Wicket complains with an error message like "WicketMessage: Markup of type 'html' for component 'com.cheesr.Index' not found." When you get this error, Wicket is unable to find the markup template. Typically, this happens when your IDE isn't configured to copy the markup files to the classpath. For instance, Eclipse doesn't automatically copy the HTML files. You can easily configure this by modifying the project settings so no filters are set for the source folder.

As we discussed in section 3.1, our page will inherit from the common base class CheesrPage (shown in listing 3.4). The Java code for our page is shown in listing 3.7, where we've added the identified components.

Listing 3.7   Index.java: Class implementing the front page

```
public class Index extends CheesrPage {
    public Index() {
        add(new ListView("cheeses", getCheeses()) {            ❶ Add
                                                                  ListView    ❷ Called
                                                                                for each
            @Override                                                          cheese
            protected void populateItem(ListItem item) {
                Cheese cheese = (Cheese) item.getModelObject();  ❸ Get cheese
                item.add(new Label("name", cheese.getName()));
                item.add(new Label("description",                              ❹
                                            cheese.getDescription()));         Add
                item.add(new Label("price", "$" + cheese.getPrice()));         labels

                item.add(new Link("add", item.getModel()) {

                    @Override                                                  ❺
                    public void onClick() {                                    Add to
                        Cheese selected = (Cheese) getModelObject();           cart
                        getCart().getCheeses().add(selected);                  link
                    }
                });
            }
        });
    }
}
```

We pass the list of cheeses into the ListView constructor ❶ so the ListView knows which items to render. For each cheese in our list, the ListView creates a ListItem and calls the populateItem method ❷, where we add our components to the List-Item to show the details of each cheese. The ListItem is used as the container for each repeated component: the components must be added to the ListItem, not the ListView. Figure 3.6 shows the structure of the ListView.

Each will have a cheese associated with it in its model: item 0 will contain cheese 0 from the list, item 1 will contain cheese 1 from the list, and so forth. To get at the cheese object, we have to retrieve the model object from the item ❸. Then we can use it to create the remaining components. In this case, we add three label components to the list item: the name, description, and price labels ❹.

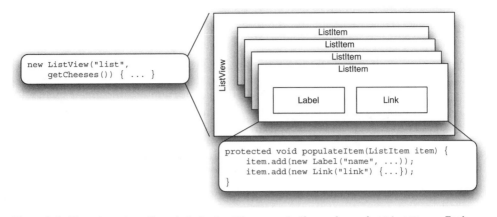

Figure 3.6 The `ListView` dissected. A `ListView` repeats the markup using `ListItems`. Each `ListItem` is populated with the repeated components in the `populateItem` method. In this example, each `ListItem` gets a `Label` and a `Link`. Chapter 5 will go into more detail concerning the `ListView` and its cousins.

Finally, we added a `Link` component to the list item ❺. In the `onClick` event handler, we want to add the selected cheese to the shopping cart. That's why we provide the link with the list item's model object: this way, the link will know which cheese to add when it's clicked. In the `onClick` event, we retrieve the cheese and add it to the shopping cart. Wicket will re-render the page, because we didn't tell it to do otherwise. Figure 3.7 shows how the page looks in a browser.

Figure 3.7 The Cheesr front page. It shows our company logo and the selection of available cheeses, with price tags and a link to add cheeses to the shopping cart.

Clicking the Add link to add a fine piece of Edam cheese to our shopping cart causes the page to refresh, but the shopping cart still looks empty: we haven't implemented the shopping-cart functionality.

3.2.2 Adding the shopping cart

Now that customers can look at our grand collection of fine cheeses and add them to their shopping cart, it's time to show the cart's contents on the front page. Figure 3.8 shows the page and the markup that belongs to the shopping cart.

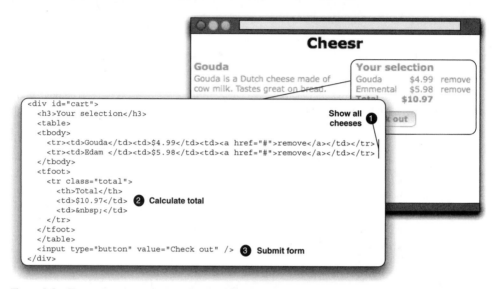

Figure 3.8   The markup for the shopping cart. We use a table to lay out the items in the shopping cart. Try to identify the repeating bits before reading further, and imagine how you would implement this cart.

In the example markup in figure 3.8, we left out some of the repeating bits; however, you can see that the table row tr is repeated for all elements in the shopping cart ❶. Inside each table row are two labels and a link. The labels show the name of the item and the price. The link gives the customer the option of removing elements from the shopping cart.

It's nice to show the total value of the customer's shopping cart so he doesn't have to add the prices himself; ❷ displays the total value of the cart. When the customer wants to order the items in the shopping cart, he can click the Check Out button, which takes him to the checkout page ❸. We'll implement the Check Out button in the next section.

Now that we've identified the components, it's time to work on our markup and add the Wicket identifiers; see listing 3.8.

Listing 3.8   Adding the shopping cart's markup to Index.html

```
<html>
...
<body>
<div id="container">
    <div id="header">...</div>
    <div id="content">
        <div id="main">...</div>
        <div id="cart">
            <h3>Your selection</h3>
            <table>
            <tbody>
                <tr wicket:id="cart">
                    <td wicket:id="name">Gouda</td>
                    <td wicket:id="price">2.99</td>
                    <td><a wicket:id="remove" href="#">remove</a></td>
                </tr>
                <wicket:remove>
                <tr>
                    <td>Emmental</td>
                    <td>$1.99</td>
                    <td><a href="#">remove</a></td>
                </tr>
                </wicket:remove>
            </tbody>
            <tfoot>
                <tr class="total">
                    <th>Total</th>
                    <td wicket:id="total">$1.99</td>
                    <td> </td>
                </tr>
            </tfoot>
            </table>
            <input type="button" value="Check out" />
        </div> <!-- cart -->
    </div> <!-- content -->
</div> <!-- container -->
</body>
</html>
```

1 ListView repeats contained markup

2 Removed from final markup

3 Show total cost

Looking closely at the markup, you'll notice that we attach the Wicket identifiers for the name and the price directly to the `td` tags instead of introducing a `span` or `div` element. The label component used to show the data doesn't require a particular tag to do its job: as long as the tag has a body, the label will replace it with its value.

It's time to create Java components to go with the markup. The next snippet implements the shopping-cart functionality for our front page:

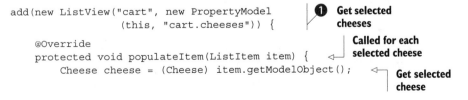

```
add(new ListView("cart", new PropertyModel
                  (this, "cart.cheeses")) {

    @Override
    protected void populateItem(ListItem item) {
        Cheese cheese = (Cheese) item.getModelObject();
```

1 Get selected cheeses

Called for each selected cheese

Get selected cheese

```
        item.add(new Label("name", cheese.getName()));
        item.add(new Label("price", "$" + cheese.getPrice()));

        item.add(new Link("remove", item.getModel()) {

            @Override
            public void onClick() {
                Cheese selected = (Cheese) getModelObject();
                getCart().getCheeses().remove(selected);
            }
        });
    }
});
add(new Label("total", "$" + getCart().getTotal()));
```

② Add labels

Add Remove link ③

Get selected cheese **④**

Here we show only the cheeses the customer has added to the shopping cart **①**. At first it's empty, but with each click of the Add link, a new item is added.

In the `populateItem` method, we add label components to each list item to display the cheese's name and the price **②**. We also add a link to remove the cheese from the shopping cart **③**. Because the link needs to know which item to remove from the list, we provide the link with the same model as the list item. This allows us to get to the selected cheese when the link is clicked **④** and remove it from the cart. The label showing the total value of the selected cheeses in the cart is the last component we add.

We're ready to start up the server and run the application. Now, when we click the Add link, we can see items added to our shopping cart. Figure 3.9 shows a before and after screenshot of our front page.

In the after screenshot, you can see one small problem: the total amount isn't correct. In fact, it hasn't changed from the initial value (shown in the before shot). If you open your debugger and check the value of the `getTotal` method in the shopping cart each time you add a cheese to the cart, you'll see that `getTotal` returns the correct value every time. We have a method that works as advertised, but what we see isn't what we expect. What is happening here?

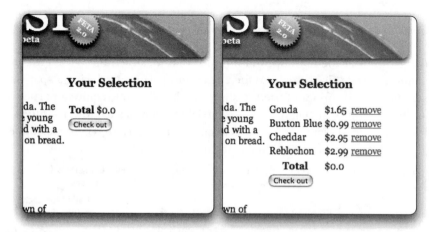

Figure 3.9   Before and after screenshots of our shopping cart when adding cheeses

If you take a closer look at the way we add the label, you may spot the problem:

```
public class Index extends CheesrPage {
    public Index() {
        /* ... */
        add(new Label("total", "$" + getCart().getTotal()));
    }
}
```

To make things clearer, you can set a break point on this line and add some cheeses to your shopping cart. You'll notice that the debugger stops here only once: the first time you hit the page in a session.

The problem is caused by the fact that in this code, we determine and set the value of our label *at construction time*. The constructor for the page is called only the first time we request the page. After we've added our first cheese, the constructor isn't called, unless we explicitly invoke it. Our label doesn't know the value has changed. We need to be able to update the value on each request.

In chapter 4, we'll discuss the differences between static models and dynamic models (the issue at hand) in greater depth. For now, we'll solve the problem by providing the label with a model that calculates its value every time it's requested:

```
add(new Label("total", new Model() {
    @Override
    public Object getObject() {
        NumberFormat nf = NumberFormat.getCurrencyInstance();
        return nf.format(getCart().getTotal());
    }
}));
```

We override the getObject method to return the display value of the price: every time the label renders itself, it calls this method. In this case, we format the value using a NumberFormat and return the formatted string. If we run the store after we've updated this piece of code, the amount is updated whenever we add or remove items. See figure 3.10.

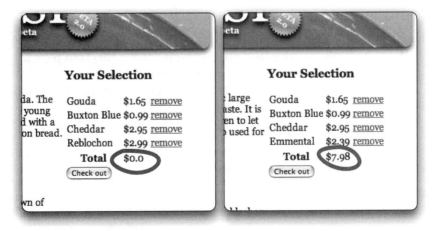

Figure 3.10 The shopping cart before and after we fixed the total amount

In these screenshots, you can see the Check Out button. Clicking the button doesn't accomplish anything yet. In the next section, we'll implement the Check Out button and provide a starting point to build our checkout page.

3.2.3 Going to check out

An online shop without a checkout page is of little value to its owners. Let's implement a way to get to the checkout page. First, we need to create the page we'll link to: our first assignment is to create an empty checkout page. In section 3.3, we'll implement the page functionality. For now, we create two files: a Java file with an empty class that extends our `CheesrPage`, and an HTML file based on our standard layout, as shown in listing 3.9.

Listing 3.9 CheckOut.java and CheckOut.html implementing an empty page

```
/* CheckOut.java */
public class CheckOut extends CheesrPage {
    public CheckOut() {
    }
}

<!-- CheckOut.html -->
<html>
    <head>
        <title>Cheesr - checkout</title>
        <link href="style.css" rel="stylesheet" />
    </head>
    <body>
        <div id="container">
            <div id="header"><h1>Cheesr</h1></div>
            <div id="contents">
                <div id="main"></div>
                <div id="cart"></div>
            </div>
        </div>
    </body>
</html>
```

We haven't added Wicket identifiers to the markup yet: the page doesn't provide any functionality. Now that we have the bare minimum for the checkout page in place, we can create a link to it. The link is the Check Out button described in figure 3.7, where we showed the markup for the shopping cart. The markup for our Check Out button, including a Wicket identifier, is as follows:

```
<input type="button" wicket:id="checkout" value="Check Out" />
```

We'll use a `Link` component to implement the behavior for this button. The `Link` is added to our Index page in the following snippet:

```
public Index() {
    /* ... */
    add(new Link("checkout") {
        @Override
        public void onClick() {
```

```
        setResponsePage(new Checkout());
      }
    });
  }
```

Just as with our previous `Link` components, we need to subclass the link and provide it with our own implementation of the `onClick` event. In this case, we set the response page to a new instance of our checkout page. Wicket renders the freshly created checkout page and returns it to the browser.

HIDING THE CHECK OUT BUTTON FOR AN EMPTY CART

To make things even nicer, we can hide the button when there is nothing in the shopping cart. This way, our users can't go to the checkout page without a valid reason. To do this, we have to override the `isVisible` method on the link (the `isVisible` method is defined for the root `Component` class and is therefore available to all components to override as they wish) and change the visibility based on the number of items in the cart. The following snippet shows how this can be done in Java code:

```
public Index() {
    /* ... */
    add(new Link("checkout") {
        @Override
        public void onClick() {
            setResponsePage(new Checkout());
        }

        @Override
        public boolean isVisible() {          Hide button for
            return !getCart().getCheeses().isEmpty();   empty cart
        }
    });
}
```

Now, if we restart the application and navigate to the store front, we see the left screenshot from figure 3.11: a shopping cart without the Check Out button. When we

Figure 3.11   The Check Out button appears after we add cheese to our cart.

add cheese to the shopping cart, the Check Out button magically appears, as shown
on the right.

Our customers can now put our prime selection of cheeses in their shopping carts
and immediately see the cost of their purchases. If their weekly cheese budget of $10
isn't used up, they can scroll down to the Roquefort and add it to the cart. But what
happens if we have more than 100 cheeses in our collection? Or if we reach 1,000?
Let's make the store more user friendly by adding the ability to browse through our
collection page by page—instead of having to scroll through a long list.

3.2.4   *Adding pagination to the list of cheeses*

There are a lot of cheeses in the world, and if we want to provide the full spectrum,
the front page could take a while to load. We need to limit the number of cheeses
shown per request. We'll do this by adding pagination to the front page—more specifically, to the list of our cheeses. When you look at the mockup of the front page in figure 3.4 you can see that we have to add a pagination component.

The pagination component at the bottom seems like a lot of work. Fortunately,
Wicket provides this pagination component out of the box: the `PagingNavigator`. It is
nothing but a Wicket `Panel` on which several components are bundled and working
together. The navigator contains links to each of the pages, links to navigate to the
previous or next page, and links to the first and last pages in the list. Let's add this
component to our markup. You might expect something like this:

```
<div class="cheese" wicket:id="cheeses">
    <h3 wicket:id="name">Gouda</h3>
    <p wicket:id="description">Gouda is a Dutch ...</p>
    <p>
        <span wicket:id="price">$2.99</span>
        <a wicket:id="add" href="#">add to cart</a>
    </p>
</div>
<div id="paginator">
    <a href="#" wicket:id="first">&lt;&lt;</a> 
    <a href="#" wicket:id="prev">&lt;</a> 
    <a href="#" wicket:id="page1">1</a> 
    <a href="#" wicket:id="page2">2</a> 
    <a href="#" wicket:id="next">&gt;</a> 
    <a href="#" wicket:id="last">&gt;&gt;</a> 
</div>
```

But that isn't how the `PagingNavigator` should be added. Because the `PagingNaviga-
tor` is a panel, we can't add its markup to the page. First, doing so would violate the
DRY principle. If we did this, we'd need to copy the markup of all our components
into the final page, which would be brittle. A change in a component would require us
to update the markup of all pages where the component was used. What should we
add? Just a `span` or `div` element as a placeholder for the component, with a wicket
identifier for referencing it. In our this case, we use a `div`. Let's see how this looks in
the markup:

```
<div class="cheese" wicket:id="cheeses">
    <h3 wicket:id="name">Gouda</h3>
    <p wicket:id="description">Gouda is a Dutch ...</p>
    <p>
        <span wicket:id="price">$2.99</span>
        <a wicket:id="add" href="#">add to cart</a>
    </p>
</div>
<div wicket:id="navigator"></div>          Add paging
                                           navigator
```

This looks a lot more civilized than the previous example. At the very least, we won't
have to add all those links to the page ourselves: the navigator takes care of that.

NOTE The ability to preview the page suffers a bit because the navigator component markup isn't shown. This can be alleviated by adding some mock
markup between the div tags, which is replaced at runtime; but usually it
isn't worth the effort. Particularly when a panel consists of a lot of
dynamic components, it's generally hard to maintain the previewability
of the page where the panel is used.

Now, let's look at the Java side of things. We already said we're going to use the Paging-
Navigator component. This component can work only on a *pageable component* implementing the IPageable interface.

Unfortunately, the ListView component we used in our page doesn't implement
this interface. However, Wicket supplies a PageableListView that implements the
required interface. When we change our page in such a way that the current ListView
becomes a PageableListView, and we add the navigator to the page, we should be all
set. Let's see how this plays out in the next snippet:

```
public Index() {
    PageableListView cheeses                          ❶ Enable
        = new PageableListView("cheeses", getCheeses(), 5) {    pagination
            @Override
            protected void populateItem(ListItem item) {
                Cheese cheese = (Cheese) item.getModelObject();
                item.add(new Label("name", cheese.getName()));
                item.add(new Label("description",
                                            cheese.getDescription()));
                item.add(new Label("price", "$" + cheese.getPrice()));

                item.add(new Link("add", item.getModel()) {

                    @Override
                    public void onClick() {
                        Cheese selected = (Cheese) getModelObject();
                        getCart().getCheeses().add(selected);
                    }
                });
            }
    };
    add(cheeses);                                      ❷ Add pagination
    add(new PagingNavigator("navigator", cheeses));       component
    /* ... */
}
```

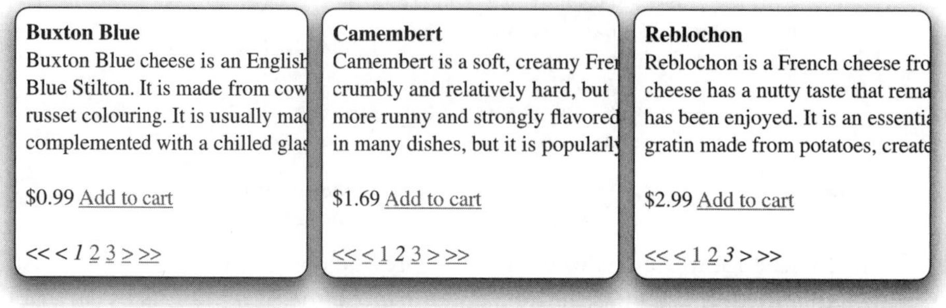

Buxton Blue Buxton Blue cheese is an English Blue Stilton. It is made from cow russet colouring. It is usually mad complemented with a chilled glas $0.99 Add to cart << < *1* 2 3 > >>	**Camembert** Camembert is a soft, creamy Frer crumbly and relatively hard, but more runny and strongly flavored in many dishes, but it is popularl $1.69 Add to cart << < 1 2 3 > >>	**Reblochon** Reblochon is a French cheese fro cheese has a nutty taste that rema has been enjoyed. It is an essenti gratin made from potatoes, create $2.99 Add to cart << < 1 2 *3* > >>

Figure 3.12   Screenshots using the paging navigator, showing pages 1, 2, and 3

We change the `ListView` into a `PageableListView` ❶ and add one extra parameter to the constructor: the number of items to show per page (in this case, 5). We also add the `PagingNavigator` to the page and provide the navigator with the list view ❷. The results of this hard work are shown in figure 3.12, where you can see the navigator in action.

Our front page is now complete: customers can browse our vast collection of cheeses and place items in the shopping cart. They can remove items, and they don't have to calculate the value of the shopping cart themselves. Now it's time to lighten our customers' wallets.

3.3   *Creating the checkout page*

The checkout page is the final step in a visit to our shop. It requires the customer to fill in several fields for billing information, and it shows the selected cheeses. The customer can cancel the checkout and return to the front page with all the items still in her shopping cart. When she clicks the Order button, the order is processed. Figure 3.13 shows a mockup of this page.

All the fields are required for a successful completion of the order. When the customer forgets to fill one or more, we'll highlight the fields that require a value. In addition, the ZIP code field must be numeric.

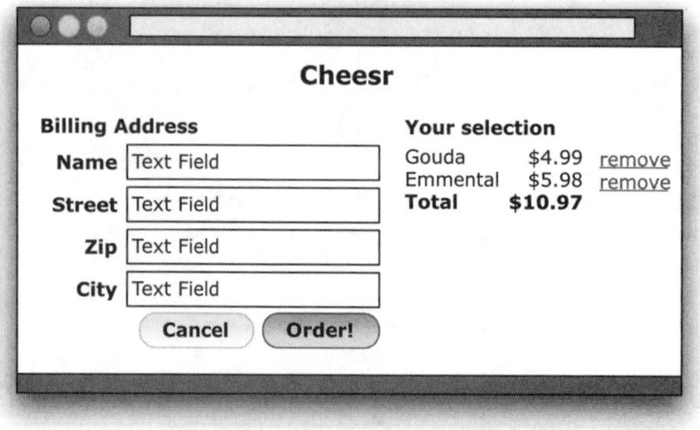

Cheesr

Billing Address   **Your selection**

Name [Text Field]   Gouda $4.99   remove
                           Emmental $5.98   remove
Street [Text Field]   **Total $10.97**

Zip [Text Field]

City [Text Field]

(Cancel) (Order!)

**Figure 3.13
A mockup of the checkout page**

3.3.1 Adding the billing address form

Almost all websites need users to enter and submit information, and our web shop is no exception to this rule. In order to close the deal, we need a form with input fields and buttons. Our current implementation of the checkout page (created in the previous section) is merely a stub. It contains only the logo and no components. In its current state, it's unlikely to generate any revenue for us. We'll fix that and show how to create a billing address form for our customers and add validation to the mix. Recall the markup for this page from listing 3.9:

```
<html>
    <head>
        <title>Cheesr - checkout</title>
        <link href="style.css" rel="stylesheet" />
    </head>
    <body>
        <div id="container">
            <div id="header"><h1>Cheesr</h1></div>
            <div id="content">
                <div id="main"> ❶ </div>          Form goes
                <div id="cart"></div>              here
            </div>
        </div>
    </body>
</html>
```

The billing address form should go into the main area ❶. Figure 3.14 shows how the markup for the form part should look like to get the desired page.

The example markup embeds a form inside the main area. Inside the form, we put all the input fields required for us to complete the checkout: the name, street, ZIP

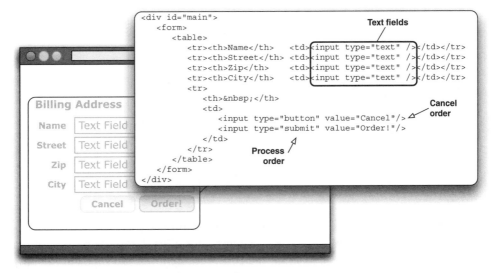

Figure 3.14   The markup of the billing address form

code, and city. The user can cancel the order by clicking the Cancel button or confirm the order by clicking the Order button.

Listing 3.10 shows the form markup, but now with Wicket component identifiers attached to the tags identified previously.

Listing 3.10   Billing address form with component identifiers

```
<div id="main">
<form wicket:id="form">     ⟵— Form component
<h3>Check out</h3>
<p>Please enter your billing address.</p>
<table>
    <tr>
        <th>Name</th>
        <td>
            <input wicket:id="name" type="text" />       ⟵┐
        </td>
    </tr>
    <tr>
        <th>Street</th>
        <td>
            <input wicket:id="street" type="text" />     ⟵┤
        </td>
    </tr>
    <tr>                                                        TextField
        <th>Zip code</th>                                       components
        <td>
            <input wicket:id="zipcode" type="text" />    ⟵┤
        </td>
    </tr>
    <tr>
        <th>City</th>
        <td>
            <input wicket:id="city" type="text" />       ⟵┘
        </td>
    </tr>
    <tr>
        <th> </th>                                         Link component
        <td>
            <input type="button" wicket:id="cancel" value="Cancel" />  ⟵┘
            <input type="submit" wicket:id="order" value="Order!" />   ⟵┐
        </td>
    </tr>                                                       Button component
</table>
</form>
</div>
```

If you open the page from the file system in a browser, you can see that it's beginning to look a lot like the page we're going to build. In the markup, we add component identifiers to the form, its input fields, and the buttons. Let's look at the Java code for the form and the fields first.

ADDING THE FIELDS TO THE BILLING ADDRESS FORM

The Java code for the form and the fields is basic, as shown in listing 3.11.

> **Listing 3.11 CheckOut.java: Checkout page with form components added**

```java
public class CheckOut extends CheesrPage {
    public CheckOut() {
        Form form = new Form("form");
        add(form);
        Address address = getCart().getBillingAddress();

        form.add(new TextField("name",
                        new PropertyModel(address, "name")));
        form.add(new TextField("street",
                        new PropertyModel(address, "street")));
        form.add(new TextField("zipcode",
                        new PropertyModel(address, "zipcode")));
        form.add(new TextField("city",
                        new PropertyModel(address, "city")));

    }
}
```

Even though the listing is short, lots of things happen. First, we add the form to the page, and then we add the text fields to the form. The fields need to be part of the form; otherwise, their input won't be submitted with the form. Each field is bound to its corresponding `Address` property using a `PropertyModel`. The `PropertyModel` retrieves the value of the property when the field is rendered and pushes the input value of the field into the `Address` object's property when the form is submitted. But what happens to the input when the form is submitted?

When a form is submitted, all the input fields' values are submitted with the HTTP request. Wicket processes the request and assigns the correct request parameter to each form component. Then, the form processing kicks in. It involves the following steps:

1 Check to be sure the required fields have input.
2 If so, convert the input to the new value for the model.
3 If converted, validate the new converted value using any registered validators.
4 If all previous steps have been successful for all fields, set the new value on the model of each field.

The conversion in step 2 is needed because the HTTP protocol transmits all request parameters using strings. In Java, we typically have `Date`, `Integer`, `Double`, and other values that aren't string types. Step 2 converts the string value of the request parameter into the actual type of the model. In our example, the ZIP code is converted into an `Integer`.

When the conversion step is successful, each field on the form (and the form itself) calls the registered validators. Examples of using validators include checking the length of a name field and validating the format and checksum of a Social Security number. If step 1, 2, or 3 fails, step 4 isn't executed, to prevent invalid data from ending up in our data objects. Wicket then renders the page again, retaining the users' input in the form components. This, in a nutshell, is how Wicket form fields populate their models. If you want to crack the nutshell and learn about its innards, see chapter 6.

Now that we have this cleared up, we imagine you're anxious to see the results in the application. But wait! Have you ever seen a web page with buttons that don't do anything?[1]

ADDING THE BUTTONS TO THE BILLING ADDRESS FORM

We still have to implement two buttons on our form: Cancel and Order. The Cancel button can be a link, because its job is only to return to the front page without doing anything else. We can skip all formalities of converting and validating the input: we won't use it anyway.

The Order button is a whole other beast. It does have to validate and convert the input. Therefore, we'll use a `Button` component for the Order button to submit the form. In listing 3.12, we leave out the processing of the order, because the art of packaging and shipping cheese isn't in the scope of this book (phew!).

Listing 3.12   Adding the Cancel and Order buttons to the checkout form

```
public Checkout() {
    Form form = new Form("form");
    ...
    form.add(new Link("cancel") {
        @Override
        public void onClick() {
            setResponsePage(Index.class);
        }
    });
    form.add(new Button("order") {
        @Override
        public void onSubmit() {
            Cart cart = getCart();

            // charge customers' credit card
            // ship cheeses to our customer
            // clean out shopping cart
            cart.getCheeses().clear();

            // return to front page
            setResponsePage(Index.class);
        }
    });
}
```

You may be surprised by the value of the parameter we set the response page to: `Index.class` instead of `new Index`. It instructs Wicket to redirect the browser to our front page. This generates a bookmarkable URL. The sidebar "Explaining setResponse-Page" explains more of the inner workings of the `setResponsePage` method.

---

[1] Except the 1996 classic "The really big button that doesn't do anything," at http://www.pixelscapes.com/spatulacity/button.htm.

Explaining setResponsePage

When you want to tell Wicket to render a different page than the current one, you have to tell the framework which page to render. Server-side request handling usually consists of two phases:

- *Request listener handling*—Invokes a server-side listener, such as a link-click listener, a form-submit listener, or an Ajax behavior

- *Rendering*—Renders the response to the browser (for example, the current page, a new page, an Ajax response, or possibly a PDF, image, or other resource)

During the listener-handling phase, you can tell Wicket which page should be rendered as the response. If no response is specified, Wicket renders the current page. The method `setResponsePage` tells Wicket which page should be rendered in the rendering phase. The last page that is specified is used, so you can call the method multiple times.

`setResponsePage` comes in two flavors. In the first, you instantiate the page that will be rendered, as shown in the following snippet:

```
setResponsePage(new CheeseDetailsPage(selectedCheese));
```

This renders the `CheeseDetailsPage` showing the selected cheese and sets the URL in the browser to something like

http://cheesr.com/app/?wicket:interface=:21::::

This URL tells Wicket that the page that was requested is page number 21 relative to the start of the user's session. It's session relative and isn't bookmarkable because the URL doesn't contain information about the page that was requested or the selected cheese—this state is stored in the user's session on the server, which is lost when the session is invalidated.

The second form of `setResponsePage` instructs Wicket to create the page for you and generate a bookmarkable URL:

```
setResponsePage(CheeseDetailsPage.class,
            new PageParameters("cheese="+cheese.getName()));
```

This form tells Wicket to redirect the browser to a bookmarkable URL that encodes some state: the page that needs to be rendered and the selected cheese. When the browser receives the redirect, it requests the page, and Wicket creates the `Cheese-DetailsPage` automatically. The generated URL looks different, depending on whether the page was mounted and which URL coding strategy was used (see chapter 14 for more information). When the page isn't mounted, Wicket generates the following URL:

http://cheesr.com/?wicket:bookmarkablePage=:com.cheesr.CheeseDetailsPage&cheese=edam

Most of the time, you can use a `BookmarkablePageLink` component instead of using the bookmarkable form of `setResponsePage`. `BookmarkablePageLink` is discussed in chapter 5 along with several other link components.

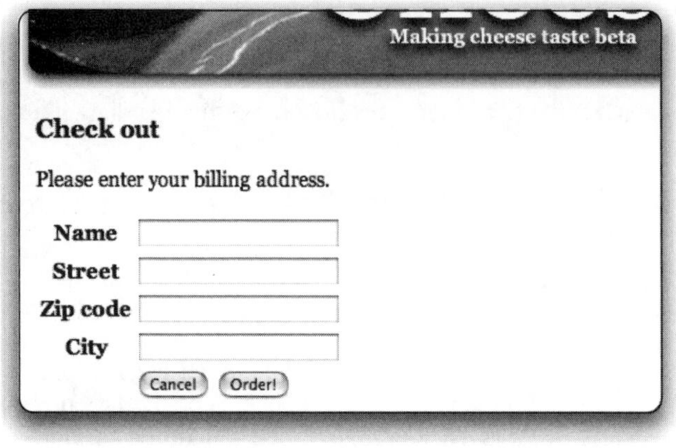

Figure 3.15
**The Check Out page with
the billing-address form**

Now that we have the buttons in place, we can fire up our application, start our browser, and order some cheese. Figure 3.15 shows the Check Out page with the billing-address form in place.

If we don't fill in our personal data, but we click the Order button, what do you think happens? At best, we'll be shipping several kilos of cheese to the bit bucket, because where would we ship the cheese without an address? More likely, we'll be presented with a stack trace containing a `NullPointerException`, because our order-processing code doesn't expect empty data. To make sure our customers get what they ordered, we must guide them to fill in the data correctly. In the next section, we'll add validations to our form components and provide internationalized feedback messages to our users.

3.3.2   *Adding validation to the billing-address form*

Nothing is more frustrating when using a website (or any application, for that matter) than making a mistake while typing and getting no response, a detailed stack trace, or a crashed application. One of the things that should be high on the priority list of any application builder is validating users' input and providing proper feedback. In this section, we'll add feedback to our checkout page. First we'll check that all required fields are completed. Next, we'll check whether the ZIP code value is a number.

MAKING THE FIELDS REQUIRED

The validation for required fields is performed before conversion and before other validations are triggered. An input value fails the required check when it's empty: either it isn't present in the request, or it consists only of whitespace. You make a field required by setting the `required` flag, as illustrated in the next snippet:

```
public class CheckOut extends CheesrPage {
    public CheckOut() {
        Form form = new Form("form");
        add(form);
        Address address = getCart().getBillingAddress();
```

```
form.add(new TextField("name", ...).setRequired(true));
form.add(new TextField("street", ...).setRequired(true));
form.add(new TextField("zipcode", ...).setRequired(true));
form.add(new TextField("city", ...).setRequired(true));
    ...
}
}
```

If we now start the application, go to the checkout page, and try to submit the form without setting any values, we no longer exit the page. It looks as if clicking the button has no effect, but actually the required validation prevents the form from being submitted. Unfortunately, we don't see any hint why we can't submit the form. To do that, we need a way to display feedback.

ADDING A FEEDBACK PANEL

Wicket uses a feedback queue to store feedback messages. You can add messages to the queue by calling info(), warning(), or error() on any component. The message is stored in the queue until it's read by a feedback component. Wicket provides the FeedbackPanel component, which reads messages from the queue and displays them in a list. If necessary, the messages can be filtered so that a particular feedback panel shows messages only from a specific component, and no messages from other components. But that is too advanced for our purposes here.

In the next snippet, we add a plain FeedbackPanel to our page. The feedback panel needs a place in the markup:

```
<div id="main">
<div wicket:id="feedback" class="feedback"></div>     ◁─┐ Feedback
<form wicket:id="form">                                   │ goes here
<h3>Check out</h3>
<p>Please enter your billing address.</p>
    ...
```

We add the feedback panel as the first component inside the main area. Now, we have to add the panel to the page, as illustrated in the next snippet of Java code:

```
public class CheckOut extends CheesrPage {
    public CheckOut() {
        add(new FeedbackPanel("feedback"));
        Form form = new Form("form");
        add(form);
        ...
    }
}
```

In this snippet, we add the feedback panel to the page. Now that the feedback panel is in place, we can look at it in the browser. Restart the application, and try to submit the checkout form without filling in any values. If you enter a value that isn't a number in the ZIP code field, the result should resemble figure 3.16, depending on the country you live in and which language you set as a default in your operating system (or browser).

These messages are provided by Wicket out of the box for over a dozen languages, including Dutch, Finnish, Swedish, Thai, Simplified Chinese, Japanese, Hungarian,

Figure 3.16 International feedback messages. Wicket provides translated basic feedback messages for over a dozen languages, including English, Dutch, and Japanese.

German, French, and of course English. Almost all validators that Wicket supplies have translated messages available. Chapter 12 goes into detail about Wicket's internationalization and localization capabilities.

You can get more validations by adding them to the form component that you want to validate. For instance, if we want to ensure that the name is at least 5 and at most 32 characters long, we add a LengthValidator to the Name field, as shown in the next snippet:

```
field.add(StringValidator.lengthBetween(5, 32));
```

More validators are available. You can use your IDE to quickly locate them (Eclipse users, select Navigate > Open Type in Hierarchy, and type IValidator in the pop-up box), or you can look at table 6.2 in chapter 6 to see all the currently available validators. Chapter 6 also shows you how to customize the validation messages for your own application.

Turning our attention back to our page, we aren't finished yet: even though we're now able to send invoices to our customers, our customers like to see what they're going to receive in return for their hard-earned money. Let's add the shopping cart to our checkout page.

3.3.3 *Creating a reusable shopping cart*

One of the great advantages of Wicket is the ability to create reusable components without much fuss. Until now, we've only reused components provided by Wicket: all the Label, Link, TextField, and ListView components we added to our pages. The most complex component we've reused so far is the PagingNavigator, added to the front page in section 3.2.3. How hard would it be to create your own, rich component? We've dedicated chapters 8 and 10 to this subject, not because it's difficult, but because we think the ability to easily create rich components is one of Wicket's best features. To give you a taste of creating reusable components, we'll create a reusable shopping-cart component using the cart from the front page, and add it to our checkout page. Figure 3.17 shows what this means.

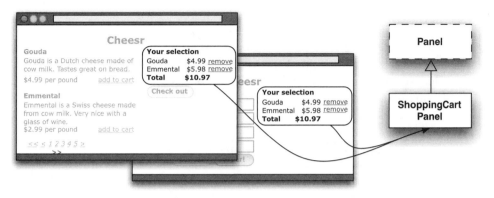

Figure 3.17 Extracting common components into a `Panel` for reuse in multiple pages

When you want to create a custom component, the best option is to use a `Panel`. A `Panel` is a Wicket component that has its own associated markup, just like a `Page`. The difference is that you can include a `Panel` anywhere on any page, include it in other panels, or even add it recursively to itself. Let's first create our `ShoppingCartPanel` Java class and markup file and put them next to the `Index` page's files. Listing 3.13 shows the Java file without components.

Listing 3.13   ShoppingCartPanel.java: Base for the reusable panel

```java
/**
 * Panel for displaying the contents of a shopping cart. The cart
 * shows the entries and the total value of the cart. Each item
 * can be removed by the user.
 */
public class ShoppingCartPanel extends Panel {
    private Cart cart;
    public ShoppingCartPanel(String id, Cart cart) {
        super(id);
        this.cart = cart;
    }

    private Cart getCart() {
        return cart;
    }
}
```

The shopping-cart panel takes two parameters in its constructor: the component identifier and the cart. Wicket uses the component identifier to identify the component in the markup, just as we've consistently done with our labels and links. In this case, we pass the identifier on to the superclass and let Wicket take care of that. In general, it's important to allow users to pass the component identifier in a custom component, because it makes it possible for the component to be reused several times on the same page, and you don't force others to use a particular identifier in the markup.

The cart is stored with the panel as a property. We also add a method to access the contents of the shopping cart. This makes it easier to move the shopping-cart code from the front page that depends on this getter method—our base page (the Cheesr-Page) provides the same method. Because our ShoppingCartPanel isn't a subclass of our CheesrPage, we need to implement this method ourselves.

Now that we have a simple Java class that does nothing much, let's add our markup file. We create a ShoppingCartPanel.html file next to the Java class, and put the following in it:

```
<html>
<body>
<wicket:panel>
</wicket:panel>
</body>
</html>
```

In this markup file, you'll notice the wicket:panel tags. These tags demarcate the specific boundaries of the panel's markup. Anything outside of these tags is discarded when the component is rendered; anything inside these tags is processed by Wicket and rendered into the final markup. Chapter 7 provides more information on these and other Wicket tags. Now, when we move the markup specific to the shopping-cart functionality (excluding the Check Out button) into this file and within the wicket:panel tags, the markup file looks like that in listing 3.14.

Listing 3.14   ShoppingCartPanel.html: Markup for a reusable shopping cart

```
<html>
<body>
<wicket:panel>
   <h3>Your selection</h3>
   <table>
   <tbody>
      <tr wicket:id="cart">
         <td wicket:id="name">Gouda</td>
         <td wicket:id="price">2.99</td>
         <td><a wicket:id="remove" href="#">remove</a></td>
      </tr>
      <wicket:remove>
      <tr>
         <td>Emmental</td>
         <td>$1.99</td>
         <td><a href="#">remove</a></td>
      </tr>
      </wicket:remove>
   </tbody>
   <tfoot>
      <tr class="total">
         <th>Total</th>
         <td wicket:id="total">$1.99</td>
         <td> </td>
      </tr>
   </tfoot>
   </table>
```

```
</wicket:panel>
</body>
</html>
```

When you compare this markup to the markup from the front page, you'll see that everything inside the cart div has been moved into our panel, except the Check Out button. The button is specific to the front page and shouldn't be included on our generic panel.

A similar selection can be made with the Java code for our shopping-cart panel. Recall the components: a list view that iterates through the cheese items in the cart, two labels and a remove link for each item in the list, and a label for displaying the total value. When we move the shopping cart code from the Index page into our panel constructor, it looks like the following:

```
public ShoppingCartPanel(String id, Cart cart) {
    super(id);
    this.cart = cart;
    add(new ListView("cart", new PropertyModel(this, "cart.cheeses")) {
        @Override
        protected void populateItem(ListItem item) {
            Cheese cheese = (Cheese) item.getModelObject();
            item.add(new Label("name", cheese.getName()));
            item.add(new Label("price", "$" + cheese.getPrice()));

            item.add(removeLink("remove", item));
        }
    });
    add(new Label("total", new Model() {
        @Override
        public Object getObject() {
            NumberFormat nf = NumberFormat.getCurrencyInstance();
            return nf.format(getCart().getTotal());
        }
    }));
}
```

Because we added the getCart method to our panel, the code compiles immediately. The only thing we have to do now is use the panel in our pages. First let's adjust our front page. The markup for the cart area of the front page is changed to this:

```
<div id="cart">
    <div wicket:id="shoppingcart"></div>
    <input type="button" wicket:id="checkout" value="Check out" />
</div>
```

We replace the relevant parts for the shopping cart with a div and a Wicket identifier. This is where our panel will render its markup. Before that is possible, we need to replace the old code in the page as well:

```
add(new PagingNavigator("navigator", listview));
add(new ShoppingCartPanel("shoppingcart", getCart()));
add(new Link("checkout")
{
    @Override
    public void onClick()
```

```
    {
        setResponsePage(new CheckOut());
    ...
});
```

Wasn't reusing the shopping-cart panel easy? In this part of the page's constructor, we replace the code for the shopping-cart list view and the label for displaying the total value with just one line of code: a call to our panel's constructor.

We're now ready to test our new panel. As you can see in your browser, the front page looks the same. We'll leave adding the shopping cart to the checkout page as an exercise for you.

3.4　*Summary*

A cheesy web shop is probably not the first thing that comes to your mind when you want to build the next Web 2.0 killer app. It is, however, a great way to see in action the different facets of developing a web application using any new technology such as Wicket.

Using the concepts introduced in chapter 2, we created the Application class that functions as our in-memory data store. To store customers' shopping-cart information, we created our own custom Session with the cart as an attribute. The minimum scaffolding that you need to build for any Wicket web application includes the Application class and a home page. A real-life application would of course have more pages and panels with the corresponding Java code and markup.

We used a simple web design to create mock HTML files for our pages. Using these files, we created our Wicket pages step by step: first, we presented a list of cheeses. We showed how you can repeat a group of components using a ListView. While building our shopping cart, we ran into a small bug: the total price field didn't update as we added more cheese to our cart. We solved the problem by giving the total price label a model that dynamically calculates the total amount on each render of the page. You learned how to control the visibility of components: in our case, the Check Out button is hidden until something is added to the shopping cart.

While building the checkout page, we introduced you to an important means of interacting with customers: form processing. We glanced at the way forms are processed, and we added validation and feedback to our checkout form. Using a PropertyModel, we were able to update the billing address with the user input when the form was successfully submitted.

We introduced the Panel component as a way to quickly create your own custom components. We extracted the shopping-cart code and markup from the front page and integrated it in our own ShoppingCartPanel. This opened up the opportunity to reuse the shopping cart on both the front page and the checkout page, while having only one implementation.

This chapter covered a lot of material and a variety of topics in a relatively short time. In the coming chapters, we'll expand and deepen the knowledge and experience you've gained in this chapter, starting with one of the most basic and important concepts: models.

Part 2

Ingredients for your Wicket applications

Now that you have a high-level understanding of Wicket, we're ready to dive into the details. In this part of the book, you'll learn the components, models, and behaviors that are available to you and how to put them to good use. Armed with this knowledge, you'll be ready to learn any new Wicket component within minutes.

Before we begin exploring components, chapter 4 discusses models. Models are the glue between the Wicket components and your domain model. As such, they're an important part of using Wicket.

Chapter 5 introduces components for displaying text and navigating to other websites and to pages in your application, links that are able to respond to user actions, and components that repeat their markup. The chapter ends with ways you can manipulate your components: modifying their visibility and manipulating their markup.

Processing form input is covered in chapter 6, together with validation and providing feedback to your users.

Creating and using components is one thing; combining them into reusable chunks that can act as a composite component is another. Chapter 7 explores grouping components and creating maintainable and consistent layouts using panels or markup inheritance.

Understanding models 4

With all those cheese stores sprouting on the web, soon we'll be able to buy lots of cheese online. And our business plan wouldn't be complete without a way to use that cheese. Cheese features as a main ingredient in many recipes, especially Italian recipes. Lasagna is not only a great Italian dish featuring heaps of cheese, it's also suitable as a metaphor for software: a lasagna gets better as you add more layers—but only to a point. (Spaghetti is also a great Italian dish that's improved by the addition of cheese, but somehow we're reluctant to use it as a metaphor for building great software.)

In the previous chapters, we've given you a grand overview of the Wicket framework. We introduced it and used it to build a simple online cheese store. Basically, we've shown you what a lasagna is, so you can get a taste for it quickly.

But knowing what a lasagna is and how it tastes isn't enough to create your own lasagna. You need to know which ingredients are required and when and how to apply them. The next few chapters will tell you about the ingredients for cooking your own Wicket application. By the time we're finished, you'll be able to roll your own lasagna noodles and cook your own tomato sauce instead of buying them from the local supermarket.

The structure of the coming chapters is such that you can read them individually—learning about ingredients for your applications—or in sequence. You can skip this chapter and read about components, and then come back to models. That said, we think that learning about models is important to get the most out of Wicket, and we encourage you to read this chapter first.

This chapter will discuss Wicket models. We discussed them in chapter 2, and you saw them in various examples in the first part of this book. But this time, we'll go into detail. Let's first recap what models are and why you should care about them.

4.1   What are models?

Remember that we talked about the Model View Controller (MVC) pattern in chapter 2? You learned that Wicket components represent the View and Controller in this pattern, and your domain objects represent the Model role. Figure 4.1 (adapted from chapter 2) shows how the MVC pattern is implemented in Wicket.

Taking the lasagna ingredients metaphor further, you can think of Wicket models as the lasagna noodles. They separate your domain layer (customer, cheese, cart) from things in the view layer (text field, page, label, form) but also bind them together to make a cohesive and neatly layered structure.

Wicket models allow the components to retrieve their data when they need to render their contents, and to convert and store user input when some event is received. From the perspective of a component, Wicket models fulfill the role of the Model in the MVC pattern.

Why are Wicket models so important that we dedicate a full chapter to them? Models are arguably the most crucial part of Wicket to understand because they can

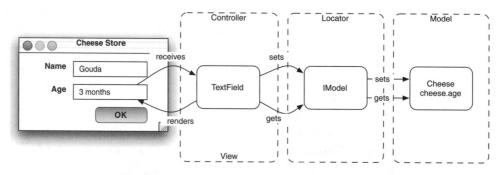

Figure 4.1   The Model-View-Controller pattern as it's implemented by Wicket. The component implements the roles of the Controller and View, and the Wicket model plays the role of the Model.

significantly affect your application's performance and memory requirements. You'll see how you can control this to your advantage when we discuss detachable models (section 4.3).

The choice of models also makes a huge difference in the number of lines of code you have to write. We all like to type less, so being able to write less code is a great benefit. Cutting down on code also makes reading the code easier, thus improving the code's maintainability.

Because Wicket models mediate between the view and domain layer, they enable you to apply transformations on your data before you display it, or before you accept user input and propagate it to your domain layer. Although Wicket provides a full-fledged localization and conversion mechanism for general use, it's often handy to quickly apply a conversion at a local level, as we did when we displayed the prices of cheeses in chapter 3.

Finally, models are important because Wicket components are tightly bound to them (at the level of the Java class hierarchy). The class diagram in figure 4.2 indicates that all components have a model property. Not all components do something with their model: several components work fine with no model value.

Figure 4.2 shows the IModel interface. The interface publishes two methods:

- getObject returning the value of the model
- setObject for setting the value of the model

From the point of view of the component, IModel acts as a bean property: it has a getter and a setter. Depending on the model implementation, the value can be local and self-contained within the model, or it can be looked up dynamically and come from a domain object. The model implementation can be as flexible as you want and get the domain object from a database, a web service, the session, or anywhere. The component doesn't know where the data is coming from or where it's stored—it just needs to be able to call getObject and setObject.

Conversely, from our point of view, the model acts as the actual value of the component. Instead of asking the component for its value, you ask the model; and instead of setting the value on the component, you change the model value. As a user

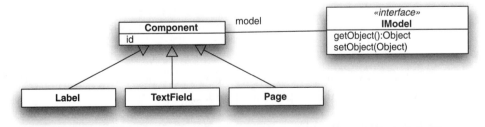

Figure 4.2 A class diagram showing the relationship between Component **and** IModel**. All Wicket components are ultimately descendants of** Component**, and all Wicket models implement the** IModel **interface.**

of the framework, as long as you have a reference to the model (or know where to find it), you have access to the value associated with the component and can even change it if required.

An interface is nice, but without an implementation you can't do much with it. It's possible to implement the interface yourself directly, but it's better to use or extend one of the standard Wicket models. In the following sections, we'll show several standard implementations of the IModel interface.

4.2   A taste of the standard models

Wicket provides a number of useful model implementations out of the box. We'll cover only a subset of the provided models because going through all of them would take a lot of space in this book. Fortunately, with the knowledge you gain from the discussed models, you should have no problem understanding those that remain.

Out of the full set of models provided by Wicket, you'll most likely use only those listed in table 4.1. Your choices aren't limited to this list, but it provides a good overview of the available commonly used models. The list is ordered from a simple model that serves as a storage container to a full-blown internationalization machine. In the following sections, we'll discuss all these models except ResourceModel and StringResource-Model; we'll discuss them in chapter 12, when we talk about internationalization.

Table 4.1   The most commonly used model classes provided by Wicket

Model	Description
Model	Simple model used to store static content, or used as a base class for quick dynamic behavior.
PropertyModel	Uses a property expression to dynamically access a property in your domain objects.
CompoundPropertyModel	Uses component identifiers as property expressions to bind components to its domain object.
LoadableDetachableModel	Abstract model for quickly creating detachable models.
ResourceModel	Easy-to-use model for retrieving messages from resource bundles.
StringResourceModel	Advanced model for retrieving messages from resource bundle; supports property expressions and MessageFormat substitutions.

We'll discuss the models in the order they're presented in table 4.1. Without further ado, we'll start with the simplest of all: Model.

4.2.1   Using the simple Model

You may not have realized it, but you've seen the simplest use of models already: in every one of our examples that features a label displaying text. Every time we've written code like this

```
...
new Label("firstname", customer.getFirstName());
new Label("lastname", customer.getLastName());
new Label("street", customer.getAddress().getStreet());
...
```

we've been doing this behind the scenes:

```
...
new Label("firstname", new Model(customer.getFirstName()));
new Label("lastname", new Model(customer.getLastName()));
new Label("street", new Model(customer.getAddress().getStreet()));
...
```

The Label component has a convenience constructor that wraps the passed-in text in a model, as shown in the following code taken from the Label class:

```
public class Label extends WebComponent {
    public Label(String id, String text) {        ❶ Wrap String
        this(id, new Model(text));                   in Model
    }
    public Label(String id, IModel model) {       Alternate constructor
        super(id, model);                         ❷ receiving IModel
    }
}
```

The label constructor takes the string and wraps it in a Model ❶ before passing it to the superconstructor ❷. This enables you to directly put strings into the label components without having to wrap the objects yourself.

Taking a closer look at the previous example, we see some issues in the code:

```
...
add(new Label("firstname", new Model(customer.getFirstName())));
add(new Label("lastname", new Model(customer.getLastName())));
add(new Label("street", new Model(customer.getAddress().getStreet())));
...
```

First, this approach only works for string properties, because there is only one convenience constructor for a Label. This doesn't pose a huge problem, but it can be annoying when you have to display a date field. Converting a date field to a string isn't exactly rocket science, but it can be cumbersome, especially if you have to take localization into account. Using Wicket's property models and converters solves this problem because they hook directly into Wicket's localization system.

The second and potentially fatal issue is the possibility of null values. If the customer object is null or the getAddress method returns null, we'll present our user with a NullPointerException, which isn't a pretty sight. So, we have to check for those values. If we were to embark on such a mission, the previous example would look something like the following:

```
...
add(new Label("firstname", (cust==null) ? "" : cust.getFirstName()));
add(new Label("lastname", (cust==null) ? "" : cust.getLastName()));
```

```
add(new Label("street", (cust==null||cust.getAddress()==null)
              ? "" : cust.getAddress().getStreet());
...
```

All this `null` checking is cumbersome, error prone, and not fun. A framework should help. In the next section, we'll look at a way to remedy this situation using the `Property-Model`. When you use `Model` as a storage facility for property values (wrapping the value), you use it as a so-called static model. We touched on the subject of static versus dynamic models in section 3.2.2 and promised a closer look. Because understanding the differences between static and dynamic models will be important when we discuss property and detachable models later, we'll discuss this subject before we continue with the models from table 4.1.

STATIC VS. DYNAMIC MODELS

To give you a better understanding of the differences between static and dynamic models, we'll create a page that shows the time in a label. Whenever the page is refreshed, the clock shows the current time. The following markup and Java code create a static clock and provide a link to refresh the page, thereby updating the time:

```html
<html>
<body>
    Current time: <span wicket:id="clock"></span> <br />
    <a href="#" wicket:id="refresh">refresh</a>
</body>
</html>
```

```java
public ClockPage extends WebPage {
    public ClockPage() {
        SimpleDateFormat df = new SimpleDateFormat("hh:mm:ss");
        String time = df.format(new Date());
        Model clock = new Model(time);          ◀──❶ Clock model     ❷ Link to
        add(new Label("clock", clock));                                 refresh
        add(new Link("refresh"){ public void onClick() {}});  ◀──┘      page
    }
}
```

We create a model for our label and give it the current time ❶. Our refresh link ❷ does nothing in its `onClick` handler, causing Wicket to refresh the page.

When you run this example and click the Refresh link, you'll see that the clock doesn't update as expected. The static time in figure 4.3 shows the result of our clock (identified by the Static Time field). Our current clock model is static.

To make the clock show the current time on each page refresh, we have to update the value of the clock model with each refresh. For instance, we could update the

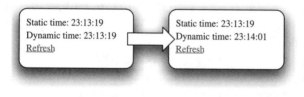

Figure 4.3
A clock as an example of the difference between static and dynamic labels. When the Refresh link is clicked, only the dynamic time is updated.

clock in the `onClick` handler of the Refresh link. But that approach will fall apart when someone clicks Refresh in her browser (or presses F5, CTRL-R, or CMD-R)—which causes the browser to request the current URL associated with the page—because the link's `onClick` handler isn't triggered in that case.

Instead of using a static (hard-coded) model to create the clock, we can make the clock model dynamic. The idea is to update the value each time the `getObject` method is called—or, more specifically, to override the `getObject` method. The following example shows how this works:

```
public ClockPage() {
    Model clock = new Model() {
            @Override
            public Object getObject() {
                SimpleDateFormat df = new SimpleDateFormat("hh:mm:ss");
                String time = df.format(new Date());
                return time;
            }
        };
    add(new Label("clock", clock));
    add(new Link("refresh"){ public void onClick() {}});
}
```

Instead of creating a new `Model` and providing it with the current date, we now create an anonymous subclass of `Model` and override the `getObject` method. The `getObject` method returns a fresh date each time it's called—and this call occurs whenever the component is rendered. This way, we always display the up-to-date time, and in this sense the model is dynamic. The Dynamic Time field in figure 4.3 shows the results of our dynamic clock before and after clicking Refresh.

Figure 4.4 summarizes the differences between static and dynamic models. With a static model, *you* are responsible for keeping the model in sync with the domain objects. This isn't a problem per se, but it's one of those things that can keep you busy before you've had your second cup of coffee for the day, leaving you wondering why

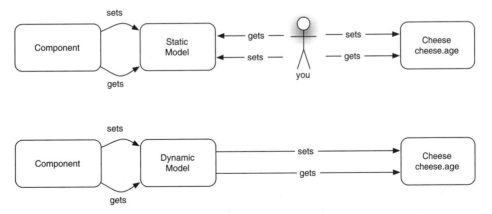

Figure 4.4 **The difference between static and dynamic models: with static models, you're responsible for keeping the domain objects in sync with your model.**

the page doesn't show the updated value of your domain object. Dynamic models can get access to updated values from your domain objects all by themselves, saving you the effort of keeping them in sync.

The fact that the Model class typically behaves in a static manner isn't the only thing to notice. Because a static Model stores its value, the value must be serializable. There is a good reason for this requirement.

SERIALIZING MODELS

Wicket components keep a reference to their associated model. At the end of the request, after the markup has been sent to the browser, Wicket stores the page, component hierarchy, and associated models (the state) in the *page store*. Depending on which type of store is configured, it can go to disk, to a database, or into the HTTP session. Most, if not all, page-store implementations use serialization to store the state.

> ### Serialization
>
> *Serialization* is a way for Java to write objects to a stream. This streaming is typically used either to store the state of an object or to transport the state to another process. Java has built-in support for serialization and uses the marker interface java. io.Serializable as a way to identify objects that support serialization.
>
> In web applications, serialization is typically used to transfer objects between the various tiers—especially when they're on separate JVMs, to synchronize session state between nodes in a cluster or to preserve session state by storing it in case a server goes down. In the latter case, the sessions can be restored when the server goes live again, and customers can continue shopping.

Because components and their associated models are serialized, objects stored in models need to implement the Serializable interface as well; otherwise the page and components can't be stored in the page store. You'll notice these errors as java. io.NotSerializableExceptions in your console or server log.

At best, users won't notice anything when such serialization errors happen. In most application setups, the only time a user may run into a problem is when he uses the browser's Back button and sees a Page Expired message. If Wicket tries to restore the page from the page store but can't find it (because it couldn't be stored due to the Not-SerializableException), Wicket shows a Page Expired message. In the worst case, you can't synchronize the state across the cluster, and your failover or load-balancing strategy fails.

Fortunately, there are ways to cope with situations where you have objects that can't be serialized, or when serialization has too big an impact on CPU and memory usage. In this chapter, we'll discuss several ways to overcome this limitation. As a final sidetrack before we return to the models from table 4.1, we'll look at how you can use Model to overcome the serialization problem.

WORKING AROUND THE SERIALIZATION PROBLEM USING MODEL

When your model value isn't serializable and can't be made serializable due to reasons beyond your control, you need to find a way to make the components work with your model value. Using Model as a generic storage facility for components is one way to work around the serialization problem: all text that you need to display is ultimately a String. But how does that work when you want to process user input and transfer the values to your domain layer?

We discuss form input in detail in chapter 6, but there is no harm in using a form as an example of how you can use Model to work around the serialization issue. Listing 4.1 shows a quick way to create a form for receiving and processing user input.

> **Listing 4.1   Using Model to store form values**

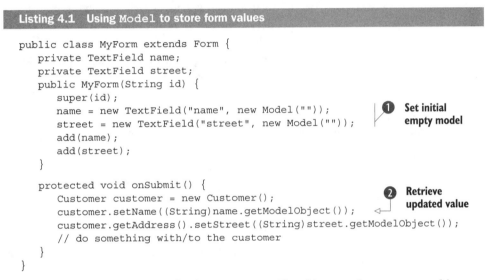

```
public class MyForm extends Form {
    private TextField name;
    private TextField street;
    public MyForm(String id) {
        super(id);
        name = new TextField("name", new Model(""));        ❶ Set initial
        street = new TextField("street", new Model(""));        empty model
        add(name);
        add(street);
    }

    protected void onSubmit() {
        Customer customer = new Customer();                  ❷ Retrieve
        customer.setName((String)name.getModelObject());   ◁──  updated value
        customer.getAddress().setStreet((String)street.getModelObject());
        // do something with/to the customer
    }
}
```

For capturing user input, we don't use any specific object or the Customer object we have—just a form with a couple of text fields ❶. Initially, the form displays empty fields. When the user fills in the fields and submits the form, we retrieve the value of each field in the onSubmit handler ❷ and copy the values across to our customer object.

NOTE   We use shorthand to retrieve the model value of the component: component.getModelObject() is shorthand for component.getModel().getObject(). To retrieve the model value as a String, you can also use component.getModelObjectAsString()

Using a simple Model is a nice way of building a quick form without much ceremony. And overriding the getObject method on the model is a great (and quick) method to get dynamic behavior in place. But it isn't that great when your form is more complex than, say, a login form with two input fields. In our day-to-day programming, we don't like this way of working with models and forms: it's tedious and repetitive. It's an interaction-driven way of coding: you have to manually mediate between the components and your model objects. In most cases, you're working with existing domain objects such as a `Customer` object, so you already have the properties, and you'd like the components to read from and write to these fields directly. This is also known as *form binding*.

Let's return to the models from table 4.1 and see how you can use `PropertyModels` to glue your components to your domain objects.

4.2.2 *Using PropertyModels for dynamic models*

As we showed in the previous section, manually binding the properties of your Java objects to Wicket components can be laborious and error prone. In this section, we'll look at a special model that takes away the disadvantages of doing it yourself: the `PropertyModel` class. We briefly discussed `PropertyModel` in chapters 1 and 3.

`PropertyModel` uses a property expression to examine your object and retrieve or set the value of the object's field. These property expressions are simple in nature; they look the same as if you were traversing your objects' public Java fields. Table 4.2 shows some example expressions.

Table 4.2 `PropertyModel` **examples**

Java public field expression	PropertyModel equivalent
`user.firstName`	`new PropertyModel(user, "firstName")`
`user.lastName`	`new PropertyModel(user, "lastName")`
`user.address.street`	`new PropertyModel(user, "address.street")`
`user.address.zipcode`	`new PropertyModel(user, "address.zipcode")`
`user.children[0].name`	`new PropertyModel(user, "children[0].name")`

The expression is the second parameter of the property model constructor. One big advantage of `PropertyModel` is it's `null`-safe: it won't throw an exception when one of the expression components turns out to be `null`. In the case where a value is being read, it returns an empty string when a `null` is encountered.

When setting the value, `PropertyModel` tries to create objects using the default constructor when possible. If this fails, a `WicketRuntimeException` is thrown.

NOTE The automatic procedure isn't clairvoyant, and it can only instantiate new objects of the type of the property itself. For instance, it isn't possible to autocreate a property with the type `java.util.List<String>`. How would Wicket know which implementation of the `List` to create? Should Wicket create an `ArrayList<String>` or a `LinkedList<String>`?

Remember the example with all the `null` checks? Here's a reminder:

```
...
add(new Label("firstname", (cust==null) ? "" : cust.getFirstName()));
add(new Label("lastname", (cust==null) ? "" : cust.getLastName()));
```

```
add(new Label("street", (cust==null||cust.getAddress()==null)
                ? "" : cust.getAddress().getStreet());
...
```

Now, let's see how this looks using property models:

```
...
add(new Label("firstname", new PropertyModel(customer, "firstName")));
add(new Label("lastname", new PropertyModel(customer, "lastName")));
add(new Label("street", new PropertyModel(customer,"address.street")));
...
```

This looks a lot cleaner, doesn't it? Using property models offers a definite advantage. Not only do they remove the need for null checks, they also make it much easier to update your Java objects inside forms. You don't have to query the form component for a value and set it yourself on your domain objects: just bind your domain object to the form component using a property model, and you're done. Wicket takes care of the rest. Let's revisit the form example from listing 4.1 and alter it to use the property model (see listing 4.2).

Listing 4.2 Using `PropertyModels` to store form values

```
public class MyForm extends Form {
    public MyForm(String id) {
        super(id);

        Customer customer = new Customer();
        setModel(new Model(customer));            ← Bind to
        add(new TextField("name",                    customer.name
                new PropertyModel(customer, "name")));   ←
                                                           Bind to
        add(new TextField("street",                        customer.
                new PropertyModel(customer, "address.street")));  ← address.
    }                                                        street

    protected void onSubmit() {
        Customer customer = (Customer)getModelObject();  ← Get customer
        String street = customer.getAddress().getStreet();  from form
        // do something with the value of the street property
    }
}
```

In this example, we create the form and provide it with a new customer object. The form text fields are bound to the customer object's fields using property models. When the form is submitted, the property models update the customer's appropriate fields.

Now that you've seen that property models can clean up code considerably, let's look at the next model from table 4.1. CompoundPropertyModel will save you from even more typing.

> ### Are property models the ideal son-in-law?
>
> Property models do have some quirks. We mentioned the first issue: property models can't perform magic and will probably create wrongly typed objects when there are multiple candidate classes (for example, creating a `Person` instead of an `Employee` when `Employee` extends `Person`) or even fail when no suitable class can be instantiated.
>
> Another quirk is that the expressions aren't safe when you're refactoring. Imagine that the customer's `address` field is renamed `homeAddress`. This means the field, getter, and setter must be renamed, along with all occurrences of them throughout your application. However, your refactoring tool probably won't notice the text inside the property expression. Your mileage may vary, depending on how smart your refactoring tool is.
>
> Finally, just as with the `Model` class, property models require the object that is used as the root of the expression to be serializable.

4.2.3   *Saving code with CompoundPropertyModels*

In everyday Wicket usage, we see a drive for consistency: when users create pages displaying the properties of domain objects, the component identifiers typically are equal to the property names that are displayed. For instance, when we display a person object, we typically have label components with identifiers such as `firstName`, `lastName`, `street`, `zipcode`, `city`, `birthdate`, `ssn`, and so forth. There is nothing wrong with this approach, because it emphasizes the meaning of a component in the markup file and in the Java file. Using cryptic names for component identifiers makes understanding and debugging an application difficult.

Early in the development of Wicket, we saw an opportunity to use this tendency to name things the same. If we take the label example from the previous section, let's see how we can save more code:

```
...
add(new Label("firstname", new PropertyModel(customer, "firstName")));
add(new Label("lastname", new PropertyModel(customer, "lastName")));
add(new Label("street", new PropertyModel(customer, "address.street")));
...
```

In this example, the component identifiers are almost the same as the attributes of the customer and the `address` objects. Let's first align them to be identical:

```
...
add(new Label("firstName", new PropertyModel(customer, "firstName")));
add(new Label("lastName", new PropertyModel(customer, "lastName")));
add(new Label("address.street",
                 new PropertyModel(customer, "address.street")));
...
```

This isn't exactly rocket science, but we're getting somewhere. The component identifiers now perfectly match the property names of the `customer` object. Don't forget to rename the `wicket:id` attributes in your markup file as well!

Next, the following example introduces the `CompoundPropertyModel`:

```
...
setModel(new CompoundPropertyModel(customer));
add(new Label("firstName"));
add(new Label("lastName"));
add(new Label("address.street"));
...
```

❶ Set model on parent

❷ No explicit models

We first set the model of the parent component (typically a page, panel, or form) to a `CompoundPropertyModel` that wraps our customer object ❶. Next, we remove the explicit models for all label components ❷. When a component needs its model value but doesn't have a model assigned (such as the labels in our example), it traverses its component hierarchy for a parent with a `CompoundPropertyModel`. The component then uses its component identifier as the property expression on the `CompoundProperty-Model`'s value for retrieving the property's value to display.

In this example, the first label retrieves the `firstName` property from the `customer` object supplied by the `CompoundPropertyModel`. The second label retrieves the `lastName` property from the customer; and the third label first gets the `address` object from the customer and then gets the value of the `street` property from the `address` object.

Let's revisit the form example and apply our knowledge of the `CompoundProperty-Model` to it. We've taken the code from the form example in listing 4.2 and modified it to use the `CompoundPropertyModel`; see listing 4.3.

Listing 4.3 Using a `CompoundPropertyModel` to store form values

```
public class MyForm extends Form {                         Set inheritable
    public MyForm(String id) {                                 model
        super(id, new CompoundPropertyModel(new Customer()));
        add(new TextField("firstName"));
        add(new TextField("address.street"));     Binds to
    }                                             customer.address.street

    protected void onSubmit() {
        Customer customer = (Customer)getModelObject();
        String street = customer.getAddress().getStreet();
        // do something with the value of the street property
    }
}
```

When you compare this example with the form example in the previous section, you can see that the code in the form constructor is much cleaner. We now take advantage of the fact that our component identifiers match the properties of our domain model.

Let's shine some light on what we refer to as *inheritable models* by examining how this works with nested components. For instance, what if we have an extra container component between the parent holding the `CompoundPropertyModel` and our component looking for an inheritable model? Listing 4.4 illustrates this example: ask yourself what is displayed by the label.

Listing 4.4   The effect of nested components on inheritable models

```
public class NestedExamplePage extends Page {
    public NestedExamplePage() {
        Customer customer = new Customer();
        customer.setAddress(new Address());
        customer.getAddress().setStreet("Penny Lane");

        setModel(new CompoundPropertyModel(customer));
        WebMarkupContainer parent = new WebMarkupContainer("address"));
        add(parent);
        parent.add(new Label("street");
    }
}
<html>
<body>
<address wicket:id="address">
    <span wicket:id="street"></span>
</address>
</body>
</html>
```

Will this example display "Penny Lane" in your browser? You would think so: the label with identifier street is a child of the container with the identifier address. If you combined those component identifiers, you might expect the whole expression to become address.street. But it doesn't work this way. Instead, you'll get an exception explaining that a Customer doesn't have a street property. Let's see how this works.

Because the label doesn't have a model of its own, it searches up the component hierarchy until the first inheritable model is encountered. Its immediate parent component (the WebMarkupContainer) doesn't have an (inheritable) model, so that one is skipped, and its parent (the page) is queried. This one has an inheritable model, so the label now tries to resolve its identifier (street) against the customer. But because the customer doesn't have such a property, Wicket can't do anything other than throw an exception.

You're probably wondering how to fix this issue. Remember that the component identifier is reused as a property expression. We need to change the label's component identifier to address.street, as illustrated in listing 4.5 (don't forget to change it in the markup as well).

Listing 4.5   The effect of nested components on inheritable models

```
public class NestedExamplePage extends Page {
    public NestedExamplePage() {
        Customer customer = new Customer();
        customer.setAddress(new Address());
        customer.getAddress().setStreet("Penny Lane");

        setModel(new CompoundPropertyModel(customer));
        WebMarkupContainer parent = new WebMarkupContainer("address"));
```

```
        add(parent);
        parent.add(new Label("address.street"));    ◁─┐
    }
}                                                        Changed
<html>                                                   component
<body>                                                   identifier
<address wicket:id="address">
    <span wicket:id="address.street"></span>        ◁─┘
</address>
</body>
</html>
```

This gets the expected "Penny Lane" result in your browser.

In summary: each component without a model searches up its parent hierarchy for an inheritable model. Once the model is found, the component uses its own identifier as is for the property expression needed to query the model. Any other components that lie between the component and the parent with the inheritable model don't make a difference.

With all this praise, you may wonder whether the CompoundPropertyModel is the mother of all models. Although we enjoy the clean code this model enables, some disadvantages remain.

Just as with the PropertyModel, property expressions aren't safe for refactoring. And this time, the problem is bigger: the component identifiers are now the property expressions, so you have to keep track of them in both your Java code and your markup files. This isn't the end of the world, but it's something you should be aware of. And with the advent of Wicket-aware plug-ins, this may become something the IDE will take care of, instead of you.

Even if someday IDE support for refactoring property expressions becomes available, how can you use the CompoundPropertyModel and provide an alternative property expression when you can't change the component's identifier?

USING BIND FOR ALTERNATIVE BINDINGS

In the previous examples featuring the CompoundPropertyModel, we only used the component identifier as the property expression. Sometimes you don't have the ability to change the component's identifier, but you do want to reuse the compound model that was set on the page or form. The bind method of the CompoundProperty-Model gives you the flexibility to add alternative bindings between components and the model object.

To illustrate this, look at the form example in listing 4.6. Assume for the moment that for some reason we can't modify the component identifier of the street text field.

> Listing 4.6 Using the bind method for more flexibility in component paths

```
public class MyForm extends Form {
    public MyForm(String id) {
        super(id);
```

```
CompoundPropertyModel model =
        new CompoundPropertyModel(new Customer());
setModel(model);           ◁——————— Set model
add(new TextField("name"));
add(new TextField("street", model.bind("address.street")));   ◁—┐
}                                                                 │
                                               Bind component    │
    protected void onSubmit() {                to address.street ❶
        Customer customer = (Customer)getModelObject();
        String street = customer.getAddress().getStreet();
        // do something with the value of the street property
    }
}
```

Because we can't modify the component identifier of the street text field, we have to bind the text field in a different way compared to our customer object's address. This is achieved by using the bind method on our CompoundPropertyModel ❶ to bind the text field to the customer's address.street property.

There remains one open issue with compound property models. Just as with PropertyModel, CompoundPropertyModel requires that the object it queries for the properties implement Serializable. There is a way to use property models (including the compound models) to circumvent the serializability requirement. In the next section, you'll learn how you can use detachable models to avoid serializing your model values.

4.3   *Keeping things small and fresh: detachable models*

Lasagna is a nice dish, but it's on the heavy side. If you look at Garfield, an anthropomorphic feline lasagna lover, you can see what eating loads of lasagna can do to you. Wouldn't it be great if there were an ingredient that allowed you to eat all the lasagna you could manage, and still preserve your supermodel figure? In the real world of béchamel sauce, salami, and cheese, it's unfortunately an impossibility; but when we cross the metaphor boundary, we have such an ingredient. Detachable models keep your applications lean and mean, no matter how often you consume them.

Let's first look at what *detaching* is. After that, we'll present a standard model that takes care of most of the work related to detaching.

4.3.1   *What is detaching?*

At the end of each request to your application, when the response HTML has been fully rendered to the client browser, Wicket invokes a detach sequence during which all components and models that took part in the request have the option to clean up any data they want to get rid of. This detaching is performed to minimize the in-memory state of the application and to leave out references to non-serializable objects. When the time comes for the application state to be serialized on the server, fewer objects must be converted, and objects that aren't serializable aren't encountered.

To illustrate how detaching works, we'll extend the Wicket Model class to create a CheeseModel that retrieves Cheese objects from a database and discards them when they're no longer needed. Until now, we've discussed the getter and setter of the

Minimizing state

A major difference between traditional thick client development and web development is the need to keep things scalable. When you build a Windows 32 (or Cocoa, GTK, or QT) client application, you usually have a whole PC at your disposal. Sometimes a user will file a bug report on your application's memory consumption, but hey, we're in an age where memory is cheap and the days of 640 KB computers are long gone. You can code your application to use 10 MB of memory and not worry. Not bad, considering that iTunes can easily take up 145 MB.

If you port your application to the web, what will happen when 100 users start using it? Your memory requirements will shoot up to 1 GB! If your application is popular and attracts thousands of users ... you can see where this is going. Either you'll have to invest in a lot of hardware, or you'll need to find a way to manage your application's memory requirements.

The total amount of available RAM isn't the only limiting factor. When your application runs in a cluster, the session state must be synchronized across the cluster. The more state your application contains, the more information must be communicated. Typically, this synchronization is done using—yes—serialization, and that's an expensive undertaking. Minimizing the amount of data that needs to be sent over the cluster is usually a great way to remove a bottleneck in your architecture.

`Model` class. But we've left one method out of our discussions: `detach`. The class diagram in figure 4.5 shows that the `Model` class implements the `IModel` interface, which in turn extends the `IDetachable` interface (note that we omitted the `IDetachable` interface in previous diagrams for clarity).

If you look at the `IModel` interface, you see that it exposes the getter and setter methods to interact with Wicket components. The inherited interface `IDetachable` adds `detach` as the third method in the contract between a component and the model. The `Model` class implements the methods of these interfaces and has one field: the value that is returned from `getObject` and modified with `setObject`.

Let's see what happens when a component needs data. Typically, a component queries its model for data during rendering or when a request is targeted at the

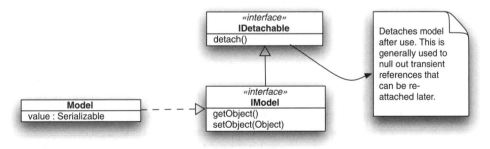

Figure 4.5   A class diagram of the `Model` class and the interfaces it implements

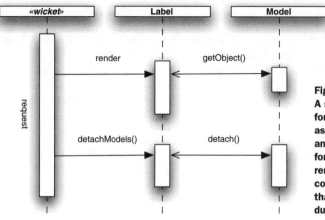

Figure 4.6
A simplified sequence diagram for processing a request. Wicket asks the Label to render itself, and the Label queries its model for the data to render. After rendering, Wicket asks the component to release any data that was temporarily cached during the detach phase.

component (for example, an onClick event for a link). Note that the getObject method can be called multiple times during a request (especially when the model is shared with multiple components). At the end of the request, when the response has been sent to the client, Wicket calls detach on all components that have been used during the request. Figure 4.6 shows a simplified sequence diagram of the interaction between Wicket, a Label component, and a Model.

If an exception occurs during the detach phase, Wicket logs the exception and continues to detach the models. At this time, the response has already been sent to the browser, so it isn't possible to notify the user that anything went wrong (not that your average Joe is interested in the failure of detaching your data).

We previously discussed the issue that objects stored in models need to be serializable. We also showed that using Model as a generic property for components is a solution to the serialization problem (see section 4.2.1). It turns out that detachable models are also helpful in working around this issue.

4.3.2 *Working around a serialization problem with detachable models*

The cause of the serialization problem lies in the fact that models hold a reference to the non-serializable value. If we could clean up that reference before serialization occurred, and reconstitute the object when it was necessary again, we'd have an elegant solution.

To illustration this solution, let's implement a detachable model that gets a Cheese object. Assume for now that the Cheese class doesn't implement the Serializable interface, and we can't change the Cheese class definition. So, we can't hold a reference to a cheese, because doing so would result in serialization errors. Let's also assume that our Cheese objects are stored in a database and that they can be retrieved on demand by using their unique identifier (primary key). The code in listing 4.7 shows a model that works around the fact that a Cheese object isn't serializable.

Listing 4.7 Detachable cheese model that works around serialization problems

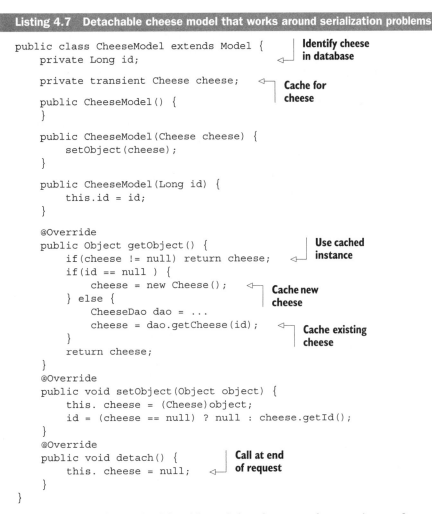

```
public class CheeseModel extends Model {          Identify cheese
    private Long id;                              in database

    private transient Cheese cheese;         Cache for
                                             cheese
    public CheeseModel() {
    }

    public CheeseModel(Cheese cheese) {
        setObject(cheese);
    }

    public CheeseModel(Long id) {
        this.id = id;
    }

    @Override
    public Object getObject() {               Use cached
        if(cheese != null) return cheese;     instance
        if(id == null ) {
            cheese = new Cheese();        Cache new
        } else {                          cheese
            CheeseDao dao = ...
            cheese = dao.getCheese(id);      Cache existing
        }                                    cheese
        return cheese;
    }
    @Override
    public void setObject(Object object) {
        this. cheese = (Cheese)object;
        id = (cheese == null) ? null : cheese.getId();
    }
    @Override
    public void detach() {            Call at end
        this. cheese = null;          of request
    }
}
```

In this model, we keep the identifier of the cheese and a transient reference to our `Cheese` object. When a component requests the cheese, our model has several options. If no identifier is available, we create a new cheese and return it. If an identifier is available, but the associated object isn't retrieved yet, we get the cheese from the DAO and store the results for subsequent calls. When the request has finished and the component no longer needs the cheese, the call to `detach` nullifies our reference, solving the serialization problem.

NOTE This model reloads the cheese from the database on each request (or creates a new `Cheese` object). If you want to retain data across requests, but you don't want to persist it (yet), you should make the domain object serializable or store the data in a different, serializable object as a temporary measure until you're able to persist the data.

This isn't a lot of code, but using this approach for a lot of different classes (one project of ours has about 200 entity classes, and counting) is asking a lot of your keyboard. Fortunately, LoadableDetachableModel takes care of a lot of the things we just presented in CheeseModel. Let's look at where the grass is greener.

4.3.3 *Using LoadableDetachableModel*

LoadableDetachableModel makes it easy to work with detachable models. It's modeled after a common use case for detachable models. Let's first look at how Loadable-DetachableModel is used. In the next example, we'll create a web page that displays a list of cheeses. For the sake of brevity, we've kept the example simple and omitted the retrieving from the database. Our page lists only the names of the cheeses:

```
public class ListCheesesPage extends WebPage {
    public ListCheesesPage() {
        IModel model = new LoadableDetachableModel() {       ❶ Required
            @Override                                            subclass
            protected Object load() {        ⟵ ❷ Get users from
                CheeseDao dao = ...                 database
                return dao.getCheeses();     ⟵
            }                                  ❸ List users
        };
        add(new ListView("cheeses", model) {
            protected void populateItem(ListItem item) {
                Cheese cheese = (Cheese)item.getModelObject();
                item.add(new Label("name", cheese.getName()));
                ...
            }
        };
    }
}

<html>
<body>
<ul>
<li wicket:id="cheeses"><span wicket:id="name"></span></li>
</ul>
</body>
</html>
```

LoadableDetachableModel ❶ requires you to implement one method: load ❷. This method should retrieve and return the object the model will hold: in our example, it retrieves the list of cheeses ❸. LoadableDetachableModel keeps a transient reference to our list and releases it when the model is detached. The getObject method returns the transient object when the model is in the attached state. At the end of the request, the model is detached: LoadableDetachableModel discards our list of cheeses.

When a new request comes in, and the ListView needs the list of cheeses again, it calls getObject on its model. The loadable detachable model notices it's still in a detached state and calls load to get the contents of the list again. The result of the load call is cached for the remainder of the request until the model is detached again.

Detaching, performance, and caching

You're probably wondering about the performance implications of going to the database with each request to save memory. Storing the domain objects directly with the components provides the best performance, but even so, this approach (in general) isn't preferred. We've discussed several problems with storing domain objects directly with components: the serialization issue (this costs CPU time, I/O time, and bandwidth), and increased memory usage.

Each user session keeps a copy of the objects in the history. These copies can quickly get out of date, especially when the user uses the Back button. With many users, there will be many copies of the same object in memory. This is a waste of RAM that could be used to serve more data to even more users.

We prefer to offload the caching of domain objects to the data tier. Using a cache ensures that only one logical copy of an object is stored in memory. This way, you can reduce your application's memory footprint. A cache can be configured to use only a limited amount of memory, thus freeing space for handling requests and making it possible to accommodate more users.

It's also possible to initialize the model in an attached state: provide the object you already have to the constructor, and the model uses that instance until it's detached. In the previous example, we didn't have any state in our detached model—we retrieved the full read-only list of cheeses on each load. Let's look at how the model works for a single object. Consider the following model class:

```
public class LoadableCheeseModel extends LoadableDetachableModel {
    private Long id;                                         ➊ Hold object
                                                                identifier
    public LoadableCheeseModel(Cheese cheese) {
        super(cheese);                      ➋ Create
        id = cheese.getId();                  attached state
    }

    public LoadableCheeseModel(Long id) {
        super();
        this.id = id;
    }

    protected Object load() {                    ➌ Create new object
        if(id == null) return new Cheese();        when id is unknown
        CheeseDao dao = ...          ➍ Get object
        return dao.get(id);             from database
    }
}
...
add(new Form("cheeseForm", new LoadableCheeseModel(user)) {
    ...
});
```

In this example, we define a subclass of the `LoadableDetachableModel` that stores the object identifier of the `Cheese` object **❶**. The identifier is the only data stored (or serialized) when this model is in a detached state, so it's efficient in terms of memory usage. The model's constructor takes an existing `Cheese` object and uses it to initialize in an attached state **❷**. In this case, the model won't use the `load` method until after it's detached. The `load` method returns a new `Cheese` object if there was no identifier **❸** or uses the identifier to retrieve the `Cheese` object **❹**.

If you need more control when the model is attached and detached, the `Loadable-DetachableModel` provides the `onAttach` and `onDetach` methods, respectively, which you can override. These methods are optional and are necessary only when you create intricate models.

In section 4.2, we discussed how property models require their values to be serializable, and we said we'd provide a solution to that problem. Detachable models work around the serialization issue by storing just enough information to recreate the non-serializable object on demand. You've seen the advantages of using property models—for example, they save you a lot of typing. How can you get the memory-saving benefits of detachable models in those cases where you want to use property models? It happens that many models, including property models, support nesting.

4.4   *Nesting models for fun and profit*

A Matryoshka doll consists of a set of dolls of decreasing sizes that can be placed inside one another. You (or your parents or an aunt) probably have a collection stashed in a cupboard, gathering dust. The nice thing about these dolls is that you can put one inside another and not know that there is one inside. The dolls have no function other than being decorative (and helping to move small colored pieces of paper between tourists and merchants, thus making them both happier). How do Russian dolls relate to Wicket models?

Property models and detachable models solve different problems: property models cut down on code size and generally make dynamic updates a walk in the park, and detachable models solve the tricky part of minimizing memory usage and enable you to use objects that aren't serializable. Approaches such as combining their functionality in Java would result in an explosion of the number of classes (imagine classes like `LoadableDetachableCompoundPropertyModel`).

Fortunately, some models allow you to nest a model, creating a chain of model functionality. The outside world (for instance, a component) sees and works with only the outermost model and remains oblivious to what is happening on the inside. The outer model uses the inner, nested model as its source of data and applies its own special functionality to that data before providing it to the outside world. The inner model can contain another model, and so forth, stacking and combining their benefits. Although the models don't need to get smaller to be nested inside one another, the outer model does need to be aware that it's working with another model and not a domain object.

To continue with the Matryoshka analogy, if you play with the dolls, you can open one and see what's inside. This is also possible with models that support nesting: they implement the `IChainingModel` interface and provide access to the nested (or rather, *chained*) model.

Let's see how nesting works with an example that puts a detachable model inside a property model:

```
LoadableCheeseModel cheeseModel = new LoadableCheeseModel(cheeseId);
PropertyModel nameModel = new PropertyModel(cheeseModel, "name");
String name = (String)nameModel.getObject();      ◁┐  Attach nameModel
nameModel.detach();      ◁┐  Detach nameModel   ❶  and cheeseModel
                         ❷  and cheeseModel
```

In this example, we create a `LoadableCheeseModel` in a detached state by giving it the object identifier of a cheese that exists in our database. The actual cheese isn't loaded at this point. Next, we create a `PropertyModel` that binds to our `CheeseModel` and retrieves the name of the cheese. Obtaining the name by asking the property model for its object ❶ sets in motion a chain of actions, as illustrated in figure 4.7. The property model in turn calls `getObject` on the cheese model, and the cheese model queries the cheese DAO, which goes to the database and retrieves the `Cheese` object. The cheese model returns the `Cheese` object to the property model, which now uses it to ask for the `name` property. When we've finished using the data in the component, we detach the models ❷; doing so discards the `Cheese` object.

Note that not all models support nesting, nor is it natural for some to do so. The `LoadableDetachableModel`, for example, is intended to retrieve an object (or a list of objects) from a persistent data store, so it doesn't make sense to nest another model

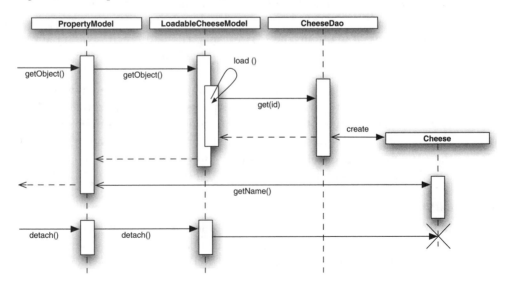

Figure 4.7 Sequence diagram for retrieving the model value of a nested detachable model inside a property model

inside it. Property models, on the other hand, allow unlimited nesting, as demonstrated in the next example:

```
Customer customer = new Customer();
customer.getAddress().setStreet("White Abbey Road");

PropertyModel addressModel = new PropertyModel(customer, "address");
PropertyModel street = new PropertyModel(addressModel, "street");

System.out.println("Street: " + street.getObject());
```

The output is, of course, "Street: White Abbey Road". In this example, we nest one property model inside another. The use of this trick isn't limited to playing with models. Take, for instance, the form in listing 4.8.

Listing 4.8   An example of using nested models in a form

```
public class CustomerForm extends Form {
    public CustomerForm(String id, IModel customer) {
        super(id, customer);
        add(new TextField("name", new PropertyModel(customer, "name")));
        add(new TextField("street",
                            new PropertyModel(customer, "address.street")));
    }
    ...
}
```

In this example, we let the user of the CustomerForm provide the model type. This can be a LoadableDetachableModel, a HibernateObjectModel, or a MyOwnCustomerModel. The form doesn't care what type the model is—it only cares that the model returns a Customer object. In Wicket 1.3 (the version this example was written for), we don't have the luxury to provide a type parameter with the IModel interface, because the framework is built to run in a Java 1.4 (or newer) environment. With newer versions of Wicket, you'll be able to specify that the IModel needs to provide a Customer, using generics like IModel<Customer>.

Being able to build chains of models opens up many different ways to assemble the data needed for your components and pages. You can have one model focus on retrieving your domain objects in an optimal way, using as little memory as possible, and also have a compound property model that saves writing oodles of code. Chaining these two models gives you the best of both worlds: minimal memory usage and up-to-date data together with less code to write. You can have the lasagna and eat it, too.

4.5   *Summary*

In this chapter, you entered a new phase in learning about Wicket development. The previous chapters followed a more introductory approach and touched on the various subjects without going into much detail. From this point on, we'll go into much more detail about each subject.

This chapter tackled one of the most challenging concepts you'll encounter when using Wicket: models. Models are a way to provide components with data to act on:

they bridge the gap between the components that make up your pages and your domain objects. You learned that models can do a lot of things. They're used to store and retrieve data, to get data from a database, and to transform data coming from a data source into something else.

We discussed various standard models provided by Wicket. We started with the simple `Model` class and used it as a means to quickly set up a form. We discussed the differences between static and dynamic models and how to make `Model` more dynamic. You learned the benefits and the downsides of property models. They can save code but make refactoring complicated and require the associated data to be serializable.

Using detachable models, you learned how to circumvent the serialization requirement and how to keep memory usage to a minimum. By using a `LoadableDetachableModel` to store only an object's database key and retrieve and discard it with each request, you can keep memory usage to a minimum and, as an added benefit, ensure that the data being used in your model remains fresh.

By nesting models, you can, for example, get the benefits of both property models and detachable models. You learned how to nest a `LoadableDetachableModel` with a `CompoundPropertyModel`.

With Wicket models as noodles, you now have the means to create neatly layered lasagna. The models from this chapter let you keep your domain objects decoupled from user-interface code but still bind them to Wicket components, thus forming a cohesive package.

It's time to look at more ingredients. The next chapter will discuss the basic components that make a great base for your lasagna—umm, application.

Working with components: labels, links, and repeaters

In the previous chapter, we started building our own lasagna beginning with the noodles that separate each layer. But we haven't talked about the ingredients that go in each layer. This chapter and the next two are divided into sections that discuss the ingredients that make up your pages: components. There are lots of components, so we've divided them into categories based on their usage. Table 5.1 provides an overview of these categories and some components that fall into each.

This list may seem short, but that's because we're saving some components for the next chapter when we talk about forms. And if we listed all the components—well, the table would be too long.

Before we start with our first category, we'll first briefly reacquaint you with Wicket components.

Table 5.1 Categories (use cases) and their corresponding components

Component	Description
Displaying text	
`Label`	Displays text, numbers, dates, and so forth.
`MultiLineLabel`	Displays multiline text and handles whitespace correctly in a browser.
`VelocityPanel`	Uses the Velocity templating engine to render text.
`<wicket:message>`	Markup tag for displaying text from resource bundles (see chapter 12).
Navigating using links	
`ExternalLink`	Links to external URIs.
`BookmarkablePageLink`	Links to internal pages; can be stored by users for future reference.
`<wicket:link>`	Creates `BookmarkablePageLinks` in markup automatically.
Responding to client actions	
`Link`	Receives an `onClick` server-side event.
`AjaxLink`	Similar to `Link`, but sends a request using Ajax.
`AjaxFallbackLink`	Uses Ajax when JavaScript and Ajax are available; falls back to normal `Link` behavior otherwise.
Repeating markup	
`RepeatingView`	Low-level repeater that repeats markup for the components added.
`RefreshingView`	Refreshes its contents on each request.
`ListView`	Higher-level repeater that repeats markup for each item in the model list.
`DataView`	Repeater that is designed to work with database queries.
`DataTable`	Flexible database driven table that promotes the use of toolbars and columns.
Processing and validating user input (chapter 6)	
Grouping components (chapter 7)	
`WebMarkupContainer`	No-op component that groups components or modifies tag attributes.
`Panel`	Reusable grouping component with its own markup file.
`Fragment`	Embedded panel that doesn't have its own markup file.
`Page`	Standard working unit in Wicket that groups all components and has its own markup file.

5.1 What are components?

When the web began, using it was a novel but boring experience. All pages consisted of static text and links between the documents. It was like a giant collection of linked

Word documents. It wasn't long before people started to add dynamic content to their pages. This dynamic content ranged from fields coming from database tables, to full articles from content-management systems, to fields from patients' medical records, to videos of Chinese guys imitating popular music videos, and much more.

In Wicket applications, components provide the dynamic content. For example, a component may render a patient's name, birth date, illnesses, or date of last visit. Another component may fill a drop-down box with available movies, let you select a movie, and store the selected value in a theater's reservation system. This list of dynamic content examples could go on indefinitely.

In chapter 2, we introduced the MVC pattern to show how components act as the View and Controller and domain objects act as the Model (with the help of the previous chapter's model classes). Figure 5.1 shows Wicket's implementation of the MVC pattern using components and models.

As we discussed in chapter 2, components encapsulate the minimal behavior and characteristics of Wicket widgets: for example, how they're rendered, what events they listen to, how models are managed, how authorization is enforced, and whether they're visible. To make a long list of responsibilities short, components display information and possibly react to events. When and how they do so is up to the components.

You also saw the component triad in chapter 2. A Wicket component needs three things to function:

- *A Java class* (the how)—Determines the component's behavior and implements its responsibilities.
- *A markup counterpart* (the where)—Determines where the component displays its dynamic content.
- *A model* (the what)—Provides the data to the component. The component can use the model to display information or use it when processing an action such as the click of a link.

Each component is given an identifier in the Java code and has a counterpart in the markup file with the same identifier. The location of the component's markup counterpart ultimately determines where the component is rendered in the final markup

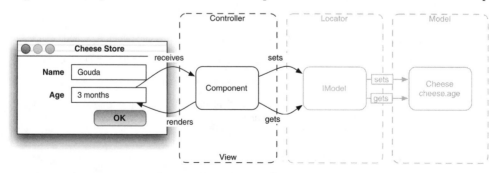

Figure 5.1   The Model-View-Controller pattern as it's implemented by Wicket, with the component fulfilling the role of both Controller and View

that is sent to the browser. The component hierarchy is constructed by adding components to a page and to other components. For instance, in most of our examples, we've added labels and forms to the page, and form fields to the form, creating a hierarchy of parents and children. As you learned in chapter 2, the tree structure of the component hierarchy and the identifier hierarchy in the markup must match.

This summarizes the concept of a component in an abstract way. Let's get started with more tangible components to solve your everyday needs. One of the basic things web applications need to do is display text, so we'll start with that.

5.2 *Displaying text with label components*

As we mentioned earlier, the first incarnation of the web was static: all pages consisted of hard-coded text, with links between the pages. Soon people wanted to show dynamic text on their websites, such as visitor counters, the current date, news headlines, product data from a database, and so forth. In this section, you'll see different components that display dynamic text. The first component is one you've seen already on numerous occasions: the Label.

5.2.1 *Using the Label component to render text*

The Label component is used to display text. The text can be anything: for example, the name of a customer, a description of a cheese, the weight of a cheese, the number of items in a shopping cart, or a fully marked up Wikipedia article. In previous chapters, we've presented many examples that show the Label in action. For instance, the front page of our cheese store contains many labels. Figure 5.2 identifies the labels on a screenshot of that page.

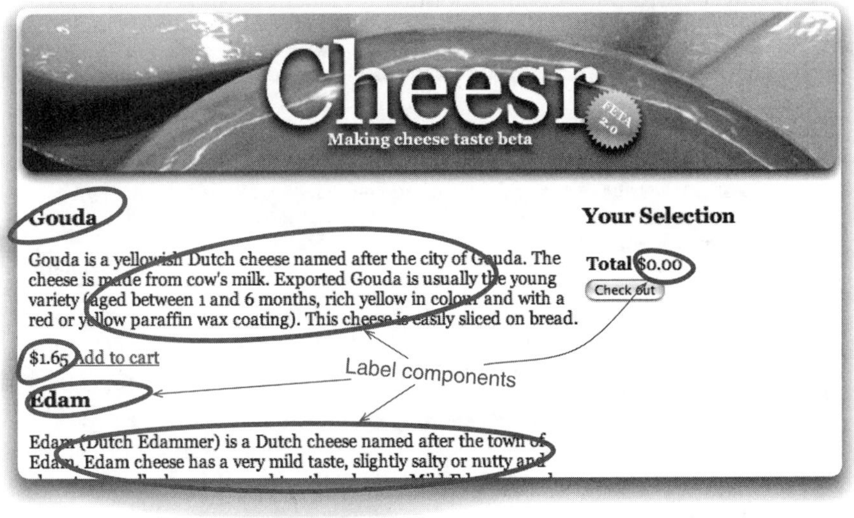

Figure 5.2 Identifying Label components on the front page of chapter 3's cheese store. Each label is responsible for displaying a single aspect: the cheese's name, description, or price.

As a reminder of how labels work in code, let's return to the Hello World! example shown in listing 5.1.

```
<!-- markup file -->
<span wicket:id="message">text goes here</span>

// java code
add(new Label("message", "Hello, World!"));

<!-- final rendered markup -->
<span wicket:id="message">Hello, World!</span>
```

The Label component is bound to the span tags in our markup using the component identifier message. The contents of the span tags are replaced by the text we provide in the Java code, as evidenced by the final markup. In this example, we provide the label directly with a string, but this isn't the only way for a label to obtain the text to display. You can pass in any model implementation—for example, you could use the compound property model, which would use the component identifier to give the label access to the display text (see also section 4.2.3). When the model value isn't a String, Wicket converts the model value to a String using the registered converters. When no converter can be found, Wicket calls the model value's toString method to convert the model value to a String. See chapter 12 for more information on converters.

In our examples, we often use the span tag to create a label, but labels aren't limited to the span tag. You can add a label to almost any tag in your markup. The only caveat is that the markup must have a content body. For instance, it doesn't make much sense to attach a Label component to img tags. Listing 5.2 shows some possible markup choices for a Label component.

```
<!-- markup -->
<span wicket:id="label1">Will be replaced</span>
<td wicket:id="label2">[name]</td>
<h1 wicket:id="label3">title goes here</h1>
Name: <span wicket:id="name"></span>
<div wicket:id="label4"></div>

/* Java code */
add(new Label("label1", "Hello, World!"));
add(new Label("label2", new PropertyModel(person, "name")));
add(new Label("label3", "Wicket in Action"));
add(new Label("name"));
add(new Label("label4", new ResourceModel("key", "default")));

<!-- output -->
<span wicket:id="label1">Hello, World!</span>
<td wicket:id="label2">John Doe</td>
<h1 wicket:id="label3">title goes here</h1>
Name: <span wicket:id="name">Parmesan</span>
<div wicket:id="label4">standaard waarde</div>
```

Internationalized text

Dutch for "default"

As you can see, the label works the same way even when attached to different markup tags. The Label component replaces anything inside it with the text that comes from the provided model (in this example, the provided strings). Listing 5.2 also shows several ways to provide the text to display: a static string, a property model, a compound property model, and a resource model (used to provide internationalized messages, as discussed in chapter 12).

NOTE You can nest example markup for preview purposes within a label's tags, but you can't nest Wicket components inside a label. If you do, the result will be an exception. At render time, the label replaces everything between the start and end tags, including any markup if present.

A Label component is great for displaying short amounts of text such as names, weights, dates, and prices. But how do you display longer text, such as descriptions, and preserve multiple lines?

5.2.2 *Displaying multiple lines using a MultiLineLabel*

Often, you'll get text from a user (for instance, through a comment form on a blog) that contains basic formatting created using newlines. As you may know, HTML ignores most whitespace if it isn't contained in <pre> tags. How can you display strings that aren't HTML but that contain basic formatting in the form of newline characters? Listing 5.3 shows a page that exhibits this problem.

Listing 5.3 Displaying a preformatted message that spans multiple lines

```
/* java code */
public MyPage extends Webpage {
    public MyPage() {
        add(new Label("message", "Hello,\nWorld!\nI'm super!"));
    }
}

<!-- markup -->
<html>
<body>
<span wicket:id="message">Text goes here</span>
</body>
</html>
```

In this example, we want to display the text "Hello, World! I'm super!" across three lines. If you run the example, you'll see that this doesn't happen. Your browser reformats the text and puts it all on the same line. To solve this problem, Wicket has a special Label component that takes into account multiple text lines: the MultiLineLabel.

The MultiLineLabel inserts line breaks (br tags) for single-line breaks in your text and paragraph tags (p tags) for multiline breaks in your text. In our example, the code renders as follows:

```
<span wicket:id="message"><p>Hello,<br/>World!<br/>I'm super!<br/></p></span>
```

Figure 5.3
Comparing the output of a normal label and a multiline label when using Java formatting inside the model text

This gives the desired result, as shown in figure 5.3, which displays the output of a normal label and a multiline label next to each other.

Now that you know how to render plain text containing basic formatting, how can you render text that needs to be bold or italic, or a heading inside a label?

5.2.3 *Displaying formatted text using labels*

Sometimes, you want to display more than just the name of a cheese. You may want to stress part of your message or display user-generated formatting. Because you're working in a web environment, and the lingua franca for controlling formatting is HTML, it's logical to provide the label with HTML markup inside the text.

What happens when you give the label some markup in its model? Look at the following snippet:

```
<!-- markup -->
<span wicket:id="markup"></span>

/* Java code */
add(new Label("markup", "<h1>Hello!</h1>"));
```

Using this code, we expect the text "Hello!" to be displayed in big, bold letters. But this isn't the case. Figure 5.4 shows the undesired result together with the desired output.

The left screenshot isn't what we expect: instead of big, bold text, we get the cryptic markup we put in the label. The tags we put into the label have been escaped, presenting us with the verbatim contents instead of the properly formatted value. In the following, you can see how Wicket has rendered the contents in the final markup:

```
<span wicket:id="markup">&lt;h1&gt;Hello!&lt;/h1&gt;</span>
```

Wicket has escaped the < and > characters and replaced them with their corresponding XML entities (< and > respectively). By setting a flag on the component, you can tell Wicket to render the contents without escaping. Look at the next Java snippet:

```
add(new Label("markup", "<h1>Hello!</h1>").setEscapeModelStrings(false));
```

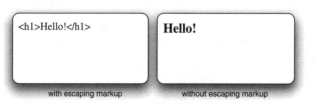

Figure 5.4
Label with and without escaped markup. Using `setEscapeModelStrings`, you can tell Wicket not to escape markup tags and to display formatted HTML the way it was intended.

The call to `setEscapeModelStrings` tells Wicket not to escape the contents of the provided string, and to render the contents into the resulting markup. This does the trick, as you can see in the right screenshot in figure 5.4. Note that this setting is available on all Wicket components, but it's primarily useful on labels.

Beware of script-injection attacks

When you give your users the ability to enter HTML markup into your application, through either a text input field or a text area, and you render this directly back to the client, the users can play dirty tricks by injecting JavaScript into your pages. Such tricks can range from opening pages on other websites (spam) to more dangerous exploits like key loggers recording credit-card information and passwords. Most browsers prevent cross-site scripting (XSS), but you can't be careful enough when it comes to security.

As an example, if we change the model of our label to the following, and escaping is turned off, clicking the message results in a popup:

```
"<h1 onclick='alert(\"clicked!\");'>Click me</h1>"
```

Be careful when you open up this possibility, and filter the markup to remove any scripting before you store it.

Displaying text on the web is rewarding in its own, but if your users are unable to navigate to the page that contains the text, it's virtually useless. Let's return to table 5.1 and continue with the next category of components: navigational links.

5.3 Navigating using links

Taking a stroll down memory lane, the internet was once called the *information superhighway* (yes, we're that old). If we use that term, it isn't hard to imagine that the exits are formed by links. On a normal highway, an exit takes you off the highway to places where you stop to do things: shop, work, relax, or see a movie. The same holds for links: they may take users to our cheese store, where they can buy cheese for lasagna; to an administrative system that will help them work; or to YouTube for some Friday afternoon entertainment.

Wicket provides several abstractions for links. There are links suited to perform an action (and navigate afterward), links that navigate only to another part of an application, and links that navigate to another website. In this section, we'll take a closer look at the navigation links listed in table 5.1. Let's first discuss static links to external websites.

5.3.1 Linking to documents using static links

In plain markup, you typically link between pages using the `<a href>` tag. This tag contains the URL of the document you're linking to. For instance, `<a href="http://wicket.apache.org">Wicket</a>` is an example of a link to the Wicket home page. You can use this type of link directly in your Wicket pages.

Static links can be useful in web applications or websites. Perhaps you want to link to the Wicket website by displaying a Powered by Wicket logo, or provide a link to your corporate intranet site or another web application. As long as the link is static, in the sense that you don't need to retrieve the link from a database or construct it using Java code, you can add the link directly to the markup of your page. Let's see how that looks on our Hello World! page by adding a Powered by Wicket link. Listing 5.4 shows the corresponding markup.

> **Listing 5.4   An example of a static link in the markup of a Wicket page**

```
<!-- markup -->
<html>
<body>
<h1 wicket:id="message">[text goes here]</h1>
<a href="http://wicket.apache.org">Powered by Wicket</a>
</body>
</html>

/* Java code */
public HelloWorldPage extends WebPage {
    public HelloWorldPage() {
        add(new Label("message", "Hello, World!"));
    }
}
```

As you can see, the `<a href>` tag doesn't contain a Wicket component identifier, and it's seen by Wicket as static markup. The Java code for this page only adds the `Label` component: there is no Java counterpart for the static link.

This is fine when you know the exact URL up front and the URL remains static, but how can you create links to an external site when the URL comes from an external data source (such as a database)?

5.3.2   *Using ExternalLink to render links programmatically*

To enable our plan for world cheese domination, wouldn't it be nice to link to recipes using each cheese? This would definitely increase sales, because our customers could immediately see ways to use a particular cheese. Say we find a partner that already has a recipe website with many recipes containing cheese. All we need to do is link our cheeses to the recipes. We add a recipe concept to our domain model, including a name and the URL to the recipe.

Now that we have a way to store a URL to the recipe, how can we render it into our page? Using the `ExternalLink` component, we can link to any URL on the web and have the URL come from anywhere. The next snippet shows how to link to a recipe that uses a cheese:

```
add(new ExternalLink("link", recipe.getUrl(), recipe.getName()));
```

In this example, we generate the URL and the contents of the link. For a good lasagna recipe, this would generate the following:

```
<a href="http://recipes.com/lasagna">lasagna</a>
```

If you don't provide contents for the link, it keeps what is in the original markup template. It's also possible to use models with the external link for both the URL and contents:

```
add(new ExternalLink("link", new PropertyModel(recipe, "link"),
                new PropertyModel(recipe, "name")));
```

The external link is an easy way to create links to external content from within your Java code. Static links are handy to link to externally available resources, but how do you link to pages inside your Wicket application? Several possibilities exist for navigating between pages, including `BookmarkablePageLinks`.

5.3.3 Linking to Wicket pages with BookmarkablePageLinks

Imagine a highway on which you can create your own exits—exits that take you directly to your destination, without detours. The links you've seen thus far give you access to predefined locations, usually outside your control. With the `BookmarkablePageLink` component, you can give others direct access to locations inside your application.

When you create a `BookmarkablePageLink` to point to a Wicket page, it renders a link that enables Wicket to create the page later, without having any previous knowledge of where the user has been. The link can be shared with other people and can be retrieved at any time, even when the user hasn't visited the site in a long time. For example, your home page, the details page for a cheese, a blog entry, and a news article are all prime examples of good pages to link to. Basically, anything your customers want to share with one another—typically by sending a link over email—or want to remember for future reference is a good candidate to be accessed through a `BookmarkablePageLink`.

Generating a link to a page for use in email

When you want to send a user a link to a page in your application, you can use the `urlFor` method to generate the URL to the page. The next snippet generates a link to a registration confirmation page:

```
String url = urlFor(ConfirmRegistrationPage.class,
                new PageParameters("id=" + registrationId));
String msg = "Click on the following link:\n\n"
        + url + "\n\nto confirm your registration.";
```

The `urlFor` method is also used to generate URLs to event listeners or resource listeners. It's a method of the `Component` class, so you can use it almost anywhere.

As an example, we'll add a details link to each cheese on the front page. The link will point to a details page for each cheese; this page will show information about the linked cheese. Using this example, we'll show the various ways of creating links to Wicket pages.

We need a link tag in our markup file and a corresponding `Bookmarkable-PageLink` component in our Java file. Listing 5.5 shows how to create a bookmarkable link to the details page.

Listing 5.5   Creating a bookmarkable link

```
<!-- markup -->
<a href="#" wicket:id="link">more information</a>

/* java code */
add(new BookmarkablePageLink("link", CheeseDetailsPage.class));
```

The `<a href>` tag has an `href` attribute containing #. This is done to show a proper link in the document when we preview it in the browser; Wicket will replace it with the URL of the page the link is pointing to. The Java code adds the link to the component hierarchy and tells Wicket to create the `CheeseDetailsPage` page when the link is clicked. Figure 5.5 shows how our front page looks after we've added the More Information link.

Our current implementation of the link has one problem: we haven't specified the cheese for which we want to show details! When the cheese details page is created, how do we know which cheese's details should be shown? We need to provide the details page with more information. The link generates a URL that contains all the information needed to create the page. URLs can contain request parameters that are passed to the page, so the page can react to that information. Wicket encapsulates those request parameters in `PageParameters`.

ADDING PARAMETERS TO A BOOKMARKABLE PAGE LINK
First we need to consider what you can put into URL parameters. According to internet standard RFC-1738, a URL may consist only of alphanumerics: 0-9, a-z, and A-Z. Special characters and whitespace must be escaped. This means you have to convert Java objects into string representations before you can use them as URL parameters.

Given the URL's limitations, we can't simply put a cheese object into the URL. Even if it were possible to pack all the details of the cheese into the URL, doing so wouldn't be appropriate, considering that the URL can be bookmarked and stored for a long time. If

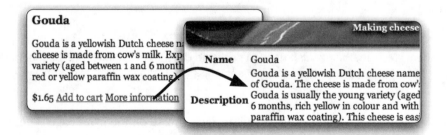

Figure 5.5   Adding a bookmarkable link to the front page of our cheese store. It links to a details page for each cheese. The screen on the right shows the details page after we clicked the link.

someone bookmarks a cheese with a discount price of, say, $1 and then opens the bookmark two months later when the price has returned to $2.50, that would be a bummer. Plus, a malicious user could attempt to modify the URL and change the price directly. Instead of storing the whole object into the URL, you can store a unique property based on which you can reconstitute the object. The object identifier is a good candidate, as is a more businesslike key such as a customer number or, in our case, the name of the cheese.

Let's assume we can load a cheese based on its name. We add the parameter to the URL in the following code:

```
PageParameters pars = new PageParameters();
pars.add("name", cheese.getName());
add(new BookmarkablePageLink("link", CheeseDetailsPage.class, pars));
```

Because the parameters are stored and rendered as strings, you can only add string values to the parameters. You can add as many parameters to the link as you want, as long as you don't exceed the maximum URL length (about 2,000 characters for Internet Explorer and 4,000 for other browsers).

Without any specific configuration, Wicket generates the URL shown in figure 5.6.

Figure 5.6   The URL as generated by the bookmarkable link. The URL contains all the information needed to create the details page and retrieve the cheese object based on its name.

This is by many standards an ugly URL. It looks complicated, it's long, and it shows information we'd rather hide from our users, such as the package name. In chapter 14, we'll look at ways to generate prettier URLs.

Now that we have the link side covered, what happens when someone clicks the link? As you can see in figure 5.6, the class name of the page is contained within the URL. Wicket tries to create that page. For this to work, the page needs to be bookmarkable.

GETTING YOUR PAGE TO WORK WITH BOOKMARKABLEPAGELINKS
A page is considered bookmarkable if

- It has a constructor that has no arguments (also known as a *default constructor*), or
- It has a constructor that takes a `PageParameters` instance as the only argument

These are the only two constructors Wicket can invoke on its own.

A page can have both constructors and additional constructors with other parameters. But when called upon to instantiate a page, Wicket prefers the constructor with `PageParameters` if it's available. The next example shows a page with three constructors where two fall into the bookmarkable category:

```
public class CheeseDetailsPage extends WebPage {
    public CheeseDetailsPage() {
```

❶ **Bookmarkable constructor**

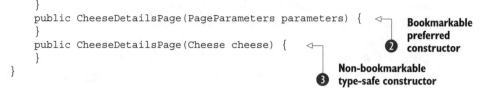

```
        }
        public CheeseDetailsPage(PageParameters parameters) {
        }
        public CheeseDetailsPage(Cheese cheese) {
        }
    }
```

Bookmarkable preferred ❷ **constructor**

Non-bookmarkable ❸ **type-safe constructor**

In this example, Wicket doesn't use the default constructor ❶, because Wicket always prefers the constructor with `PageParameters` ❷. But the default constructor is still useful inside your code, because it makes it (a bit) easier to create the page yourself. As long as the page has either of these two constructors, it can be used successfully in a bookmarkable link.

If the page had only the constructor with a `Cheese` parameter ❸, it wouldn't be possible to reference it in a bookmarkable link—or, to be more precise, Wicket wouldn't know how to create a new instance of the page with only the `Cheese` constructor, and would generate an error. This is the case because Wicket can't determine which cheese needs to be passed in as a parameter. You can still use this constructor if you know how to get a cheese instance based on the page parameters. Listing 5.6 shows how to parse `PageParameters` and use the type-safe constructor.

Listing 5.6   Parsing page parameters to retrieve a `Cheese` object

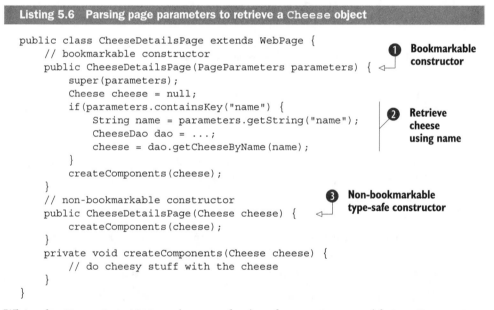

```
public class CheeseDetailsPage extends WebPage {
    // bookmarkable constructor
    public CheeseDetailsPage(PageParameters parameters) {
        super(parameters);
        Cheese cheese = null;
        if(parameters.containsKey("name") {
            String name = parameters.getString("name");
            CheeseDao dao = ...;
            cheese = dao.getCheeseByName(name);
        }
        createComponents(cheese);
    }
    // non-bookmarkable constructor
    public CheeseDetailsPage(Cheese cheese) {
        createComponents(cheese);
    }
    private void createComponents(Cheese cheese) {
        // do cheesy stuff with the cheese
    }
}
```

❶ **Bookmarkable constructor**

❷ **Retrieve cheese using name**

❸ **Non-bookmarkable type-safe constructor**

When the `CheeseDetailsPage` is created using the constructor with `PageParameters` ❶ we parse the parameters and retrieve the value for the parameter name ❷. We call the `createComponents` method to create the component hierarchy. This method is also called in our non-bookmarkable constructor ❸ to avoid code duplication.

We've covered a lot of ground and let many concepts and components pass by. Let's take a break and let Wicket do all the heavy lifting for us. All the links we've

---

Parsing PageParameters

The `PageParameters` class lets you get converted parameters from the URL. For example, `PageParameters` has a `getInteger(key)` method that looks up the key in the URL and tries to convert its value to an integer. If this fails, it throws a conversion error.

People like to modify the URLs in their browser bar, so you may get strange requests to your pages. Wicket shows a default error page if it encounters such malice. To show a friendlier page at a local level, you should surround the querying of the page parameters with a `try-catch` block. In our example, we could show a page that proposes, "Sorry we couldn't find the cheese you were looking for, but how about this Beenleigh Blue for just $10?"

---

discussed so far require you to add links in both the markup and the Java file. For simple links to pages and resources, it would be nice to automate this process.

5.3.4 Adding bookmarkable links automatically with wicket:link

Previously, we showed you how to create bookmarkable links to pages in your web application. To make this work, you have to add the links to the markup and add a `BookmarkablePageLink` component to the page class. If you have many pages that are accessible through bookmarkable links, this is a lot of work to do by hand. The special `wicket:link` tags in a markup file instruct Wicket to automatically create bookmarkable link components for the links inside the tags.

Let's see how this works with auto-linking to two pages. First, look at the markup file in the next example:

```
<html>
<body>
<wicket:link>                                              Link to
<ul>                                             com.wia.package1.Page1
    <li><a href="package1/Page1.html">Page1</a></li>    ◁┐   Auto-link
    <li><a href="package2/Page2.html">Page2</a></li>    ◁┤   block
</ul>
</wicket:link>                                             Link to
</body>                                           com.wia.package2.Page2
</html>
```

Wicket automatically creates components for these links when they point to existing pages based on the value of the `href` attribute. In this example, Wicket auto-creates two bookmarkable links—one to `com.wia.package1.Page1` and the other to `com.wia.package2.Page2`—when the current page is in package `com.wia`.

Note that a link is rendered as disabled when it would point to the current page. Figure 5.7 shows how this might look in your browser.

You can also use this auto-link facility to add links to packaged resources such as stylesheets and JavaScript files (you can learn more about this subject in chapter 9).

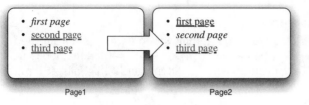

Figure 5.7
Auto-linking in action. The link to the current page is rendered as disabled by replacing the link tag with a span, and rendering the text using an em-tag (this is configurable).

`wicket:link` saves manual labor: you don't have to add the bookmarkable links yourself. Note that `wicket:link` is not refactoring safe: when you move pages between packages, you should modify the links inside the `wicket:link` section in your markup as well. `wicket:link` is a convenience rather than an all encompassing solution to your linking problems—especially when the links have to respond to user actions.

Let's continue with the next component category from table 5.1 and look at responding to client actions.

5.4   *Responding to client actions with a link*

Links are useful for more than navigating the web and going from one page to another. They also represent a way to perform an action when the user clicks a link. For instance, the user could add one kilo of Parmesan cheese to a shopping cart or select a course of action in an online text adventure.

All the links we've discussed until now don't provide a way to act on the event of the link click. External links divert our users from our site, and bookmarkable links don't provide a context to work in: they create a page and render it to the client. They don't give you a way to do any processing in response to a user action. In contrast, Wicket's `Link` component provides a way to perform an action when a user clicks the link; combined with the `setResponsePage` method, `Link` even allows you to travel to another destination.

In this section, we'll look at two link implementations: a `Link` class that uses the old Web 1.0–style request/response cycle, and an Ajax `Link` class that uses the hip Web 2.0–style request/response cycle that doesn't refresh the entire web page. We'll start with the old-fashioned `Link`.

5.4.1   *Using Link to respond to client actions*

The `Link` component is an abstract class, requiring that you implement the `onClick` method. The `onClick` event is called when the user clicks that link. In this event, you can do a lot of things, such as saving an object to the database, deleting it from the database, calculating a value, creating and returning a document (PDF, Excel, image, and so forth), starting a background thread, sending an email message, or going to another page.

Let's look a basic link example in which we navigate to a new page in the `onClick` event. Listing 5.7 shows the markup and Java code.

Don't use hyperlinks to make deletions and changes

Automated clients such as search-engine bots typically harvest information by parsing the documents they find on your website. They follow all links, regardless of whether the link says START WORLD WAR 3 or My Dear Pony Poem.

You may have heard the urban legend of a website owner who had a fully filled Wiki published on the internet, including a Delete link in each article. When the Google bot passed by to index this website, it faithfully followed all links, including the Delete links. Rumor has it that the owner got the contents of the website back using a dump from the Google index.

This story serves as a warning for all web application developers, including those who choose to use Wicket. Using normal hyperlinks to delete items or modify the contents of your database on a public part of your website is dangerous and could lead to unwanted results.

Listing 5.7 Using a link and `setResponsePage` to navigate to another page

```
<!-- markup file -->
<html>
<body>
<a href="#" wicket:id="link">click me</a>
</body>
</html>

/* Java file */
public class MyPage extends WebPage {
    public MyPage() {
        add(new Link("link") {
            public void onClick() {
                // ... do something useful ...            Create page
                Page next = new SomeOtherPage();      ◁─┘ manually
                setResponsePage(next);     ◁─┐  Respond with
            }                                 │  next page
        };
    }
}
```

Just as in the previous link examples, the markup is nothing special: an ordinary link tag with a Wicket identifier. In the server-side `onClick` event, we create the new page and instruct Wicket to respond using that page. Using this type of navigation gives us full control over how the page is constructed. We can create a constructor for the page with a `Cheese` object as parameter, as opposed to passing in an identifier using `PageParameters`.

A link component can also be attached to other tags than `<a href>`: images, spans, table cells, and table rows; you can attach the link component to any tag that can have a JavaScript `onclick` event. There is one caveat: the browser must have JavaScript enabled for this to work, because the link behavior is implemented using a short Java-Script snippet.

Table 5.1 lists several options for responding to client actions. Next to the `Link` component, it lists two other link components: `AjaxLink` and `AjaxFallbackLink`. They're similar, so we'll discuss the link that has the broadest use: the `AjaxFallbackLink`.

5.4.2   *Using AjaxFallbackLink to respond to client actions*

The `Link` we discussed in the previous section causes a full request/response cycle to take place, during which the entrance page is rendered again if you don't direct to another page. This approach has some drawbacks: rendering a full page costs time and bandwidth, downloading the full markup of the page takes time too, and the browser needs to re-render the full page in its window. All this time, the user is waiting for something to happen.

With Ajax, it's possible to send a request to the server asynchronously from the main browser thread. This keeps the browser responsive to user actions because the main thread isn't blocked waiting for a server response. The server can send a small response back to the browser that updates only those parts of the page that have been changed. This typically results in more requests being fired on your server, but each request usually places a lower load on the server because less data has to be gathered and transmitted per request. The overall user experience is richer than if the entire page were being refreshed with each action.

`AjaxFallbackLink` is a link component that works in a browser regardless of whether Ajax and JavaScript are available. In the fallback scenario, the link uses the normal request/response cycle and refreshes the entire page in the browser window as a normal `Link` component would. To work in the Ajax scenario, the link also generates a JavaScript `onclick` event handler in the markup, in which the Ajax callback is performed. The `onclick` handler is called only when the browser supports JavaScript. This way, `AjaxFallbackLink` works in all browsers.

This dual mode for `AjaxFallbackLink` makes it a hybrid of the normal `Link` component (which works even in older browsers or when JavaScript is disabled) and `AjaxLink` (which can operate only when the browser supports JavaScript and Ajax).

As an example of performing Ajax updates using `AjaxFallbackLink`, we'll return to the cheese store and make adding a cheese to the shopping cart take place using Ajax. Figure 5.8 shows what we want to do.

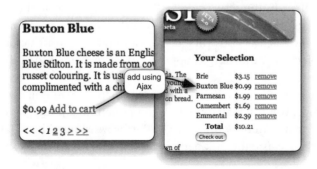

Figure 5.8
Updating our shopping cart using Ajax. The Add link is replaced with an `AjaxLink`. When clicked, it updates only the `ShoppingCartPanel` on the page, asynchronously.

To implement this, we don't have to modify the markup at all; and only the Java code needs to be modified for the page to do Ajax tricks. Changing the page to make it perform Ajax tricks requires us to change only the Java code. Listing 5.8 shows the final Java code with annotations for each modification.

Listing 5.8 Front page of the shop using Ajax to add items to the shopping cart

```
public class Index extends CheesrPage {
    private ShoppingCartPanel shoppingcart;          ◁━┐  Added for
                                                      ❶  easy access
    public Index() {
        PageableListView cheeses = new PageableListView("cheeses",
            getCheeses(), 5) {                               Changed to   ❷
            @Override                                    AjaxFallbackLink
            protected void populateItem(ListItem item) {
                Cheese cheese = (Cheese) item.getModelObject();
                item.add(new Label("name", cheese.getName()));
                item.add(new Label("description",cheese.getDescription()));
                item.add(new Label("price", "$" + cheese.getPrice()));

                item.add(new AjaxFallbackLink("add", item.getModel()) {   ◁─
                                                  Added parameter target  ❸
                    @Override
                    public void onClick(AjaxRequestTarget target) {   ◁────
                        Cheese selected = (Cheese) getModelObject();
                        getCart().add(selected);
                        if(target != null) {                     ❹  Refresh
                            target.addComponent(shoppingcart);          shopping cart
                        }
                    }
                });
            }
        };
        add(cheeses);
        add(new PagingNavigator("navigator", cheeses));

        shoppingcart = new ShoppingCartPanel("cart", getCart());
        shoppingcart.setOutputMarkupId(true);    ◁━┐  Ensure
        add(shoppingcart);                        ❺  DOM id

        add(new Link("checkout") { ... });
    }
}
```

The page remains largely the same as the final result from chapter 3. We add the shopping-cart panel to the page as a private variable ❶ so we can easily reference it when we want to update it in the Ajax link ❹. We replace the Link with an AjaxFallbackLink ❷; AjaxFallbackLink works in browsers with and without Ajax capabilities. If the browser sends an Ajax request, the target parameter ❸ won't be null, and we can add to it the components that require updating. If a normal request is sent, the target parameter is null and we have to refresh the whole page.

When you update a component using Wicket's Ajax capabilities, the component's markup is rendered anew and sent back to the browser. Wicket's Ajax mechanism needs to be able to find the old markup in the browser's DOM to replace it with the new markup. So, we need to render a markup identifier for the component that we want to replace using Ajax ❺. The method `setOutputMarkupId` instructs Wicket to generate such a markup identifier for us; Wicket takes care of generating an `id` attribute that is guaranteed to be unique within the HTML document.

NOTE   `AjaxRequestTarget` lets you update multiple components at one time. All you need to do is add all of them to the target—and don't forget to give them a markup identifier. `AjaxRequestTarget` also allows you to run JavaScript before and after the component updates. This way, you can easily integrate any of the available JavaScript libraries or widget toolkits to add Web 2.0 effects to your components. Wicket doesn't provide a Java-Script effects library yet, but there are plenty to be found on the web or in the Wicket Stuff project.

The observant reader may notice that the Total field doesn't update with each addition to the cart using Ajax. It's left as an exercise for you to implement this feature as well as turn the delete link in the `ShoppingCartPanel` into an Ajax link.

With the `AjaxFallbackLink`, you have a component that creates modern, responsive web-based UIs and doesn't hang users out to dry when their browser doesn't support JavaScript or Ajax. You now have a reasonably complete overview of the possibilities when using the various links. You can navigate to external documents on the web, create a navigation structure within an application, and create links that respond to user actions. In the next section, we'll look at the components from table 5.1 that enable you to repeat markup and components.

5.5   *Using repeaters to repeat markup and components*

When you're layering lasagna, you do the same thing over and over: you might create a thin, smooth layer of sauce; add slices of salami; add cheese; cover it all with lasagna noodles; and repeat until the lasagna tray is full. You repeat the ingredients according to a specific recipe. As analogies go, Wicket also has a couple of components that repeat ingredients, or rather components. These components are generally called *repeaters*, and Wicket provides several, each with a specific goal.

As with most components discussed so far, you've already seen the `ListView` used to render the list of cheeses and the contents of the shopping cart in the online cheese store. In this section, we'll revisit the `ListView` and introduce the `Repeating-View` as a do-it-yourself way to repeat components and their markup.

5.5.1   *Using the RepeatingView to repeat markup and components*

The `RepeatingView` is a component that doesn't do anything except write out the components that are added to it. The concept of the repeating view is best explained using a simple example:

```
<!-- markup -->
<ul>
    <li wicket:id="rv"></li>
</ul>
```

```
// java, in e.g. constructor of page
RepeatingView rv = new RepeatingView("rv");
add(rv);
for(int i = 0; i < 5; i++) {
    rv.add(new Label(String.valueOf(i), "Value " + i));
}

<!-- rendered markup -->
<ul>
    <li wicket:id="rv">Value 0</li>
    <li wicket:id="rv">Value 1</li>
    <li wicket:id="rv">Value 2</li>
    <li wicket:id="rv">Value 3</li>
    <li wicket:id="rv">Value 4</li>
</ul>
```

When you compare the original and the rendered markup in this example, you can see that the markup is repeated five times, each with different contents. Note that you first add the repeating view to the page hierarchy; otherwise it can't render its children. In the for loop, we repeatedly add a Label component to the repeating view. The view renders its markup against its child components. In this example, each label is paired to the li tag. Note that we add each label with a unique identifier, which we derive by converting the loop counter into a string. Because the labels are added as children to the repeating view at the same level in the hierarchy, we have to ensure that the identifiers are unique. The repeating view provides the newChildId method for generating these identifiers, so you can use that instead of conjuring the identifiers yourself.

How can you use the repeating view in a setting where you have to render a more complex component hierarchy, such as a menu? An application menu is typically created using an unordered list (menu tags have been deprecated in the HTML specification) and some links. By applying CSS and background imagery, you can make the menu look any way you want. Figure 5.9 shows one example of transforming the unordered list to something more appealing using CSS. Many websites are dedicated to creating CSS-styled menus, so we'll skip the CSS and focus on the Wicket end of creating the menu.

To create this menu, we need a list of menu items with captions and destinations. We then have to loop through that list and create the markup elements for each item. Each element consists of a link to the destination page and a label containing the

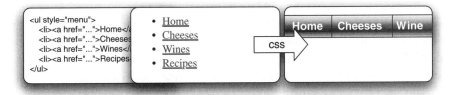

Figure 5.9 Creating a menu using a repeating view and an unordered list. Sprinkle in some CSS, garnish with some images, and get an appetizing menu.

caption. Listing 5.9 shows how to render a (basic) menu using a repeating view, illustrating a more complex hierarchy.

Listing 5.9 Generating a menu using a repeating view

```
/** Class for modeling a menu item for our application. */
public class MenuItem implements Serializable {
    /** the caption of the menu item */
    private String caption;

    /** the (bookmarkable) page the menu item links to */
    private Class destination;

    // ... getters/setters omitted
}

<!-- markup file for page with menu bar -->
<html>
<body>
    <ul>
        <li wicket:id="menu">
            <a href="#" wicket:id="link">
                <span wicket:id="caption"></span>
            </a>
        </li>
    </ul>
</body>
</html>

/** Page with menu bar */
public class PageWithMenu extends WebPage {
    public PageWithMenu(List<MenuItem> menu) {
        RepeatingView rv = new RepeatingView("menu");
        add(rv);
        for(MenuItem item : menu) {
            WebMarkupContainer parent =
                new WebMarkupContainer(rv.newChildId());
            rv.add(parent);
            BookmarkablePageLink link =
                new BookmarkablePageLink("link", item.getDestination());
            parent.add(link);
            link.add(new Label("caption", item.getCaption()));
        }
    }
}
```

1 Menu item markup

2 Extra component level

3 Generate unique identifiers

In this example, we create an object-oriented abstraction of a menu item and provide our page with a list of menu items. There are two things to note in this example. First is the use of the `newChildId` method to generate unique identifiers for the children added directly to the repeating view **3**. The second, possibly more confusing, thing is the extra component between the link and the repeating view.

This extra component, a `WebMarkupContainer` called `parent` **2** is introduced because we need to repeat a nesting of components. The `BookmarkablePageLink` needs to be attached to a `<a href>` tag. But the menu item consists not only of the link tag, but also of the surrounding list item (li) tags ❶. So, we introduce the generic WebMarkupContainer as a parent for our link.

The WebMarkupContainer is a generic component that in itself doesn't do much. It can contain child components, so it's a handy tool to group components or use as an intermediate layer when you need to group more markup for a component. Grouping and organizing components is discussed in chapter 7.

Taking a step back from the menu implementation, the repeating view also doesn't do much. It repeats the markup it's attached to, and you need to maintain the one-to-one relationship between the markup and component hierarchy. The component structure of the repeating view is static. Once the components have been added and the contents of your list change, you have to reconstruct the repeating view. This isn't a bad thing, but it's something you have to be aware of.

Updating the contents of a RepeatingView

When you need to refresh the contents of a repeating view—for instance, when menu items are added or updated—you have two choices: update the repeating view's component structure to reflect your changes (for example, remove the second menu item, replace the third, and add a fifth item), or remove all the children and repaint the view completely.

This meddling with the children of the RepeatingView component is best done by overriding the repeating view's onPopulate event. The following code shows how to replace the contents:

```
@Override
protected void onPopulate() {         removes all child
    removeAll();                  ⏎   components
    for(MenuItem item : menu) {
        WebMarkupContainer parent =
            new WebMarkupContainer(newChildId());
        add(parent);
        BookmarkablePageLink link =
            new BookmarkablePageLink("link",
                    item.getDestination());
        parent.add(link);
        link.add(new Label("caption", item.getCaption()));
    }
}
```

In this example, we first remove all children and then recreate the menu items. Note that the onPopulate callback is a member of the RepeatingView; when we add the parent, we add it to the RepeatingView directly.

The repeating view is a low-level approach to create lists of components—maybe too low. The ListView component offers a more complete out-of-the-box approach to building lists in your pages.

5.5.2   *Using a ListView to repeat markup and components*

Ultimately, both the `RepeatingView` and the `ListView` components solve the same problem: they repeat component hierarchies and markup. The list view is different in that it encapsulates the logic you must perform with a repeating view. In this section, we'll compare the repeating and list views. We'll look inside the list view and see what you can customize, and we'll also give you an idea of things to watch out for when you're working with database-backed lists.

First, let's implement the menu from listing 5.9 to see how the `ListView` component is different from the `RepeatingView`. Listing 5.10 shows our implementation using a list view. We omitted the menu item class, because it hasn't changed between the two implementations.

> **Listing 5.10   Building a menu with a `ListView` vs. a `RepeatingView`**

```
/** Page with menu bar */
public class PageWithMenu extends WebPage {
    public PageWithMenu(List<MenuItem> menu) {
        ListView lv = new ListView("menu", menu) {
            @Override
            protected void populateItem(ListItem item) {
                MenuItem menuitem = (MenuItem)item.getModelObject();
                BookmarkablePageLink link =
                    new BookmarkablePageLink("link", menuitem.getDestination());
                link.add(new Label("caption", menuitem.caption));
                item.add(link);
            }
        };
        add(lv);
    }
}
```

The `ListView` component iterates through the items in the supplied list. For each item in the list, it create a `ListItem` object. The `ListItem` is given the *N*th element of the list as a model. The list view then calls `populateItem` to give us a chance to add components to the `ListItem`. Effectively, the `ListItem` fulfills the role of the `Web-MarkupContainer` from listing 5.9.

When you compare listings 5.9 and 5.10, you can see that the `ListView` component saves code. You don't have to run the loop yourself to add components, and you don't have to add a `WebMarkupContainer` because the `ListItem` provides that role. The list view also rebuilds itself each time it's rendered. So, you can change the contents of the list, and the rendered list view shows the updated contents (try it: add two links to the page, and add/remove menu items in their `onClick` events).

When you display the results of a database query in your list view, you typically want to recreate the whole list instead of manipulating the elements of the list. The handiest way to handle this is to wrap your list and its retrieval in a `LoadableDetachableModel` (as we described in chapter 4). For instance, the code in listing 5.11 reloads the collection of cheeses from the database using a DAO and displays the names using a list view.

Listing 5.11 Refreshing a `ListView` using a `LoadableDetachableModel`

```
public class CheesesPage extends WebPage {
    public class CheesesModel extends LoadableDetachableModel {
        protected Object load() {
            CheeseDao dao = ...
            return dao.list();
        }
    }
    public CheesesPage() {
        add(new PropertyListView("cheeses", new CheesesModel()) {
            @Override
            protected void populateItem(ListItem item) {
                add(new Label("name"));
            }
        }
    }
}
```

Using the `CheesesModel`, we retrieve the list of cheeses on each request and cache it during the request processing; typically, it doesn't affect performance. Depending on your caching strategy, the results are also cached at the data access layer or in the database itself.

You may have noticed the use of a `PropertyListView` component instead of a normal `ListView`. The `PropertyListView` wraps the model of each item in a `CompoundPropertyModel`, which is why we can use the label without specifying an explicit model.

You can override the default way in which Wicket gets the model used for each list item. This is usually a good idea when you add links with each list item that perform some logic on the selected item—for instance, deleting the item. The default list view works by assuming that the list doesn't change between requests, and uses an indexed approach to accessing the elements. If someone changes the contents of the database—for example, by adding a new cheese to the collection—this can change the order of the list. Perhaps on the next request item 12 from our collection of cheeses is no longer the expected raejuusto cheese, but turns out to point to the Venezuelan beaver cheese.

To remedy such unfortunate misunderstandings, you should change the list item's model to store the object identifier instead of the index in the list. Fortunately, you can override the creation of the list item's model, as shown in listing 5.12.

Listing 5.12 Replacing the default item model of a `ListView` with our own

```
add(new ListView("cheeses", new CheesesModel()) {
    @Override
    protected void populateItem(final ListItem item) {
        add(new Label("name"));
        add(new Link("delete") {
                protected void onClick() {
                    Cheese cheese = (Cheese)item.getMod
                    CheeseDao dao = ...
                    dao.delete(cheese);
```

```
                }
            });
    }
    @Override
    protected IModel getListItemModel(IModel listViewModel, int index) {
        Cheese cheese = ((List<Cheese>)listViewModel).get(index);
        return new CompoundPropertyModel(new CheeseModel(cheese));
    }
}
```

We override the list view's `getListItemModel` factory method and provide our own model implementation for each list item. This example reuses the `CheeseModel` from chapter 4 (a `LoadableDetachableModel` that reloads the cheese based on the cheese's object identifier). By nesting it in a compound property model, we keep the benefits of not having to specify a model with each component in the list item. Note that we could change the type of the list view back to a normal `ListView`, because we provide our own `CompoundPropertyModel`.

> ## Working with large collections
>
> When the lists you want to show aren't too large, the `ListView` is a good choice; but when the list gets so large that you need it to be paged, the `ListView` becomes burdensome. The problem is that the `ListView` uses a list as its model. The whole list needs to be loaded in memory for it to work. Even the `PageableListView` (featured in chapter 3) loads the whole list in memory before it renders items 41 through 50 of 200. To mitigate this problem, you should consider the `DataView` and its cousins. These components are much better suited for working in a database-backed environment.

`ListView` and `RepeatingView` are the basic repeating components and a valuable asset to your Wicket toolbox. Together with labels and links, they're the key ingredients for any Wi...

...gh table 5.1's allotted goals for this chapter, we want ...ledge before diving into the next chapter. You may ...using the components we just introduced, such as ...ge or modifying attributes of markup tags. The next ...mmon tasks.

...ith components

...nly in the ingredients but also in the way you pre-...y, prime cut steak into a chunk of tough leather if ...way. The analogy holds for programming as well: ...guage, or libraries, if you use them incorrectly, the ...be able to use ingredients or tools appropriately, ...ith them.

In the next couple of sections, we'll discuss ways you can prepare your components while building your application. You'll learn how to manipulate the attributes of the markup, how to remove excess markup, and how to remove those special Wicket tags. First, let's look at how to change the visibility of components.

5.6.1   Hiding parts of a page

A common requirement is to hide part of a page because some condition isn't met. The reasons for hiding parts of a page can be diverse. For example, in our cheese store from chapter 3, we didn't show the Checkout button until the user had a product in the shopping cart. Another example is a gold Member badge that should be visible only to repeat customers with a spending habit of more than \$18,000 per month. Or consider a list of humorously shaped vegetables, visible only to visitors over 18 years of age.

A simplistic approach to hide part of the page is to not add it to the component hierarchy. But in Wicket's case this doesn't work, because the component hierarchy and the markup need to match: anything that is a component in the markup must have a Java counterpart. You can tell a component to become invisible, which removes the component's markup from the output. You're still required to add the component to the hierarchy, but you can hide it from the final output.

Hiding any component is simple. Each component has a method to set visibility, as shown in the next snippet, where we toggle the visibility of a label:

```
label.setVisible(false);      // hide the label
label.setVisible(!label.isVisible()); // toggle the visibility
```

The effect of making a component invisible is that its markup and the markup of its children are completely removed from the rendered page. For instance, when you make a panel, a form, or a page invisible, all markup for that component and its children is removed. In the case of a page, you see an empty response without any markup.

Setting the flag to determine visibility is a static way of working. When the visibility of a component can change dynamically, it's usually better to override the isVisible method and determine the visibility each time it's queried. The following example shows a label that is visible only on weekdays:

```
add(new Label("label", "I'm only visible on weekdays!") {
    @Override
    public boolean isVisible() {
        int day = Calendar.getInstance().get(Calendar.DAY_OF_WEEK);
        return day != Calendar.SATURDAY && day != Calendar.SUNDAY;
    }
});
```

The isVisible method can be called several times during a request, so it's best to ensure that you don't perform heavy processing here. Using the override, you can do all kinds of visibility tricks: for instance, you can toggle the visibility of two components so one hides when the other is visible and vice versa.

When you want to hide more than just the markup of the component, such as neighboring components and the markup surrounding them, you can use a special Wicket tag in the markup to group them. Listing 5.13 shows an example.

Listing 5.13   Hiding surrounding markup and sibling components

```
<html>
<body>
    <h1>Billing information</h1>
    <table>
        <wicket:enclosure child="name">
            <tr><th colspan="2">Billing address</th></tr>
            <tr><th>Name</th><td wicket:id="name"></td></tr>
            <tr><th>Street</th><td wicket:id="street"></td></tr>
        </wicket:enclosure>
    </table>
</body>
</html>
```

The enclosure is wrapped around three table rows that contain information for the billing address. We tell Wicket that the entire enclosure should be hidden when the name component isn't visible, by specifying the child identifier that regulates the visibility for the whole enclosure. You can specify only one identifier.

The `wicket:enclosure` tag doesn't have an explicit Java counterpart: Wicket automatically adds the necessary component to the hierarchy and makes sure that the component hierarchy remains in one-to-one correspondence.

Changing the visibility of components using Ajax

If you're thinking of modifying the visibility of your components using Ajax, be aware that you need to do more than set the visibility to false. Because the markup for a hidden component is absent from the final markup, you won't be able to make the component visible again using Ajax if you don't take precautions.

A hidden component leaves a special placeholder tag in the markup to enable Ajax visibility changes when you set `setOutputMarkupPlaceholderTag` to true. The placeholder still renders invisible in your markup with the use of CSS:

```
<span wicket:id="label1" style="display:none" id="label1" />
```

Wicket's Ajax functionality is discussed in greater detail in chapter 10.

The visibility of components isn't always controlled by data or computation. Often, it's linked directly to the role of the user and her authorization level. In chapter 11, you'll learn how to implement authorization strategies to control the visibility of components.

Let's look at another way of manipulating components and see how you can change the attributes of the component's tag in the markup.

5.6.2 Manipulating markup attributes

With Wicket, you can specify markup attributes directly in the HTML template. This approach is static: there is no way to change attributes by putting something inside the template. But you can use a couple of techniques to modify the attributes of the component tags:

- Override the onComponentTag method
- Use attribute modifiers

We'll discuss these methods next. We'll use the Hello World! example from chapter 1 as our example case and change the font color of the text programmatically. Listing 5.14 recaps the code from chapter 1.

Listing 5.14 Hello World! example from chapter 1

```
<html>
<body>
<h1 wicket:id="message">Text goes here</h1>
</body>
</html>

public class HelloWorldPage extends WebPage {
    public HelloWorldPage() {
        add(new Label("message", "Hello, World!"));
    }
}
```

As you can see, this text is boring. Let's make the text red from inside the Java code. To do so, we need to modify the h1 tag such that it renders like the following markup:

```
<h1 style="color:red">Hello, World!</h1>
```

Figure 5.10 shows an example of how this would be rendered.

We could add the style attribute to the markup and be done, but that would be cheating. Let's open our Hello-WorldPage class and try to modify the attribute using Java code.

Figure 5.10   Transforming black text to red

MODIFYING ATTRIBUTES USING ONCOMPONENTTAG

Overriding the onComponentTag method is the first option to modifying the attributes of the component tag. The onComponentTag method is called when Wicket is rendering the component's start tag. This is the moment to add or modify any attributes on the component tag. Here's the code that makes our message red:

```
public class HelloWorldPage extends WebPage {
    public HelloWorldPage() {
        add(new Label("message", "Hello, World!") {
            @Override
            protected void onComponentTag(ComponentTag tag) {
```

```
            super.onComponentTag(tag);
            tag.put("style", "color:red");
        }
    });
    }
}
```

Change color → Don't forget super

Using this technique, we have to remember to call the parent onComponentTag, because the parent component (in this case, the Label), may need to modify the tags itself. Just like the attributes, you can change the tag. For instance, we can change the h1 tag to a h3 tag:

```
@Override
protected void onComponentTag(ComponentTag tag) {
    super.onComponentTag(tag);
    tag.setName("h3");
    tag.put("style", "color:red");
}
```

Change tag

This is a powerful way to work with component markup from inside your server-side Java code. With this power comes responsibility, as well: don't forget to call onComponentTag on the super class, or you'll break something eventually.

This approach has one problem: it requires you to subclass your components to manipulate the tags. Can't you extend a component without subclassing it? Attribute modifiers let you access the attributes of your components.

MODIFYING ATTRIBUTES USING ATTRIBUTE MODIFIERS

The attribute modifier is an example of the concept of behaviors, which we discussed in chapter 2. The attribute modifier manipulates the component tag on a more general level. You can create an attribute modifier to add JavaScript to a component tag and reuse it for different components. The next example uses an AttributeModifier to modify our label's style tag:

```
public class HelloWorldPage extends WebPage {
    public HelloWorldPage() {
        add(new Label("message", "Hello, World!").add(
            new AttributeModifier(
                "style",
                true,
                new Model("color:red"))));
    }
}
```

Attribute name
Add if not present
Attribute value

The AttributeModifier uses an IModel for the attribute value. This means you can retrieve the attribute value at a later time from any place—for example, a database or a resource file. This enables you to add localized messages to accessibility markup features, such as the title and alt attributes.

As another example to show the power of attribute modifiers, let's add a JavaScript confirmation dialog to a link. Requesting confirmation for expensive or dangerous operations is one way to improve the usability of your applications. Listing 5.15 shows a basic implementation of adding confirmation behavior to a link in a generic way.

Listing 5.15   Adding a confirmation popup to a link

```
<html>
<body>
<h1>WOPR</h1>
<a href="#" wicket:id="link">Play global thermonuclear war</a>
</body>
</html>

public class MyPage extends WebPage {
    public MyPage() {
        Link link = new Link("link") {
            @Override
            protected void onClick() {
                System.out.println("Link clicked");
            }
        };
        add(link);
        link.add(new SimpleAttributeModifier("onclick",
                "return confirm('Are you sure?');"));
    }
}
```

In this quick example, we add a link to the page that logs a message to the console. The link is fitted with an attribute modifier that adds an `onclick` event to the link's tag. The browser asks for confirmation with the message "Are you sure?" If the user clicks OK, the browser sends the request to the server; if the user clicks Cancel, nothing happens. Figure 5.11 shows how this looks in the browser.

This example shows how you can use attribute modifiers to add JavaScript events to existing components in an elegant way without much effort. When we discuss creating rich components in chapter 10, you'll see how you can use attribute modifiers to pull your Web 1.0 application into the twenty-first century with Ajax and superfluous effects.

You may have wondered about the markup in our examples carrying some extra weight when rendered to the browser: the `wicket:id` and, in some cases, the label's tags. Let's travel light by removing that excess baggage.

Figure 5.11
A screenshot of the confirmation link created by adding an attribute modifier to a `Link` component

5.6.3   *Removing excess markup*

In all our previous examples, the label's open and close tags appear in the final output. Sometimes you want to remove those tags to produce smaller markup, or to remove tags that cause layout problems when they appear out of context in the HTML. Take the following, chewed-up Hello World! example:

```
<!-- original markup -->
<html>
<body>
<span wicket:id="message">Message</span>
</body>
</html>

/* Java code */
add(new Label("message", "Hello, World!"));

<!-- final markup -->
<html>
<body>                                        ⎤ Excess
<span wicket:id="message">Hello, World!</span>  ⊲⎦ span tags
</body>
</html>
```

In the final markup, the span tags and the Wicket identifiers are still rendered. If you want to remove the span tags from the final output, you can use the following setting on the Label component: setRenderBodyOnly(boolean value). This setting is part of all Wicket components, and it works on almost all of them in a similar way. Exceptions are the Page component and components that don't have their own markup but repeat the attached markup, such as repeating views and list views.

Let's see how this setting works on our label in the following example. Here we've altered the Java code to hide the Wicket-specific tags:

```
/* Java code */
add(new Label("message", "Hello, World!").setRenderBodyOnly(true));  ⊲⎤
                                                              Render ⎦
<!-- final markup -->                                      body only
<html>
<body>
Hello, World!     ⊲⎤ Span no
</body>             ⎦ more
</html>
```

In the final markup, the span tags have disappeared, along with the Wicket identifiers. This is a nice way to clean up the excess markup that is sometimes necessary to construct a working page.

In some cases, you need to add markup in a place where it's illegal to do so. Consider the following markup example:

```
<table>
<span wicket:id="rows">
    <tr>
        <td wicket:id="cols1">...</td>
```

```
    </tr>
    <tr>
        <td wicket:id="cols2">...</td>
    </tr>
</span>
</table>
```

The span tags in this example are illegal as per the HTML specification: the only tags that are allowed as children of a table tag are the tr, tfoot, tbody, and thead. For those who want to keep their markup clean, Wicket provides a special Wicket tag for these situations: wicket:container. Because the tag resides in the wicket namespace, replacing span with the wicket:container tag produces valid markup. The next example shows what this looks like:

```
<table>
<wicket:container wicket:id="rows">
    <tr>
        <td wicket:id="cols1">...</td>
    </tr>
    <tr>
        <td wicket:id="cols2">...</td>
    </tr>
</wicket:container>
</table>
```

Using the wicket:container tag has the benefit of passing a validator, which is a requirement for some projects and companies. Keep in mind, though, that all Wicket namespaced tags are removed from the final markup if you run your application in production mode. We'll discuss configuring your Wicket application for production in chapter 14.

5.7 Summary

In this chapter, we looked at a some components: basic ingredients that enable you to build web applications using Wicket. You learned how to render plain text, formatted text, and text containing HTML to the browser. Although rendering text containing HTML is handy and gives you and your users great power, you shouldn't ignore the safety concerns that stem from this approach. Your site won't be the first to fall prey to insertion attacks.

Displaying content is important for any web application, but an application is more than a set of pages without relationships. Using links, you can navigate to other websites or within your own application. With bookmarkable links, you let users store a bookmark to a particular spot of interest in the application or site (for instance, an article).

Links are also suited to respond to users' actions, such as removing all the data from a database or performing an action and navigating to another page. The AjaxFallbackLink is instrumental in transforming an old-style link-based page to a Web 2.0, Ajax-enabled page, while still providing support to browsers that shun JavaScript or Ajax.

Next, we showed how to repeat components to render lists of data. Using a RepeatingView component, we created an example menu for web applications. The menu serves as an example to contrast the hands-on approach of the repeating view with the more abstract and flexible approach enabled by the list view.

With the basic components covered, we discussed several operations you can perform on them. Hiding a component completely removes it from the markup (unless you tell the component specifically to leave a placeholder tag, using `setOutputMarkupPlaceholderTag`). Using attribute modifiers, you can change all the markup attributes of your component tags: we showed how to modify a label's color and how to add extra JavaScript to a link, asking for confirmation before the request is sent to the server. Finally, you learned how to clean up the extra markup generated by components in places where you don't want it—for instance, to make the rendered markup valid.

The components and operations we've discussed should allow you to build a basic Wicket application. But unfortunately, this isn't enough for many web applications: most applications need more methods of interacting with users, such as checkout forms, comments, and profile edit pages. The next chapter will discuss how to add forms and form components to your application.

Processing user input using forms

In this chapter:

- How Wicket processes HTML forms
- Creating HTML forms with Wicket components
- Submitting forms using Ajax
- Validating user input with validators
- Providing feedback to users

In the previous chapter, we discussed several ingredients for lasagna. But for a recipe to be complete, it needs a set of directions for creating the lasagna. Steps in our particular recipe include preheating the oven, cooking the lasagna sauce (don't be shy with the garlic!), layering the lasagna in the oven dish, and letting it simmer in the oven for half an hour at 190°C (375°F).

Working with forms is like following a set of directions. First, you need to add a form and form components. Next, you must be able to react when user input is sent to the server. You need to validate that the input is correct, or at least be in the format you want. And finally, you should provide feedback to the user when the input is incorrect.

In this chapter we'll discuss forms and how they're processed. We'll look at the various form components you can use to receive input from your users. You'll learn

139

different ways to submit the form using buttons, links, and Ajax. We'll show you how you can validate user input and, finally, how you can give feedback.

We have to cover a lot of topics, so it isn't surprising that this is a long chapter. Let's get started.

6.1   *What are forms?*

In everyday life, you encounter forms: for example, when you want to buy a car, apply for insurance, or fill in a lottery ticket. Most web applications are a reflection of or a replacement for these everyday forms.

What is a form in Wicket applications? The `Form` component groups controls that take user input and processes them when they're submitted. A form has an HTML part and a Java (Wicket) part. A form is used to get input from users in the form of text fields, selection boxes, radio buttons, check boxes, buttons, and more. The form groups input controls and processes all of them together when the form is submitted.

Usually, the form itself is invisible to the user—at least, when CSS hasn't been used to highlight it in some way. Unfortunately, you can't skip the form because it's essential in processing user input: without the form to group input controls, you wouldn't receive the input.

A `Form` component needs to be bound to a `form` tag. Listing 6.1 shows the markup and corresponding Java code for creating a form.

Listing 6.1   Markup and Java code for creating a form containing a text field

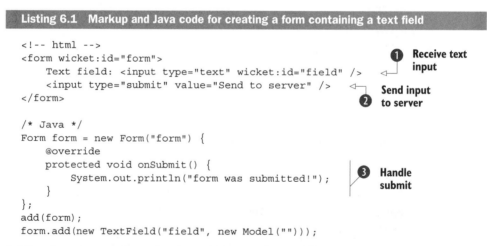

```
<!-- html -->
<form wicket:id="form">
    Text field: <input type="text" wicket:id="field" />      ❶ Receive text input
    <input type="submit" value="Send to server" />           ❷ Send input to server
</form>

/* Java */
Form form = new Form("form") {
    @override
    protected void onSubmit() {
        System.out.println("form was submitted!");           ❸ Handle submit
    }
};
add(form);
form.add(new TextField("field", new Model("")));
```

Adding input controls to the form is as simple as adding components to a page or panel. Our example adds a text field to the mix ❶. A form needs to be submitted in order to have the user input processed. The HTML specification defines a special-purpose input control to submit a form to the server ❷. The submit button shows the value as its caption—in this case, the text *Send to server.*

The submit button doesn't need to be a Wicket component. In this example, we haven't added a Wicket identifier to the `input` tag. How can we react to a user clicking the submit button? There are several options, which we'll discuss in more detail in section 6.5. For now, our example shows the simplest approach: subclassing the Form component and overriding the onSubmit method **❸**.

Because Wicket's Form component is just another Java class, you can extend it and override its methods. This example's onSubmit implementation prints a message to the console. In a real application, you can do anything, such as saving an object in a database, searching cheeses, or sending a confirmation launch code for a thermonuclear strike.

If something goes wrong during the processing of the input, Wicket doesn't call onSubmit but instead calls onError. You can optionally override onError and provide your own error handling.

The next section will show what can possibly go wrong during processing.

6.2 How does form processing work?

When a form is processed, there are two sides to the story. First, the client (browser) submits the values of the form components to the server, then the server processes these values into meaningful domain values and conjures a response. Figure 6.1 shows how this process works.

Let's first look at the client-side of things.

6.2.1 Submitting a form from the browser to the server

A form must be submitted to the server so the application can process the input. For that, the form tag gets an action attribute in the markup that contains a URL where the values of each input control should be sent. Wicket takes care of generating this

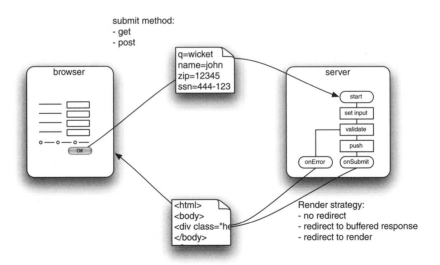

Figure 6.1 Diagram of submitting a form, processing it on the server, and sending the response. The submittal can be performed using the get or post method. The response can be generated using different render strategies: no redirect, redirect to buffer, or redirect to render.

URL and putting it in the `action` attribute—you don't have to do so when creating the markup.

SUBMITTING A FORM USING GET

A form can be sent using either of two HTTP protocol methods: `get` or `post`. The `get` method sends a request by encoding the input controls' values using URL parameters. This method is typically used for forms where the results need to be bookmarkable, such as search engines. The `get` method is limited (by URL length) in the amount of data that can be submitted and the fact that you can't upload files using this method.

Although it usually isn't apparent to users, a form that uses the `get` method is considered *safe*. This means the request shouldn't have an adverse effect on the state of the server. For instance, processing a customer order using a `get` method isn't advised, especially on the public-facing part of your site (or you may end up shipping a lot of cheese to Google headquarters). An example of a get request is shown in figure 6.2.

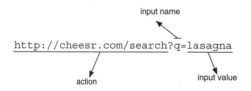

Figure 6.2
A get URL dissected. The action part is used in the form tag's `action` attribute. The input name and value come from the input controls that are embedded inside the form tags.

SUBMITTING A FORM USING POST

Conversely, the `post` method is used for forms when the size of the submitting request will exceed the URL limit, a file needs to be uploaded, or consequences will result from submitting the form. Instead of encoding the input values in the URL, the request's document body is used to transfer the input values. This lets you submit larger forms that aren't restricted to the maximum URL length. Because the input is contained within the request body, the request can't be stored in a bookmark. This also means users can't easily mess with the input values by modifying the URL. But you still shouldn't completely trust the input—there are plenty of ways to modify the input values, although it's harder to do.

Unless told otherwise, Wicket uses the `post` method by default to submit forms. You can change the default behavior by either setting the `method` attribute of the `form` tag in the markup file to `get` or overriding the form's `getMethod` method and returning the `Form#METHOD_GET` constant. When you change the method to `get`, you should also turn off redirection (`setRedirect(false)` in the `onSubmit` handler). Doing so gives users the ability to bookmark the resulting page.

The `post` method is also known for the infamous popup that users get when they reload a page generated with a post form (see figure 6.3). The usual practice to stop users from resubmitting a possibly damaging action (such as depleting their credit card or your database) is to redirect the browser to a safe URL using the `get` method just after the submission. This pattern is called *redirect after post*.

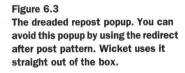

Figure 6.3
The dreaded repost popup. You can
avoid this popup by using the redirect
after post pattern. Wicket uses it
straight out of the box.

REDIRECT AFTER POST

The redirect after post pattern causes the browser to send two requests to the server: one submitting the form and one retrieving the result page. When you use detachable models in your application, this typically means that objects are loaded twice for a single form submission: one time to process the form, and one time to generate the result. But Wicket uses a special implementation of the redirect after post idiom to optimize this behavior: the response markup is generated in the same request as the post, and stored in a buffer. Then, the browser is redirected and served with the buffered response directly without having to regenerate it.

Wicket supports three strategies for handling form submissions, configured at the application level:

- *No redirect*—Renders the response directly; doesn't prevent reposting of the form (see IRequestCycleSettings#ONE_PASS_RENDER)
- *Redirect to buffer*—Renders the response directly to a buffer, redirects the browser, and prevents reposting of the form (see IRequestCycleSettings# REDIRECT_TO_BUFFER)
- *Redirect to render*—Redirects the browser directly; renders in a separate request (see IRequestCycleSettings#REDIRECT_TO_RENDER)

The default strategy of Wicket applications is to redirect to the buffer, because doing so yields the best of both worlds: the performance of handling everything in one request and the benefit of not resubmitting forms.

NOTE The redirect is useful for more than posting forms. Wicket uses the redirect pattern for all event listeners. When you create a Link and implement an action in the onClick handler that should be done only once, you're safe with the default render strategy. After processing the event handler, Wicket redirects the browser to a URL that displays the result.

Now that you've seen how values are transmitted to the server, let's look at what happens there.

6.2.2   *Processing the form submission on the server*

Form processing deals mostly with checking that the provided input is valid. When Wicket receives the form-submission request, it decodes the request and stores the submitted value of each form component in the component's input buffer. HTML input controls only known strings, so the input is stored as string values.

When each Wicket component has received its input, validation kicks in. Validation is a multistep process, as you can see in figure 6.4.

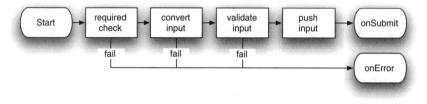

Figure 6.4   The steps in server-side form processing. When a step fails, Wicket calls the form's `onError` method. When all steps are successful, Wicket calls the `onSubmit` method.

In this figure, you can see that a failure in a step stops further processing for the field that failed. When even one field has failed any step, the last step (push input) isn't performed for any of the fields, and `onError` is called. Let's take a closer look at each of these steps.

CHECKING REQUIRED INPUT

When a form is submitted, the first thing Wicket checks after setting the raw input on each form component is whether all required values are present in the request. If a field has been set to be required, it must have input.

When a required field doesn't have input, the field is marked as invalid and an error message is registered. No other validations are performed on this field. When a value was supplied (or the field was marked as not required), the input is converted in the next step.

CONVERTING THE INPUT FROM STRING TO THE MODEL TYPE

The input for a form component is delivered to it in the form of a string. But often you want to edit a date that isn't just a string—perhaps the value is a ZIP code, a weight, a measure, an age, or a date. These types can also be in a locale-specific format. For example, Dutch ZIP codes are formatted *1234 AA*, whereas US ZIP codes are formatted *12345*; and large monetary values are written $1,000,000.00 when the locale is the US but €1.000.000,00 in the Dutch locale.

Each converter has two modes: converting from string to a particular type and converting from a particular type back to string. The former is used to convert incoming request parameters into model values. Browsers don't know about ZIP codes, weights, and other domain types, so the conversion from model value to string is used when the response is generated and the input controls need to display their value.

When the conversion fails, Wicket registers an error message. When the conversion succeeds for a field, Wicket runs the registered validators using the converted input.

VALIDATING THE CONVERTED INPUT

A validator checks the converted input to see if it conforms to some restrictions. These restrictions can be anything: a valid credit-card number, a minimum age, or a limited golf handicap to keep hobbyists off the green. Section 6.6 lists the available validators and shows you how to create custom validators.

A failed validation registers the error using its resource key to allow for later internationalization of the feedback message. Table 6.2 in section 6.7 lists all the information you need to create your own feedback message. When a validator fails, it stops the validation for the component. However, other fields on the form being processed are still validated.

PUSHING THE CONVERTED VALUE TO THE MODEL

The purpose of form processing is that ultimately the user's input is stored in the domain objects. When all validation has passed, Wicket pushes the converted value to the component's model by calling `getModel().setObject(convertedValue)`. This stores the converted value in the model, regardless of what the model does under the covers (see chapter 4 to learn more about models).

This step is skipped when any of the previous steps failed for any component of the form. No input is pushed to the model when there is invalid input.

CALLING ONSUBMIT OR ONERROR

The last thing to do is to call any submit listeners. When any of the previous steps failed for any child component of the form that was submitted, `onError` is called on the form and the submitting button as well (if there was a submitting button). Otherwise, `onSubmit` is called on the form and the submitting button.

What happens after this is up to you. It depends on what your implementation of `onSubmit` and `onError` does. If your `onSubmit` handler doesn't set a new response page, the current page with the form on it is rendered again, showing the new model values. But when validation errors occur and your `onError` handler (if you've overridden the default implementation) doesn't set a new response page, Wicket retains the user's input and shows the feedback messages. This gives the user the ability to fix any errors before submitting the form again. When you set a new response page, Wicket renders that page instead.

You've seen how you can create forms and how the user input gets processed. How can the user provide you with input? Let's look at the input controls at your disposal. First, you'll learn how to create and use text components.

6.3   *Components for text input*

The most common form of input for web applications is to submit some form of text. Most applications store textual data in a database and let users work with that data, be it personal information for students, customers, employees or patients; liabilities; contracts; product information; rebates; and so on. Figure 6.5 shows the basic components that provide textual input to your application.

Figure 6.5   The basic text components. The text field is useful for single-line input. A password field obscures its value to ensure privacy. The text area shows a basic multiline editor without any formatting possibilities.

In the following sections, we'll discuss each of the text components in figure 6.5 and how you can use them.

6.3.1   Using a TextField to process single-line text

The simplest form component for processing text is the TextField. You use a text field when you have single-line, limited-length input. You can use a TextField to process any type of textual input: strings (for example, a name, an email address, a website URL, or a title), numbers (Social Security number, price, weight, number of people in a party), and dates. The following example shows how to create a TextField in markup and in Java code:

```
<!-- markup -->
<input wicket:id="name" type="text" maxlength="32" />

<!-- Java -->
add(new TextField("name", new PropertyModel(person, "name")));
```

The text field component must be bound to an input tag with the type "text", as shown in the example. It isn't possible to couple the text field component to any other markup tag.

The text field is a simple component; all you have to do is add it to a form, or a child of a form, and provide it with a model. Just like any component, the text field also works with inheritable models such as CompoundPropertyModel (see chapter 4 for more information).

In HTML, you can limit the number of characters the field allows. You do so using the maxlength attribute. If the value of maxlength is determined at runtime, you can use an AttributeModifier to change the attribute from inside the Java code. This comes in handy when you're building a dynamic form and are able to retrieve the maximum column length of the property—for instance, using a javax.persistence (Java Persistence API [JPA]) annotation. How you retrieve the property using annotations is beyond the scope of this book; for now, the next example shows how to constrain the length of the text field to 32 characters programmatically:

```
add(new TextField("name", PropertyModel(person, "name"))
        .add(new SimpleAttributeModifier("maxlength", "32")));
```

Note that this restriction doesn't limit the length of the input on the server-side. As always, you should double-check the input using a length validator, because malicious users may try to tamper with your input fields.

Preventing SQL injection: trust your users as far as you can throw them

When you're creating a publicly facing website, you should always mistrust input from your users. This means rigorously adding validations, because the web is no longer as nice as in 1992 (you can find a great comic regarding this issue here: http:// xkcd.com/327/). Probably the most important advice we can give you is to always use `query` parameters instead of string concatenation when you build your SQL queries. If you use concatenation, you're opening up your application to SQL injection attacks. This way, a simple query such as

```
String query = "SELECT * FROM persons WHERE name='" + name + "'";
```

gives malicious users the ability to drop tables from your database (if the user rights aren't correctly managed). For example, the following `name` value drops the USERS table!:

```
"'; DROP TABLE USERS; --"
```

This risk is easily mitigated by using `query` parameters. The query becomes

```
String query = "SELECT * FROM persons WHERE name=?";
```

and you need to bind the `name` value to the SQL statement. This not only improves your security but also gives your database system ample opportunity to cache a compiled version of your query, increasing the performance of your application as a whole.

`Query` parameters are also referred to as *bind variables* or *placeholders*.

You can use an attribute modifier to modify programmatically any attributes supported by the `input` tag. The most useful tags for modifying are `maxlength`, `readonly`, `size` (although CSS styling is preferable for controlling size), and `title`.

The text field is used to show text to the user and to give the user the ability to modify the text. But how can you prevent bystanders from seeing what the user is typing in—for example, a password?

6.3.2 *Using a PasswordTextField to process a password*

The `PasswordTextField` form component is primarily used for entering passwords on a sign-in form. Typically, the user has to provide a username and password combination that is checked against the database before the user is granted access. But there are other situations in which bystanders shouldn't be able to read the password—for instance, when the user is changing her password.

The HTML `input` tag with type `"password"` is just what the doctor ordered. This tag instructs the browser to obscure the input, rendering it unreadable. The browser also prevents copying the field's contents to the clipboard, increasing security slightly (remember that people still can view the page's source!). Figure 6.5 shows an example of how a password field obscures the input.

Creating a `PasswordTextField` is as simple as creating a `TextField`, as shown in the following example:

```
<!-- markup -->
<input wicket:id="password" type="password" />

/* Java */
PasswordTextField pw = new PasswordTextField("password", new Model(""));
add(pw);
```

The `PasswordTextField` behaves differently from the normal `TextField`. For starters, the password field is by default *required*. This means a user is required to provide input in the field. You can easily modify this behavior by setting the `required` flag on the password component to `false`.

Another difference from the normal text field is that, again by default, the `PasswordTextField` clears its input on each request. This ensures that the password is initially empty on sign-in forms, but doesn't prevent password managers from filling in the password. The following line of code lets the field retain the input if you want it to:

```
pw.setResetPassword(false);
```

The last way the `PasswordTextField` differs from other form components is that it doesn't support storing its value in a cookie using `setPersistent(true)`. Storing a password on a client system in a cookie is insecure, even when you encrypt the value. If you want to store a client-authentication token, it's best to create your own cookie and use a one-way hash with a salt as the value to identify the user. (There is, of course, a lot more to write about security; chapter 11 is dedicated to securing your application.)

Storing form values on the client side with cookies

All form components (except the `PasswordTextField`) have the ability to store their value on the client using cookies. All you need to do is tell Wicket to make the field persistent using `field.setPersistent(true)`. This will set a client-side cookie for the particular component filled with the model value of the component.

With a `TextField` component, you can receive single-line input; and with a `PasswordTextField`, you can make it secure. How can you receive multiline input?

6.3.3   *Using a TextArea to process multiline text*

In many applications, it's necessary to provide users with a way to enter multiline text: for instance, to edit the description of cheeses in our cheese store, or to provide comments with a recipe. The HTML text area input control provides this ability; you use the `TextArea` form component like its Wicket counterpart.

The HTML input control is basic: it allows only line breaks as formatting options. There are no provisions for user-enabled formatting of the text except by adopting one of several JavaScript libraries that are available to provide enhanced formatting options. TinyMCE and FCKeditor are the two most popular libraries and provide an almost-Microsoft-Word-like experience inside the browser.

Using the text area is as simple as using the (password) text field:

```
<!-- markup -->
<textarea wicket:id="description" cols="120" rows="6"></textarea>

<!-- Java -->
add(new TextArea("description",
                 new PropertyModel(cheese, "description")));
```

The markup for the text area requires you to provide the number of columns and rows; otherwise, your markup won't be valid HTML. Fortunately, your browser corrects omissions by using default values for these attributes, but it's up to the browser to determine what values are used. Typically, the values for these attributes are specified in the markup, because they have a profound influence on the layout of the page: more columns mean a wider input box, and more rows mean a higher box. You can manipulate them at runtime with attribute modifiers.

You've learned how to create editing controls for free text and add them to your forms. But free text isn't the only way to provide input. Often, the number of valid input choices is limited (for instance, male or female). Using selection controls, you can restrict user input to a list of choices.

6.4 Selecting from a list of items

There are many ways in which users can interact with forms. We just looked at a free-format way of receiving textual input. In this section, we'll examine ways to select items from a list of choices. In our cheese store, we might implement a credit-card checkout form and list the number of supported credit cards, or provide something as simple as being able to select a gender (to address the customer correctly).

First, we'll look at selecting a single value from a list, and then we'll move on to selecting multiple values.

6.4.1 Selecting a single value from a list of choices

Wicket has several components that allow you to select a single value from a list of choices. They all work basically the same way but show a different form control to the user. The input controls are limited to what the HTML specification has to offer, although some JavaScript libraries provide additional controls. Wicket provides support only for the standard controls, so we'll limit our discussion to those in the coming sections. Figure 6.6 shows examples of the provided single-select components.

As an example, we'll add a field to our cheese store that lets users select the category of the cheese: fresh, whey, goat or sheep, hard, and blue vein. We'll use this list to create a cheese category selection component. Let's look at the first component from figure 6.6: the ListChoice.

Figure 6.6   An overview of the single-select components provided by Wicket. Each component allows a user to select one value from a list of choices.

USING THE LISTCHOICE TO SELECT A SINGLE VALUE

A ListChoice is a selection control that displays a box with a number of rows inside. The user can select only one item. The following example shows how to add a ListChoice in markup and Java:

```
<!-- html -->
<select wicket:id="category" size="6">
   <option>Hard</option><option>Soft</option>
</select>

/* Java */
List<String> categories = Arrays.asList("Fresh", "Whey",
                        "Goat or sheep", "Hard", "Blue vein");
form.add(new ListChoice("category",
           new PropertyModel(cheese, "category"),    <─┘ Bind selected value
           categories));                             <─┐ Provide choices
cheese.setCategory("Blue vein");    <─ Set selected value
```

The markup shows that we need to use the select tag. Inside the tag, we can include example markup for previewing the page. The markup contained within the select tag is replaced with the options we generate in the Java code.

The ListChoice is added to the form and provided with a model from which to retrieve the selected value and in which to store the selected value. We also provide the ListChoice with the available choices—in this case, the list of categories. The list of choices can also be a model, giving you the ability to manage the list dynamically using models. For instance, you can use a LoadableDetachableModel to load the list of categories from the database.

Note that the ListChoice and all selection components require you to provide the choices. When you use a ListChoice in combination with a CompoundPropertyModel, you still have to provide the list of choices, whereas you can omit an explicit model for the selected value of the component. The following Java code shows you how this works:

```
Form form = new Form("form", new CompoundPropertyModel(cheese));
add(form);
form.add(new ListChoice("category", new CategoriesModel()));
```

In this example, the ListChoice uses the CompoundPropertyModel idiom to bind to the cheese's category property (category is the component identifier of the List-Choice) and the CategoriesModel to load the list of categories from the database.

The number of visible rows is configurable from the Java code, but that property is best left to the designer and specified in the markup (the size attribute in our example). The number of rows can have a profound effect on the layout of your page, so it's best not to change it too much. That said, you can choose to alter the number of rows using setMaxRows(), provided the markup doesn't have the attribute set.

USING A DROPDOWNCHOICE TO SELECT A SINGLE VALUE

The DropDownChoice component is also used to select a single value, like ListChoice. A DropDownChoice shows the currently selected value in a single field and shows the available choices in a popup list when it's clicked. Because it's space efficient, it's probably the most commonly used selection control.

Using the DropDownChoice is similar to using the ListChoice. The following example provides the same functionality as the ListChoice but uses a DropDownChoice instead:

```
<!-- html -->
<select wicket:id="category">
    <option>Hard</option><option>Soft</option>
</select>

/* Java */
form.add(new DropDownChoice("category",
                new PropertyModel(cheese, "category"),
                categories));
```

Two changes are important. First, the select tag doesn't have a size attribute. If you put the size attribute in, it renders as a ListBox. Second, we now use the DropDownChoice component. This is all there is to it. You can use DropDownChoice and ListChoice interchangeably.

USING A RADIOCHOICE TO SELECT A SINGLE VALUE

If you have a limited number of choices and want to display them all, a RadioChoice component is perfect. It uses radio buttons to display each choice. Because the radio component shows all the choices, it takes more space than a DropDownChoice or a ListChoice. This makes it more user-friendly, though, because the values are immediately visible.

Using the RadioChoice is a bit different than using the previous selection components. Let's look at implementing our example with a RadioChoice:

```
<!-- html -->
<span wicket:id="category">
    <input type="radio" /> Hard<br />
    <input type="radio" /> Soft<br />
</span>

/* Java */
form.add(new RadioChoice("category",
                new PropertyModel(cheese, "category"),
                categories));
```

As you can see, we replace the select tag with a span and the options with the input tags. There is no official tag for grouping radio buttons—HTML doesn't prescribe one. As in the earlier examples, the contents of the outer tags are replaced with the actual values and are present only for previewing.

The `RadioChoice` renders each choice on its own line. You can alter this behavior by setting the prefix and suffix. The next snippet instructs our `RadioChoice` to render all choices on one line by removing the `br` element from the final output:

```
form.add(new RadioChoice("category",
              new PropertyModel(cheese, "category"),
              categories).setSuffix(""));
```

If you need more control over the final markup, look at the `RadioGroup` component. It doesn't generate the list of choices for you, but it serves as a wrapper around radio buttons such that they function as a `RadioChoice`.

6.4.2   *Selecting multiple values from a list of choices*

In some cases, you need to let users select more than one value. For example, Cabrales is a blue cheese from northern Spain made of cow, goat, and ewe milk. This makes the milk type property of our `Cheese` object a list (of milk types).

Wicket provides two components for selecting multiple values, as shown in figure 6.7.

As in the previous section, these components are similar. They need a model

Figure 6.7   Form components that allow multiple items to be selected from a list of choices: the `ListMultipleChoice` and the `CheckBoxMultipleChoice`, respectively.

from which to get their selected values and in which to store the selected values, and they need a list of choices. Let's first look at the `ListMultipleChoice` component.

USING A LISTMULTIPLECHOICE COMPONENT TO SELECT MULTIPLE VALUES

The `ListMultipleChoice` component is almost identical to the `ListChoice` component. It also lists the choices in a box, with each choice on a row. The difference is that the `ListMultipleChoice` allows the user to select more than one row at a time.

Let's look at an example that uses the milk types for selecting multiple values:

```
<!-- html -->
<select wicket:id="milkTypes" size="6" multiple="multiple">
    <option>Bison</option><option>Camel</option>
</select>

/* Java */
List<String> choices = Arrays.asList("Camel", "Cow", "Goat",
                         "Reindeer", "Sheep", "Yak");
form.add(new ListMultipleChoice("milkTypes",                    Bind selected
            new PropertyModel(cheese, "milkTypes"),             values
            choices));
cheese.getMilkTypes().clear();                                  Provide
cheese.getMilkTypes().add("Cow");       ❶ Select               choices
cheese.getMilkTypes().add("Yak");         choices
```

This example renders the selection box with six rows filled with the provided milk types. We selected two values by adding the values to the list of milk types on the cheese ❶, so these values are displayed as selected when the control is rendered.

USING A CHECKBOXMULTIPLECHOICE TO SELECT MULTIPLE VALUES

The CheckBoxMultipleChoice presents choices using check boxes. The user can select multiple values by clicking the preferred check boxes. Similar to the Radio-Choice, this component renders all values visible and so can take up a lot of space.

Using the CheckBoxMultipleChoice should be familiar by now: it's similar to the previous selection components, as evidenced by the following example showing the markup and Java code:

```
<!-- html -->
<span wicket:id="milkTypes">
    <input type="checkbox" /> Cow<br />
    <input type="checkbox" /> Yak<br />
</select>

/* Java */
List<String> choices = Arrays.asList("Camel", "Cow", "Goat",
                       "Reindeer", "Sheep", "Yak");
form.add(new CheckBoxMultipleChoice("milkTypes",
            new PropertyModel(cheese, "milkTypes"),
            choices));
```

This code renders each choice using a check box on a single line. You can change this (as you can the RadioChoice) by setting the prefix and suffix (using setPrefix and setSuffix methods). If you need even more control for generating the list of choices, look at the CheckGroup component.

In all our examples for selecting items from a list, we've used strings for the list of choices. But what if you want to include an actual object in the choices? The Choice-Renderer component provides a mapping between objects and choices.

6.4.3 *Mapping an object to a choice and back using a ChoiceRenderer*

The list of possible choices often isn't fixed but changes over time. In such cases, the list isn't maintained in Java code, but comes from other places. In most applications, such lists are kept in database tables and mapped to a Java class.

In our case, we could replace the milk type property with a proper class backed by a database table. This would allow us to add kangaroo milk-based cheese when that opportunity arises, without having to modify our application. Figure 6.8 shows what we're up to.

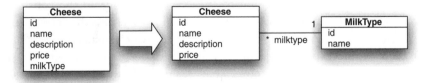

Figure 6.8   Making the MilkType a proper abstraction in our application

We're going to create a MilkType class (with an identifier and a name property) and use it for a many-to-one relation on our cheese (the milk-Type property). Let's see how each option is rendered in the markup. Figure 6.9 shows what is generated for each choice.

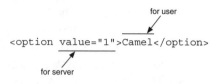

Figure 6.9   The markup that is generated for each option in a DropDownChoice component

The option has two parts: the value and the display text. The value attribute is used to identify the option when the value is submitted. By default, Wicket uses the list index to generate this value. This approach works in most cases, but it can lead to strange behavior when the order of the list changes between requests. For instance, take the case of inserting bison milk in the list: all other choices shift one position. This means someone who had chosen goat milk suddenly has picked ewe milk, instead.

We can remedy this issue by using a different value to identify choices instead of the list index. The object identifier of the MilkType is a good candidate for this task. For the display value, we want to use the name property of the MilkType.

How can we perform this mapping for our DropDownChoice component? The choice family of components uses a conversion interface called the IChoiceRenderer to transform domain objects into a display value and identifying value. When you implement the interface, you have to implement these conversions. For the general case, Wicket has a standard implementation available: the ChoiceRenderer. This renderer uses property expressions to get at the desired fields: one expression for the identifying value and one for the display text. Listing 6.2 illustrates the usage of the ChoiceRenderer in our case.

Listing 6.2   Using the ChoiceRenderer to match an object to a choice

```
List<MilkType> choices = dao.getMilkTypes();      ⬅❶ Get from database

ChoiceRenderer renderer = new ChoiceRenderer("name", "id");   ⬅
form.add(new DropDownChoice("milktype",                         ❷ Map name
          new PropertyModel(cheese, "milkType"),                  and id
          choices,
          renderer));      ⬅❸ Use renderer
```

In this example, we change our list of strings to a list of MilkType objects and fetch it from the database ❶. We create a choice renderer that maps the name property of each choice object to the display text and the id property to the option's value attribute ❷. The renderer is passed to the DropDownChoice in the constructor ❸. With a ChoiceRenderer we're able to satisfy both our users and the server: users see a meaningful description and the server knows exactly which object to select.

We've used check box components to select values from a provided list. But a check box can also be used in a more binary fashion. It's well suited to answer yes or no questions, or more generally suited to modify boolean properties.

6.4.4 *Using check boxes for boolean properties*

"Would you like spam with your cheese?" is a question we could ask our customers when they register with our cheese store. In this modern day and age, the spam wouldn't come in cans with an order of cheese (although that might make the service more attractive) but in a monthly or weekly newsletter with the latest discounts and offers of cheese. Typically, such questions are asked using a check box where customers can confirm that they wish to receive the newsletter (see figure 6.10).

Figure 6.10 Using a check box to receive spam with a cheese order

In our cheese store, we could add a boolean property to our customer object that registers whether the customer wants to receive newsletters. Binding to the customer object is then as simple as binding the customer's wantspam property to the checkbox using a PropertyModel, as shown in the following snippet:

```
<!-- markup -->
<input type="checkbox" wicket:id="wantsspam" id="wantsspam" />
<label for="wantspam">I want to receive spam with my cheese!</label>

/* Java */
form.add(new CheckBox("wantsspam",
                      new PropertyModel(cust, "wantsspam")));
```

This is one way of using the check box. But there are other use cases: for example, to toggle the visibility of a part of the UI. Figure 6.11 shows a cheese-search page with an option to search using more advanced criteria.

The idea is to hide the more advanced options from the casual user. Most users are probably happy to search for Gouda or Edam; but if a cheese connoisseur visits our site, we want to provide more search options. Listing 6.3 shows how to create such a form using an Ajax-enabled check box for toggling the visibility of the advanced options.

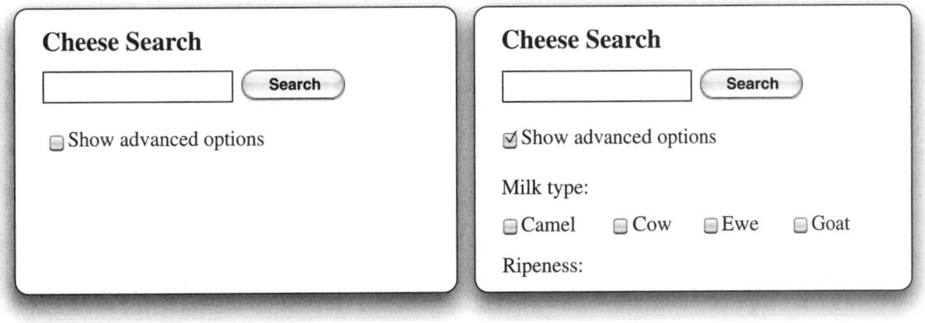

Figure 6.11 A cheese-search page with advanced options initially hidden from the user. Clicking the check box makes the advanced options visible.

Listing 6.3   Markup and Java code for an advanced search form for cheeses

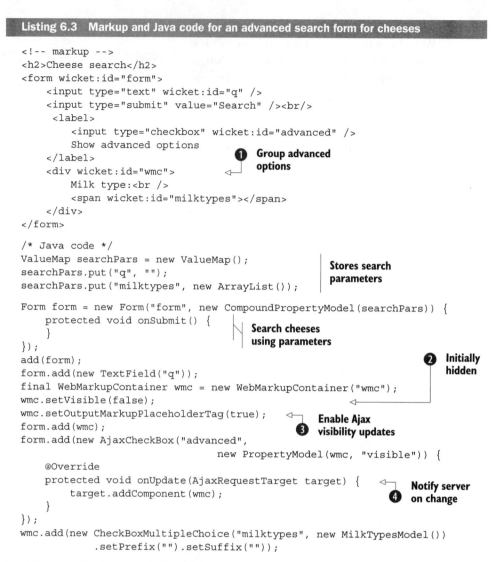

```
<!-- markup -->
<h2>Cheese search</h2>
<form wicket:id="form">
    <input type="text" wicket:id="q" />
    <input type="submit" value="Search" /><br/>
     <label>
        <input type="checkbox" wicket:id="advanced" />
        Show advanced options
    </label>                              ❶ Group advanced
    <div wicket:id="wmc">                    options
        Milk type:<br />
        <span wicket:id="milktypes"></span>
    </div>
</form>

/* Java code */
ValueMap searchPars = new ValueMap();            Stores search
searchPars.put("q", "");                         parameters
searchPars.put("milktypes", new ArrayList());

Form form = new Form("form", new CompoundPropertyModel(searchPars)) {
    protected void onSubmit() {       Search cheeses
    }                                 using parameters
});
add(form);                                                    ❷ Initially
form.add(new TextField("q"));                                    hidden
final WebMarkupContainer wmc = new WebMarkupContainer("wmc");
wmc.setVisible(false);
wmc.setOutputMarkupPlaceholderTag(true);    Enable Ajax
form.add(wmc);                              ❸ visibility updates
form.add(new AjaxCheckBox("advanced",
                         new PropertyModel(wmc, "visible")) {
    @Override
    protected void onUpdate(AjaxRequestTarget target) {    Notify server
        target.addComponent(wmc);                       ❹ on change
    }
});
wmc.add(new CheckBoxMultipleChoice("milktypes", new MilkTypesModel())
            .setPrefix("").setSuffix(""));
```

In this example, the search form has a special, separate part for the advanced search options ❶. The advanced search options are grouped using a WebMarkupContainer and hidden initially ❷. Because we're going to update the visibility using Ajax, we need to keep a placeholder in the markup ❸ (as explained in chapter 5). The container's visibility is controlled by binding the check box's model to the visibility property of the container. By using an AjaxCheckBox, we get notified of a change directly ❹; we add the markup container to the Ajax request target so it can either render itself or hide itself based on its visibility property.

You've seen several ways of letting users answer questions (would you like spam with your order?), but the answers need to be sent to the server for them to be useful.

> ## A standalone check box
>
> The check box is useful as a form component, but you can also use a check box outside a form. The only caveat is that it won't submit a form but instead sends the change request directly to the server. Any input in forms that haven't been submitted yet will be lost when you click the check box.

The next section discusses components that tell the browser to send the accumulated data to the server.

6.5 Components for submitting form data

In section 6.1, you learned how to submit a form using a normal HTML submit button without attaching or using a Wicket component. This approach works in many cases, but sometimes you need more than one button on a form. A nice example for this use case is the I'm Feeling Lucky button on the Google search page. Another use case is when you want to display a button that submits the form but that is located outside the form tags.

This section will show you various components that enable you to submit a form with more than one button on a form, using links, or using Ajax. We'll also look at disabling Wicket's form-processing logic for those cases where you don't want to validate the input or don't want to update the components' models. Let's start with buttons.

6.5.1 Using buttons to submit data

A Wicket button is a component that submits a form. When the button is clicked, it submits the form. Wicket first calls the button's onSubmit method and then (if not configured otherwise) calls the form's onSubmit method. Using the button's onSubmit method gives you the opportunity to specify different behaviors for different events. For instance, you could implement a Save button and also a Copy button. Depending on which button is clicked, a particular action is taken.

The Wicket button component can work with two different markup tags: the button tag and the input tag (of type button or submit). When you use the button tag, you must supply the contents of the tag for the label. If you use the input tag, the model value of the button is used to generate the value attribute of the tag (if the model is supplied and not empty). Providing a model allows you to render the caption of the button with internationalized text (using a ResourceModel or StringResourceModel; see chapter 12). Listing 6.4 gives a short example of the markup alternatives and Java code.

> **Listing 6.4 Markup alternatives and Java code for using a button to submit a form**

```
<!-- html -->
<form wicket:id="form">
    <input type="submit" value="Click me!" wicket:id="button1" />
    <button wicket:id="button2" type="submit">Click me!</button>
</form>

/* Java Code */
Form form = new Form("form") {
```

```
    @Override
    protected void onSubmit() {
        System.out.println("Form onSubmit is called");
    }
};
add(form);
form.add(new Button("button1", new Model("Pressing matters"))) {
    @Override
    public void onSubmit() {
        System.out.println("Button 1's onSubmit is called");
    }
});
form.add(new Button("button2") {
    @Override
    public void onSubmit() {
        System.out.println("Button 2's onSubmit is called");
    }
});
```

Model provides caption

Here we add the two buttons to the form. The first button uses a model to override the `value` attribute of the `input` tag. The second button doesn't have that option, because the contents are plain markup (although you can use a label component or a panel inside to generate the contents).

When either button is clicked, its `onSubmit` method is called; and when that is completed, the form's `onSubmit` method is called. When the user clicks `button2` from the example in listing 6.4, we first see "Button 2's onSubmit is called" and then "Form onSubmit is called".

Here we use buttons inside a form for submittal, but sometimes you may want to use a link to submit the form data, or even a button outside the form. With the `SubmitLink` component, you can.

6.5.2 Using links to submit data

The `SubmitLink` component acts like a `Button` but uses JavaScript to submit the form. The `SubmitLink` can be used with any markup that supports an `onclick` JavaScript event. When it's used in combination with an `<a>` tag, it uses the `href` attribute to generate the JavaScript necessary to submit the form. A big advantage of the `SubmitLink` over the `Button` component is that the link doesn't need to be a child of a form to submit the form. This means you can put the link anywhere on the page no matter the form's location.

The example in listing 6.5 shows two uses for the `SubmitLink`. One link is inside the form, and the other is outside.

Listing 6.5 Markup and Java code for using a `SubmitLink` inside and outside a form

```
<!-- html -->
<form wicket:id="form">
    <a href="#" wicket:id="inside">Click me!</a>
</form>
<input type="button" value="Outside!" wicket:id="outside" />
```

Can be anything supporting onclick

```
/* Java Code */
Form form = new Form("form") {
    @Override
    protected void onSubmit() {
        System.out.println("Form onSubmit is called");
    }
};
add(form);
form.add(new SubmitLink("inside") {
    @Override
    public void onSubmit() {
        System.out.println("Inside link's onSubmit is called");
    }
});
add(new SubmitLink("outside", form) {    ◁─❶ Need form
    @Override
    public void onSubmit() {
        System.out.println("Outside link's onSubmit is called");
    }
});
```

As you can see in this example, the SubmitLink is used the same way as the Button. When you use a SubmitLink outside a form, you must provide it with the form that will be submitted by the link ❶.

There is one caveat to using the SubmitLink: your visitors need to have JavaScript enabled for the link to work. The SubmitLink uses a normal request cycle to submit the form. If you want a more interactive, Web 2.0 way of submitting the form data, you may want to use Ajax.

6.5.3 *Using Ajax to submit data*

Using Ajax gives you the opportunity to provide a more responsive user experience when submitting form data. Typically, you use Ajax to submit small forms containing a couple of fields.

As an example of using an AjaxSubmitLink, we'll show an Ajax-enabled comment form for our cheeses. Visitors can submit a comment directly without having to refresh the whole page. Listing 6.6 shows how to do this in markup and Java.

Listing 6.6 Creating an Ajax-enabled comment form for a cheese detail page

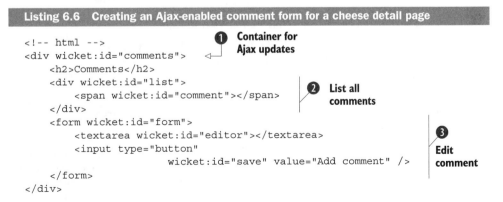

```
<!-- html -->                    ❶ Container for
<div wicket:id="comments">    ◁─   Ajax updates
    <h2>Comments</h2>
    <div wicket:id="list">
        <span wicket:id="comment"></span>    ❷ List all
    </div>                                      comments
    <form wicket:id="form">                               ❸
        <textarea wicket:id="editor"></textarea>       Edit
        <input type="button"                           comment
                    wicket:id="save" value="Add comment" />
    </form>
</div>
```

```
/* Java code */
final WebMarkupContainer parent = new WebMarkupContainer("comments");
parent.setOutputMarkupId(true);
add(parent);
List<String> comments = ...                          Generate markup    ❹
parent.add(new ListView("list", comments) {              id for Ajax
        @Override
        protected void populateItem(ListItem item) {
            item.add(new Label("comment", item.getModel()));
        }
    });

Form form = new Form("form");
final TextArea editor = new TextArea("editor", new Model(""));
editor.setOutputMarkupId(true);
form.add(editor);
form.add(new AjaxSubmitLink("save") {
        @Override
        protected void onSubmit(AjaxRequestTarget target, Form form) {
            comments.add(editor.getModelObjectAsString());
            editor.setModel(new Model(""));
            target.addComponent(parent);
            target.focusComponent(editor);
        }
    });
parent.add(form);
```

A lot happens in this example. The outer div in the markup is used to update the whole list of comments and the form in one go ❶. The example is basically split into two parts: one for showing the list of comments ❷ and one for adding a new comment to the list ❸.

In the onSubmit method of our AjaxSubmitLink, we retrieve the model value of the editor and add it to the comments list. We clear the value of the editor to begin with a clean slate. Then, we add the WebMarkupContainer that groups our list of comments and comment form to the Ajax request target. This repaints our components. Finally, we set the focus of the browser back to the comment field.

Because we update the WebMarkupContainer with Ajax, we need to give it a markup identifier. The same goes for our editor: to be able to set the focus on the element, we need its markup identifier. In this example, we instruct Wicket to generate the markup identifier for us ❹. Because we use both the WebMarkupContainer and the editor inside the anonymous class, we must make their references final; otherwise we'll get compile errors. Figure 6.12 shows the result of our labor.

We've looked at submitting the form in various ways. When the form is submitted, the automatic form processing kicks in. But sometimes you need

Comments

This cheese is great with a glass of Pinot Noir.
I like a Riesling better.
p0wn3d!

(Add comment)

Figure 6.12 A screenshot of the Ajax form that processes comments for our cheese details page

to bypass the form processing—for instance, to create a Cancel button, or to do some other processing before submitting the form (like address auto-completion based on a ZIP code).

6.5.4 *Skipping Wicket's form processing*

Imagine that you're shopping for cheese in our online cheese store. You've added a kilo of Gouda, one pound of Cheddar, and a couple of boxes of Camembert. You go to the checkout page and fill in your shipping and billing addresses. Just as you start filling in the credit-card data, you remember that there are more days in the month than expected, and your paycheck won't arrive for a couple of days. Saddened by those 31-day months, you click the Cancel button.

The Cancel button in this scenario needs to skip our validations, or you won't be able to send a request to the server. There are several ways to bypass the form processing. One is to use a normal `Link` component instead of a button. A normal, nonsubmitting link doesn't submit the form data and hence bypasses the form processing.

If you want to retain the user input in the form components, you need to submit the form (this sends the user input to the server) but not process it. To accomplish this, you have to set the default form-processing flag on the submitting component (for example, the `Button` or `SubmitLink`) to `false`. This gives you the opportunity to go to another page to let the user perform another task, and then return to the current page without losing the user's input. Listing 6.7 shows how you can achieve this.

Listing 6.7 Bypassing default form processing to retain user input

```
public Page1 extends WebPage {
    public Page1() {
        Form form = new Form("form");
        add(form);
        form.add(new TextField("q", new Model(), Integer.class));    ← Accept only integers
        Button b = new Button("do") {
            @Override public void onSubmit() {
                setResponsePage(new Page2(Page1.this));     ← ❶ Respond with new, old
            }
        };
        b.setDefaultFormProcessing(false);    ← ❷ Don't process; retain input
        form.add(b);
        form.add(new FeedbackPanel("feedback"));
    }
}

public Page2 extends WebPage {
    public Page2(final Page returnTo) {
        add(new Link("returnLink") {
            @Override public void onClick() {
                setResponsePage(returnTo);     ← ❸ Return to old page
            }
        });
    }
}
```

The button on Page1 navigates to Page2 and provides the current page as a parameter ❶. By setting the default form-processing flag to false, we won't process the user input, but keep the raw input until it can be used ❷. Page2 uses the reference when the user clicks the return link, returning to the old Page1 ❸. When you try this, you'll notice that any input in the text field of Page1 is still there. This opens up possibilities for implementing complex navigation structures—for example, using pages to look up information during a long entry process.

With the submit buttons and links from this section and the input controls discussed in the sections before, you can create forms of any size and with any complexity. But that only covers the client side of the form-processing equation. Now we need to look at the server side and make sure the data we receive is valid.

6.6   *Validating user input*

We'd like to live in a perfect world where nobody makes mistakes and where only nice and perfect people visit our websites. However, people do make mistakes, and you should do your best to ensure those mistakes don't have negative consequences.

In this section, you'll learn how to validate user input so you don't receive bad or incomplete data. In section 6.2, you learned that form processing consists of these steps:

1   Checks that required input is supplied.
2   Converts the input value from String to an actual type.
3   Validates the input using the registered validators.
4   Pushes converted and validated input to models.
5   Calls onSubmit or onError.

Steps 1 through 3 are part of the validation cycle. Step 4 is performed only when the prior steps were all successful for all fields. Wicket takes care of the validation part; you only need to tell Wicket what to check. Step 5, explained in detail in section 6.2, is obvious. Let's take a closer look at steps 1 through 3 and start with step 1: the required check.

6.6.1   *Making a field required*

How can you tell Wicket that a particular value is required? You specify a setting available on each form input control. You can set the required flag by doing the following:

```
field.setRequired(true);
```

As with most methods of form components, you can chain the method calls as in the next snippet:

```
form.add(new TextField("age")
            .setRequired(true)
            .setLabel(new Model("age"))
            .add(NumberValidator.minimum(18)));
```

This results in concise code (and, in our opinion, more readable code, provided your IDE's automatic formatter works correctly).

A required field that's left empty generates an error message. The error message is looked up using Wicket's resource-lookup strategies (see chapter 12 for more information on this subject) by searching for the resource key Required (case sensitive).

The message is localized and by default shows "Field '${label}' is required." If you need a different language—for example, Dutch—the message is "Veld '${label}' is verplicht." The ${label} expression is replaced with the offending component's label or, if a label hasn't been set, the component's identifier. If you want to provide a custom message, you can use the Required resource key in your resource bundle to override the message.

When Wicket has checked the required fields, it converts the raw input to the domain types.

6.6.2   *Converting user input from strings to domain types*

As you learned in section 6.2, the browser sends input as strings to the server. Wicket tries to convert these strings to your domain types, such as numbers, dates, and ZIP codes. The act of converting the values is discussed in chapter 12. For now, we'll look at how to help Wicket determine the domain type.

For most fields, Wicket can automatically determine the type by using reflection on the associated model. This doesn't work when the model isn't a property model and the model value is null. For instance, the following snippet doesn't give any information that helps Wicket determine what type the input needs to be converted into:

```
add(new TextField("age", new Model()));
```

When Wicket can't determine the target domain type, it assumes that String is the correct type. You can help Wicket by supplying the target domain type. In our example, we probably want to use an Integer for the age. The following code sets the correct type on the fields:

```
add(new TextField("age", new Model(), Integer.class));
add(new TextField("zipcode", new Model()).setType(ZipCode.class));
```

Wicket uses the domain type (obtained through discovery or provided by you) to look up a converter. The converter is applied to convert the raw input string. The converters are registered with the Application object (see Application#getConverterLocator).

A failed conversion is registered as a validation error using the resource key (for the feedback message) IConverter or IConverter.<typename> (substitute the type name for the conversion type, such as Long or ZipCode). For example, we could use the key age.IConverter or age.IConverter.Integer. Both keys are valid.

When the conversion is successful, Wicket checks the registered validators. Let's look at how you can add them to your fields.

6.6.3   *Using Wicket's supplied validators*

Wicket comes with several validators to make your life easier. In this section, we'll give you an idea which validators are available and how you can use them.

The NumberValidator class provides several factory methods and ready-made validators for validating numbers. It has methods for longs and doubles, but they work equally well for integers and floats, respectively. Here's an example:

```
add(new TextField("age").add(NumberValidator.minimum(18)));
add(new TextField("handicap").add(NumberValidator.range(0, 3.5)));
add(new TextField("duration").add(NumberValidator.POSITIVE));
```

You can check strings using the StringValidator class, which also specifies several factory methods. Here are some examples of its use:

```
add(new TextField("userid").add(StringValidator.lengthBetween(8,12)));
add(new TextField("comment").add(StringValidator.maximumLength(4000)));
```

If you want to check the input using a *regular expression*, you can use a PatternValidator:

```
add(new TextField("phone").add(
                new PatternValidator("^[2-9]\\d{2}-\\d{3}-\\d{4}$")));
```

Ample documentation is available about regular expressions, so we won't repeat it here.

The Wicket package includes a couple of standard pattern validators:

```
add(new TextField("email").add(EmailAddressValidator.getInstance()));
add(new TextField("url").add(new UrlValidator(new String[]{"http"})));
```

Note that you aren't limited to text fields, but they're the most commonly used form components in conjunction with validators.

Sometimes you need to compare two field values—for instance, when you want to be sure a password was entered correctly. In such a case, you need a form-level validator. The following snippet shows how to ensure that two password fields have the same value:

```
PasswordTextField field1 = new PasswordTextField("password");
field1.setResetPassword(false);
form.add(field1);

PasswordTextField field2 = new PasswordTextField("controlPassword");
field2.setModel(field1.getModel());
field2.setResetPassword(false);
form.add(field2);

form.add(new EqualPasswordInputValidator(field1, field2));
```

In this example, we make sure the password fields retain their input. We also let both fields share the same model; this way, the fields start with the same values and keep it that way. Note that the validator works on the input, not on the model values. Unless both fields have the same input value, no input is transferred to the domain object.

You can also add multiple validators to a component. For instance, you could add a length validator and a pattern validator to a text field. Doing so would give two validation errors if the input didn't conform to either validator. Usually it's beneficial to add both a length validator and a pattern validator if the pattern isn't a regulated pattern such as an ISBN or SSN.

What should you do if your own business rules call for a specific validation that isn't one of the standard, provided validators? You need to write your own. Let's take a look.

6.6.4 *Writing your own validator*

Even though Wicket comes with many validators and the PatternValidator gives you
a lot of flexibility in rolling your own validators quickly, this may not be enough. A regular expression won't help you calculate a modulo 11 proof or determine if a number
is a prime. In this section, you'll create a validator that determines whether the input
is divisible by a particular number.

A validator needs to implement the IValidator interface or, if it wants to validate
null values, the INullAcceptingValidator interface. The INullAcceptingInter-
face is a subclass of IValidator and doesn't add any extra methods.

Instead of going bare bones, we'll use some infrastructure code that is provided by
Wicket. Wicket's validators all extend AbstractValidator, and this class gives us a
nice jump start for building a custom validator. Listing 6.8 shows how to use the
AbstractValidator to implement the DivisibleValidator.

Listing 6.8 Creating a custom validator: DivisibleValidator

```
public class DivisibleValidator extends AbstractValidator {
    private final long n;
    public DivisibleValidator(long n) {
        if (n == 0) throw new IllegalArgumentException("n can't be 0");
        this.n = n;
    }
    @Override
    protected void onValidate(IValidatable validatable) {
        Number value = (Number)validatable.getValue();
        if(value.longValue() % n != 0) {
            error(validatable);            ◁┐   Report
        }                                   ❶  error
    }
    @Override
    protected String resourceKey() {              ❷  Key for error
        return "DivisibleValidator";                  message
    }
    @Override
    protected Map variablesMap(IValidatable validatable) {   ❸
        Map map = super.variablesMap(validatable);            Substitution
        map.put("divisor", n);                                variables for
        return map;                                           error message
    }
}
```

The AbstractValidator requires us to override the onValidate method. The method
has an IValidatable as a parameter. The IValidatable is the item that is to be validated, and we can get the value by calling getValue on the validatable. Here we
cast the value directly to a java.lang.Number class and use the converted value to
perform our check. When the number isn't divisible by N, we call error to inform
the validatable that the validation has failed. Note that the value of N is initialized
in the constructor so that it can be easily configured when using this validator in
the code.

The error method registers an error with the `validatable` and provides it with a configured `IValidationError` message ❶. The `IValidationError` contains all the necessary information to construct an internationalized error message based on Wicket's resource bundle lookup mechanisms. By default, Wicket uses the class name as the key to look up the corresponding error message, but you can provide your own resource key by overriding `AbstractValidator`'s `resourceKey()` method in the custom validator ❷. Usually, the default implementation is good enough—if you can live with the default class name, then there is no need to override the method. In our case, `DivisibleValidator` is used as the key.

The error message can contain multiple variables that are substituted by the validator. You can add your own variables to the default list of `"label"`, `"input"`, and `"name"`. For instance, the minimum validator for numbers adds the `"minimum"` substitution variable, replacing `${minimum}` in error messages with the value provided to the validator. In our example, we add the `"divisor"` substitution key with the value of our divisor ❸. Any occurrence of `${divisor}` is replaced with the value of our divisor in the error messages.

You now have the means to check users' input and make sure it's valid. But how can you communicate the errors of their ways?

6.7　*Providing feedback*

Nothing is more frustrating than getting a message that an error occurred and having to restart the process of filling in fields. Until now, we've discussed how to get input from users and how to ensure the data is correct. But we haven't provided a way to tell visitors what they did wrong.

In this section, we'll show how you can provide your own messages for failed validations and how to provide *flash messages*. We'll also look at the different ways to present the messages to your visitors. Let's start with providing feedback messages.

6.7.1　*Feedback messages*

Wicket comes with many feedback messages in various languages. Some may not be to your liking; and when you create a custom validator, you'll need to provide your own message.

Feedback messages are provided in *resource bundles.* There are various ways to store resource bundles, and the Wicket default is to use property files on the class path. You can put the bundles several places. In searching for a resource bundle, Wicket starts looking in the most specific place and searches in more generic places until the requested resource for the correct locale is found. In more specific cases, the name of the page or component being rendered is used when attempting to retrieve the appropriate property file (see table 6.1).

If you don't like a message that Wicket provides, and you want to customize it for your entire application, you have to override it in your application's resource bundle by creating a YourApplication.properties file.

Table 6.1 Location of feedback messages in the order they're picked up by the framework

Location next to...	Order	Description	Example
Page class	1	Messages specific to a page	Index.properties Index_hu.properties
Component class	2	Messages specific to a component	AddressPanel_hu.properties CheckOutForm.properties
Your `Application` class	3	Default application-wide message bundle	CheesrApplication_nl_BE.properties CheesrApplication_nl.properties CheesrApplication.properties
Wicket's `Application` base class	4	Default messages provided by Wicket	Application_nl.properties

The most common way to provide your own messages is to create a properties file next to your page's markup file: for instance, Index.properties next to Index.html. If you need more languages, you can append the specific locale information to the filename (before the extension): for example, Index_nl.properties for the Dutch language or even Index_nl_BE.properties for the Belgian variation of Dutch. You can learn more about localization and internationalization in chapter 12.

The following example shows a form with a couple of required fields and the contents of a properties file where we override Wicket's required validation message with something less formal:

```
/* Index.java */
Form form = new Form("myform");
form.add(new TextField("name").setRequired(true));
form.add(new PasswordTextField("password").setRequired(true));
form.add(new TextField("phonenumber").setRequired(true));

# Index.properties
Required=Provide a ${label} or else...
myform.name.Required=You have to provide a name.
password.Required=You have to provide a password.
phonenumber.Required=A telephone number is obligatory.
```

This example shows a couple of variations of providing alternative feedback messages. First, we can override the general message identified with the key `Required`. Next are a couple of different messages with prefixes before the resource key. Wicket uses component paths to give you the option to override the message for a single component. The message with the most specific path is displayed. For instance, when the text field with identifier `name` in the form with identifier `myform` flags an error, it displays "You have to provide a name". This message is chosen over "Provide a name or else..." because the component path in Index.java matches `myform.name.Required`, and it's more specific than `Required`.

As you can see, the resource key of a validator is important when you want to supply your own validation error messages. Table 6.2 shows the resource keys for all the validators built into Wicket and the variables that can be substituted in each message.

Table 6.2   A list of the available validators and their resource keys, and provided variables for creating your own custom messages (or providing messages in a language that isn't supported out of the box).

Validator	Resource key	Variables
Required fields	`Required`	`label, name`
Conversion errors	`IConverter` `IConverter.<type>`	`Iabel, name, input, type`

NumberValidator (surrounding class)

Validator	Resource key	Variables
`RangeValidator`	`NumberValidator.range`	`label, name, input,` `minimum, maximum`
`MinimumValidator`	`NumberValidator.minimum`	`label, name, input,` `minimum`
`MaximumValidator`	`NumberValidator.maximum`	`label, name, input,` `maximum`
`DoubleRangeValidator`	`NumberValidator.range`	`label, name, input,` `minimum, maximum`
`DoubleMinimumValidator`	`NumberValidator.minimum`	`label, name, input,` `minimum`
`DoubleMaximumValidator`	`NumberValidator.maximum`	`label, name, input,` `maximum`

StringValidator (surrounding class)

Validator	Resource key	Variables
`ExactLengthValidator`	`StringValidator.exact`	`label, name, input,` `length, exact`

`LengthBetweenValidator`	`StringValidator.range`	`label, name, input,`
		`minimum, maximum,`
		`length`

`MaximumLengthValidator`	`StringValidator.maximum`	`label, name, input,` `maximum, length`
`MinimumLengthValidator`	`StringValidator.minimum`	`label, name, input,` `minimum, length`

DateValidator (surrounding class)

Validator	Resource key	Variables
`RangeValidator`	`DateValidator.range`	`label, name, input,` `minimum, maximum`
`MinimumValidator`	`DateValidator.minimum`	`label, name, input,` `minimum`
`MaximumValidator`	`DateValidator.maximum`	`label, name, input,` `maximum`

Table 6.2 A list of the available validators and their resource keys, and provided variables for creating your own custom messages (or providing messages in a language that isn't supported out of the box). *(continued)*

Validator	Resource key	Variables
Other validators		
CreditCardValidator	CreditCardValidator	label, name, input
PatternValidator	PatternValidator	label, name, input, pattern
EmailAddressValidator	EmailAddressValidator	label, name, input
UrlValidator	UrlValidator	label, name, input
EqualInputValidator	EqualInputValidator	label0, name0, input0, label1, name1, input1
EqualPasswordInput-Validator	EqualPasswordInput-Validator	label0, name0, input0, label1, name1, input1

All these standard messages can save you a lot of time writing out (and translating) your own. But often you need to convey information other than validation errors. For instance, when an object has been saved to the database, a message like "The changes to cheese Gouda have been saved" will reassure the user that all is well. To provide free-form messages, you can use the info, error, and warn methods.

6.7.2 *Using the info, error, and warn methods for general messages*

All the feedback discussed until now has been part of the form processing. But sometimes you want to notify a visitor that something has happened, such as saving account information successfully. The following form example displays a message on a new page (SomePage) shown after the person saved successfully, or an error message (on the current page) when something went wrong:

```
add(new Form("form", new Model(person)) {
    @Override
    protected void onSubmit() {
        Person p = (Person)getModelObject();
        try {
            p.save();
            getSession().info(p.getName() + " was saved.");
            setResponsePage(SomePage.class);
        } catch (Exception e) {
            error(p.getName() + " was not saved: " + e.getMessage());
            // do something to rollback the transaction
        }
    }
});
```

There are different levels of severity for this type of messages (also known as *flash messages*): information, warning, and error. You can add a message with a specific severity by calling the corresponding method, as illustrated with the following example:

```
info("This message is an informative message");
warn("This message is a warning");
error("This message is an error");
```

These methods are part of the public interface of the Component class. You can call them anywhere when you have access to a component. You can also call them on a specific component and use feedback filters to only display those messages (see the next section for more information on feedback filtering).

When you want the message to display when the user navigates to a different page, you should register the messages with the session instead. The next example shows how to do this:

```
@Override
protected void onSubmit() {
    // ... do something useful ...
    getSession().info("Is stored until OtherPage is rendered");
    setResponsePage(OtherPage.class);
}
```

When you want to localize the displayed message, you can use the Component.getString method to gain access to the specific message. Here's how:

```
/* java */
info(getString("hello"));

# properties
hello=Hello, World!
```

With all these possibilities to generate messages for visitors, we almost forgot to show you how to display them. Let's look at displaying feedback messages.

6.7.3 Displaying feedback messages using a FeedbackPanel

Until now, we've only shown you how to change Wicket's feedback messages and how to provide your own messages outside form processing. Let's now look at how to display the messages.

The easiest way to display feedback messages is to add a FeedbackPanel to your page. The FeedbackPanel reads the messages from Wicket's message queue and displays them with appropriate styling information. The message queue contains messages resulting from form-validation processing as well as any messages in flash scope supplied to the session. The feedback panel also lets you filter for certain kinds of messages.

The following example adds a feedback panel to a page:

```
<!-- html -->
<div wicket:id="feedback"></div>

/* Java */
add(new FeedbackPanel("feedback"));
```

This simple code catches and displays all feedback messages that are available when the panel is rendered. The output looks like this:

```
<ul class="feedbackPanel">
  <li class="feedbackPanelERROR">
    <span class="feedbackPanelERROR">Field 'name' is required.</span>
  </li>
</ul>
```

This markup and style information should give web designers ample possibilities to turn this simple list into something beautiful (red crosses, warning signs, and so forth). If you need to override the markup, you can create your own subclass of FeedbackPanel.

Wicket supplies three feedback message filters for the most common use cases:

- ComponentFeedbackMessageFilter—Gives only messages for a specific component
- ContainerFeedbackMessageFilter—Gives only messages for a specific container component and its children
- ErrorLevelFeedbackMessageFilter—Gives only messages at a certain level (or higher)

For example, if we want to display only messages that are generated for a specific form, we can apply the ContainerFeedbackMessageFilter to our feedback panel in the following way:

```
add(new FeedbackPanel("feedback",
            new ContainerFeedbackMessageFilter(form)));
```

This feedback panel only shows feedback messages generated by the form and its children. Similarly, the ComponentFeedbackMessageFilter only displays the feedback messages for the assigned component.

When you want to indicate which form field failed a validation, you can use a FormComponentFeedbackBorder component. The border displays a red asterisk when a validation message is registered for its form component (you can override the red asterisk by supplying your own markup). The following snippet shows how to use the border:

```
<label>SSN:
    <span wicket:id="border">
        <input type="text" wicket:id="ssn">
    </span>
</label>

form.add(
    new FormComponentFeedbackBorder("border").add(
            new TextField("ssn")));
```

Note that we add the text field to the border. The border is a component that can render other components before and after its child components. In this case, it renders the red asterisk after the text field when a feedback message is registered. Figure 6.13 shows the result.

Now that you have the ability to display feedback messages, you've closed the form-processing loop: you can receive input, convert and validate it, and tell users what is wrong so they can fix their input.

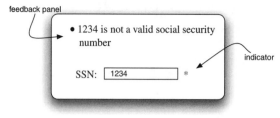

feedback panel

- 1234 is not a valid social security number

SSN: [1234]   *

indicator

Figure 6.13
The `FeedbackPanel` **and**
`FormComponentFeedbackBorder`
components working together to give
the user a clear message about which
component has invalid input

6.8   *Summary*

Working with forms is a primary task for most if not all web application developers. Forms and form-input controls are the main means of gathering input from users. In this chapter, we continued our discussion of Wicket components by introducing the `Form` and the components that capture the user input.

Forms encapsulate and group input controls and provide a way to convey user input to the server. Using the `get` method, you can provide users with a bookmarkable results page for search queries. Using the `post` method (Wicket's default), you can even upload files to the server and overcome input limits imposed with the `get` method. To prevent the nefarious popup, when a user revisits a page generated by a post submission, Wicket uses the redirect after post pattern. You've learned how to submit a form using buttons and links. We showed how to use Ajax to submit a form and how to disable form processing when you don't want the input to be validated or propagated to your domain objects.

Using text fields, radio buttons, check boxes, and drop-down boxes, you can provide users with a variety of input controls. Although controls provide basic insurance that the data is in good shape, you should check the input before you send it to the domain layer. Wicket validation is a multistep process that checks the availability of input, converts the input, and validates the converted input before propagating it to the domain layer. Only when all supplied input is valid is the input transferred to the domain layer.

Providing feedback to users is just as important: it's frustrating to see something fail without knowing why. When any input is invalid or missing, processing stops, and the failed validations generate error messages. A feedback panel will show the feedback messages in the user's language.

In the next chapter, we'll look at how to compose pages by grouping components.

Composing your pages

One of the biggest challenges of designing and building a lasagna is to create as many layers as you can possibly fit in the baking dish, without turning the lasagna in one giant noodle. Years of empiric research have shown that the best lasagna has between five and seven layers. According to our recipe, this means stacking a thin layer of sauce, a couple of salami slices, cheese slices, a thin layer of spinach, and a layer of lasagna noodles on top of each other, and repeating until the only thing we have room for on top is a thin layer of sauce.

The secret to a great lasagna lies in how thick you make each layer and how you distribute the ingredients. The thickness of the layers and the careful distribution of the ingredients make the difference between a solid, perfect slice of lasagna that stands on your plate ready to be cut to pieces, and a lasagna that turns into Italian soup when you dish it up.

The same applies to building Wicket applications: the way you group and distribute the components on and across your pages determines whether your application can stand the test of time and be maintainable, even for guest developers. For instance, while building the cheese store in chapter 3, you saw that it's easy to create a reusable shopping cart panel and save yourself from writing duplicate code.

Grouping components in reusable units is only part of the equation. The way you distribute them across your pages is the other part. In this chapter, we'll explore the options available for grouping and distributing our components to maximize reuse and minimize maintenance costs. We'll start with grouping components and work our way up to composing pages.

7.1   *Grouping components*

One of the major benefits of using Wicket is that you can create component hierarchies in which you can nest components at will. This gives you control over how your pages are composed and what elements are visible and active. In this section, we'll look at how to group components and how to make them reusable across pages. Figure 7.1 gives an outline of the options available to group components.

This figure shows the following options:

- No grouping
- Grouping using a `WebMarkupContainer`
- Grouping using a `Panel`
- Grouping using a `Fragment`

This section will build on the two labels visible in figure 7.1. The example in listing 7.1 shows the markup and Java code for the page without any grouping. The two labels contain quotes from the "Big Cheese" episode of the cartoon *Dexter's Laboratory.*

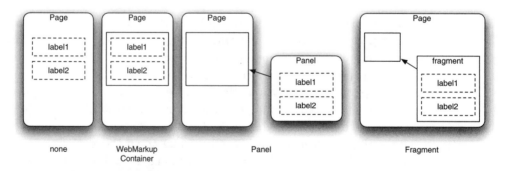

Figure 7.1   The different ways to group components: no grouping; or using a web markup container, a panel, or a fragment. The panel requires its own class and HTML file, whereas the fragment is embedded in the page's markup and class.

Listing 7.1 A page with two labels and no grouping

```
<html>
<body>
    <blockquote wicket:id="dexter"></blockquote>
    <blockquote wicket:id="deedee"></blockquote>
</ol>
</body>
</html>

public class GroupingPage extends WebPage {
    public GroupingPage() {
        add(new Label("dexter", "Omelette du fromage"));
        add(new Label("deedee", "That's all you can say!"));
    }
}
```

As you can see, we attach the labels directly to the blockquote elements. You may remember from chapter 6 that the Label component isn't picky about the tags it's attached to, and we take advantage of that feature here.

We'll use this example as a basis for the coming sections, where we'll group the labels using the techniques from figure 7.1. Let's start with grouping components using a WebMarkupContainer.

7.1.1 Grouping components on a page: WebMarkupContainer

Wicket lets you create component hierarchies by nesting components, putting them inside one another. This grouping of related components allows you to perform common actions on the group as a whole. Examples of such actions are hiding or showing the components, repainting a section on a page using Ajax, and replacing all components with new components.

The WebMarkupContainer is well suited for this kind of use because it only attaches itself to the markup tags and doesn't modify them unless you tell it to by using behaviors or by overriding onComponentTag or onComponentTagBody. The WebMarkupContainer lets you add child components without limits, making it ideal for grouping components.

Listing 7.2 groups the two labels using a WebMarkupContainer.

Listing 7.2 Grouping labels using a WebMarkupContainer

```
<html>
<body>                              ❶ Group labels
<div wicket:id="group">   ◁┐          (HTML)
    <blockquote wicket:id="dexter">[label1]</blockquote>
    <blockquote wicket:id="deedee">[label2]</blockquote>
</div>
</body>
</html>

public class GroupingPage extends WebPage {
    public GroupingPage() {
```

```
    WebMarkupContainer group = new WebMarkupContainer("group");
    add(group);
    group.add(new Label("dexter", "Omelette du fromage"));
    group.add(new Label("deedee", "That's all you can say!"));
  }
}
```
Group labels (Java) ❷

We introduce a `div` in the markup to group the two labels ❶. Because Wicket requires a one-to-one match between the components in the markup and the Java hierarchy, we need to provide additional markup and an additional component ❷ to group the labels. In this example, we create a new instance of a `WebMarkupContainer` to act as our grouping component. By adding the labels to the group component, we create the necessary component hierarchy that mirrors the component structure in the markup file.

USING THE GROUP AS A WHOLE

Now that we've defined our group of components, we can use the group as a whole. As an example, we'll add a link to the page that shows and hides the group:

```
public GroupingPage() {
    final WebMarkupContainer group = new WebMarkupContainer("group");
    add(group);
    group.add(new Label("dexter", "Omelette du fromage"));
    group.add(new Label("deedee", "That's all you can say!"));

    add(new Link("link") {
        @Override
        public void onClick() {
            group.setVisible(!group.isVisible());
        }
    });
}
```

In this example, we only call `setVisible` on the group component. This is sufficient to hide the group and all its child components.

We can also hide and show the group using Ajax:

```
public GroupingPage() {
    final WebMarkupContainer group = new WebMarkupContainer("group");
    add(group);
    group.add(new Label("dexter", "Omelette du fromage"));
    group.add(new Label("deedee", "That's all you can say!"));

    group.setOutputMarkupPlaceholderTag(true);          ◁— Ensure Ajax
    add(new AjaxFallbackLink("link") {                ❶ operability
        @Override
        public void onClick(AjaxRequestTarget target) {
            group.setVisible(!group.isVisible());
            if(target != null) {                        ◁— Check Ajax
                target.addComponent(group);           ❷ availability
            }
        }
    });
}
```

We ensure that the group can be updated by telling it to output a placeholder tag ❶ when it's hidden (see section 6.6 for more information). The Ajax link we use in this example is a fallback link that works even in browsers that don't support Ajax or Java-Script. So, we need to check whether the request is an Ajax request ❷.

We just demonstrated the basic recipe for performing partial updates of pages. In this example, we not only toggled the visibility, we also updated the contents of the container. If you modify the contents of a label to display the current time, you'll see it update with each refresh.

How does the `WebMarkupContainer` help when you want to reuse a group of components?

REUSING THE GROUP OF COMPONENTS

One of the ideals of component-oriented development is to create reusable components. Although the `WebMarkupContainer` is a perfect starting point for developing your own custom components (Wicket uses this container as a base to create many of the core components), it isn't suited to create reusable groups of components. This section illustrates why the `WebMarkupContainer` isn't a good fit to create reusable groups of components.

In listing 7.2, we created a new instance of the `WebMarkupContainer`. If you have larger groups of components, it makes sense to create a custom class to prevent copy/paste programming. The next example turns our container with its labels into a custom, self-contained class that extends `WebMarkupContainer`:

```
public class GroupingPage extends WebPage {
    public class LabelsGroup extends WebMarkupContainer {        ⎫
        public LabelsGroup(String id) {                         ⎪
            super(id);                                          ⎪ Group
            add(new Label("dexter", "Omelette du fromage"));    ⎬ class
            add(new Label("deedee", "That's all you can say!")); ⎪
        }                                                       ⎪
    }                                                           ⎭
    public GroupingPage() {              Group
        add(new LabelsGroup("group"));   ⎤ instance
    }                                    ⎦
}
```

Here we clean up the code within the constructor of the `GroupingPage` page considerably by creating a custom `LabelsGroup` class for the group. Because the `LabelsGroup` is a normal Java class, we can add properties and methods and do anything we'd normally do when building Java classes. You can even move such a custom class to a top-level class in its own file, but you'll run into problems if you do so unprepared.

If you move a custom class like `LabelsGroup` to its own Java file, you may feel tempted to use the component on another page as well. There is no law against doing so, and Wicket doesn't prohibit it, so let's see where it leads. Assuming that the `LabelsGroup` class is now in its own file, we can use it on another page; let's call the page `SecondGroupingPage`. The following example shows how:

```
public class SecondGroupingPage extends WebPage {
    public SecondGroupingPage() {
```

```
        add(new LabelsGroup("group"));
    }
}
```

We create a new instance of the LabelsGroup component and add it to the page. This is nothing special, and we don't have any problems yet. How does the markup look? Here's the SecondGroupingPage.html file:

```
<html>
<body>
<div wicket:id="group">
    <blockquote wicket:id="dexter">[label1]</blockquote>    Exact copy from
    <blockquote wicket:id="deedee">[label2]</blockquote>   GroupingPage.html
</div>
</html>
```

In this file, we have to copy the markup from the GroupingPage.html file shown in listing 7.1 and match it exactly with respect to the component structure. We could add extra markup or extra components (we'd have to remember to add them to the Java structure as well). But at least the *dexter* and *deedee* labels must be present in the markup and should be inside the div tags of our group component.

What happens when we (or someone else) change the structure of the Labels-Group component—for instance, by adding a label or link? Then we have to change both GroupingPage.html and SecondGroupingPage.html. This is a violation of the DRY principle: we broke the encapsulation of the LabelsGroup component by moving the Java code to its own file, but not the markup. If we could also move the markup to its own file, then we would only have to change that markup—all pages that used the LabelsGroup component would automatically use the new markup.

The WebMarkupContainer is an interesting basis for creating custom components, and it's well suited for creating group components that act as a whole. But you shouldn't reuse a group of components created by a WebMarkupContainer, because you'd need to duplicate the markup everywhere it's used. This is where panels come in handy.

7.1.2   *Reusing grouped components by creating a Panel*

A Panel component is a WebMarkupContainer with its own markup file associated with it (just like a page). When you use a panel in a page, the content of the panel's markup file is inserted within the component tags in the page where the panel is attached. Just like a page, a panel's markup file has to have the same, case-sensitive filename as the Java class (with the extension .html). Before we convert our running example into a panel, let's take a closer look at the panel itself.

Let's start with an example that illustrates most of the concepts of a typical panel:

```
<html>
<head>                    ❶ Add to page's
<wicket:head>               head section
    <wicket:link>                                                   ❷ Link to
        <link href="ExamplePanel.css" rel="stylesheet" />            stylesheet
    </wicket:link>                                                   on classpath
```

```
</wicket:head>
</head>
<body>
<h1>Example Panel</h1>
<p>This panel is an example of Wicket's panels.</p>
<wicket:panel>
    <h3 wicket:id="title"></h3>
</wicket:panel>
</body>
</html>
```

❸ **Get included
when used**

This markup consists of two parts: the head and the panel. The head (identified by the wicket:head tags ❶) is added to the page's head section where the panel is used. In this case, we add an auto-link to a stylesheet that is in the same directory as our markup on the classpath ❷. The wicket:link creates the correct link to this resource. We can open the panel's markup and preview it in a browser. This is an easy and convenient way to add links to resources used locally for your components. The coming chapters will further discuss custom components and working with resources.

The body (the part between the wicket:panel tags ❸) is rendered at the position where you use the panel. All markup that is outside the wicket:panel tags doesn't appear in the final markup when the page containing the panel is rendered. We can freely add extra markup and text to this file, as long as it's outside the panel tags.

Before we can use the panel, we should create a Java class to go with the markup:

```java
public class ExamplePanel extends Panel {
    public ExamplePanel(String id) {
        super(id);
        add(new Label("title", "Example Panel"));
    }
}
```

The Java class for the panel isn't difficult to understand: we extend Wicket's Panel class and, in the constructor, add our components to the panel. Using our example panel is as simple as adding to the page and creating and adding the component in the appropriate location:

```html
<!-- ExamplePage.html -->
<html>
<body>
    <div wicket:id="panel">this gets replaced</div>
</body>
</html>
```

```java
/* ExamplePage.java */
public class ExamplePage extends WebPage {
    public ExamplePage() {
        add(new ExamplePanel("panel"));
    }
}
```

When we run this example it produces the following markup:

```html
<html>
<head>
```

```
       <link href="[some path]/ExamplePanel.css" rel="stylesheet" />
</head>
<body>
       <div>
       <h3>Example Panel</h3>
</div>
</body>
</html>
```

Our example panel is used in the page, and its markup is inserted inside the `div` tags associated with the panel. The contents of the `div` tags in our page are replaced with the contents of the panel's `wicket:panel` tags: the "this gets replaced" text is gone from the final markup. Also note that the markup outside the `wicket:panel` tags in our panel markup file is gone: only the content inside the `wicket:panel` tags is used. The stylesheet reference we included in the head section is added to the final markup of our page, making any styles defined in our panel available to the included panel content. Wicket's header-contribution mechanism makes this possible; it's discussed in detail in chapter 8.

Armed with this fresh knowledge about panels, let's return to the *omelette du fromage* example from listing 7.1 and move the quote labels into a panel. Listing 7.3 shows the resulting markup and code for the converted group.

Listing 7.3 `LabelsGroup` converted to a panel

```
<html>
<body>
<wicket:panel>
    <blockquote wicket:id="dexter">[label1]</blockquote>
    <blockquote wicket:id="deedee">[label2]</blockquote>
</wicket:panel>
</body>
</html>

public class LabelsGroup extends Panel {
    public LabelsGroup(String id) {
        super(id);
        add(new Label("dexter", "Omelette du fromage"));
        add(new Label("deedee", "That's all you can say!"));
    }
}
```

In the markup, we omit the outer `div` that grouped the labels in listing 7.2. This extra tag isn't necessary in our panel because it's provided by the page that uses this panel. But sometimes it can be helpful to group components on a panel using a markup container—for instance, when you're building Ajax-enabled components. Nothing prevents you from doing so.

How does this look when you want to use the group component in a page? Let's adjust `GroupingPage` to use our new panel. The following example shows what's left of the page:

```
<html>
<body>
<div wicket:id="group"></div>
```

```
    </body>
    </html>
    public class GroupingPage extends WebPage {
        public GroupingPage() {
            add(new LabelsGroup("group"));
        }
    }
```

What's interesting in this example is that the labels and their markup are invisible in the page's markup and Java code. All we know is that we're using a LabelsGroup component; we attach it to a div tag without having to know anything about the markup's internals. This is the major advantage of using panels: they hide their implementation details from their users.

NOTE Should you use div or span tags to attach a panel? You can use any tag to attach a panel: td, form, or p. The panel is forgiving in that regard. But browsers tend to like standards-compliant documents much more than invalid documents, especially when it comes to replacing parts of the document using Ajax, or traversing the DOM in JavaScript. We advise you to use the correct tag for the context in which you want to put your panel, and to do so you'll need to study the (X)HTML specification.

Another advantage is that you can replace one panel with a different one without getting into trouble. We modify not only the component hierarchy on the Java side, but also the markup hierarchy by providing the panel's alternative markup. This makes the component hierarchy consistent with the markup again.

Consider Wicket's EmptyPanel: the panel, being empty (hence the name), is typically used to occupy a spot and is replaced by a panel that gives users more functionality. When clicked, the link implementation in the following example swaps our grouping panel with the empty panel and vice versa:

```
    public class GroupingPage extends WebPage {
        private Component group;
        public GroupingPage() {
            group = new LabelsGroup("group");
            add(group);
            add(new Link("swap") {
                private Component alternate = new EmptyPanel("group");
                @Override
                public void onClick() {
                    Component temp = group;
                    group.replaceWith(alternate);
                    group = alternate;
                    alternate = temp;
                }
            });
        }
    }
```

When you run this example, you can see that we swap the LabelPanel made up of two labels with the EmptyPanel that doesn't have any child components. Here we modify the component hierarchy in a drastic way, and we don't get an error. It's worth mentioning that the component identifier must be the same when we replace a panel with another; as you can see in this example, the EmptyPanel is also given the identifier group.

Panels are versatile and do a good job of grouping and reusing components, even across pages. But they require a lot of work: you have to create a separate Java class and markup file. If you don't want to reuse the grouped components in other pages, but you do need to modify the hierarchy in a single page, you can use fragments.

7.1.3 *Grouping components using fragments*

Fragments are basically inline panels. They behave the same as panels, but their associated markup resides in the markup of the page (or panel) where they're defined and used. Fragments can't be reused outside the page where they were defined, but they're intended for a different purpose. They're a convenience for those moments when you'd have to create panels if fragments didn't exist. Let's see what fragments look like and how you can use them.

In the following example, we group the Label components inside the Fragment class:

```
public class GroupingPage extends WebPage {
    public class LabelsFragment extends Fragment {
        public LabelsFragment(String id) {
            super(id, "fragment", GroupingPage.this);
            add(new Label("dexter", "Omelette du fromage"));
            add(new Label("deedee", "That's all you can say!"));
        }
    }
    public GroupingPage() {
        add(new LabelsFragment("group"));
    }
}
```

This looks similar to the Panel component. There are two differences: we extend from Fragment, and the call to the super fragment constructor takes extra parameters: the markup identifier and a reference to the markup container that contains the fragment's markup. The purpose of this identifier becomes clear when we look at the markup for this page in the following snippet. The container is necessary because otherwise Wicket wouldn't know where to find the fragment's markup in the file:

```
<html>
    <body>
        <div wicket:id="group"></div>          ❶ Use
    </body>                                       fragment
    <wicket:fragment wicket:id="fragment">
        <blockquote wicket:id="dexter"></blockquote>    ❷ Define fragment
        <blockquote wicket:id="deedee"></blockquote>       markup
    </wicket:fragment>
</html>
```

In ❶ we use the fragment just as we'd use a panel. The special Wicket tag wicket: fragment demarcates the part of the page where the fragment's markup can be found ❷. The fragment is identified by a markup identifier, just like the component. This markup identifier corresponds to the second identifier of the fragment constructor. The fragment needs its own markup identifier because you can create multiple fragments on the page; the identifier makes it possible to distinguish the various fragments.

This example explains the basic usage pattern for fragments. They're most commonly used in highly dynamic pages. Suppose you have to show a list of contacts, but you need to render different markup depending on the relationship with the contact (a friend might show more information than an acquaintance). In this case, a fragment may be useful, especially if the rendering of the contact information is local to that page. If the contact information will be used in other pages of your application, you should consider creating panels instead.

Table 7.1 provides a summary of the grouping options discussed in this section.

Table 7.1   The different component grouping mechanisms and when to use them

Grouping	Description	When to use
WebMarkupContainer	Groups components directly in the markup and Java code. No extra files are necessary.	When the grouped components aren't reusable, but they need to act together for Ajax updates or visibility changes. This approach is also helpful to modify attributes of a markup tag.
Panel	Groups components in a separate markup file and Java class.	When the grouped components are to be reused in different pages, or contributions to the header are necessary.
Fragment	Groups components in a separate component hierarchy outside the normal hierarchy, but inside the markup file. Also known as an inline panel.	When the grouped components are inherent to the page/panel they're part of and aren't reusable in other pages/panels.

Now that you've learned to group components into reusable parts, let's go up the ladder and see how to create reusable page structures that cut back even more on the copy/paste approach to programming.

7.2   *Page composition: creating a consistent layout*

When discussing the cheese store in chapter 3, we didn't pay much attention to creating a consistent layout for all the pages. We did make both pages look the same, at the expense of duplicating all the common layout markup and components across all pages. In this section, we'll look at options to make pages more maintainable by reducing this duplication and keeping things organized. You can compose pages three ways (these approaches aren't mutually exclusive):

- *Using plain pages*—Copy the common components from one page to another.
- *Using markup inheritance*—Move the common bits of your pages to a base class, including the markup, and let concrete pages provide the custom portion.

- *Using panels*—Use a single page that contains the common markup and has a panel for the main content. Depending on the actions, the main content panel can be swapped with other panels to show different content.

In this section, we'll discuss these strategies in their pure forms to make a clear distinction between them. But you can combine the strategies: for example, you can use panels inside panels, or use panels inside a markup-inherited page, or apply markup inheritance to panels. For now, we'll keep things simple. First, we'll look at how to build an application the traditional way using plain pages.

7.2.1 Creating consistent layouts using plain pages

Building applications using plain pages is the approach we've discussed so far in this book. Each page focuses on doing one thing: showing a list of cheeses, ordering cheeses, and so forth. The pages don't contain shared elements like a navigational menu. Let's look at an example that includes two pages and uses the plain-pages approach. Figure 7.2 shows the general layout of the pages we'll construct in the coming sections.

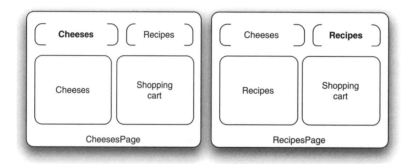

Figure 7.2   The layout of the Cheeses page and the Recipes page. The basis of this example comes from chapter 3; we added the top menu to let users switch between the two pages. Notice that the shopping cart is present on both pages.

Each page should display (for now) two menu items: Cheeses and Recipes. When the user selects one menu item, the corresponding page (`CheesesPage` or `RecipesPage`) is displayed.

Let's first build the `CheesesPage` using plain pages. Listing 7.4 shows the markup.

Listing 7.4   `CheesesPage` markup using the plain pages approach

```
<html>
<head>
    <title>Cheesr - we make cheese taste beta</title>
    <link rel="stylesheet" href="style.css" />
</head>
<body>
<div id="container">
```

```
    <div id="header">
        <h1>Cheesr</h1>
    </div>
    <div id="contents">
        <wicket:link>
            <a href="CheesesPage.html">Cheeses</a>        Menu
            <a href="RecipesPage.html">Recipes</a>        links
        </wicket:link>
        <div id="main">
            <div wicket:id="cheeses">
                <h3 wicket:id="name"></h3>                Main
                <p wicket:id="description"></p>            section
            </div>
        </div>
        <div wicket:id="cart" id="cart"></div>    ⊲─   Shopping
    </div>                                                cart
</div>
</body>
</html>
```

The markup for the Cheeses page has three interesting parts. The menu is present on all pages, which means duplicating this markup. The list of cheeses is specific to this page and isn't repeated on other pages (although the structure may be similar). Finally, the shopping cart is present on each page, so it must be duplicated as well. Let's look at the Java code for this page:

```
public class CheesesPage extends WebPage {
    public CheesesPage() {
        List<Cheese> cheeses = /* get cheeses */
        Cart cart = /* get cart */
        add(new PropertyListView("cheeses", cheeses) {
            @Override
            protected void populateItem(ListItem item) {
                item.add(new Label("name"));
                item.add(new MultiLineLabel("description"));
            }
        });
        add(new ShoppingCartPanel("cart", cart));
    }
}
```

In this class, all we have to do is add the list of cheeses with its two labels as our repeating contents, and add the shopping-cart panel. Wicket autogenerates the menu using the wicket:link tags.

Now that we have a finished Cheeses page, let's look at the Recipes page. The markup for this page is listed in listing 7.5.

Listing 7.5 RecipesPage markup using the plain pages approach

```
<html>
<head>
    <title>Cheesr - we make cheese taste beta</title>
    <link rel="stylesheet" href="style.css" />
</head>
```

```
<body>
<div id="container">
    <div id="header">
        <h1>Cheesr</h1>
    </div>
    <div id="contents">
        <wicket:link>
            <a href="CheesesPage.html">Cheeses</a>        Menu
            <a href="RecipesPage.html">Recipes</a>        links
        </wicket:link>
        <div id="main">
            <div wicket:id="recipes">
                <h3 wicket:id="name"></h3>
                <p wicket:id="serves"></p>
                <h4>Ingredients<h4>                       Main
                <ul>                                       section
                    <li wicket:id="ingredients"></li>
                </ul>
                <p wicket:id="instructions"></p>
            </div>
        </div>
        <div wicket:id="cart" id="cart"></div>     ◁⌐ Shopping
    </div>                                              cart
</div>
</body>
</html>
```

This is exactly the same markup as for the Cheeses page, except for the main section. Now let's look at the Java class for this page:

```java
public class RecipesPage extends WebPage {
    public RecipesPage() {
        List<Recipe> recipes = /* get recipes */
        Cart cart = /* get cart */
        add(new PropertyListView("recipes", recipes) {
            @Override
            protected void populateItem(ListItem item) {
                item.add(new Label("name"));
                item.add(new Label("serves"));
                RepeatingView view = new RepeatingView("ingredients");
                item.add(view);
                 for(String ingredient : recipe.getIngredients()) {
                    view.add(new Label(view.newChildId(), ingredient));
                }
                item.add(new MultiLineLabel("instructions"));
            }
        });
        add(new ShoppingCartPanel("cart", cart));
    }
}
```

The RecipesPage class looks almost identical to the CheesesPage class. We change some identifiers and implement the list view a bit differently, but that's it. The menu (in the markup) and the shopping cart are the same. If we fire up our application in the browser, we see something like the screenshots in figure 7.3.

Figure 7.3   Screenshots from the Cheeses and Recipes pages

Using the plain-pages technique, we created our pages' markup, added components, and provided the links between the pages to navigate the site. We've duplicated a lot of markup and code in our pages. Now imagine that we have to add a new page and provide a link to it. Then, consider doing this for a 500+ page website with the current setup. Fortunately, several options are available to mitigate this maintenance nightmare. Let's see how we can improve this approach by using inheritance.

7.2.2 Creating consistent layouts using markup inheritance

In programming languages, one benefit of using object orientation is the ability to share common code using inheritance. Even though inheritance can (and will) be misused, it's a powerful construct. Because you can create common component hierarchies for your pages and components, this question pops up: "How do I keep my markup under control?" Enter markup inheritance. This Wicket feature lets you create a markup hierarchy that mirrors your class hierarchy, as illustrated in figure 7.4.

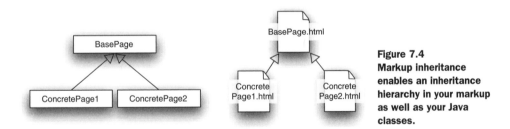

**Figure 7.4
Markup inheritance enables an inheritance hierarchy in your markup as well as your Java classes.**

Figure 7.4 proposes a common base class for your page and that concrete pages inherit from the base. Let's see how this works in listing 7.6, which shows the HTML and Java code for the base page.

Listing 7.6   `BasePage` markup and Java code using markup inheritance

```
<html>
<head>
    <title>Cheesr - we make cheese taste beta</title>
```

```
    <link rel="stylesheet" href="style.css" />
</head>
<body>
<div id="container">
    <div id="header">
        <h1>Cheesr</h1>
    </div>
    <div id="contents">
        <wicket:link>
            <a href="CheesesPage.html">Cheeses</a>
            <a href="RecipesPage.html">Recipes</a>
        </wicket:link>
        <div id="main">
            <wicket:child />
        </div>
        <div wicket:id="cart" id="cart"></div>
    </div>
</div>
</body>
</html>

public abstract class BasePage extends WebPage {
    public BasePage() {
        Cart cart = /* get cart */
        add(new ShoppingCartPanel("cart", cart));
    }
}
```

Menu
links

Main
section

Shopping
cart

The base page contains the components common to all pages: in this case, the menu, the shopping cart, and the supporting markup. Take a closer look at the markup for BasePage, and you'll see that we introduce a special Wicket tag: wicket:child. This tag tells Wicket where to include the markup of the child page: in this example, the list views that display the cheeses and the recipes.

Let's look next at how to create the Cheeses and Recipes pages. Listing 7.7 shows the refactored Cheeses page.

Listing 7.7 CheesesPage markup and Java code using markup inheritance

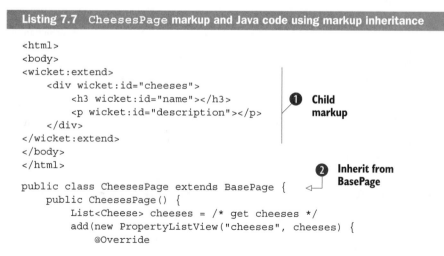

```
<html>
<body>
<wicket:extend>
    <div wicket:id="cheeses">
        <h3 wicket:id="name"></h3>
        <p wicket:id="description"></p>
    </div>
</wicket:extend>
</body>
</html>

public class CheesesPage extends BasePage {
    public CheesesPage() {
        List<Cheese> cheeses = /* get cheeses */
        add(new PropertyListView("cheeses", cheeses) {
            @Override
```

❶ Child
markup

❷ Inherit from
BasePage

```
                protected void populateItem(ListItem item) {
                    item.add(new Label("name"));
                    item.add(new MultiLineLabel("description"));
                }
            });
        }
    }
```

We introduce another new Wicket tag: `wicket:extend` ❶. These tags are like the `wicket:panel` tags: Wicket doesn't use anything outside them. Here, the `wicket:extend` tags demarcate the area that is used in the parent's `<wicket:child />` tag. Instead of extending `WebPage`, we now extend from our common base class `BasePage` ❷. By moving the common markup and the common components to our base page, we're able to clean up our Cheeses page considerably. It now contains only the markup and components directly associated with its purpose. We leave implementing the `RecipesPage` using markup inheritance as an exercise for you.

Markup inheritance also works with multiple layers. You can nest a `wicket:child` tag inside your `wicket:extend` tags and create hierarchies of common, layered layouts. You can also let your subpages contribute markup such as CSS or JavaScript references to the header of the page by using the `wicket:head` tags we discussed earlier. Anything inside the `wicket:head` tags is included in the final page.

WRAPPING A COMPONENT AROUND THE CHILD MARKUP

When you define a component—for instance, a `WebMarkupContainer` or a `Form`—and you want to wrap it around the child area, you get into trouble. In other words, when you nest the child area within a tag attached to a Wicket component, the child pages add their components to the page, not to the wrapper around the child area. This causes an inconsistency in the component hierarchy, and Wicket shows an error instead of your page. Listing 7.8 provides a concrete example of this problem.

Listing 7.8   Base page wrapping a `WebMarkupContainer` around the child page

```
<!-- BasePage.html -->
<html>
<body>
<div wicket:id="wrapper"><wicket:child /></div>          ◁─┐ Wrap around
<a href="#" wicket:id="refresh">Refresh</a>                │ child markup
</body>
</html>

/* BasePage.java */
public class BasePage extends WebPage {
    private WebMarkupContainer wrapper;
    public BasePage() {
        wrapper = new WebMarkupContainer("wrapper") {
            @Override
            public boolean isTransparentResolver() {       ❶ Resolve missing
                return true;                                   children from
            }                                                  siblings
        };
        wrapper.setOutputMarkupId(true);
```

```
        add(wrapper);
        add(new AjaxFallbackLink("refresh") {
            @Override
            public void onClick(AjaxRequestTarget target) {
                if(target != null) {
                    target.addComponent(wrapper);
                }
            }
        });
    }
}
```

```
<!-- ChildPage.html -->
<wicket:extend>
Nr of refreshes: <span wicket:id="nr"></span>     ⊲┘  Become
</wicket:extend>                                       wrapper's child
```

```
/* ChildPage.java */
public class ChildPage extends BasePage {
    private int nr = 0;
    public ChildPage() {                                       Become
        add(new Label("nr", new PropertyModel(this, "nr")));  ⊲┘ page's child
    }

    public int getNr() {
        return nr++;
    }
}
```

The `BasePage` in this example shows a link to update the main contents using Ajax. To update the main content embedded in the subclasses of our base page, we wrap the `wicket:child` tag with a `WebMarkupContainer`. In the `ChildPage`, we specify a label that increments its value each time it's accessed via the `getNr` method. The label is added to the child page, not the wrapping markup container. Adding the label to the page violates the component hierarchy as we set it up in the markup.

So, we need to add the label to the wrapper, which means exposing the wrapper to all the child pages, perhaps as a protected variable. Each child page will then be responsible for adding its components to the wrapper instead of the page. Take, for instance, the following replacement for the `ChildPage`'s constructor:

```
public ChildPage() {
    wrapper.add(new Label("nr", new PropertyModel(this, "nr")));
}
```

Needless to say, this approach is error prone: it's natural to add components to the page instead of some mysterious object defined in a superclass. Instead of taking this route, we can make the wrapping `WebMarkupContainer` a *transparent resolving component* ❶. Such components will resolve components that are added to the transparent resolver's parent, but are defined inside the transparent resolver's markup. In other words: when components are added to the parent of a transparent resolver, they can be automatically attached to the transparent resolving component instead. For example, the following markup transparently resolves the `foo1` and `foo2` components to be inside the bar's markup:

```
<ul wicket:id="bar">
    <li wicket:id="foo1"></li>
    <li wicket:id="foo2"></li>
</ul>

add(new WebMarkupContainer("bar") {
    @Override
    public boolean isTransparentResolver() {
        return true;
    }
});
add(new Label("foo1", "Hello, World!"));
add(new Label("foo2", "How are we doing?"));
```

We add the `foo1` and `foo2` labels to the parent of the container `bar`. Normally, this would generate an error because the component hierarchy doesn't match the hierarchy in the markup. But because we made the container into a transparent resolver, the container looks for its missing children (according to the markup) among its siblings.

With markup inheritance, you instantly get more maintainable pages. The base page provides the framework for the subpages in the markup and adds common components. Each subpage only has to add the components it needs to provide its unique functionality.

This concludes our demonstration of the second strategy to compose pages. Let's look at the final option: using panels.

7.2.3 Creating consistent layouts using panels

In the previous sections, we used different page classes to display different content: a page for cheeses and a page for recipes. But there is another way to maintain a consistent layout using a single page. In this scenario, you swap parts of the page with new content using panels. Figure 7.5 shows how this works for our example.

To convert our running example into a single page that swaps panels, we need to do some work. First, we must create the two panels that contain our cheeses and recipes. Creating these panels is left to you. Armed with the knowledge from section 7.1

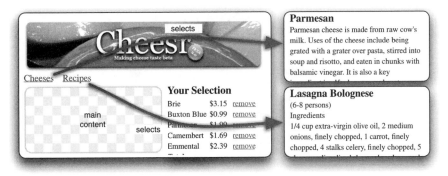

Figure 7.5 Swapping the main content using panels. When the user clicks the Cheeses link, the main content is replaced with the Cheeses panel. The Recipes link replaces the main content with the Recipes panel.

and the `CheesesPage` example markup and Java code from the previous section, you shouldn't find it difficult to convert those pages into panels.

Next, we need to create the single page. Listing 7.9 shows the markup and Java code.

Listing 7.9   Using panel replacement to swap the main content of a page

```html
<html>
<head>
    <title>Cheesr - we make cheese taste beta</title>
    <link rel="stylesheet" href="style.css" />
</head>
<body>
<div id="container">
    <div id="header">
        <h1>Cheesr</h1>
    </div>
    <div id="contents">
        <a href="#" wicket:id="cheeseslink">Cheeses</a>       ❶ Menu
        <a href="#" wicket:id="recipeslink">Recipes</a>          links
        <div wicket:id="main" id="main"></div>       ◁
        <div wicket:id="cart" id="cart"></div>      ❷ Main
    </div>                                              section
</div>
</body>
</html>
```

```java
public class CheesrPage extends WebPage {
    private Panel cheesesPanel = new CheesesPanel("main");
    private Panel recipesPanel = new RecipesPanel("main");
    private Panel current = cheesesPanel;    ◁┐  ❸ Track active
                                                    panel
    public CheesrPage() {
        add(new Link("cheeseslink") {
            @Override
            public void onClick() {
                current.replaceWith(cheesesPanel);    ◁┐ Swap in
                current = cheesesPanel;               ❹ cheese panel
            }
            @Override
            public boolean isEnabled() {
                return current != cheesesPanel;
            }
        });
        add(new Link("recipeslink") {
            @Override
            public void onClick() {
                current.replaceWith(recipesPanel);
                current = recipesPanel;
            }
            @Override
            public boolean isEnabled() {
                return current != recipesPanel;
            }
        });                        ❺ Add current
                                      panel
        add(current);    ◁┘
```

```
            Cart cart = /* get cart */
            add(new ShoppingCartPanel("cart", cart));
        }
    }
```

Going from top to bottom in this listing, notice first in the markup that we replaced the `wicket:link` tags with actual Wicket components ❶. We need to swap the panels when the link is clicked. The auto-link isn't suited for this purpose because it doesn't provide `onClick` event handlers, so we replace them with `Link` components. Next, we use the main section `div` ❷ to swap the cheeses with the recipes ❹.

In the Java code, we have three references to panels: two for the panels and one to keep track of which panel is currently active ❸. Finally we add the current panel to our page ❺. The menu links swap the current panel with their respective content panel and disable themselves when their panel is active, to mimic the auto-link behavior.

The panel-swapping strategy takes more initial effort to implement than the multi-page strategy using markup inheritance. Swapping panels can create complex pages without much more effort than it took to create this example.

We've shown you the ways in which you can compose pages. The obvious question now becomes, which of the proposed solutions is the best?

7.2.4 *Which is the best?*

Because we presented three strategies to compose your pages, it's logical to ask which is best. To find out, let's define some criteria we can use to evaluate each strategy. Typical criteria like performance and memory usage won't vary among the proposed strategies. Performance-wise, retrieving the data that needs to be displayed will usually take longer than composing your page on the server using any of the techniques. When you're concerned with memory usage, the benefit of a carefully designed and tested panel outweighs the couple of bytes that are saved when you inline the panel's contents into the page.

We'll skip these criteria and instead consider the following list:

- *Previewability*—Can you preview the end result by opening the markup file directly in the browser without starting the application?
- *Duplication*—How much markup and code do you need to duplicate to get a consistent layout throughout the application?
- *Navigation*—Can you create an easy navigation structure using links?
- *Bookmarkability*—Can users bookmark each page to revisit the specific location later?

Let's go through each of these criteria and see how the strategies hold up. When you're reading these evaluations, note that we're considering extreme implementations of each strategy—nothing is stopping you from mixing the strategies to your benefit.

PREVIEWABILITY
With Wicket, you can preview pages without having to start your application (at least, to a certain extent). One issue is that without starting your application, no data is

available from the server. Another is that the stylesheet information isn't usually located side-by-side with your pages and Java classes when you open the markup file directly in a browser.

The best preview result is achieved by including as much markup and dummy text in your HTML file as possible. Using plain pages is the best strategy when previewability is important, because this strategy provides the browser with the most information.

With markup inheritance, you need to do a bit more. For previewability, the `wicket:child` tag in the base pages must be filled with mock markup; and in the child pages, you need to surround the `wicket:extend` tags with the markup from the base page to achieve the right result. Although the amount of markup is practically the same as with the plain-pages approach, duplicating the available markup without using it will quickly cause it to get out of sync. In our experience, it isn't worth keeping the example markup outside the `wicket:extend` tags after the initial development of the page.

The same holds true for the strategy of swapping panels. Because each panel provides different markup, the main page's previewability is limited. You can include example markup inside the tags associated with the panel and provide context markup surrounding the `wicket:panel` tags, but the effort required to get good previewability is worthwhile only in the early stages of development.

DUPLICATION

One of the cardinal sins of software development is copy/paste programming. Once code (and in web applications, markup counts as code) is duplicated, you've doubled your maintenance requirements. Not only do you need to maintain code in two places, but anyone new coming to your project must know where the code is duplicated when he wants to change something. When your application consists of two Wicket pages, this isn't too great a concern. But when you have hundreds of pages, and you want to change, for example, the stylesheet reference, you have to modify all the pages instead of just one.

The plain-pages approach to Wicket development results in a lot of duplication when you want to maintain a consistent layout across the application. You need to copy the page structure and add the appropriate stylesheet and JavaScript files to each page's header. Due to this duplication, this approach is workable with applications consisting of at most 10 pages. Anything beyond that number will quickly run into copy/paste errors.

The situation improves considerably when you use pages with markup inheritance. The structure goes into your base page, and only the specific markup and components end up in the child pages. This structure provides excellent reuse of templates, as you saw in section 7.2.2.

Replacing panels gives you the same benefit as using markup inheritance. You have a single base page for the layout and provide specific markup and components by swapping panels in and out of the base page. The difference with markup inheritance is that you can swap multiple parts of your page instead of only the `wicket:child` part.

NAVIGATION

One of the key ingredients of web applications is the ability to navigate through your application: for example, browsing the online cheese catalogue, browsing recipes, or clicking a link to learn more about Parmesan cheese or find similar cheeses.

Both the plain-pages and markup-inheritance strategies provide easy navigation between pages. It's natural to create links directly to a page or links that set the response page to a new page.

Creating a navigation plan for the swapping-panels approach is more complex. You need to swap one panel with another to achieve some form of navigation. Instead of creating a new page, you must get hold of the old panel and swap it with a new panel. This swapping can easily be altered to work through Ajax links, making the updates almost seamless to the user.

BOOKMARKABILITY

Closely related to navigation is the ability for users to create bookmarks that link to pages they've visited. This is especially useful when a user discovers a particular cheese and wants to share it with friends.

The page-oriented strategies provide the best support for bookmarking. By using `BookmarkablePageLinks` to navigate between the pages, users can bookmark and share links with friends to their hearts' content.

Achieving bookmarkability with the panel-replacement strategy is much harder. You have to encode a way to select the active panel in the bookmarkable URL, which tends to fall apart when you have more than a couple of panels that can be replaced.

AND THE WINNER IS?

Surprisingly, we aren't able to declare a clear winner. If you ask us which strategy is best, our answer is, "It depends."

The plain-pages strategy is a good way to start: it provides ample opportunities to create a mockup of your final application and to sprinkle real components across the pages. When the mockup has served its purpose, you can migrate to any of the other strategies by refactoring and moving parts to panels and creating a hierarchy of pages. The end result for your application will probably be a mix of markup inheritance and panel replacement.

7.3   Summary

This chapter concludes part 2 of this book. In the previous chapters, you learned about components and how to put them to good use. In this chapter, you learned how to group these components. Grouping components enables you to hide or show parts of pages by setting the visibility flag of one component: the grouping container. There are three grouping containers: `WebMarkupContainer`, `Panel`, and `Fragment`. Each of these containers has a different use case, and each is best suited for a particular task. Table 7.1 lists the grouping containers and when to use them.

You learned that using panels provides opportunities to reuse code and markup across pages. But even when you reuse a menu panel across pages, you're still duplicating a lot of code. We therefore looked at composing pages to cut down on code duplication.

We discussed three ways of composing pages. Using plain pages is the most basic approach; you don't take any precautions to prevent code and markup duplication. This strategy is best for small applications and at the start of projects.

When the design has settled and the number of pages in your application increases, it's best to apply markup inheritance to factor out the common bits and create a hierarchy of pages. The base page defines the common layout, and the child pages provide the specific functionality.

We also looked at composing pages by replacing panels on a single base page. This strategy provides a great way to create highly interactive applications where Ajax is used to swap functionality in the application.

By grouping common components using a panel, you can create a custom component. However, panels aren't the only way to create custom components; nor did we touch all aspects of custom component creation. The next chapter will discuss custom components in detail.

Part 3

Going beyond Wicket basics

Now that you know how to use the components that come with Wicket, it's time to take the plunge and build components yourself. In chapter 8, you'll learn how to create custom reusable components. Chapter 9 gives you insight into working with resources such as images, JavaScript files, stylesheets, and CSV files. Chapter 9 also covers integration with third-party libraries to generate dynamic content using a captcha example.

Creating custom components is great, but creating rich components is more fun. Chapter 10 introduces Ajax and discusses how to use Ajax in your applications. You'll learn how to create your own rich, Ajaxified components.

Developing
reusable components

8

In this chapter:

- Learn the advantages of creating custom components
- Create complex compound components that include their own navigation

In chapter 7, we looked at group components strategies. You learned that panels are particularly well suited for creating components that can be reused in a variety of contexts, without the need to know anything about their internal structure.

In this chapter, we'll look at creating reusable components. The more generic and context-independent components are, the easier it is to reuse them. We'll first look at examples of generic components. We'll start with a locale component, which is simple; later, we'll add features to illustrate how you can create compound components. After that, we'll discuss how to develop a date-time panel, to illustrate how you can create compound components that participate in form processing.

In the second half of this chapter, we'll examine a domain-specific component: a discount list for the cheese store example. It will illustrate that components can have their own independent navigation. The discount list will also use some of the components developed earlier in this chapter, and it will be the component we'll build upon in the chapters that follow.

Before we get back into coding, let's look at why you should take the time to create reusable components.

8.1   Why create custom reusable components?

Creating custom reusable components takes effort. You need to think about the proper abstractions, encapsulations, and couplings, and you have to design an API, document it, and so on. Why go through the effort? Here are a few good reasons:

- *To battle code duplication.* Code duplication (also known as *copying and pasting*) is one of the larger evils in software engineering. You'll get into situations where you fix a bug in one place but forget about duplicate code elsewhere. Code duplication is a telltale sign of software that isn't well thought out.

- *To save time.* If you solved a problem once and need to address a similar problem somewhere else, being able to reuse a component can be a huge time-saver. Even if the component needs to be tweaked to fit in this new use case, it's typically cheaper to do this than to solve the problem again from scratch. Often, the further your project progresses, the more time you'll save by being able to reuse components you wrote at an earlier stage.

- *To improve quality.* Less code means fewer bugs. And instead of implementing a quick (and often dirty) solution, you take a step back to think about what you really need to solve. That process often results in better code. On top of that, reusing components gets them more exposure (testing hours), so issues are often found more quickly.

- *To divide tasks more easily.* Breaking pages into sets of components enables you to better delegate development tasks across multiple team members.

- *To achieve better abstraction.* One of the main ideas behind modularization in programming is that you can manage complexity by breaking big problems into smaller ones. Custom components can help you tackle issues one at a time. Imagine a component that combines a search panel, a pageable results list, filters, and sort headers. Once you have that, you only have to focus on how you connect the data.

The remainder of this chapter looks at examples of creating custom components. We'll start with a component for switching a user's locale.

8.2   Creating a component that selects the current locale

Java's `Locale` object represents the combination of a language and country. Examples of locales are Thai/Thailand, English/USA, and English/UK. Wicket utilizes the user's locale to perform date and number conversions, do message lookups, even determine which file the markup is loaded from. We'll take a closer look at such capabilities in chapter 12, where you'll use them as part of a user properties panel.

Before we start implementing the `Locale` object, let's see what we mean by developing custom reusable components.

8.2.1　*What are reusable custom components?*

It sounds exciting to learn about authoring custom components, but you've already seen quite a few in previous chapters. For instance, this code fragment is a custom component:

```
add(new Link("add") {
  public void onClick() {
    setResponsePage(new EditContactPage(new Contact()));
  }
});
```

It isn't a reusable custom component, because the only way to put this functionality into another page is to copy it. But making it a reusable component is easy:

```
public class AddLink extends Link {

  private AddLink(String id) {
    super(id);
  }

  public void onClick() {
    setResponsePage(new EditContactPage(new Contact()));
  }
}
```

Because the second code fragment is defined in its own public class, you can put it on any page or any panel by instantiating it and adding it.

Another example of a reusable component is a required text field. Without it, we'd define a text field that enforces input like this:

```
TextField f = new TextField("name");
f.setRequired(true);
```

If we did that for 10 fields, we'd get a lot of code bloat. To avoid that, we can create a custom component that hides the call to `setRequired`. Listing 8.1 shows the code for such a component.

Listing 8.1 `RequiredTextField` component

```
public class RequiredTextField extends TextField {

  public RequiredTextField(String id) {
    super(id);
    setRequired(true);
  }

  public RequiredTextField(String id, IModel model) {
    super(id, model);
    setRequired(true);
  }
}
```

Using this code, we can declare a required component in one line:

```
RequiredTextField f = new RequiredTextField("name");
```

This component is trivial. But the need to hide implementation details becomes more obvious when we look at the implementation of a date format label (see listing 8.2). This component prints the date of its model object in MEDIUM notation as used in `java.text.DateFormat`.

Listing 8.2   The `DateFmtLabel` component

```
public class DateFmtLabel extends Label {

  public DateFmtLabel(String id) {
    super(id);
  }

  @Override
  public final IConverter getConverter(Class type) {
    return new StyleDateConverter("M-", true);
  }
}
```

If we have this component, we can do this:

```
add(new DateFmtLabel("until"));
```

Assuming a date value is provided—say, through a compound property model—it's formatted as follows: Sep 26, 2007. Internally, a format converter that can handle dates is configured, and the implementation details are hidden from those who wish to reuse this component. With preconfigured components like these, you can easily enforce consistency in your projects.

In the next section, we'll develop a custom component that displays the current locale and lets users change to another one.

8.2.2   *Implementing the locale-selector component*

In action, the locale-select component looks like the drop-down menu shown in the partial screen shot in figure 8.1.

Figure 8.1   The locale-select component in action

The current locale is English. If we select Thai from the drop-down menu, the display changes as shown in figure 8.2.

Figure 8.2   The locale changed to Thai

Listing 8.3 shows how the component is implemented.

Listing 8.3   Implementation of the locale select component

```java
public class LocaleDropDown extends DropDownChoice {

  private class LocaleRenderer extends ChoiceRenderer {            ◁── Render
                                                                       choices
    @Override
    public String getDisplayValue(Object locale) {              ◁── Display in
      return ((Locale) locale).getDisplayName(getLocale());         current
    }                                                               locale's
  }                                                                 language

  public LocaleDropDown(String id, List<Locale> supportedLocales) {
    super(id, supportedLocales);
    setChoiceRenderer(new LocaleRenderer());
    setModel(new IModel() {                    ◁── Use
                                                   custom-
      public Object getObject() {                  defined
        return getSession().getLocale();           model
      }                                                          Use session's
                                                                 locale directly
      public void setObject(Object object) {
        getSession().setLocale((Locale) object);
      }

      public void detach() {
      }
    });
  }

  @Override
  protected boolean wantOnSelectionChangedNotifications() {
    return true;
  }
}
```

`ChoiceRenderers` are used by components such as the drop-down menu to determine what should be rendered as visible values for users and what as internal identifiers. Letting the `wantOnSelectionChangeNotifications` method return `true` results in a postback every time a user changes the selection in the drop-down menu.

The nice thing about this code is that there isn't much to it. By extending the drop-down menu component, we let that component do the heavy lifting, and we can focus on the specific functionality we need.

Again, this is an example of how you can fairly easily build custom components by hard-wiring a particular component configuration. Instead of creating a custom class, we could have instantiated a drop-down menu and set the choice renderer and model on it directly. If we needed this functionality only once, that would be a fine choice. But if we might need the functionality multiple times, a single line of code now suffices:

```java
add(new LocaleDropDown("localeSelect", Arrays
    .asList(new Locale[] { Locale.ENGLISH,
        Locale.SIMPLIFIED_CHINESE, new Locale("th") })));
```

It's nice that the component lets you switch from English to Thai; but if your Thai language skills are lacking, you suddenly won't understand what was on the page. Suppose, as an exercise, we provide a link that resets the session's locale to the value it had when the component was constructed. We

Figure 8.3   The drop-down menu with a Reset link

want the link's display to be transparent to the user; the component should be a single entity that can be constructed as you just saw.

Figure 8.3 shows the locale-select component with a Reset link.

How do you create a component that consists of two components? The next section explains.

8.2.3   Creating a compound component

As you learned in chapter 7, panels are a good choice to create compound components. Panels can easily be reused in separate contexts without requiring users to know about their internal structure. That comes in handy here, because we're about to create a combination of components: the drop-down menu and a Reset link. We don't want users to have to include the markup for both components in their pages; we make it possible for them to use, say, a <span> tag as a placeholder.

The code in listing 8.4 is the first step in developing the compound component. We wrap the locale drop-down menu we developed in the previous section in a panel.

Listing 8.4   Locale drop-down menu nested in a panel

```
public class LocaleDropDownPanel extends Panel {

  private static class LocaleDropDown extends DropDownChoice {

    private class LocaleRenderer extends ChoiceRenderer {

      @Override
      public String getDisplayValue(Object locale) {
        return ((Locale) locale).getDisplayName(getLocale());
      }
    }

    LocaleDropDown(String id, List<Locale> supportedLocales) {
      super(id, supportedLocales);
      setChoiceRenderer(new LocaleRenderer());
      setModel(new IModel() {

        public Object getObject() {
          return getSession().getLocale();
        }

        public void setObject(Object object) {
          getSession().setLocale((Locale) object);
        }

        public void detach() {
        }
      });
    }
```

```
      @Override
      protected boolean wantOnSelectionChangedNotifications() {
        return true;
      }
    }

  public LocaleDropDownPanel(String id, List<Locale> supportedLocales) {
    super(id);
    add(new LocaleDropDown("localeSelect", supportedLocales));
  }
}
```

And here's the code for LocaleDropDownPanel.html:

```
<wicket:panel>
  <select wicket:id="localeSelect">
    <option value="nl">Dutch</option>
    <option value="en">English</option>
  </select>
</wicket:panel>
```

Pretty straightforward, isn't it?

The option elements in the markup will be discarded. They're here so you can preview the markup in an arbitrary editor—or even your browser—and have an idea what the panel will look like. If we don't care about the preview, we can do this:

```
<wicket:panel>
  <select wicket:id="localeSelect" />
</wicket:panel>
```

The instantiation works much the same as before:

```
add(new LocaleDropDownPanel("localeSelect",
  Arrays.asList(new Locale[] { Locale.ENGLISH,
        Locale.GERMAN, Locale.SIMPLIFIED_CHINESE })));
```

But the markup used as a placeholder for the component is now something like this

```
<span wicket:id="localeSelect" />
```

rather than this:

```
<select wicket:id="localeSelect">
  <option value="nl">Dutch</option>
  <option value="en">English</option>
</select>
```

If we tried the latter, the resulting markup would be as follows:

```
<select>
  <select name="localeSelect:localeSelect"
  onchange="window.location.href='?wicket:interface=
  5:localeSelect:localeSelect::IOnChangeListener::&amp;localeSelect:locale
  Select=' + this.options[this.selectedIndex].value;">
    <option selected="selected" value="0">English</option>
    <option value="1">German</option>
    <option value="2">Chinese (China)</option>
  </select>
</select>
```

A `select` tag nested within another `select` tag isn't valid HTML, so the output is wrong. The HTML looks this way because panels replace what is between the tags they're attached to, not the tags themselves.

If we care about previewability, we can use tags. Here we've added dummy markup for a `select` next to where our panel (which in turn contains a `select`) will be replaced:

```
<span wicket:id="localeSelect" />
<wicket:remove>
  <select>
    <option value="nl">Dutch</option>
    <option value="en">English</option>
  </select>
</wicket:remove>
```

These `<wicket:remove>` tags instruct Wicket to skip everything between them, so you can insert any markup you want for the purpose of previewability.

In case you think this is a half-baked solution, we can do something smart to let users use a `<select>` tag as a placeholder for our panel. Using our panel (which essentially is a specialized select) feels like using a normal `select`. At runtime, we can convert the tag to something harmless (like a `<span>` tag) by putting this in our panel:

```
@Override
protected void onComponentTag(ComponentTag tag) {
  super.onComponentTag(tag);
  tag.setName("span");
}
```

The `name` property of `ComponentTag` is mutable and determines what the actual HTML tag is when it's rendered. If we render the component with this code in place, the output is as follows:

```
<span>
  <select name="localeSelect:localeSelect"
onchange="window.location.href='?wicket:interface=
5:localeSelect:localeSelect::IOnChangeListener::&amp;
localeSelect:localeSelect=' +
 this.options[this.selectedIndex].value;">
    <option selected="selected" value="0">English</option>
    <option value="1">German</option>
    <option value="2">Chinese (China)</option>
  </select>
</span>
```

This is the case regardless of what tag is used in the markup: it's always set to `<span>`.

Most components shipped with Wicket don't alter tags like we just did. You have fewer surprises that way, which increases the chance that you'll write robust programs. But changing the tag can be a convenient trick to facilitate better previewability in your projects.

The locale-select component currently has the same functionality it had before, but now it's wrapped in a panel. In the next section, we'll add the Reset link.

8.2.4 *Adding a Reset link*

The Reset link implements the functionality to change the locale back to what the user's locale was when the component was instantiated. The first step is to save the locale before it is changed. In this example, we do that lazily through the model (see listing 8.5).

Listing 8.5 `setObject` implementation that saves the current locale

```
public void setObject(Object object) {
  Session session = getSession();
  Locale keep = (Locale) session.getMetaData(SAVED);
  if (keep == null) {
    session.setMetaData(SAVED, getLocale());
  }
  session.setLocale((Locale) object);
}
```

We store the locale as session metadata. Metadata exists for components, request cycles, sessions, and applications; you can use it to store arbitrary objects such as configuration data, authorization data, or just about anything you wish. In this example, it makes sense to use this facility so we don't have to force users of our component to provide a custom session that stores the initial locale as a property.

The metadata key is defined like this:

```
static MetaDataKey SAVED = new MetaDataKey(Locale.class) { };
```

Now, we can add to the panel a link that uses this metadata to reset the locale (see listing 8.6).

Listing 8.6 Implementation of the Reset link

```
add(new Link("reset") {
  @Override
  public void onClick() {
    Session session = getSession();
    Locale keep = (Locale) session.getMetaData(SAVED);
    if (keep != null) {
      session.setLocale(keep);
      session.setMetaData(SAVED, null);
    }
  }
});
```

The link gets the saved locale from the session, if it exists, and if so, sets the locale to that value and nulls the metadata entry.

Here's the panel template:

```
<wicket:panel>
  <select wicket:id="localeSelect" />
  <a href="#" wicket:id="reset">[reset]</a>
</wicket:panel>
```

Let's look at what we've achieved so far. We created a component that lets users switch their locale. To use this component, you don't have to know anything about how it's implemented; nor does it have to know anything about what else is on the page it's placed on. The component can handle input, such as selection changes or a click of the Reset link, independent of what is on the page. The component is truly self-contained. You'll see it again in chapter 12 on localization.

Remember the `DateFmtLabel` component from the beginning of this chapter? In the next section, we'll develop an input-receiving and time-enabled counterpart, which will show how you can develop composite components that participate in form processing.

8.3   *Developing a compound component: DateTimeField*

Our goal in this section is to create a component, `DateTimeField`, that provides the user with separate input fields for the date, hours, and minutes. The component should hide from users the internal implementation details; users should provide a model that works as a date and be done with it.

When it's finished, you'll be able to use the component as shown in listing 8.7.

Listing 8.7   Example of how `DateTimeField` can be used

```java
public class DateTimeFieldPage extends WebPage {

  private Date date = new Date();

  public DateTimeFieldPage() {
    Form form = new Form("form") {
      @Override
      protected void onSubmit() {
        info("new date value: " + date);
      }
    };
    add(form);
    PropertyModel model = new PropertyModel(this, "date");
    form.add(new DateTimeField("dateTime", model));
    add(new FeedbackPanel("feedback"));
  }
}
```

Here's the markup:

```html
<form wicket:id="form">
  <span wicket:id="dateTime">[date time field here]</span>
  <input type="submit" value="set" />
</form>
<div wicket:id="feedback">[feedback here]</div>
```

When rendered in a browser, it looks like figure 8.4.

As you can see, this component is a composite. Let's examine how to implement it.

Figure 8.4
The `DateTimeField` component as rendered in a browser

8.3.1 *Composite input components*

Things can get tricky when you want to create compound components that act like form components. You can nest form components in panels, and their individual models will be updated without any problem; but the model of the panel isn't automatically updated. That often isn't an issue: the locale drop-down menu we developed works fine embedded in a normal panel, and the panel doesn't need to have a model of its own. But consider a date-time field that works on a model (which produces a date) and which internally breaks dates into separate date (day of month) and time (hours and minutes) fields. You could let each of these nested components update its part of the model, but then you wouldn't have a single action for updating the model object of the outer component. Also, because validation is only executed for form components, you would have to pass validators to nested components—and that would bloat your component's API and expose implementation details.

The solution is to use a special kind of component that is both a panel and a form component: `FormComponentPanel`. Like normal panels, form component panels are associated with markup files; but unlike panels, they participate in form processing. We'll base the date-time field on this special component. In the next section, we'll start by embedding the form components that do the real job of receiving input for us.

8.3.2 *Embedding form components*

The first part of writing the date-time field is straightforward. We already know that we need to nest three text-field components: one for the date, one for the hours, and one for the minutes. These components should work with their own models, and the date-time field should use these model values to update its own model as an atomic operation. In other words, the component should update its model only when all the inputs of the nested components are valid and can be combined to form a date that passes the component's validation.

We'll look next at how a date-time field component can be implemented. The code is extensive, so it's broken up over several sections. Listing 8.8 shows the first part.

> **Listing 8.8 `DateTimeField` embedding the form components**

```
public class DateTimeField extends FormComponentPanel {

  private Date date;
  private Integer hours;
  private Integer minutes;
  private final DateTextField dateField;
  private final TextField hoursField;
  private final TextField minutesField;

  public DateTimeField(String id) {
    this(id, null);
  }

  public DateTimeField(String id, IModel model) {
    super(id, model);
```

```
setType(Date.class);
PropertyModel dateFieldModel = new PropertyModel(this, "date");
add(dateField = newDateTextField("date", dateFieldModel));
dateField.add(new DatePicker());
hoursField = new TextField("hours", new PropertyModel(this,
    "hours"), Integer.class);
add(hoursField);
hoursField.add(NumberValidator.range(0, 24));
hoursField.setLabel(new Model("hours"));
minutesField = new TextField("minutes", new PropertyModel(
    this, "minutes"), Integer.class)
add(minutesField);
minutesField.add(NumberValidator.range(0, 59));
minutesField.setLabel(new Model("minutes"));
}
```

Each field works on its own model object (date, hours, and minutes). Note that we don't have to add getters and setters for the private members date, hours, and minutes, because property models can work on them directly. We can decide to regard such fields as implementation details and not expose them via getters and setters.

The component exposes two constructors. The one without a model argument is useful when you want to use the component with compound property models.

The hours and minutes text fields both have validators attached to ensure valid input, and they have labels set for error reporting. You've seen how this works in earlier chapters.

A last interesting bit from this fragment is the use of a factory method that produces the date text field:

```
add(dateField = newDateTextField("date", dateFieldModel));
```

By default—in this component—this factory method is implemented like this:

```
protected DateTextField newDateTextField(String id,
    PropertyModel dateFieldModel) {
  return DateTextField.forShortStyle(id, dateFieldModel);
}
```

By delegating the construction of the date text field to a factory method, we enable users to provide their own versions or configurations of the text field. They could, for instance, specify a date pattern by overriding the factory method like this:

```
dateTimeField = new DateTimeField("dateTime", model) {
  @Override
  protected DateTextField newDateTextField(String id,
      PropertyModel dateFieldModel) {
    return DateTextField.forDatePattern(id, dateFieldModel,
        "dd-MM-yyyy");
  }
};
```

There are no surprises in the first part of the date-time field. Next, we'll look at how to synchronize the models of the nested components with the model of the top component.

This wasn't relevant for the locale-selection component earlier, because it works with its own model and isn't meant to interface with a model provided by users. This component, however, is meant to be used as follows:

```
form.add(new DateTimeField("dateTime", model));
```

Users will expect the date-time field to use the provided model object. If the model produces a date like 12 January 2008, 11:00 AM, they will expect the date and time fields to display values accordingly; and if end users change these fields and submit them as part of a form, the users will expect the date to be changed properly.

We need to synchronize the models that are used by the embedded components in a separate step so the change is atomic: either all nested fields validate and the date is updated properly, or the nested fields don't validate, in which case the date isn't updated. The next section shows how to do this.

8.3.3 Synchronizing the models of the embedded components

To keep the models of the nested components and the top component synchronized, we need to override two methods: onBeforeRender, which prepares for rendering, and convertInput, which handles receiving input. onBeforeRender is defined at the level of the Component base class. We'll use it as a hook into the component lifecycle so that we can synchronize the internal models right before the nested components are rendered (see listing 8.9).

Listing 8.9 `DateTimeField` preparing for rendering

```
@Override
protected void onBeforeRender() {
  date = (Date) getModelObject();
  if (date != null) {
    Calendar calendar = Calendar.getInstance(getLocale());      Synchronize
    calendar.setTime(date);                                     member
    hours = calendar.get(Calendar.HOUR_OF_DAY);                 variables
    minutes = calendar.get(Calendar.MINUTE);
  }                                                    Synchronize
  dateField.setRequired(isRequired());            ◁── required flag
  super.onBeforeRender();              ◁─┐ Call super
}                                         (required)
```

This code reads the current value of the model object—which should be a date—and extracts the days, hours, and minutes values from it so they can be used by the nested text fields. It's important to realize that the date-time field doesn't "own" its model or model value. The model is a reference to some data passed in, so it may have been changed from the outside between requests. For instance, in the Date-TimeFieldPage example (listing 8.7), we could include a link in the page to set the date-time to "now":

```
add(new Link("now") {
  @Override
  public void onClick() {
```

```
        date = new Date();
    }
});
```

In this case, the date used by the model of the date-time field would be changed without our direct knowledge. So, it's a good idea to determine the current model value right before rendering, assuming it might have been changed since the last time we checked (and saved) it, which explains the call to getModelObject().

Notice two other things in the method implementation: we have to remember to call the super-implementation of the onBeforeRender method (although in this case it doesn't matter whether that is done toward the start or end of the method), and we set the required bit of the date text field according to whether the component is required. In this case, hours and minutes are always optional.

The second method, convertInput, handles the receiving of user input. Listing 8.10 defines this method.

Listing 8.10 DateTimeField receiving input

```java
@Override
protected void convertInput() {
    Date date = (Date) dateField.getConvertedInput();
    if (date != null) {
        Calendar calendar = Calendar.getInstance(getLocale());
        calendar.setTime(date);
        Integer hours = (Integer) hoursField.getConvertedInput();
        Integer minutes = (Integer) minutesField.getConvertedInput();
        if (hours != null) {
            calendar.set(Calendar.HOUR_OF_DAY, hours % 24);
            calendar.set(Calendar.MINUTE,
                    (minutes != null) ? minutes : 0);
        }
        setConvertedInput(calendar.getTime());
    } else {
        setConvertedInput(null);
    }
}
```

The convertInput method is called during the first phase of component validation (before any validators are executed). Implementations should parse user input and either set the converted input using setConvertedInput or report that the input couldn't be interpreted directly. A form component panel typically doesn't receive user input directly. But because its nested components do, and because it wants to update its own model value accordingly, we override this method.

Form processing functions like validating and updating models are done using depth-first (*postorder*) traversals of the component tree. In effect, this means the children of compound components are processed before the top component. That is exactly what we need here, because we want to construct the date from the already-processed nested components. The tricky thing is that when Wicket calls convertInput, form processing hasn't finished performing validation, and the models of the nested components aren't yet updated. We can't use the date, hours, and minutes member variables to construct the date. Instead, we can manually call getConverted-Input on the nested components. We can safely do that because convertInput is called only when a form component is marked "valid" (meaning it passed all validation), and the method to determine that (isValid) returns true only when all children are valid. We can implement convertInput assured that the input of the nested components is valid.

After doing a bit of date calculation, we set the converted date. Note that because we can assume all the validators of the nested components executed successfully, we know that the hours and minutes values we get from the nested components are valid: we added validators to them to enforce that.

One last method will make the component well-rounded:

```
@Override
public String getInput() {
   return dateField.getInput() + ", " + hoursField.getInput() + ":"
       + minutesField.getInput();
}
```

This method is used by the default implementation of convertInput. It's also useful at various locations for error reporting (for example, for validators with messages that use the ${input} variable).

We'll use this component in the next and last sections of this chapter, where we'll develop another custom component: the discount list.

8.4 Developing a discount list component

The locale-select component and date-time field are both examples of generic components; they can function in a large variety of contexts. In this section, we'll develop a component that is specific for a certain domain. We may be able to reuse it across our domain—the cheese store—but even if we use it only once, developing it as a separate component still makes sense. Doing so allows us to focus on problems one at a time; and once we have the component, we can place it on any page or panel. That also makes refactoring a lot easier.

The component we're about to develop lists discounts and has an administration function for editing those discounts. Switching between the normal list and editing is handled by the component.

The domain model can be described as follows. A discount consists of a reference to a cheese, a description, a discount (which is a percentage), and a date from/until when the offer is valid. Figure 8.5 shows a UML diagram.

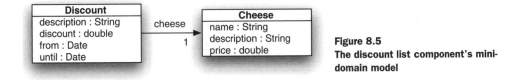

Figure 8.5
The discount list component's mini-domain model

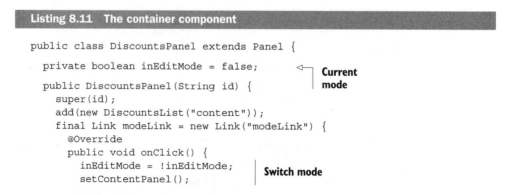

Figure 8.6   The layout of the discount list component

Schematically, the layout of the discount-list component can be drawn as shown in fig-ure 8.6.

The component's top section has a static title and a link that displays either Edit or Display, depending on the component's state. The rest of the section (Display) displays either a read-only list with discounts or a form with a list of input fields to directly edit those discounts.

When the component is in list mode, it displays the discounts, and the link says Edit. If the link is clicked, the display changes to a form in which the list can be directly edited and which has buttons for adding and removing rows. In edit mode, the link in the title section says Display; when clicked, it changes the display back to the normal list.

In the next section, we'll look at the top-level component that contains the header and list sections.

8.4.1   *The container*

The container, `DiscountsPanel`, nests the header and list components and needs to track whether it's in edit mode (if not, it should display the read-only list). Listing 8.11 shows the code for the container component.

Listing 8.11   The container component

```
public class DiscountsPanel extends Panel {

  private boolean inEditMode = false;          ⊲──┐ Current
                                                    │ mode
  public DiscountsPanel(String id) {
    super(id);
    add(new DiscountsList("content"));
    final Link modeLink = new Link("modeLink") {
      @Override
      public void onClick() {
        inEditMode = !inEditMode;      │ Switch mode
        setContentPanel();
```

```
        }
      };
      add(modeLink);
      modeLink.add(new Label("linkLabel", new AbstractReadOnlyModel() {
        @Override
        public Object getObject() {
          return inEditMode ? "[display]" : "[edit]";
        }
      }));
    }

    void setContentPanel() {
      if (inEditMode) {
        addOrReplace(new DiscountsEditList("content"));
      } else {
        addOrReplace(new DiscountsList("content"));
      }
    }
  }
}
```

← **Mode-dependent link label**

Add or replace child

As you can see, the component initially nests the DiscountList component (inEdit-Mode starts out being false). Whenever the mode link is clicked, the mode is switched and the content component is replaced accordingly.

Reflect on what we've achieved. Using component replacement, we created a component that can perform its own self-contained navigation. We created a portlet-like miniapplication that can function in any page without further configuration. This is quite a contrast to many of Wicket's competitors, which force you to do everything with page navigation.

As great as component replacement is in many cases, you need to keep a couple of things in the back of your mind.

COMPONENT-REPLACEMENT GOTCHAS

Consider that as soon as you start applying component replacement, you lose book-markability. In order to provide Back button support, Wicket records versions of pages that make structural changes; that way, if the Back button is clicked, Wicket can roll back to a previous structure.

Also keep in mind that the identifiers of the replacement and replaced components must be the same. Unless your component actively changes the tag it's linked to (as in section 8.1.4), you have to be careful that the replacement is compatible with the structure of the component it replaces. For instance, you can't replace a text field with a list view. But if you use panels and fragments as we do in this example, you'll never run into this problem.

The last thing we need to finish the top-level part of the component is the markup. As you can see, it's straightforward:

```
<wicket:panel>
  <div>
    <div>
      Special discounts  
```

```
      <a href="#" wicket:id="modeLink">
        <span wicket:id="linkLabel">[label]</span>
      </a>
    </div>
    <span wicket:id="content">[panel content here]</span>
  </div>
</wicket:panel>
```

Mode-switch link

Content section

The first part of the component is finished. Using the component is as simple as this:

```
add(new DiscountsPanel("discounts"));
```

In the next two sections, we'll develop the discount list panels, which will be placed one at a time in the content section of the component we just built. We'll start with the default panel: the read-only discounts list.

8.4.2   *The read-only discounts list*

In view mode, the read-only list is the component that is displayed as the content. Figure 8.7 shows the discount list in view mode. It displays discounts the way end users would see them, except that it has an Edit link embedded.

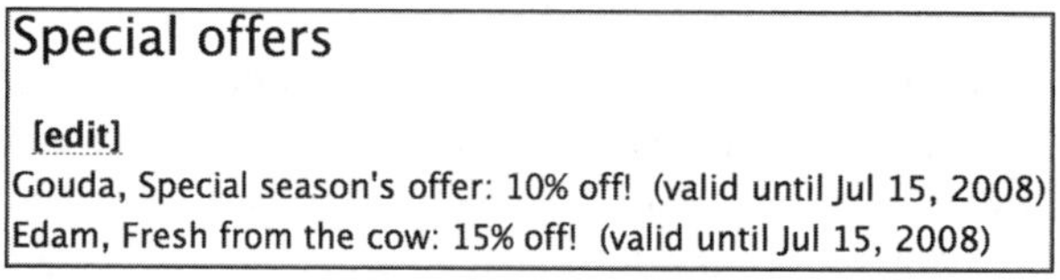

Special offers

[edit]
Gouda, Special season's offer: 10% off! (valid until Jul 15, 2008)
Edam, Fresh from the cow: 15% off! (valid until Jul 15, 2008)

**Figure 8.7
The discount list component
in view mode**

For the implementation, we'll embed a refreshing-view component (a list that recalculates its children on every render) in a panel, so we can easily use the list elsewhere without having to worry about what the internal structure looks like. Listing 8.12 shows the implementation.

Listing 8.12   Implementation of the read-only list component

```
public class DiscountsList extends Panel {

  public DiscountsList(String id) {

    super(id);
    add(new RefreshingView("discounts") {

      @Override                                        Wrap discounts list
      protected Iterator getItemModels() {
        return new ModelIteratorAdapter(MyDataBase.getInstance()
            .listDiscounts().iterator()) {
          @Override
          protected IModel model(Object object) {
            return new CompoundPropertyModel((Discount) object);
          }
        };                                             CompoundPropertyModel
      }

      @Override
      protected void populateItem(Item item) {
```

```
            item.add(new Label("cheese.name"));
            item.add(new PercentLabel("discount"));
            item.add(new Label("description"));
            item.add(new DateFmtLabel("until"));
        }
    });
  }
}
```

The `getItemModels` method needs to return an iterator that produces `IModel` objects. The `ModelIteratorAdapter` wraps the iterator of the discounts list, and we wrap each object that is produced by the iterator in a compound property model. Because every list item will have a compound property model set, we can add components without explicitly providing their models; the child components will use their identifiers as property expressions on those models.

Listing 8.13 shows the markup for the read-only list.

Listing 8.13 Markup for the read-only list component

```
<wicket:panel>
  <li wicket:id="discounts">
    <strong><span wicket:id="cheese.name">name</span></strong>,
    <span wicket:id="description">description</span>:
    <span wicket:id="discount">discount</span> off! 
    (valid until <span wicket:id="until">until</span>)
  </li>
</wicket:panel>
```

Note that we use another custom component: a label that formats its model value as a percentage. As an exercise, think about how you would implement that, and compare it to the component available in the code that comes with this book.

Now that we've implemented the read-only list for view mode, we're ready to look at the edit list for the discount-list component's edit mode.

8.4.3 The edit-discounts list

The edit list provides a form for bulk editing discounts; it includes a button for creating a new discount and links for removing discounts. When we're done, it will look like figure 8.8.

Let's start with the simple part and create a panel with a form, a button for a new discount, and a save button that persists the bulk changes. You can see the implementation in listing 8.14.

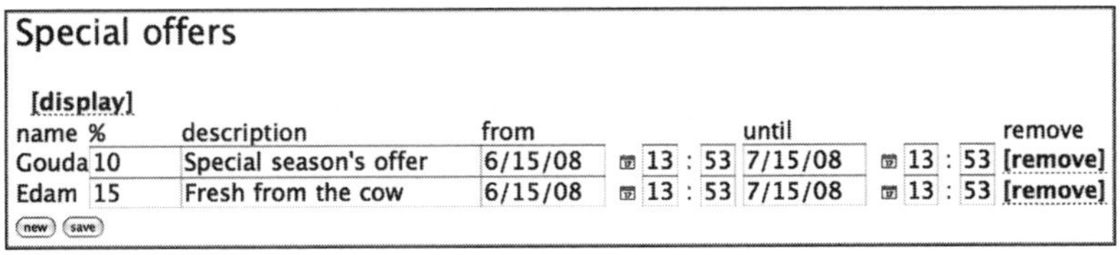

Figure 8.8 A screenshot of the edit-discounts list

Listing 8.14   Form portion of the list-editing component

```
public final class DiscountsEditList extends Panel {

  private List<Discount> discounts;

  public DiscountsEditList(String id) {

    super(id);
    Form form = new Form("form");
    add(form);
    form.add(new Button("newButton") {
      @Override
      public void onSubmit() {
        DiscountsEditList.this.replaceWith(                    Replace
          new NewDiscountForm(DiscountsEditList.this.getId()));  self
      }
    });
    form.add(new Button("saveButton") {
      @Override
      public void onSubmit() {                       Save list
        MyDataBase.getInstance().update(discounts);  contents
        info("discounts updated");
      }
    });
    form.add(new FeedbackPanel("feedback"));
  ...
```

The Wicket part of this code should hold no secrets by now. To make the example somewhat realistic, we're keeping a reference to a list of discounts retrieved from the database, which after updating is saved back to the database.

It's more interesting to look at the use of replaceWith. This method, which is defined on the component base class, is shorthand for doing getParent().replace(..), where replace is a method defined on MarkupContainer. Either form is fine.

The first part of the repeater is implemented as shown in listing 8.15.

Listing 8.15   Repeater's iterator

```
RefreshingView discountsView = new RefreshingView("discounts") {

  @Override
  protected Iterator getItemModels() {
    if (discounts == null) {
      discounts = DataBase.getInstance().listDiscounts();
    }
    return new ModelIteratorAdapter(discounts.iterator()) {
      @Override
      protected IModel model(Object object) {
        return EqualsDecorator
            .decorate(new CompoundPropertyModel((Discount) object));
      }
    };
  }
```

This is almost the same as the way we defined `getItemModels` in the read-only list. If it were exactly the same, we probably would have made a common base class for it. But here we assign the discounts list we get from the database to the discounts member. Because the database returns a snapshot of its current contents when servicing `list-Discounts` calls, we in effect keep a reference to a working copy of the database contents. The Save button's `onSubmit` method synchronizes the working copy with the database contents by calling the database's `update` method.

Also, because we're working in a form, we don't want the repeater to discard its child components every time rendering completes (the default behavior when refreshing a view). Instead, it should refresh only when the model objects are changed. We can configure this by setting the item-reuse strategy, as follows:

```
discountsView.setItemReuseStrategy(
  ReuseIfModelsEqualStrategy.getInstance());
```

That, together with wrapping the model with `EqualsDecorator`—which returns a model proxy that implements `equals` and `hashCode` using the model object—makes the repeater refresh only when the underlying model changes. Listing 8.16 shows the implementation of `EqualsDecorator` (an elaborate explanation of it is outside the scope of this book).

Listing 8.16   Model proxy that implements `equals` and `hashCode`

```
public final class EqualsDecorator {

  private EqualsDecorator() { }

  public static IModel decorate(final IModel model) {
    return (IModel) Proxy.newProxyInstance(model.getClass()
        .getClassLoader(), model.getClass().getInterfaces(),
        new Decorator(model));
  }

  private static class Decorator implements
      InvocationHandler, Serializable {

    private final IModel model;

    Decorator(IModel model) { this.model = model; }

    public Object invoke(Object proxy, Method method, Object[] args)
        throws Throwable {
      String methodName = method.getName();
      if (methodName.equals("equals")) {
        if (args[0] instanceof IModel) {
          return Objects.equal(model.getObject(), ((IModel) args[0])
              .getObject());
        }
      } else if (methodName.equals("hashCode")) {
        Object val = model.getObject();
        return Objects.hashCode(val);
      } else if (methodName.equals("writeReplace")) {
```

```
        return new SerializableReplacement(model);
      }
      return method.invoke(model, args);
    }
  }

  private static class SerializableReplacement implements
      Serializable {
    private final IModel model;

    SerializableReplacement(IModel model) { this.model = model; }

    private Object readResolve() throws ObjectStreamException {
      return decorate(model);
    }
  }
}
```

The last code fragment of the list-editing component is shown in listing 8.17: the populateItem implementation.

Listing 8.17   Repeater's `populateItem` implementation

```
@Override
protected void populateItem(Item item) {
  item.add(new Label("cheese.name"));
  item.add(new PercentageField("discount"));        ⟵  Another custom
  item.add(new RequiredTextField("description"));        component
  item.add(new DateTimeField("from"));
  item.add(new DateTimeField("until"));

  final Discount discount = (Discount) item.getModelObject();
  final Link removeLink = new Link("remove") {
    @Override
    public void onClick() {
      MyDataBase.getInstance().remove(discount);
    }
  };
  item.add(removeLink);
  removeLink.add(new SimpleAttributeModifier("onclick",
      "if(!confirm('remove discount for "
         + discount.getCheese().getName()
         + " ?')) return false;"));
}
```

What, another custom component? That's what happens once you get the hang of it: custom components everywhere!

The percentage field is implemented in listing 8.18.

Listing 8.18   Implementation of the percentage field

```
public class PercentageField extends TextField {

  public PercentageField(String id) {
    super(id, double.class);        ⟵  Type is
  }                                    double
```

```
    public PercentageField(String id, IModel model) {
      super(id, model, double.class);
    }

    @Override                                                    Fixed
    public final IConverter getConverter(Class type) {    <─┘  converter
      return new IConverter() {

        public Object convertToObject(String value, Locale locale) {
          try {
            return getNumberFormat(locale).parseObject(value);
          } catch (ParseException e) {
            throw new ConversionException(e);    <─┐  Conversion
          }                                         exception
        }

        public String convertToString(Object value, Locale locale) {
          return getNumberFormat(locale).format((Double) value);
        }

        private NumberFormat getNumberFormat(Locale locale) {
          DecimalFormat fmt = new DecimalFormat("##");
          fmt.setMultiplier(100);
          return fmt;
        }
      };
    }
  }
```

If we had used a regular text field, we would have seen 0.20 or something similar for a discount of 20%. That isn't exactly user-friendly. The percentage field component translates 0.20 to 20 and back again, so the user doesn't have to calculate back and forth. It uses a converter to perform that calculation, and the converter in turn uses a decimal formatter.

Converters are responsible for converting model values to user-facing output and user input back to model values. The percentage field component sets up the converter to be used for itself by overriding the getConverter method and making the method final to prevent misuse. We'll take another look at converters in chapter 13.

We'll leave the component's markup and the implementation of the new discount form to your imagination (or you can look it up in the source code that comes with this book). It's time to wrap up the chapter.

8.5   Summary

In this chapter, we looked at how to create custom reusable components for Wicket, and why you would want to do so. The first few examples packaged component configuration into new classes. That can be an effective strategy to hide complexity, to enforce consistency throughout your project(s), and to reduce code duplication.

The locale-select component and date-time field component are examples of generic components that can be used in many different contexts. The locale-select component with a Reset link is an example of a composite component that acts as a single self-contained unit for its users. Users don't have to know that the component combines a drop-down menu and a link: a single line of Java code and a single line of markup are enough to use the component.

The date-time field extends that concept and is a composite component that participates in form processing (it's updated on form submits) and that automatically updates its model depending on the input of its nested form components.

The last example in this chapter created a domain-specific cheese store discount list. It reused some of the components we developed earlier, and it showed how by using component replacement, components can implement their own independent means of navigation, even for editing data.

In the next chapter, we'll discuss Wicket resources, which you can use to include things like images, JavaScript, and CSS references in your custom components.

Images, CSS, and scripts: working with resources

9

In this chapter:

- Including images, scripts, and stylesheets using packaged resources
- Providing downloadable content with dynamic resources
- Integrating third-party libraries using resources

Up to now, we've mainly been talking about components. As powerful as they are, there are some things you can't do with them. For example, you can't render PDFs with them, and they don't provide a direct answer to how images or CSS files should be handled.

This is where Wicket resources come in. Wicket *resources* are objects that can process requests independently from pages. They typically represent things like images and files (for instance, JavaScript and CSS files); but as you'll see in this chapter, they aren't limited to that.

In the first part of this chapter, we'll look at what we call *packaged resources* and show how they can be used to develop custom components that ship with their own images and other dependencies. After that, we'll investigate three ways to use Wicket resources to build functionality for downloading cheese discounts in a file of comma-separated values (CSV). The final part of this chapter examines how you can use Wicket resources to integrate third-party software that generates PDFs, images, and so on.

First, let's look at a concept you'll likely be using soon: packaged resources.

9.1 Using packaged resources

In the previous chapter, we developed a discount-list component with edit functionality. Figure 9.1 shows this component in edit mode.

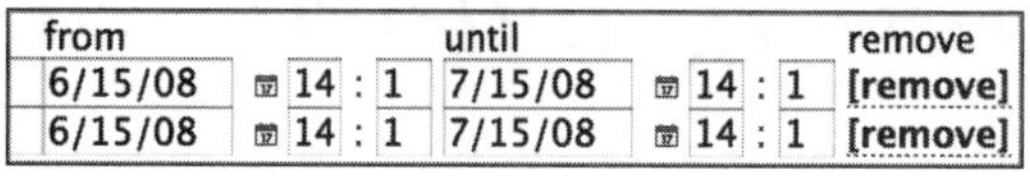

from			until			remove
6/15/08	🗓 14 : 1		7/15/08	🗓 14 : 1		[remove]
6/15/08	🗓 14 : 1		7/15/08	🗓 14 : 1		[remove]

Figure 9.1
The discount-list component in edit mode

The link to remove a row currently displays the text *[remove]*. Our goal in this section is to replace that text with an image, so that it looks like figure 9.2.

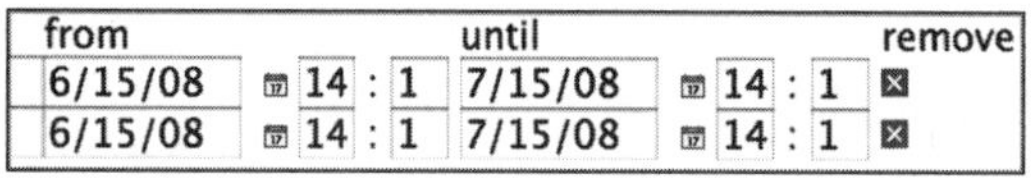

from			until			remove
6/15/08	🗓 14 : 1		7/15/08	🗓 14 : 1		☒
6/15/08	🗓 14 : 1		7/15/08	🗓 14 : 1		☒

Figure 9.2
The discount-list component in edit mode, now using an image for the Remove link

Doing so is straightforward if you know your HTML. If you have this link

```
<a href="delete">click me</a>
```

you replace the "click me" message with an image as follows:

```
<a href="delete"><img src="images/remove_icon.gif" /></a>
```

Then, you place the image remove_icon.gif in the web application's images subdirectory, and you're finished.

But something doesn't feel quite right in that last part. So far, we've been able to keep our Java and HTML side by side and avoid the configuration hassle that characterizes so many other Java frameworks. Now, we need to know that the component expects the image to be in the web app directory, and make the image available. And this is just one image, for one component. You can see that you'd end up spending a considerable amount of time setting up dependencies if all components were written this way.

For example, consider the date picker we use in the discount list. To attach a date picker to a text field, all we need to do is this:

```
textField.add(new DatePicker());
```

If you investigate the date picker closely, you'll find that it uses multiple images—the clickable calendar icon that is rendered as part of the date picker, for instance—Java-Script, and CSS dependencies. Yet you don't have to copy or configure a single thing to be able to use the date picker.

The date picker ships with the dependencies it needs. The images, JavaScript, and CSS files are put in the classpath (for example, directly in WEB-INF/classes or embedded in a jar file), and Wicket makes it possible for these dependencies to be accessed. Wicket has a special terminology for this: *packaged resources.*

To make the Remove icon a packaged resource, we need to place it in—or relative to—the same package as the component it's meant for. You can see this for the discounts list in figure 9.3.

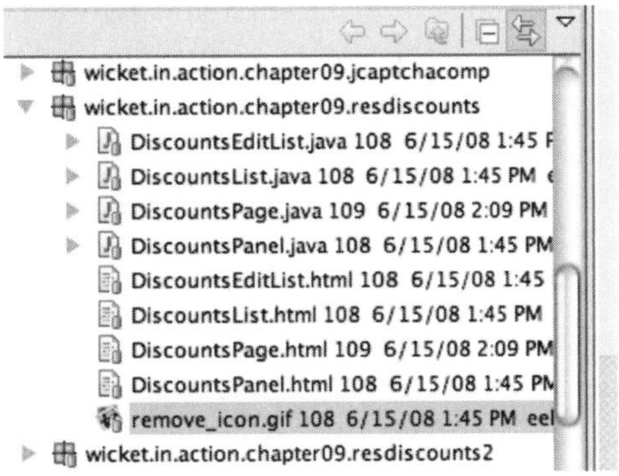

Note that you should configure your IDE and build process to copy these resources to the same classpath or jar file it compiles the Java classes to. An IDE like Eclipse does this by default.

Next, we add the image to the link and give it a `wicket:id` identifier:

```
<a href="#" wicket:id="remove">
  <img wicket:id="icon" /></a>
```

Figure 9.3 The `remove_icon` image is placed in the package.

The `img` tag is coupled to a component with the identifier `icon`. That component is constructed and added to the link as follows:

```
removeLink.add(new Image("icon",
    new ResourceReference(DiscountsEditList.class, "remove_icon.gif")));
```

The resource reference is created with two parameters: the class that should serve as a base from which to perform a relative lookup, and the resource's relative name.

Wicket looks for the remove_icon.gif file in the same package where the `DiscountEditList` class resides.

NOTE   The use of navigational double dots (`..`) to navigate up one level currently isn't supported, but going into subdirectories is. For instance, this is permitted:

```
new ResourceReference(MyClass.class, "some/sub/directory/
my_image.jpg")
```

Instead of using a resource reference, you can use a resource directly. The class to use when you're referencing resources from the classpath is `PackageResource`:

```
removeLink.add(new Image("icon",
    PackageResource.get(DiscountsEditList.class, "remove_icon.gif")));
```

This class is used internally by resource references, and in many cases it can be used instead of them. Resource reference is primarily an abstraction that hides how to get the resource; it offers the slight advantage that if you set the locale or style, or invoke the `invalidate` method directly on it, it recalculates its resource without losing the reference. If you're using a packaged resource directly, and you change the locale or style, you have to get a new packaged resource object yourself.

Including packaged resources is such a common task that Wicket supports autolinking for images, JavaScript files, and CSS files.

9.1.1 *Including packaged resources using auto-linking*

You already learned that you can use auto-link regions to automatically set the href attributes of anchor tags (<a>) that are nested in each region. Wicket determines whether the href attributes match any existing pages; if they do, Wicket replaces the href attributes to refer to those pages.

In addition to links, auto-link regions can also be applied to <link> tags (CSS), script references, and images. Instead of explicitly adding an image component as we just did, we can include the image in an auto-link region like this:

```
<wicket:link>
  <a href="#" wicket:id="remove"><img src="remove_icon.gif" /></a>
</wicket:link>
```

No Java code is needed. Wicket tries to match the value of the src attribute with a resource relative to the component that loaded the markup (DiscountsEditList). If src can't be resolved to a packaged resource, Wicket leaves the attribute alone. In this example, it matches the image we've placed in the package of the page, so Wicket changes the attribute value to something like this:

```
<img src="resources/com.foo.DiscountsEditList/remove_icon_en.gif"/>
```

The _en is part of how Wicket handles localization and can be ignored for now; Wicket automatically falls back to the base name (remove_icon.gif) when it loads the image.

Packaging resources is a great way to develop self-contained components. We'll use this technique in the next chapter, which is about developing rich components. In the next section, we'll develop new functionality for the discounts list to show a very different use of Wicket resources.

9.2 *Building export functionality as a resource*

In this section, we'll build functionality for exporting the discounts list to a CSV file. We'll add a link to the main discounts panel that, when clicked, downloads the discounts in CSV form to the client. When we're finished, the panel will look like figure 9.4.

This section discusses three distinct ways to achieve this result: with a component-scoped resource, with a shared resource, and without a resource. First, let's implement the resource.

Figure 9.4
The discounts panel with a link for exporting the discounts to a CSV file

9.2.1   Creating the resource

The first thing we need to do is build a function in the database class that creates a string with the discounts separated by commas (see listing 9.1).

Listing 9.1   Method that produces a CSV representation of the discounts

```java
public CharSequence exportDiscounts() {
  StringBuilder b = new StringBuilder();
  for (Discount discount : discounts) {
    b.append(discount.getCheese().getName()).append(',');
    ... (etc)
    b.append(discount.getDescription()).append('\n');
  }
  return b;
}
```

Next, we need to implement the Wicket resource that directly streams these exports (see listing 9.2).

Listing 9.2   Resource that streams the CSV representation of the discounts

```java
WebResource export = new WebResource() {

  @Override
  public IResourceStream getResourceStream() {
    CharSequence discounts = MyDataBase.getInstance()
        .exportDiscounts();
    return new StringResourceStream(discounts, "text/csv");
  }

  @Override
  protected void setHeaders(WebResponse response) {
    super.setHeaders(response);
    response.setAttachmentHeader("discounts.csv");   ⟵─┐ Trigger download
  }                                                       dialog
};
export.setCacheable(false);
```

`WebResource` is a base resource class. The `getResourceStream` method is abstract in this base class, so we had to define it here. This method must return a resource stream, which in turn is responsible for producing whatever is to be streamed to the client. Here, we return a convenience implementation of the resource stream interface, `StringResourceStream`. That implementation produces the string passed in during construction; the second argument—the content type—is sent to the client so that it can properly interpret the stream.

The export resource also overrides the `setHeaders` method, in which it calls one of `WebResponse`'s methods: `setAttachmentHeader`. This method sets a special header in the response: `Content-disposition: attachment; filename=x`, where *x* will be replaced by the argument that is passed in. Setting this header triggers the browser to pop up a download dialog as well as set the selected name of the file to save the download to.

That's the resource. Next, we need to create a link that users can click to download the export. You can expose the resource in two ways: through a component or in a slightly more direct manner as a shared resource. The next section shows how to expose the resource using a component.

9.2.2   *Letting a component host the resource*

Wicket has a convenient link component for referencing resources: `ResourceLink`. It's used like this:

```
new ResourceLink("exportLink", export);
```

The link hosts the resource. The `href` attribute of the export link is rendered as follows:

```
?wicket:interface=:1:discounts:exportLink::IResourceListener::
```

When the link is clicked, Wicket looks up the component that is reachable with the component path `1:discounts:exportLink`, which arrives at the export link. Wicket then executes the method `onResourceRequested` of `IResourceListener` on it (`ResourceLink` implements that interface). The implementation of that method in `ResourceLink` delegates the call to the embedded Wicket resource—the export resource. Figure 9.5 shows this process.

The resource is available only through a host component, which is fine in this case but may not always be what you want. The two primary disadvantages of component-hosted resources are that they aren't bookmarkable (which means they can't be crawled, but also can't be cached by browsers), and they inherit the fact that components are synchronized on the session (chapter 2 covers thread-safety).

In the next section, we'll look at resources that can be reached independently from components: shared resources.

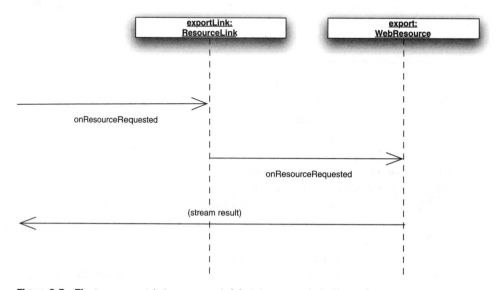

Figure 9.5   The `ResourceLink` component delegates requests to the real resource.

9.2.3   *Making the export available as a shared resource*

Shared resources are resources that don't need host components. They're stored in a special object of type SharedResources, which is managed by the application class. Unlike component-hosted resources, they have stable URLs, which makes them suitable for indexing by web crawlers and caching by web browsers. And—especially important with images and resources such as JavaScript or CSS files—they aren't synchronized on the session, which means they can be loaded asynchronously.

The packaged resources you saw earlier in this chapter are an example of shared resources. Unlike the application-wide shared resources we're discussing now, you don't need to explicitly configure packaged resources, because Wicket tries to discover them when their URLs are requested.

Lazy initialization is applicable to packaged resources—Wicket loads them only when they're requested (the first time) by a page or component being rendered. If you want to make other resources globally available, you can get access to the shared-resource object directly like this:

```
SharedResources res = Application.get().getSharedResources();
```

One way to register shared resources is to add them to the application's shared resources object. To add the Export resource, for instance, we do this:

```
WebResource export = ... (like earlier example)
Application.get().getSharedResources().add("discounts", export);
```

The resource is then available through a stable URL (/resources/discounts), independent of components.

If we want to make this shared resource available through a link that needs to appear on a page or, for example, on our discount panel, we can change the Discount-Panel code as follows:

```
ResourceReference ref = new ResourceReference("discounts");
add(new ResourceLink("exportLink", ref));
```

The single-argument resource-reference constructor you see here references application scoped/shared resources by name. The generated href attribute contains this:

```
resources/org.apache.wicket.Application/discounts
```

The resources/ bit is a reserved path in Wicket applications. The form of the resource URLs is as follows:

```
"resources/" scope "/" name
```

scope is the class that functions as the root for looking up the resource in the classpath, and name is either the name of a packaged file or an arbitrary name when the resource is registered as a shared resource at the application level. As you may have guessed, the scope Application is always recognized as a shared resource.

NOTE It's important to realize that shared resources aren't thread-safe. For this example, that isn't a problem, because the discounts export isn't dependent on specific sessions, and the resource doesn't have mutable state. But if you ever need shared resources that must be thread-safe, look at `DynamicWebResource`. An excellent example is `UploadStatusResource`, which is used by the Ajax-enabled upload progress bar available in the Wicket extensions project.

If you want to make resources globally accessible, you need to register them as shared resources. In the next section, we'll look at how to do this.

9.2.4   *Initializing the shared resource*

Shared resources must be registered before they're available through their own URLs. One way to do this is to add the resource in the application's `init` method. But doing so conflicts with the idea of self-contained components. This is especially true if the resource is part of a component, which may be provided by a third party. You don't want to keep track of all the resources needed by various components just because you have to register them properly in one place.

Fortunately, there is a way to automatically initialize components during startup: Wicket initializers.

INITIALIZERS

When Wicket starts up an application, it scans the classpath roots, looking for files named wicket.properties. It reads every wicket.properties file it finds, and it instantiates and executes the initializers (of type `IInitializer`) defined in those files.

For our example, the wicket.properties file (which should be packaged in the root of the classpath) contains this line:

```
initializer=my.package.DiscountsExport$Initializer
```

The initializer can be implemented like this:

```
public class DiscountsExport extends WebResource {

  public static class Initializer implements IInitializer {

    public void init(Application application) {
      SharedResources res = application.getSharedResources();
      res.add("discounts", new DiscountsExport());
    }
  }
  ...
```

Resources added this way are available immediately after the Wicket application is started. You can type the path to the resource (resources/org.apache.wicket.Application/discounts) in your browser and get it directly.

Note that you can define only one `IInitializer` per library (jar). If you want to initialize multiple resources in a library, you can implement the `IInitializer` to delegate to other initializers:

```
public class MyInitializer implements IInitializer {
  public void init(Application application) {
    new FooInitializer().init(application);
    new BarInitializer().init(application);
  }
}
```

This first half of the chapter has given you an idea how resources work. Sometimes you can achieve the same thing without relying on Wicket resources. Just for the heck of it, let's look at how to implement the Export function using a special request target.

9.2.5 *An alternative implementation*

If you ever want to stream something to the client, such as part of a form submit, you can use an alternative approach to achieve what you'd otherwise do with a component-hosted resource. Remember from chapter 2 that request targets are responsible for what is streamed back to the client? You can use that knowledge and write a variant of the Export function that directly sets a request target as part of handling a form submit. You can see this implemented in listing 9.3.

Listing 9.3 An export form

```
Form form = new Form("exportForm");
add(form);
form.add(new SubmitLink("exportLink", new Model("export"))) {

  @Override
  public void onSubmit() {
    CharSequence export = MyDataBase.getInstance()
      .exportDiscounts();
    ResourceStreamRequestTarget target =
      new ResourceStreamRequestTarget(
        new StringResourceStream(export, "text/plain"));
    target.setFileName("discounts.csv");
    RequestCycle.get().setRequestTarget(target);      ⟵┐ Set request
  }                                                     │ target directly
});
```

Request targets are typically resolved by the implementation of IRequestCycle-Processor's resolve method; but as you can see, you can set one directly.

The request cycle holds a stack of request targets; every time one is set, the new request target is put on top of the stack. When Wicket renders the request, the request target from the top of the stack is popped and used for rendering (Wicket cleans up all the request targets on the stack so resources can be freed if necessary).

Using request targets directly is powerful. But resources are more suitable for reuse, because they can be defined as shared resources, and the same resource can be exposed in multiple ways.

Resources are great for creating components with dependencies, such as images and stylesheets, and for creating export functionality as we just did. They're also suitable for integrating third-party libraries, as we'll investigate in the next section.

9.3   *Resources and third-party libraries*

As you've seen, resources can handle requests independently and stream responses back to the client any way they like. This makes them suitable for streaming content that isn't rendered by Wicket. Such libraries, for instance, can generate PDF reports, Excel sheets, Rich Text Format (RTF) documents, or images. Using Wicket resources, you can easily integrate such libraries. As an example, in this section we'll look at how to integrate a third-party library called library JCaptcha.

9.3.1   *A JCaptcha image component*

Captcha, which is an acronym for *Completely Automated Public Turing test to tell Computers and Humans Apart,* and which is trademarked by Carnegie Mellon, is an authentication test to determine whether users are human. It's a recent effort to fight spam, particularly on public forms like blog comments. Figure 9.6 shows a captcha form in action.

Figure 9.6   Captcha authentication

With a little effort, you should be able to recognize the text *whiker* in the image on the form. Because the image is distorted in several ways, it's difficult for *bots* (computer programs) to "read" the text. If the text entered in the form doesn't match the image, you can assume it was submitted by a bot on behalf of some unscrupulous spammer trying to advertise her wares.

JCaptcha is a versatile open source Java implementation that provides an efficient image generator and a secure validation mechanism. You can integrate JCaptcha with an application by using, for instance, a servlet. Listing 9.4 shows a slightly modified version of the servlet that JCaptcha recommends on its website.

> **Listing 9.4   JCaptcha integration using a servlet**

```
public class ImageCaptchaServlet extends HttpServlet {

  private static final ImageCaptchaService captchaService =
    new DefaultManageableImageCaptchaService();

  protected void doGet(                                        ◁─┐ Handle POST and
    HttpServletRequest request, HttpServletResponse response)    │ GET requests
      throws ServletException, IOException {
    byte[] captchaChallengeAsJpeg = null;
    ByteArrayOutputStream jpegOutputStream =
        new ByteArrayOutputStream();
    String captchaId = request.getSession(true).getId();
    BufferedImage challenge = captchaService.getImageChallengeForID(
        captchaId, request.getLocale());
    JPEGImageEncoder jpegEncoder = JPEGCodec
        .createJPEGEncoder(jpegOutputStream);
    jpegEncoder.encode(challenge);
    captchaChallengeAsJpeg = jpegOutputStream.toByteArray();
```

```
response.setHeader("Cache-Control", "no-store");
response.setHeader("Pragma", "no-cache");          Prepare HTTP
response.setDateHeader("Expires", 0);              headers
response.setContentType("image/jpeg");
ServletOutputStream os = response.getOutputStream();
os.write(captchaChallengeAsJpeg);      ◁──  Write to output
os.flush();                                  stream
os.close();
    }
}
```

That code looks straightforward, doesn't it? If you want to use this servlet to integrate
JCaptcha with your Wicket application, you can. But you may prefer to use Wicket
resources instead. The servlet must be configured separately, whereas a Wicket resource
is a seamless part of a Wicket application. You also need to know how to determine the
URL to the servlet, which in turn depends on how the servlet was configured.

Listing 9.5 shows the same thing using a Wicket resource.

Listing 9.5 JCaptcha image that uses a Wicket resource internally

```
public abstract class CaptchaImage extends Image {

  public CaptchaImage(MarkupContainer parent, String id,
      final String challengeId) {

    super(id);
    setImageResource(new DynamicImageResource() {       Called when rendering
      protected byte[] getImageData() {            ◁──  DynamicImageResource
        ByteArrayOutputStream os = new ByteArrayOutputStream();
        BufferedImage challenge = getImageCaptchaService()
          .getImageChallengeForID(challengeId,
                Session.get().getLocale());
        JPEGImageEncoder encoder = JPEGCodec.createJPEGEncoder(os);
        try {
          encoder.encode(challenge);
          return os.toByteArray();
        } catch (Exception e) {
          throw new RuntimeException(e);
        }
      }
    });
  }

  protected abstract ImageCaptchaService getImageCaptchaService();
}
```

We add the abstract getImageCaptchaService to determine the actual implementation of the service. We generally prefer abstract methods over properties because they
save memory by avoiding extra object references.

The Wicket Image that we extend requires an object of type ImageResource; we
provide an implementation that can dynamically generate the image as an implementation detail. Our resulting captcha image component expects a challenge ID to be
passed in, in the constructor: it's likely that the identifier will be created from outside

the component, because it will also be used to validate user input. The resource hides details like getting, writing to, and closing the response, and how to prevent the browser from caching the image. But probably the greatest advantage of using a resource in such a case is that you don't have to worry about configuration and which URL to use. Just make sure you have the JCaptcha dependency in the classpath, and you're ready to go.

That covers the resource part of it. Let's extend this discussion and create a complete reusable component, so you get another look at how to build custom components.

9.3.2   *Implementing a complete JCaptcha form*

To make this a complete component, we need a text field for the input and a form for submitting that input. It makes sense to let the text field do the validation, because the input it receives is what we want to check. Listing 9.6 shows how the JCaptcha text field can be implemented.

Listing 9.6   JCaptcha input component that includes validation

```
public abstract class CaptchaInput extends TextField {

  public CaptchaInput (String id,
      IModel model, final String challengeId) {           ❶ Validation is
    super(id, model);                                         implementation detail
    add(new AbstractValidator() {
      @Override
      protected void onValidate(IValidatable validatable) {
        if (!getImageCaptchaService().validateResponseForID(
            challengeId, validatable.getValue())) {
          onError(this, validatable);
        }
      }
    });                                                    ❷ Same old
  }                                                            indirection

  protected abstract ImageCaptchaService getImageCaptchaService();

  @Override
  protected void onComponentTag(final ComponentTag tag) {
    super.onComponentTag(tag);
    tag.put("value", "");        ❸ Clear value each    Force clients to ❸
  }                                   request            handle errors
  protected abstract void onError(
      AbstractValidator validator, IValidatable validatable);
}
```

The text input component adds validation on the captcha form as an implementation detail ❶. It uses the same trick as our captcha image did in getting the captcha image service ❷, and it introduces even more indirection by defining an abstract method called onError ❸. By doing this, we push responsibilities to the client while, at the same time, providing for flexible reuse of the component.

Listing 9.7 defines the form that uses the image and input components.

Listing 9.7 JCaptcha form

```
public abstract class CaptchaForm extends Panel {

  private final class CaptchaInputForm extends Form {

    private String challengeResponse;

    public CaptchaInputForm(String id) {                          ❶ Shared
      super(id);                                                      challenge
      String challengeId = UUID.randomUUID().toString();     ◁─┘      identifier
      add(new CaptchaImage("captchaImage", challengeId) {
        @Override
        protected ImageCaptchaService getImageCaptchaService() {
          return CaptchaForm.this.getImageCaptchaService();
        }
      });

      add(new CaptchaInput("response", new PropertyModel(this,
          "challengeResponse"), challengeId) {
        @Override
        protected ImageCaptchaService getImageCaptchaService() {
          return CaptchaForm.this.getImageCaptchaService();
        }

        @Override
        protected void onError(AbstractValidator validator,
            IValidatable validatable) {
          CaptchaForm.this.onError(validator, validatable);  ◁─┐
        }                                                        ❷ Indirection
      });

      add(new FeedbackPanel("feedback"));
    }

    @Override
    protected void onSubmit() {
      onSuccess();
    }
  }

  public CaptchaForm(String id) {
    super(id);
    add(new CaptchaInputForm("form"));
  }

  protected abstract ImageCaptchaService getImageCaptchaService();

  protected void onError(AbstractValidator validator,
      IValidatable validatable) {
    validator.error(validatable, "captcha.validation.failed");
  }

  protected void onSuccess() {
    info(getLocalizer().getString("captcha.validation.succeeded",
        this));
  }
}
```

The challenge identifier is generated during construction ❶ and used by both the image and input component. Again, we use indirection to determine the captcha image server we use, and we use indirection with a default implementation for handling success/errors so users can override that if they wish ❷.

The HTML code for the form is straightforward, as you can see in listing 9.8.

Listing 9.8   Markup of the JCaptcha form

```
<wicket:panel>
  <form wicket:id="form">
  <p><img wicket:id="captchaImage" /></p>
  <p><wicket:message key="captcha.provide.input" /> <br />
  <input wicket:id="response" type="text" />
  <input type="submit" value="submit" /></p>
  <div wicket:id="feedback">[feedback here]</div>
  </form>
</wicket:panel>
```

Finally, we can use the component as shown in listing 9.9.

Listing 9.9   Using the JCaptcha form

```
public class CaptchaPage extends WebPage {

  @SpringBean                                          Retrieve Spring
  private ImageCaptchaService captchaService;          service

  public CaptchaPage() {
    add(new CaptchaForm("captchaForm") {

      @Override
      protected ImageCaptchaService getImageCaptchaService() {
        return captchaService;
      }
    });
  }
}
```

We depend on Spring to provide an appropriate instance of the captcha image service. (We'll look into Spring integration in chapter 13.)

9.4   *Summary*

Wicket resources are a great way to make things like images and JavaScript files available in your web application through Wicket. You can make them accessible either through host components or as shared resources. Components can automatically register shared resources they depend on using initializers defined in wicket.properties files—you don't have to do this explicitly using these components. Packaged resources are the only shared resources that don't need to be explicitly registered.

In this chapter, we enhanced our cheese shop's discount list with export-as-text functionality, and we replaced the text of the link to remove discounts with an image that is packaged with the component. You saw three ways to implement the Export function: using a resource hosted by a component, using a shared resource, and using no resource (using a request target directly).

In the second part of this chapter, we looked at how resources can help with third-party library integration. We created a reusable JCaptcha image component, which we later added to a reusable JCaptcha form.

We'll make extensive use of resources, particularly packaged resources, in the next chapter, which is about rich components and Ajax.

Rich components and Ajax

In this chapter:

- Using Ajax components and behaviors to create responsive web UIs
- Contributing JavaScript and CSS to the `<head>` section with header contributors
- Integrating third-party JavaScript libraries in your custom components
- Gotchas when using Ajax in your applications

Chapter 8 introduced you to creating custom components with Wicket. In the second half of that chapter, we developed a discount-list component, which consists of multiple panels and has different modes of operation (list, edit/delete, and add).

This chapter is about *rich components*, which typically means widgets that have richer behavior than basic ones in HTML. Examples are lists where you can reorder elements by dragging and dropping them, maps that load data in the background when you scroll, and text fields that provide a list of suggestions while you type.

The term rich components can apply to components that use anything from DHTML (typically HTML + JavaScript + CSS) to Flash to Java applets, and so forth. This book focuses on DHTML because it has the broadest support of all the options.

In this chapter, we'll explore a few things that will enable you to create killer components. You'll learn about the different ways in which you can enrich your components using JavaScript, CSS, and packaged resources, and you'll learn how to use and extend Wicket's Ajax capabilities.

As the main example of this chapter, we'll build on the discounts list from chapter 8. We'll revamp that component to display Wicket's Ajax capabilities and end up with a component that allows for a different user experience. But before we get to that, we'll look into what Ajax is and how you can use one of the enablers of Ajax support for header contributions.

10.1 *Asynchronous JavaScript and XML (Ajax)*

Suddenly, somewhere in early 2005, there was a lot of talk about a fancy new technique to make web applications more responsive. The term *Ajax* was coined by Jesse James Garret in his famous article "Ajax: A New Approach to Web Applications." In it, he describes how the company he works for, Adaptive Path, has been combining a set of technologies to get a more responsive UI. Shortly after the release of this article, Ajax was hyped to incredible heights. A plethora of new websites, books, magazines, courses, frameworks, and conferences dedicated to Ajax sprang up. Ajax was defined as a crucial part in another revolution: Web 2.0. Some famous applications served as references of what could be done with Ajax, such as Google Suggest, Google Maps, and Flickr. Today, Ajax is a fully accepted part of the developer's toolbox, although debates over the merits and dangers of this technology still rage.

Let's investigate what Ajax stands for.

10.1.1 *Ajax explained*

Ajax is an acronym for Asynchronous JavaScript and XML. It stands for a whole range of techniques that have the same goal: letting browsers perform server round-trips in the background so that web pages can be updated without doing a full reload, thus providing a more fluent user experience (as compared to doing full page reloads).

In his article, Jesse James Garrett lists the following technologies as the typical (rather than required) enablers for Ajax:

- Standards-based presentation using XHTML and CSS
- Dynamic display and interaction using the DOM
- Data interchange and manipulation using XML and XSLT
- Asynchronous data retrieval using `XMLHttpRequest`
- JavaScript binding everything together

The main difference between normal requests and Ajax requests is that normal requests cause the whole browser window (or frame) to be refreshed, showing a blank page while loading is in progress. With Ajax, requests are done in the background by an Ajax *engine* (a script that is part of the page), and responses are interpreted by that engine and typically used to replace part of the page.

Figure 10.1 shows a traditional request/response cycle.

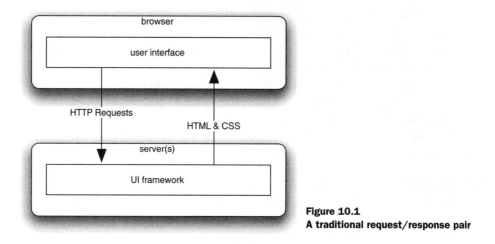

Figure 10.1
A traditional request/response pair

Figure 10.2 shows schematically how an Ajax request/response works.

The user interface here consists of the usual HTML elements: inputs, forms, links, and so forth. Instead of using those elements unaltered, we define event handlers that communicate with the Ajax engine. For instance, here's an Ajax version of a text field:

```
<input type="text" name="foo" value="bar" />
```

If it makes a round-trip to perform validation when the value is changed, it looks like this:

```
<input type="text" name="foo" value="bar"
  onchange="callToAjaxEngine(this); " />
```

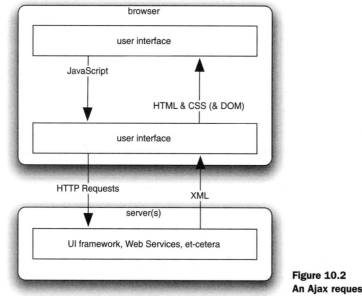

Figure 10.2
An Ajax request/response pair

A non-Ajax variant that works similarly is as follows:

```
<input type="text" name="foo" value="bar"
  onchange="myform.submit();" />
```

This has a couple of disadvantages, compared to an Ajax round-trip:

- The user has to wait for the entire round-trip to finish, possibly staring at a blank window and sandbox in the meanwhile.

- Although we're interested in validating only one text field, we either have to validate the whole form or remember to send back intermediate information that enables us to restore the values of the other form elements to as they were when the request was initiated. This is a waste of the server's CPU; and the request handling is more complex than it is with Ajax.

- Instead of receiving a response that only indicates whether the text field validated, possibly accompanied by extra information like an error message in case validation failed, we now get the HTML of the whole page, which is a waste of bandwidth.

This example should convince you that using Ajax is a good idea in at least some cases. But it has some potential disadvantages you should be aware of:

- Ajax limits the range of browsers and browser configurations you can use. The client must allow JavaScript to be executed. In addition, depending on how well the Ajax engine is built, all browsers have their own quirks that the Ajax engine must work around. With normal CSS and HTML, quirks usually result in improper display; in other cases, the failure to have a workaround in place to handle a quirk often results in the Ajax functionality not working.

- When you're using Ajax, you don't automatically support standard browser features, like the Back button, bookmarkability (the URLs don't change when executing Ajax requests), and so forth.

- With Ajax, it isn't always obvious that a request is in progress and waiting for an answer. This can result in users frantically clicking away and getting frustrated because they think the application doesn't work. The Ajax engine needs a queue to ensure orderly processing in case requests are issued while a request is running. The engine may be able to prevent new requests while running certain requests. On top of this, many Ajax engines provide a busy indicator to notify the user that a request is being processed. This may not seem like a disadvantage, but compared to the traditional model, more thought definitely should go into how the UI should react.

- Ajax relies heavily on JavaScript executed in the browser. Compared with server-side Java, this is typically a lot harder to debug. And the fact that JavaScript isn't strongly typed makes it vulnerable to typos, wrong variables passed into methods, and so forth.

Don't let all this scare you away. Just be pragmatic, and evaluate whether Ajax is useful based on the UI requirements.

Wicket's approach to Ajax is that Ajax is optional. By default, Wicket follows the traditional approach; but adding Ajax support to both existing traditional components and new components from scratch is easy, and you can do so several ways. Wicket comes with its own robust Ajax engine implementation and ships with a decent range of reusable Ajax behaviors and components. Wicket leaves enough doors open to roll your own support in case you aren't happy with what the framework provides.

The next section will provide a short overview of what Wicket's Ajax support looks like, so you won't be lost when we start revamping the discount list. Later in this chapter, we'll delve deeper so you'll know what strategies are available for building custom Ajax components or plugging in different Ajax engines.

10.1.2 *Ajax support in Wicket*

The key element of Ajax support is the Ajax engine that runs in the browser. Such an engine usually consists of one or more JavaScript libraries.

Since Ajax became popular, several specialized frameworks have emerged, including Dojo, Scriptaculous, Yahoo User Interface (YUI) library, and Direct Web Remoting (DWR). These libraries can all be used with Wicket; but because they're generic frameworks in their own right, you'll probably need to write bridging code to let the two frameworks (the Ajax engine and Wicket) work together seamlessly. You can find Ajax implementations for several of these projects in the third-party Wicket Stuff component repository (http://wicketstuff.org).

Wicket ships with a specialized Ajax engine designed to be used with Wicket's server-side components and behaviors.

WICKET'S DEFAULT AJAX ENGINE

The main goal of Wicket's Ajax engine is to integrate well with Wicket components and behaviors. This is in contrast to a JavaScript/Ajax engine like Dojo, which has a broad scope and which doesn't support any particular server-side framework. Wicket's Ajax engine is designed to be as minimal as possible and thus isn't as feature rich as some other Ajax engines. But the supported functionality should be sufficient for most common cases. The engine is geared toward the following:

- Message-handling between the client (web browser) and server
- Repainting (replacing) and hiding components
- Executing custom JavaScript sent by Ajax responses
- Dynamically adding JavaScript and CSS to the page
- Providing the means to debug/track the engine's workings
- Throttling and timeout functionality

This engine is implemented in wicket-ajax.js, which you can find in the `org.apache.wicket.ajax` package. Wicket also ships with the wicket-ajax-debug.js and wicket-ajax-debug-drag.js JavaScript components in the same package; together they provide a simple but effective debugger that shows you information about the traffic the engine handles. Figure 10.3 shows a screenshot.

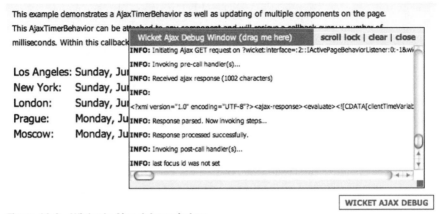

This example demonstrates a AjaxTimerBehavior as well as updating of multiple components on the page. This AjaxTimerBehavior can be attached to any component and will receive a callback every *n* number of milliseconds. Within this callback

Los Angeles: Sunday, Jun
New York: Sunday, Jun
London: Sunday, Jun
Prague: Monday, Ju
Moscow: Monday, Ju

Figure 10.3 Wicket's Ajax debug window

Another great tool when you're working with Ajax is the Firebug plug-in for the Mozilla Firefox web browser. Firebug is currently the best JavaScript debugger for client-side debugging. Firebug will help you in dealing with client-side software development, but it won't iron out cross-browser issues.

The advantage of using Wicket's Ajax JavaScript engine over more generic engines like Dojo is that it integrates better with Wicket. The engine understands the kind of server code it's communicating with, so you can avoid writing plumbing code as you'd have to do with other frameworks.

In addition to the client-side Ajax engine, Wicket's Ajax support has two important enablers: header contributions and the ability of behaviors to receive requests independently. We'll look more closely at these enablers later this chapter.

First, let's examine a few examples of Ajax components that are shipped with Wicket.

10.1.3 Ajax components

It's easiest for most end users to look up whether an existing Wicket component does what they want. Wicket ships with quite a few high-level components. Most of the Ajax components supported as part of the core project can be found in the packages `org.apache.wicket.ajax.*` and `org.apache.wicket.extensions.ajax.*`. As usual, the Examples project that ships with the Wicket distribution covers many of them.

Here are a few examples of Ajax components that are part of the distributions (in no particular order):

- AjaxLink—A generic link that does a partial request instead of a full round-trip.
- AjaxSubmitLink and AjaxSubmitButton—Partial requests that submit the form they're linked to.
- AjaxCheckBox—A check box that issues a partial request when its value is changed (the user selects it).
- AjaxEditableLabel—A label that, when clicked, changes to a text field so the value can be edited (you'll see more from this component later in this chapter).

- AutoCompleteTextField—A text field that offers choices when you start typing in it. It was made famous by Google Suggest. Finally, web applications got a smarter combo-box component without having to rely on Java applets, Flash, or other technologies.

You can use Wicket's Ajax components like any other Wicket component. From an end user's point of view, there is no difference between Ajax components and normal components, other than Ajax components result in partial page updates rather than full page loads.

Most of the Ajax components shipped with Wicket's distribution work with a special request target: `AjaxRequestTarget`. This request target is typically used as an argument of Ajax component callback methods. Listing 10.1 uses an Ajax link.

Listing 10.1   Using the `AjaxLink` component

```
private int counter = 0;

public MyPage() {
    super(new CompoundPropertyModel(this));
    final Label counterLabel = new Label("counter");
    add(counterLabel);
    counterLabel.setOutputMarkupId(true);          ◁─┐ Always output
    add(new AjaxLink("counterLabelLink")              │ markup id with Ajax
        @Override
        public void onClick(AjaxRequestTarget target) {
            counter++;
            target.addComponent(counterLabel);     ◁─┐ Re-render
        }                                             │ label
    });
}
```

Here we define an Ajax link that increments `MyPage`'s `counter` variable. Like normal links, `AjaxLink` components have an `onClick` method to do the real work. In addition to incrementing the counter, `onClick`'s implementation adds a component to the render queue. Ajax request targets have a special method for that: `AjaxRequest-Target#addComponent`. It ensures not only that the provided component is rendered using its current state, but also that the corresponding HTML tags that now reside in the client's browser are replaced by the fresh ones.

It's important to instruct Wicket to generate markup identifiers by setting the `output-MarkupId` flag on the components you want to re-render with Ajax requests to `true` (`setOutputMarkupId`). If you set that flag, Wicket outputs the unique component path of that component in its HTML identifier attribute: for example, `<a hef="..." wicket:id="foo" id="foo">`. This identifier can then be used with JavaScript, and thus by an Ajax engine, to locate tags in the DOM that browsers use to keep track of the HTML document's structure. If you don't set the component to render its markup identifier, the Ajax engine won't be able to locate the tag linked to a component. And if the tag can't be located, its contents can never be replaced.

AjaxRequestTarget has more useful methods for working with Ajax. Another convenient method in the Ajax request target is appendJavascript. For example:

```
@Override
public void onClick(AjaxRequestTarget target) {
  target.appendJavascript("alert('hello!')");
}
```
⟵ **Executed on client**

The JavaScript you add to an Ajax target using the appendJavascript method is executed on the client when the Ajax reply is interpreted. In this case, that results in displaying an alert box (JavaScript alert function) containing the text *hello!*

Now you've seen how to use Wicket's Ajax components. These components are convenient, but components aren't always the best method for adding Ajax behavior. A more flexible approach uses Ajax behaviors. Most Ajax components use Ajax behaviors internally to implement their functionality.

10.1.4 Ajax behaviors

Ajax behaviors are those that can receive Ajax requests. Such behaviors implement the IBehaviorListener interface and typically also IHeaderContributor. The IBehaviorListener interface can be implemented by behaviors that want to be able to receive requests directly. It has a single method for this purpose: onRequest. You use header contributions to include JavaScript and CSS resources in the page in which components and behaviors are placed. We'll look further at that later this chapter.

Behaviors provide a flexible means of constructing functionality (using composition rather than inheritance). Ajax is triggered through JavaScript event handlers like onclick, onchange, and the like—attributes you typically set using behaviors.

Ajax behaviors should extend AbstractAjaxBehavior, which, in addition to implementing the behavior listener and header contribution interfaces, takes care of some common behaviors. It ensures that any Ajax behavior is bound to only one component and provides access to that component so that it can be used later—for example, to get the markup identifier or the model value. AbstractAjaxBehavior also provides a method to calculate the callback URL (getCallbackUrl), and it provides adapter methods for the interface methods of the behavior listener and header contributor interfaces. You have to override only the methods you're interested in.

Wicket's default Ajax engine ships with extensive server-side support. The base class of Wicket's Ajax engine behaviors is AbstractDefaultAjaxBehavior, which you can find in the package org.apache.wicket.ajax. That package contains the core of Wicket's Ajax engine, including the JavaScript libraries in wicket-ajax.js and the two JavaScript files that contain debugging functionality for the engine. Abstract-DefaultAjaxBehavior takes care of properly including the Ajax engine in pages, and it prepares incoming requests by creating and activating an Ajax request target.

Figure 10.4 shows this class and a few implementations.

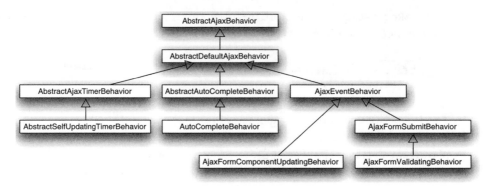

Figure 10.4   Ajax behaviors that work with the default engine

We'll look into how you can create custom Ajax behaviors later in this chapter. For now, we'll examine a few examples:

- `AjaxSelfUpdatingTimerBehavior`—Triggers a component to be redisplayed after a certain interval.
- `AjaxFormComponentUpdatingBehavior`—Updates the model of the form component the behavior is attached to whenever the specified client event—typically `onchange`—occurs. Used, for instance, by AjaxCheckBox.
- `AjaxFormSubmitBehavior`—Submits the form this behavior is coupled to when the specified client event occurs. Used by `AjaxSubmitButton` and `AjaxSubmitLink`.
- `AjaxFormValidatingBehavior`—A specialization of form-submit behavior that triggers validation of the form when the specified client event occurs.

There are many other Ajax behaviors, and their numbers are growing almost by the day. You can often use them like regular behaviors. Listing 10.2 shows an Ajax behavior used in one of the Ajax examples that ships with Wicket.

Listing 10.2   Example of a self-updating (Ajax) timer behavior

```
public class ClockPage extends WebPage {

  public ClockPage() {

    TimeZone tz = TimeZone.getTimeZone("America/Los_Angeles");
    Clock clock = new Clock("clock", tz);
    add(clock);
    clock.add(new AjaxSelfUpdatingTimerBehavior(Duration.seconds(5)));
  }
}
```

The clock component is defined like this:

```
public class Clock extends Label {

  private static class ClockModel extends AbstractReadOnlyModel {

  private DateFormat df;

  public ClockModel(TimeZone tz) {
    df = DateFormat.getDateTimeInstance(
```

```
        DateFormat.FULL, DateFormat.FULL);
      df.setTimeZone(tz);
    }

    @Override
    public Object getObject() {
      return df.format(new Date());
    }
  }

  public Clock(MarkupContainer parent, final String id, TimeZone tz) {
    super(parent, id, new ClockModel(tz));
  }
}
```

As you can see, all you have to do to let a component redisplay itself in a set interval is add the Ajax behavior to it:

```
clock.add(new AjaxSelfUpdatingTimerBehavior(Duration.seconds(5)));
```

Ajax behaviors are a great way to enrich components with additional behavior without impacting their normal behavior.

The Ajax engine is an important aspect of Ajax. As we stated earlier, the Ajax engine is a JavaScript library that runs in the client and takes care of issuing and handling partial, asynchronous requests. It needs to be included in the page—preferably just once, so the instance can be shared among the components that may use its functionality. Wicket has a *header contributions* mechanism that lets individual components include text and references in the header part of pages.

10.2 *Header contributions*

Contributing to the header section of pages is crucial for many components. This ability of individual components and behaviors to contribute to the page's header is called a *header contribution*. The HTML head section of a page, contained in <head> tags, is typically where JavaScript and CSS dependencies are declared. Such dependencies are then loaded before the page is rendered, so they can be used for rendering the body of the page.

For example, consider a Wicket page with a Tree component embedded, like the nested example in wicket-examples. The head section in the source of that page looks like this:

Normal inclusion of CSS stylesheet

```
<head>
    <title>Wicket Examples - nested</title>
    <link href="../style.css" rel="stylesheet" type="text/css"/>    ⟵
    <script type="text/javascript"
        src="resources/{package}.AbstractTree/res/tree.js"></script>
    <link rel="stylesheet" type="text/css"
        href="resources/{package}.DefaultAbstractTree/res/tree.css" />  ⟵
</head>
```

Inclusion by component

The reference to style.css is common and refers to style.css in the web application directory. The next two references—one for JavaScript and one for CSS—are contributed by the Tree component (note that {package} is an abbreviation to make this example readable).

The page the tree is placed in doesn't need to know anything about the component's JavaScript and CSS dependencies; the header-contribution system that Wicket provides takes care of inserting them in the right place. This mechanism also takes care of filtering duplicate contributions, so that no matter how many trees you place on that page, those two lines are the only ones inserted in the Page's head section for the Tree component. This allows for components that encapsulate their dependency on some complex JavaScript and CSS files.

You can make header contributions happen in several ways. We'll discuss them in the next few sections.

10.2.1 *Using header-contributing behaviors*

If we look at the Tree component, this is how the JavaScript part is contributed in AbstractTree:

```
add(HeaderContributor.forJavaScript(
    AbstractTree.class, "res/tree.js"));
```

A factory method of the utility class HeaderContributor is called that returns a behavior that takes care of contributing when the component it's attached to is rendered. This method returns a behavior that writes out a <script> tag and replaces the src attribute with the URL to the tree.js file, relative to the package that AbstractTree resides in (in the res subdirectory).

In a similar fashion, you can add CSS:

```
add(HeaderContributor.forCss(MyComponent.class, "some.css"));
```

This writes out a <link> tag, where the href attribute is replaced with the URL to some.css in the package where MyComponent.class resides.

You can also use the header-contributor utility class to contribute files that don't reside in packages. For instance,

```
add(HeaderContributor.forCss("css/sysadmin.css"));
```

refers to sysadmin.css in the web application's css directory. If you don't provide a scope argument (like AbstractTree.class), references are resolved relative to the web application context path.

Internally, HeaderContributor uses StringHeaderContributor, which contributes the model object you provide to it as a plain string to the head section. A useful subclass of StringHeaderContributor is TextTemplateHeaderContributor. This behavior lets you contribute with variable interpolation built in. This is useful when you have something to contribute that is at least partially dynamic, but you don't want to maintain it as a concatenated Java string (because that is harder to maintain, for example).

You can find an example of how to use this in the Wicket Stuff project wicket-contrib-yui, which focuses on creating Wicket adaptor components for the YUI widgets. Let's look at part of the `Slider` component in that project. For every component instance, you need to do some JavaScript initialization. The JavaScript is dynamically generated based on properties of the component. Here, we could use a `StringBuilder` to generate the necessary JavaScript, but doing so would result in code that's hard to read and maintain. Instead, we use a text template header contributor, as shown in the next code fragment:

```
IModel variablesModel = new AbstractReadOnlyModel() {       ◁──┐  Create model for
                                                                interpolation
  public Map getObject() {
    Map<String, CharSequence> variables =                      Model returns
      new HashMap<String, CharSequence>(7);                    map
    variables.put("javaScriptId", javaScriptId);
    variables.put("backGroundElementId", backgroundElementId);
    variables.put("imageElementId", imageElementId);
    variables.put("leftUp", settings.getLeftUp());
    variables.put("rightDown", settings.getRightDown());
    variables.put("tick", settings.getTick());
    variables.put("formElementId", element.getId());
    return variables;
  }
};

add(TextTemplateHeaderContributor.forJavaScript(          Add header contributor
  Slider.class, "init.js", variablesModel));              with variables model
```

This code first creates a model that returns a map with the variables we want to expose for substitution. Then, it adds the contribution using a static factory method that is useful for JavaScript; when rendered, the method interpolates any variables in the provided model with init.js from the package that contains `Slider`.

The JavaScript file looks like this:

```
var ${javaScriptId};
function init${javaScriptId}() {
  ${javaScriptId} = YAHOO.widget.Slider.getHorizSlider(
    "${backGroundElementId}", "${imageElementId}", ${leftUp},
    ${rightDown}, ${tick});
  ${javaScriptId}.onChange = function(offsetFromStart) {
    document.getElementById("${formElementId}").value=offsetFromStart;
  }
}
```

In the next section, we'll see what makes these behaviors contribute to the header.

10.2.2 *Using the header contributor interface*

In the previous section, the `IHeaderContributor` interface enables the header-contributing behaviors. This interface can be implemented by both components and behaviors, in which case the interface method `renderHead` is automatically called when the page is rendered.

The `renderHead` method is called with an instance of `IHeaderResponse` (org.wicket.markup.html` package). This interface has a `renderString` method, which is used to directly write a string to the header. It also has convenience methods for writing JavaScript and CSS.

You can find the `getResponse` method in `IHeaderResponse`. You can view it as a breakout method for rare cases in which you need to render directly to the response instead of via the other methods.

The `IHeaderContributor` interface is implemented by `AbstractAjaxBehavior`; when you write your own Ajax behaviors, you can override `renderHead` directly if you need to contribute to the head section. For instance, this fragment of an Ajax behavior does that:

```
public abstract class AbstractAutoCompleteBehavior
    extends AbstractDefaultAjaxBehavior {

  public void renderHead(IHeaderResponse response) {
    super.renderHead(response);
    response.renderJavascriptReference(new
    CompressedResourceReference(AutoCompleteBehavior.class,
      "wicket-autocomplete.js"));
  }
...
```

One more method for contributing to the page header is available to Wicket users, as we'll discuss in the next section.

10.2.3 *Using the wicket:head tag*

Doing header contributions as described in the previous sections works well for most cases. But an alternative is available that lets you define header contributions as part of the markup: `<wicket:head>` tags. In some cases, this markup is easier to read—for example, when the contribution consists of multiple lines of static text. You can use these tags for panels, borders, and pages that work with `<wicket:extend>`.

For example, consider this example, which is a panel:

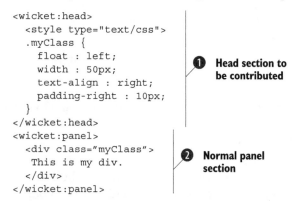

```
<wicket:head>
  <style type="text/css">
  .myClass {
    float : left;
    width : 50px;
    text-align : right;
    padding-right : 10px;
  }
</wicket:head>
<wicket:panel>
  <div class="myClass">
  This is my div.
  </div>
</wicket:panel>
```

❶ **Head section to be contributed**

❷ **Normal panel section**

In addition to the `<wicket:panel>` tags required for a panel definition, this example includes `<wicket:head>` tags ❶. Between those tags, we place a CSS definition; that definition (`myClass`) is used in the panel section ❷.

You can also use Wicket components as you would regularly. Add them to the panel in the right hierarchy, and Wicket will find them.

Auto-links also work well in head sections. For instance, we can rewrite this

```
add(HeaderContributor.forCss(MyComponent.class, "some.css"));
```

as follows:

```
<wicket:head>
  <wicket:link>
    <link href="some.css" rel="stylesheet" type="text/css" />
  </wicket:link>
</wicket:head>
```

This example assumes `MyComponent` is a panel and this is the associated markup.

As you've seen, you can perform header contributions three ways: using one of the special header-contribution behaviors, by implementing `IHeaderContributor` directly with your components or behaviors, and using `<wicket:head>` tags.

Now that we've covered the basics, let's write some Ajax code.

10.3 Ajaxifying the cheese discounts

In this section, we'll refactor the discounts example to use Ajax. We won't develop any new Ajax behaviors and components; rather, we'll reuse the ones that ship with Wicket. The purpose of this section is to give you an idea not only how to implement some basic Ajax functionality with existing components, but also how using Ajax can result in a UI that works differently compared to a traditional web interface. The next section shows what the end result will look like.

10.3.1 Implementing in-place editing

The big change for the discount-list component is that instead of having separate modes for viewing and updating records, the component will have in-place editing. We won't provide a link for switching between editing and displaying; instead, users can directly click the value they want to update.

For the sake of simplicity, we'll only make the percentage editable. Let's look at what we'll be building. Figure 10.5 should look familiar: it's the list without the [edit]/[display] link.

| Gouda, Special season's offer: 10% off! (valid until Jul 15, 2008) |
| Edam, Fresh from the cow: 15% off! (valid until Jul 15, 2008) |

Figure 10.5
The discount list

When a user clicks one of the percentages, the text changes to a text field, as shown in figure 10.6.

| Gouda, Special season's offer: 10   % off! (valid until Jul 15, 2008) |
| Edam, Fresh from the cow: 15% off! (valid until Jul 15, 2008) |

Figure 10.6
Editing the discount

When you leave the field or press Enter, an Ajax round-trip immediately updates the discount. After the discount is updated, the label is shown again instead of an editor.

If the provided value isn't correct for the field, an error message appears and the discount isn't updated. The field stays open (in edit mode) as long as no valid value is provided. You can see this in figure 10.7.

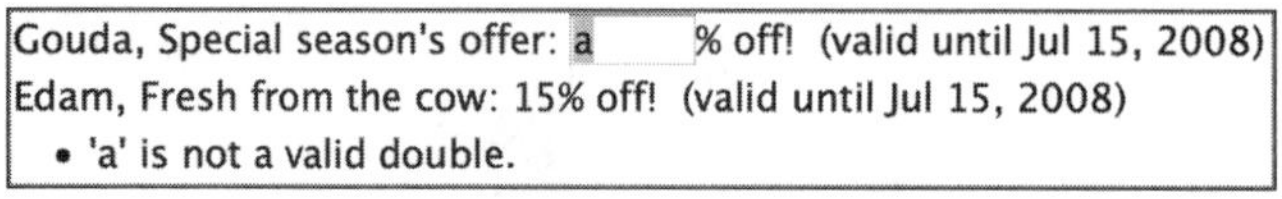

```
Gouda, Special season's offer: a      % off!  (valid until Jul 15, 2008)
Edam, Fresh from the cow: 15% off!  (valid until Jul 15, 2008)
  • 'a' is not a valid double.
```

Figure 10.7
Invalid value for the discount

This is a different UI than the one we had before we used Ajax (although different isn't always better). An Ajax UI can be more intuitive, because it requires fewer user actions to achieve the same result. In addition, users don't have to look for a link to switch to editing mode but instead can click the values they want to change. The previous UI is better suited for bulk editing and may be less confusing because the difference between displaying and editing is more explicit.

Now that you know what the end result will look like, it's time to discuss how we'll implement this new user interface.

10.3.2 *Refactoring the discount list*

With the new approach, we don't need separate panels for editing and viewing the discounts. We'll take the `DiscountsList` component (which was used to view discounts in chapter 8) and replace the `Label` component for the discount percentage with a special component that supports in-place editing. We also need a feedback panel, so we'll add that to the component as well. Listing 10.3 shows the new version of `DiscountsList`.

Listing 10.3 Discounts panel with a feedback panel and editable label

```java
public final class DiscountsPanel extends Panel {
  public DiscountsPanel(String id) {
    super(id);
    final FeedbackPanel feedbackPanel = new FeedbackPanel("feedback");
    add(feedbackPanel);
    add(new RefreshingView("discounts") {
      @Override
      protected Iterator getItemModels() {
        return new ModelIteratorAdapter(DataBase.getInstance()
            .listDiscounts().iterator()) {
          @Override
          protected IModel model(Object object) {
            return new CompoundPropertyModel((Discount) object);
          }
        };
      }

      @Override
      protected void populateItem(Item item) {
        item.add(new Label("cheese.name"));
```

```
        item.add(new EditablePercentageLabel("discount",          ◁─┐  Editable
            feedbackPanel));                                         │  label
        item.add(new Label("description"));
        item.add(new DateFmtLabel("until"));
      }
    });
  }
}
```

The interesting part is the editable label. You can see the code for that component in listing 10.4.

Listing 10.4 Editable label

```
public class EditablePercentageLabel extends AjaxEditableLabel {
    private FeedbackPanel feedbackPanel;    ◁─┐  FeedbackPanel for reporting errors

    public EditablePercentageLabel(String id, FeedbackPanel feedbackPanel) {
        super(id);
        feedbackPanel.setOutputMarkupId(true);   ◁─┐  Let Wicket
        this.feedbackPanel = feedbackPanel;         │  set identifier
    }

    @Override
    public IConverter getConverter(Class type) {
        return new PercentageConverter();
    }

    @Override
    protected void onError(AjaxRequestTarget target) {
        super.onError(target);                        Called when
        target.addComponent(feedbackPanel);           validation fails
    }

    @Override
    protected void onSubmit(AjaxRequestTarget target) {       Called when
        super.onSubmit(target);                           component is
        target.addComponent(feedbackPanel);          successfully updated
        Discount discount = (Discount) getParent().getModelObject();
        DataBase.getInstance().update(discount);
    }
}
```

Here is where things start to get interesting. We'll skip getConverterMethod for now—we'll look at converters in chapter 13—and focus on the Ajax part.

It's important to note that we pass in the feedback panel in the constructor and that we ask Wicket to re-render it using AjaxRequestTarget's addComponent method whenever an error happens (in the onError callback method).

You never have to tell which components should be rendered if you aren't using Ajax; but if you use Wicket's default Ajax implementation, you have to do so. Using Ajax, you typically want only a few areas of the page to be updated, so it wouldn't make sense to render the whole page. And because Wicket can't guess what needs to be updated, you'll have to tell Wicket explicitly.

The good news is that when you tell Wicket what needs to be updated, it takes care of the rest, including all the hard work of updating relevant areas of the client's browser. In order for Wicket to update those areas, you need to instruct Wicket to output the components' DOM identifiers. You do so by calling setOutputMarkupId with true for the components you want to update using Ajax. You don't need to do this on any children of these components: just the top-level component you want to re-render.

To understand better how Wicket works with Ajax, let's look at the implementation of AjaxEditableLabel in the next section.

10.3.3   *How AjaxEditableLabel works*

The source of AjaxEditableLabel is large, because it's a component that's meant to be used in many different contexts. A lot of that code handles corner cases and extensibility. You're interested in learning how the component works without all the extra code, so let's look at a few fragments of its code.

The AjaxEditableLabel is a Panel that has two different modes: one for displaying and one for editing. This is similar to how the non-Ajax version of the discounts list is set up. It has two nested components: a form component (called editor) for editing, and a component (called label) for displaying. At any given time, only one of the two is visible.

Let's examine these nested components separately.

THE NESTED LABEL COMPONENT

The parent component constructs the embedded display component by calling the newLabel method. The default implementation of this method is shown in listing 10.5.

Listing 10.5   Label component of the Ajax editable label

```
protected Component newLabel(MarkupContainer parent,
    String componentId, IModel model) {

  Label label = new Label(componentId, model) {

    @Override
    public IConverter getConverter(Class type) {          Pass through
      IConverter c = AjaxEditableLabel.this.getConverter(type);   parent's
      return c != null ? c : super.getConverter(type);    converter
    }

    @Override
    protected void onComponentTagBody(MarkupStream markupStream,
        ComponentTag openTag) {
      Object modelObject = getModelObject();
      if (modelObject == null || "".equals(modelObject)) {
        replaceComponentTagBody(markupStream, openTag,
            defaultNullLabel());
      } else {                                            Display when
        super.onComponentTagBody(markupStream, openTag);  model is null
      }
```

```
    }
  };                                          Print DOM
  label.setOutputMarkupId(true);  ⊏──── identifier          Add
  label.add(new LabelAjaxBehavior("onclick"));  ⊏──── AjaxBehavior
  return label;
}
```

The key thing in this code is the adding of an Ajax behavior; it attaches an `onclick` event handler to the label, which when triggered results in a callback to the behavior.

Listing 10.6 shows the implementation of `LabelAjaxBehavior`.

Listing 10.6　Label component of the Ajax editable label

```
protected class LabelAjaxBehavior extends AjaxEventBehavior {

  public LabelAjaxBehavior(String event) {
    super(event);
  }

  @Override
  protected void onEvent(AjaxRequestTarget target) {
    onEdit(target);   ⊏── onEdit defined
  }                         in parent class
}
```

This behavior extends `AjaxEventBehavior`, which builds on `AbstractDefaultAjax-Behavior`, so it uses Wicket's default Ajax engine. `AjaxEventBehavior` attaches to a JavaScript event handler (`onclick` in this example, as you can see in listing 10.5) and triggers a callback when the JavaScript event handler is executed. The label in the example is defined in the markup like this

```
<span wicket:id="label">[[label]]</span>%
```

which is expanded to

```
<span onclick="var wcall=wicketAjaxGet(...) != null;}.bind(this));"
  id="label11">15</span>%
```

when it's rendered. The `wicketAjaxGet` function is defined in the wicket-ajax.js Java-Script file, which contains most of Wicket's default Ajax implementation. You'll rarely, if ever, need to access JavaScript functions from wicket-ajax.js directly because Java-Script is abstracted away in the basic Ajax behaviors Wicket provides.

The `LabelAjaxBehavior` calls the `onEdit` method of the parent class when the event is executed. You'll recognize this as a common pattern used by components that nest other components as part of their functionality. When designing the behavior, we wanted users of the behavior to be able to override what happens when the label is clicked. The default implementation is sufficient for most cases, but you never know in what ways users will extend your component. By deferring the real work to an over-ridable method on the parent class, we keep the label an implementation detail but provide users with an easy way to customize the functionality by applying the *template method* design pattern.

The implementation of the `onEdit` method is shown in listing 10.7.

Listing 10.7   Event-handling code for when the edit label is clicked

```
protected void onEdit(AjaxRequestTarget target) {
  label.setVisible(false);
  editor.setVisible(true);
  target.addComponent(AjaxEditableLabel.this);
  target.appendJavascript("{ var el=wicketGet('"
      + editor.getMarkupId() + "');"
      + "   if (el.createTextRange) { "
      + "      var v = el.value; var r = el.createTextRange(); "
      + "      r.moveStart('character', v.length); r.select(); } }");
  target.focusComponent(editor);
}
```

We set the label to `invisible` and the editor to `visible`. The parent component, `AjaxEditableLabel`, is added to the request target for re-rendering, which results in the label and editor also being rendered (because they're visible children of the component). The JavaScript that is sent as part of the Ajax response (using the `append-Javascript` method of `AjaxRequestTarget`) is executed on the client and selects the text of the text field. The call to `focusComponent` finally asks the client to put the focus on the text field.

That's the display part. Now, let's look at how to implement the editing part.

THE NESTED TEXT FIELD COMPONENT

The parent component constructs the embedded edit component by calling the `new-Editor` method; the default implementation appears in listing 10.8.

Listing 10.8   Text field component of the Ajax editable label

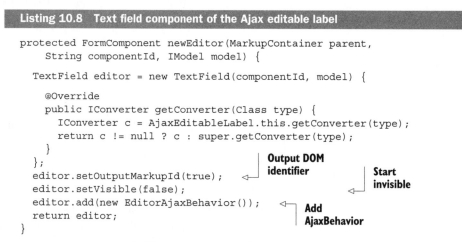

```
protected FormComponent newEditor(MarkupContainer parent,
    String componentId, IModel model) {

  TextField editor = new TextField(componentId, model) {

    @Override
    public IConverter getConverter(Class type) {
      IConverter c = AjaxEditableLabel.this.getConverter(type);
      return c != null ? c : super.getConverter(type);
    }
  };
  editor.setOutputMarkupId(true);      ◁── Output DOM identifier
  editor.setVisible(false);            ◁── Start invisible
  editor.add(new EditorAjaxBehavior());   ◁── Add AjaxBehavior
  return editor;
}
```

No surprises here. As with the label, the interesting part is found in the Ajax behavior. Let's look at `EditorAjaxBehavior`, shown in listing 10.9.

Listing 10.9   Event-handling code for the editor text field

```
protected class EditorAjaxBehavior extends
    AbstractDefaultAjaxBehavior {

  @Override
```

```
    protected void onComponentTag(ComponentTag tag) {
      super.onComponentTag(tag);

      String saveCall = "{"
          + generateCallbackScript("wicketAjaxGet('"
              + getCallbackUrl()
              + "&save=true&'+this.name+'='+wicketEncode(this.value)")
          + "; return false;}";

      String cancelCall = "{"
          + generateCallbackScript("wicketAjaxGet('"
              + getCallbackUrl() + "&save=false'")
          + "; return false;}";

      String keypress = "var kc=wicketKeyCode(event); if (kc==27) "
          + cancelCall
          + " else if (kc!=13) { return true; } else "
          + saveCall;

      tag.put("onblur", saveCall);          ◁─┐ Triggered when
                                                leaving field
      tag.put("onkeypress", keypress);      ◁─┐ Triggered when
    }                                           key is pressed

    @Override
    protected void respond(AjaxRequestTarget target) {
      RequestCycle requestCycle = RequestCycle.get();
      boolean save = Boolean.valueOf(
          requestCycle.getRequest().getParameter("save"))
          .booleanValue();

      if (save) {                           &'+this.name+'='
        editor.processInput();       ◁─┐   provides value

        if (editor.isValid()) {      ◁─┐   Add validation
          onSubmit(target);                 result
        } else {
          onError(target);
        }
      } else {
        onCancel(target);
      }
    }
  }
```

The `EditorAjaxBehavior`'s `onComponentTag` method attaches JavaScript event handlers to the text-field tag. It triggers a save on the `onBlur` event (which is triggered when the text field loses focus) and when the user presses the Enter key. When the user presses the Esc key, `cancel` is triggered.

save and cancel are Ajax calls back to the behavior, which handles them through the respond method. The calls pass a save request parameter to communicate the action that should be performed (save or cancel). The save call also sends the current value of the text field with the request. That's what this does in listing 10.9:

```
    this.name+'='+wicketEncode(this.value)"
```

The call

```
    editor.processInput();
```

lets the component pick up that value and use it to try to update its model value. When that is done, we check whether validation succeeded using the following:

```
if (editor.isValid()) { ...
```

The appropriate method `onSubmit` or `onError` is then called. Those two methods were implemented in listing 10.4.

In the first section of this chapter, we looked at what Ajax is. After that, we discussed header contributions—a crucial construct to enable transparently reusable Ajax components. In this section, we examined the implementation of an Ajax component. The next section will explore some dos and don'ts when you're creating custom Ajax components.

10.4   *Creating your own Ajax components*

The typical pattern for creating custom Ajax components starts with Ajax behaviors. You can either reuse an existing behavior or create one yourself, or even combine a few. Then, you create a component that uses such an Ajax behavior. That component typically hides the behavior and, for instance, adds the behavior to itself in its constructor.

You don't have to use behaviors to implement Ajax components—you can ultimately code everything in, for example, `onComponentTag` and friends—but doing so offers some advantages:

- Ajax behaviors hide the details of Ajax processing well and provide a good way to hook into things like header contributions.
- The range of available Ajax behaviors covers most common use cases so you don't have to implement those behaviors yourself.
- Behaviors can easily be combined and reused in other contexts (that is, other components).

Let Ajax behaviors be the starting point for creating Ajax components. The choice to make is whether to use Wicket's built-in Ajax engine or a third-party Ajax engine, such as Dojo or Scriptaculous.

10.4.1   *Using third-party Ajax engines*

If you want to use a third-party Ajax engine, you typically start by creating an abstract base class for that engine. That base class should extend `AbstractAjaxBehavior`. It's possible to go lower than that class by implementing the `IBehavior`, `IBehavior-Listener`, and `IHeaderContributor` interfaces, but that's not recommended because you'll have to implement everything yourself instead of only the interesting bits.

The minimal thing the base class then does is ensure that the proper JavaScript is contributed when the host component is rendered. You also want to be sure the common JavaScript is contributed only once for all behaviors that use the same engine, and you want to encapsulate these contributions so clients don't have to know anything about them. The behavior in listing 10.10 performs the contributions in the renderHead method, which is declared final so it's guaranteed to be called. Users can override onRenderHead if they wish.

> **Listing 10.10   Abstract behavior that contributes JavaScript dependencies**

```java
public abstract class AbstractScriptaculousBehavior extends
    AbstractAjaxBehavior {

  @Override
  public final void renderHead(IHeaderResponse response) {
    response.renderJavascriptReference(new ResourceReference(
      ScriptaculousAjaxHandler.class, "prototype.js"));
    response.renderJavascriptReference(new ResourceReference(
      ScriptaculousAjaxHandler.class, "scriptaculous.js"));
    response.renderJavascriptReference(new ResourceReference(
      ScriptaculousAjaxHandler.class, "behavior.js"));
    onRenderHead(response);
  }

  protected void onRenderHead(IHeaderResponse response) {
  }
}
```

This could be the base class for Ajax behaviors that use Scriptaculous as their Ajax engine. We use relative package resource references, so the JavaScript files can be found relative to the class in the same package. This is illustrated in figure 10.8.

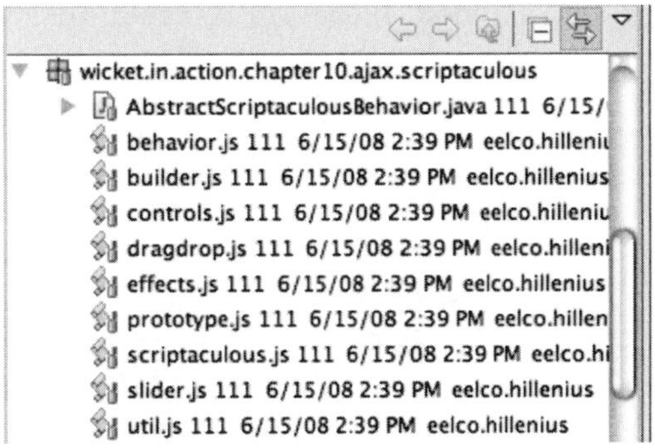

The AbstractScriptaculousBehavior class overrides renderHead to contribute prototype.js, scriptaculous.js, and behavior.js. Note that in addition to overriding that method, Abstract-ScriptaculousBehavior also declares

Figure 10.8   Example package for Scriptaculous Ajax behavior

it as final and defines another method, onRenderHead, which is called at the end of renderHead. This is a common trick to provide customizability while ensuring our own functionality remains in place. We ensure that subclasses can't override our method (renderHead), and provide a customization hook (onRenderHead) that subclasses can override to provide their own code.

The package includes more JavaScript files than are contributed, because the core JavaScript file scriptaculous.js includes the other files. These kinds of inclusions are common with larger JavaScript projects, and they typically involve dependent files that can be found relative to the main files. Fortunately, this isn't a problem for Wicket; scriptaculous.js can load its dependencies, such as builder.js and effects.js, without a problem.

Another nice feature of performing header contributions with package resources is that you don't have to do anything extra to filter double contributions: Wicket takes care of that automatically. If for some reason you're unable to use package resources, you have to do a little more work. This is how such filtering would look if you were to do filtered header contributions yourself:

```
public class SomeHeaderContributor extends AbstractBehavior implements
    IHeaderContributor {
  private static final String id = "foo";

  public void renderHead(IHeaderResponse response) {
    if (!response.wasRendered(id)) {
      response.renderString("<!-- very meaningful contribution -->");
      response.markRendered(id);
    }
  }
}
```

In the `renderHead` method, we check whether our header contributor has been rendered already by checking for our identifier `"foo"`. This identifier should be fairly unique. A typical good value would be the name of the library you're integrating or your behavior's class name.

The last thing left to implement in our custom behavior is the Ajax callback method: `IBehaviorListener`'s `onRequest` method. That method should typically set a request target specific for handling the request.

Suppose we want to be lazy and implement something that forces the subclasses to provide an answer as a plain string. The Scriptaculous base class then looks like this:

```
public abstract class AbstractScriptaculousBehavior extends
    AbstractAjaxBehavior {

  public void onRequest() {
    RequestCycle.get().setRequestTarget(                    ❶ Set simple
      new StringRequestTarget(getAnswer()));                   request target
  }

  @Override
  public final void renderHead(IHeaderResponse response) {
    response.renderJavascriptReference(new ResourceReference(
      AbstractScriptaculousBehavior.class, "prototype.js"));
    response.renderJavascriptReference(new ResourceReference(
      AbstractScriptaculousBehavior.class, "scriptaculous.js"));
    response.renderJavascriptReference(new ResourceReference(
      AbstractScriptaculousBehavior.class, "behavior.js"));
    onRenderHead(response);
  }
                                              ❷ Called when making
  protected abstract String getAnswer();         request target

  protected void onRenderHead(IHeaderResponse response) {
  }
}
```

This version of `AbstractScriptaculousBehavior` has `onRequest` implemented; it utilizes the simplest request target available with Wicket ❶. The `StringRequestTarget` renders the passed-in string as is. In this case, the string is whatever a concrete subclass returns with its `getAnswer` implementation ❷. That would be crude for a real-world implementation, but it gives you an idea of how third-party Ajax support could be built up.

So far in this chapter, we've assumed that all users have JavaScript-enabled browsers and have turned on JavaScript support. This may be a risky assumption; in some cases, it's good to find out more about the client so you can decide whether to take an alternative approach. The next section shows how you can inspect clients' capabilities with Wicket.

10.4.2 *Detecting client capabilities*

Wicket has a built-in mechanism for detecting client capabilities. You can access this information by putting the following statement in your code:

```
WebClientInfo clientInfo = WebRequestCycle.get().getClientInfo();
```

By default, the `User-Agent` header that is part of the request header is used to build the `WebClientInfo` object. This is sufficient for simple cases, but it doesn't guarantee you much when, for instance, you want to assert whether a client supports JavaScript.

Wicket ships with an enhanced client-detection mechanism that involves an intermediate page that executes tests on the client itself before sending this information back and redirecting to the original page. This should be fast enough so clients don't notice, but clients with slower connections may see a flash of the page. This is why it's turned off by default. If you want to turn it on, you have to configure the appropriate setting in the request-cycle settings:

```
getRequestCycleSettings().setGatherExtendedBrowserInfo(true);
```

Now, a bunch of extra properties are available to be read:

```
WebClientInfo clientInfo = WebRequestCycle.get().getClientInfo();
final ClientProperties properties = clientInfo.getProperties();
TimeZone timeZone = properties.getTimeZone();
properties.getBoolean(ClientProperties.NAVIGATOR_JAVA_ENABLED);
properties.getInt(ClientProperties.SCREEN_HEIGHT, -1);
properties.getInt(ClientProperties.SCREEN_WIDTH, -1);
```

NOTE If you configure Wicket to gather extended browser information, don't call `getClientInfo` in a model. If you do, and the client info isn't read, a redirect will be issued in the middle of rendering, which will be denied. Alternatively, you can make sure the redirect is performed at an early stage—for example, your front page.

The page that's used to do the extended client polling is `BrowserInfoPage` in the `org.apache.wicket.markup.html.pages` package. If you have an application that requires users to log in before they can do anything else, it makes sense to put the detecting code in the login form; you swat two flies at once, as the Dutch would say.

If you want to work with your own generic mechanism, you can also provide a custom request cycle and override the `newClientInfo` method. To do that, it may be worth taking a look at the implementation in `WebRequestCycle` and see what you can reuse.

The last option is to do something completely custom. For instance, you can make the browser polling part of your login page and send the information back using hidden fields. Then, when processing the login, you can get the client properties and set the appropriate fields.

We'll finish this chapter by listing common mistakes that people make when working with Wicket and Ajax.

10.5   *Gotchas when working with Wicket and Ajax*

When you work with Ajax, whether or not in combination with Wicket, you're likely to run into a couple of gotchas. Here's how to avoid the most common ones:

- Always let the components you want to re-render through Ajax print out their DOM identifiers. You do this by calling `setOutputMarkupId` with `true`.
- Communicate what you're doing. Latency may feel to the user as if nothing is going on. Consider using a busy indicator, and always communicate things like validation errors. See `WicketAjaxIndicatorAppender` and `IndicatingAjax-Link` for ideas on how to add busy indicators to your components.
- Be careful with Ajax and tables, because you're likely to run into browser issues (specifically, in Internet Explorer) if you combine the two. We've found it works best to repaint the entire table when working with Ajax rather than try to replace sections of it. This isn't the most efficient solution, but it seems to be the most reliable.
- Understand specific limitations of components such as `ListView` and `Repeat-ingView` when you use them with Ajax. Wicket takes care of a lot of magic, but sometimes a few rough edges are left. See the wiki on the Wicket website and mailing list archives for discussions if you run into trouble.

As an example of a gotcha, look at what happens if we try to refresh a `ListView` directly using Ajax. The following snippet shows the Java code and markup illustrating our example:

```
ListView lv = new ListView("editors",
                    Arrays.asList("Tiffany", "Mary", "Cynthia")) {
    @Override protected void populateItem(Item item) {
        item.add(new Label("name", item.getModelObjectAsString()));
    }
}
lv.setOutputMarkupId(true);
add(lv);

<!-- markup -->
<ul>
<li wicket:id="editors"><span wicket:id="name"></span></li>
</ul>
```

This example generates the following markup:

```
<ul>
<li wicket:id="editors"><span wicket:id="name">Tiffany</span></li>
<li wicket:id="editors"><span wicket:id="name">Mary</span></li>
<li wicket:id="editors"><span wicket:id="name">Cynthia</span></li>
</ul>
```

As you can see, the `ListView` doesn't produce any markup identifiers. This is because we set the flag on the `ListView` component, not on the `Item` components. You'd expect the `ul` tag to receive a markup identifier, but the `ListView` doesn't even know the `ul` tag exists. Remember that `ListView` is a component that repeats its markup and uses the `Item` as the container that receives the markup. Calling `setOutputMarkupId` on a `ListView` has no effect. This is one reason why refreshing a `ListView` directly using Ajax doesn't work. There are more technical issues, but going through them all would be boring.

The solution to this problem is easy: either let Wicket repaint a suitable parent (for example, a panel or form that is a parent of the `ListView`) or create a parent for this special purpose. We could rewrite our example as follows:

```
WebMarkupContainer wmc = new WebMarkupContainer("parent");
wmc.setOutputMarkupId(true);
ListView lv = new ListView("editors",
                    Arrays.asList("Tiffany", "Mary", "Cynthia")) {
    @Override protected void populateItem(Item item) {
        item.add(new Label("name", item.getModelObjectAsString()));
    }
}
wmc.add(lv);

<!-- markup -->
<ul wicket:id="parent">
<li wicket:id="editors"><span wicket:id="name"></span></li>
</ul>
```

In this example, we first create a `WebMarkupContainer` that functions as a wrapper around our `ListView`. Next, we tell the `WebMarkupContainer` to write out its markup identifier. Finally, we add our `ListView` to the `WebMarkupContainer`. In the markup, we attach the `WebMarkupContainer` to the `ul` tag. Using this improved example, we're now able to repaint the `ListView` by adding the `WebMarkupContainer` to an `AjaxRequestTarget`.

To prevent mistakes like those demonstrated, keep in mind that you can't add a repeater directly to an `AjaxRequestTarget` with the current Wicket version—you'll get a runtime error if you try.

Many good resources go into more detail about the issues you may run into when using Ajax, such as http://ajaxpatterns.org and http://ajaxian.com. Keep track of these sites when you use Ajax in your applications.

10.6   *Summary*

We've spent the last few chapters discussing custom components from different angles. Chapter 8 was about the basics of custom components, and this chapter examined components that use techniques like DHTML and Ajax to create a richer user experience.

We looked at what Ajax is, and we discussed Wicket's enabling technology for Ajax and other rich components header contributions. Wicket components and behaviors can contribute JavaScript and CSS to the head section of the page they're nested in. This comes in handy when you're designing self-contained components that depend on JavaScript and CSS.

The main topic of this chapter was Ajax. First, we discussed a couple of advantages and disadvantages. Then, we revamped the cheese store's discount list so you could see the difference between an Ajax approach and a traditional one in terms of both the UI and the code you end up with. We also took a peek at the internals of one of Wicket's built-in Ajax components to get an idea of how you can bridge the Java and client JavaScript worlds. We ended by looking briefly at how to get started when you want to develop Ajax components from scratch.

In the next chapter, we'll discuss how to build in security at a component level.

Part 4

Preparing for the real world

In the previous parts of this book, you learned how to use Wicket's components and make your own. Now you can start designing pages and custom components, and finally ship your application. But an evil world lurks outside. How can you make your application secure? Chapter 11 introduces Wicket's security features. You'll learn how to apply authentication and authorization to secure (parts of) your application.

But the world is not only an evil place (at least, parts of it); billions of users don't speak your language. Wicket's internationalization and localization support gives you the means to reach out to the world. Chapter 12 discusses how you can prepare your application for an international crowd.

When you build an application, chances are you're using a dependency-injection framework such as Spring or Guice. In chapter 13, you'll learn how to implement such a multitiered architecture with Spring as an example. When you use Spring or Guice, you probably use an object-relational mapping framework such as Hibernate, iBatis, Cayenne, or OpenJPA. Chapter 13 shows you how to use Hibernate together with Wicket.

Before you unleash your application on the unsuspecting world, you may want to read chapter 14. This chapter discusses how you can test your Wicket pages and components. You'll learn how to create a search-engine-friendly URL schema, how to configure your application for maximum performance, and how to monitor your application once it's in production.

11

Securing your application

In the previous few chapters, we looked at custom components while we developed the discount-list example. In this chapter, we'll take that example and secure it. The discount list has a function to edit discounts, which is currently available to all users of the web application. We'll change that so only specific users—administrators—can edit this list.

The first step in doing so is to ensure that users are who they say they are. This is called *authentication*. The simplest and most common form of authentication requires users to provide a username and password combination. This is what we'll develop in the first half of this chapter.

In addition to authenticating users, we also need to authorize them. Because we want only administrators to have access to the discount-editing functionality, normal users shouldn't be aware of the functionality. We'll discuss how to implement that kind of protection in the second half of this chapter.

We didn't want to title this chapter "Security," because that would have increased its scope considerably. But we'd like to say a few words about how Wicket is secure by default.

11.1 *Session-relative pages*

With Wicket, if you don't code using bookmarkable pages, you use *session-relative* pages—Wicket's default way of coding web applications. Page instances are kept on the server, and you ask Wicket (through your browser) for a certain page by providing the page number, the version, and the component that is the target of the request. This works contrary to the REST architectural pattern, which states that servers shouldn't keep state: clients provide servers with the relevant state when they issue requests. As you saw in chapter 1, REST is great for scalability but lousy for the programming model. Now, we get to another problem with REST: the pattern is inherently unsafe, whereas Wicket's server-state pattern is safe (although not watertight) by default.

For instance, suppose you implement the functionality of removing an object using a link like this:

```
final MyObject myObject = ...
add(new Link("remove") {
    @Override
    public void onClick() {
        myDao.remove(myObject);
    }
});
```

You never need to worry about pimple-faced 14-year-olds trying to hack your web application. To do so, they would have to hijack the session and then guess the right page identifiers and version numbers, which would be relative to the session and the relevant component paths. You'd have to be a persistent hacker to pull that off. You can make your Wicket application even more secure from the default by encrypting requests with, for instance, `CryptedUrlWebRequestCodingStrategy`.

The REST variant of building your application would use bookmarkable pages like this:

```
public DeleteMyObjectPage(PageParameters p) {
    super(p);
    Long id = p.getLong("id");
    myDao.remove(MyObject.class, id);
}
```

This example, which is similar to how you'd use *actions* or *commands* with Model 2 frameworks, is unsafe in two distinct ways. The URL of `DeleteMyObjectPage` can be guessed, thus exposing that functionality to misuse. Even if users are authorized to access that page, and allowing access itself isn't a problem, they may need to be restricted so that they can delete only certain instances of `MyObject`. Without explicit protection, they can guess identifiers or write a script to delete parts of the database. That means extra checks that need to be coded and potential security holes that may be overlooked; the session-relative approach doesn't require you to do anything extra in this respect.

The ability to secure your application by using session-relative addressing is a big advantage of Wicket over most of its competitors. But depending on session-relative addressing doesn't always cover everything you need. You may have good reasons to make functionality bookmarkable, and in that case you may need fine-grained control over how your components are rendered, for instance. We'll fill in these gaps here, starting with authentication.

11.2 Implementing authentication

In this part of the chapter, we'll build pages for signing in and signing out users, and we'll build a panel that shows users their authentication status (whether or not they're signed in).

Users' authentication status is something you should have readily available throughout the period a user is active on the site. You'll often need that information when deciding whether a user can access a page, see a link, and so forth (performing authorization). A good place to store authorization information is in the Wicket session object, because it's available throughout the user's session. Let's implement this in the next section.

11.2.1 Keeping track of the user

To store information about users, we'll create a User class. In it, we'll store the user's full name, unique username, and password, and a field that says whether the user is an administrator. A User object is created when a user successfully authenticates; the object is stored in the Wicket session. To achieve that, we need to create a custom session that keeps a reference to the currently logged-in user. If that reference is null, it means that the current user didn't authenticate (yet).

Figure 11.1 shows a diagram of the session and user classes.

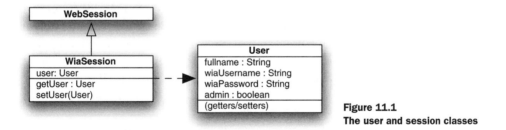

Figure 11.1
The user and session classes

The Java code for the custom session class is shown in listing 11.1.

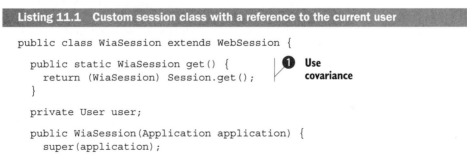

Listing 11.1 Custom session class with a reference to the current user

```java
public class WiaSession extends WebSession {

    public static WiaSession get() {
        return (WiaSession) Session.get();
    }

    private User user;

    public WiaSession(Application application) {
        super(application);
```

① Use covariance

```
  }
  public boolean isAuthenticated() {          ❷  Utility
    return (user != null);                         method
  }
  ..(getUser/setUser)
}
```

The `WiaSession` class ❶ extends `WebSession` and uses Java's covariance feature (Java 5 and up) so that clients don't have to cast the session but instead do this:

```
WiaSession s = WiaSession.get();
```

Having the `isAuthenticated` method ❷ isn't strictly necessary either, because clients could call `getUser` and check on `null`; but providing this separate method is a good way to hide this implementation detail of how `null` is interpreted.

You can instruct Wicket to use custom sessions by overriding the `newSession` method in your application class:

```
@Override
public Session newSession(Request request, Response response) {
  return new WiaSession(request);
}
```

Wicket creates sessions for users automatically.

Now that we've built the facilities for keeping the authentication information, we can build the authentication functionality.

11.2.2 *Authenticating the user*

Authentication is done many ways. These approaches are generally classified in three categories: something users have (a chip card), users' biometrics (fingerprints), and something users know (username/password). To keep things simple, we'll implement authentication based on a username/password that users enter on a sign-in page.

The sign-in page should provide the functionality to process a login attempt. It should know how to validate the input the user provides; and if the attempt is successful, it should save the relevant information in the session and redirect the user to where she wanted to go in the first place.

When we're done, the sign-in page will look like the one in figure 11.2.

Figure 11.2
The sign-in page

Let's implement this as a regular page with the form implemented as a private class. A partial implementation is displayed in listing 11.2.

Listing 11.2 The sign-in page

```
public class SigninPage extends WebPage {

  private static class SignInForm extends StatelessForm {     ◁   Stateless
                                                             ❶    form
    private String wiaPassword;
```

```
    private String wiaUsername;

    public SignInForm(String id) {
      super(id);
      setModel(new CompoundPropertyModel(this));
      add(new TextField("wiaUsername"));
      add(new PasswordTextField("wiaPassword"));
    }
  }
  ...
}
```

2 Special password component

This is a form like those you've seen many times. But two things may have caught your attention.

First, rather than a regular text field, we use a password text field **2**. This component attaches to an HTML input tag of type password, and it clears the input every time it renders so it won't be sent back to the client if authentication fails.

Second, the form extends StatelessForm **1**. It's possible (although probably rare) for a user to go to the login screen, decide to do something else for an hour, then try to log in using that page of the now-expired session, and be confronted with a session-expired message. We avoid that situation by making the login form (and page) stateful so the login functionality is bookmarkable.

What happens when the form is submitted? In the onSubmit method, we check whether the user is authenticated; if so, we redirect to the originally requested URL, if applicable (more on that later in this chapter). The implementation is shown in listing 11.3.

Listing 11.3   Logging in users

```
@Override
public final void onSubmit() {
  if (signIn(wiaUsername, wiaPassword)) {
    if (!continueToOriginalDestination()) {
      setResponsePage(getApplication().getHomePage());
    }
  } else {
    error("Unknown username/ password");
  }
}

private boolean signIn(String username, String password) {
  if (username != null && password != null) {
    User user = DataBase.getInstance().findUser(username);
    if (user != null) {
      if (user.getWiaPassword().equals(password)) {
        WiaSession.get().setUser(user);
        return true;
      }
    }
  }
  return false;
}
```

The `signIn` method checks the database for the provided username and password and saves the user in the session if the check succeeds. If it does, the method `continueToOriginalDestination` is called on the component (it doesn't matter on which component, because it ultimately passes the call to the current page map). That method finds out whether an interception URL was set prior to this call; if so, the method sets a special request target that initiates a redirect to the original URL. The method returns `true` if an interception URL was set. If no such URL was set, we don't want to keep displaying the login page; instead, we redirect to the application's home page.

And with this, users can now log in. To make the example more realistic, we should show users an indication that they're logged in. In the next section, we'll develop a user panel for this purpose.

11.2.3 *Building a user panel*

The user panel displays the message "Signed in as (user)" followed by a link the user can click to sign out. This functionality is implemented in listing 11.4.

Listing 11.4   Panel that displays the logged-in user and a sign-out link

```
public class UserPanel extends Panel {

  public UserPanel(String id, Class<? extends Page> logoutPageClass) {
    super(id);
    add(new Label("fullname", new PropertyModel(this,
        "session.user.fullname")));
    PageParameters parameters = new PageParameters();
    parameters.add(SignOutPage.REDIRECTPAGE_PARAM, logoutPageClass
        .getName());
    add(new BookmarkablePageLink("signout", SignOutPage.class,
        parameters) {
      @Override
      public boolean isVisible() {
        return WiaSession.get().isAuthenticated();
      }
    });
    add(new Link("signin") {

      @Override
      public void onClick() {
        throw new RestartResponseAtInterceptPageException(
            SigninPage.class);
      }

      @Override
      public boolean isVisible() {
        return !WiaSession.get().isAuthenticated();
      }
    });
  }
}
```

This is the HTML that goes with it (UserPanel.html):

```
<wicket:panel>
 <wicket:enclosure child="signout">
  Signed in as <i><span wicket:id="fullname">[name]</span></i>
    <a wicket:id="signout">sign out</a>
 </wicket:enclosure>
 <a wicket:id="signin">sign in</a>
</wicket:panel>
```

In the `UserPanel`, we created a model that extends `LoadableDetachableModel` for representing the current user (if any). Next, we instantiate a property model that works on that user model, with the property expression `fullname`. Property models are smart enough not to crash when target objects (the objects the expression is supposed to work on) are `null`. If there is no user in the session—in which case the model's `load` method would return `null`—nameModel returns `null`, and the label renders blank.

The `isVisible` overrides ensure that either the sign-in link is displayed when the user isn't signed in yet, or the sign-out link is displayed when the user is signed in. We also use a `<wicket:enclosure>` tag to couple the section that displays some static text and the username to the visibility of the sign-out link, so that the whole section is displayed only when a user is signed in.

NOTE You may wonder why we call the sign-out link with a parameter. The only reason is that redirecting to a specified sign-out page is such a basic facility, you probably won't want to implement it over and over again as we'd have to do if we hard-coded the location to redirect to. Alternatively, you could redirect to the application's home page.

In the next section, we'll create the sign-out page.

11.2.4 Building a page for signing out

The sign-out page is implemented in a generic fashion, so we can reuse it in multiple applications. The code of the sign-out page is shown in listing 11.5.

Listing 11.5   Generic sign-out page

```
public class SignOutPage extends WebPage {

  public static final String REDIRECTPAGE_PARAM = "redirectpage";

  @SuppressWarnings("unchecked")
  public SignOutPage(final PageParameters parameters) {
    String page = parameters.getString(REDIRECTPAGE_PARAM);
    Class<? extends Page> pageClass;
    if (page != null) {
      try {
        pageClass = (Class<? extends Page>) Class.forName(page);
      } catch (ClassNotFoundException e) {
        throw new RuntimeException(e);
      }
    } else {
```

```
        pageClass = getApplication().getHomePage();
    }
    getSession().invalidate();         ◁──┐  Invalidate
    setResponsePage(pageClass);           │  session
  }
}
```

The only thing this page does is terminate the session and redirect to a given page. We don't need anything special for markup. This is enough:

```
<html></html>
```

The interesting part in the sign-out page is the call to invalidate the session. Whenever you want to invalidate the session, you have two methods at your disposal: Session.invalidate and Session.invalidateNow. Typically, you should use the first variant, which sets a flag that's processed at the end of the request but allows the request in progress to keep accessing the session without problems. The advantage of this approach is that everything renders as usual, giving any components the chance to clean up properly, and so on. We can't think of a good reason to call invalidate-Now, unless you have, for instance, a special security constraint you want to enforce.

NOTE   Always set a bookmarkable response page after you invalidate the session. If we passed a page instance in the sign-off page, it wouldn't be available on the next request because the session it was recorded in would no longer be available.

This concludes the first part of the chapter on authentication. We built a simple user class and a custom Wicket session to hold a reference to the user, we built sign-in and sign-out forms, and we built a panel that displays the user's authentication status.

Now that we can authenticate users, we can implement authorization.

11.3   *Implementing authorization*

For our example, just authenticating users isn't enough. We also want to determine whether users may edit discounts. Checking whether a user is allowed to do or see something is what we refer to as *authorization.*

In this part of the chapter, we'll change the discount's functionality so that it's only available to authenticated users. We'll also make sure only admin users can edit discounts; normal users won't even see the Edit link, let alone be able to access the functionality.

There are multiple ways to protect your pages from unwanted access. A simple approach, for instance, is to let your pages extend a base page that checks authorization in its constructor. It can throw an exception or issue a redirect if authorization fails.

But using inheritance to take care of such things limits flexibility. It's often better to implement authorization as a cross-cutting concern. Wicket has a mechanism for doing that: authorization strategies.

11.3.1   *Introducing authorization strategies*

The IAuthorizationStrategy interface is especially designed for securing web applications. We'll create an implementation of this interface that denies unauthorized users access to the discounts page and that decides whether the Edit link is visible based on what kind of user is signed in.

The authorization strategy interface is defined in listing 11.6.

Listing 11.6 `IAuthorizationStrategy` interface

```
public interface IAuthorizationStrategy {

  boolean isInstantiationAuthorized(Class componentClass);

  boolean isActionAuthorized(Component component, Action action);

  public static final IAuthorizationStrategy ALLOW_ALL =
      new IAuthorizationStrategy() {
    public boolean isActionAuthorized(Component c, Action action) {
      return true;
    }

    public boolean isInstantiationAuthorized(final Class c) {
      return true;
    }
  };
}
```

This interface defines two separate events where authorization is checked:

- On component creation
- On specific actions on components after creation

Wicket checks component creation using component-instantiation listeners. These listeners are registered with the application class, and they're notified about every component that is constructed. Schematically, notification looks like the diagram in figure 11.3.

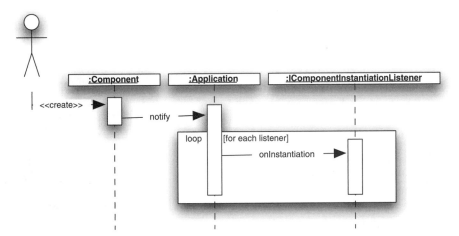

Figure 11.3 Instantiation listeners are notified when components are in the process of construction. Because the components are still in the first stage of constructing themselves, construction can be vetoed safely. Even if you execute authorization-dependent functionality in your constructor, if the listener vetoes it, that functionality won't be executed.

NOTE Be careful with component-instantiation listeners. They are called for every component, so it's important to keep your processing efficient. Also keep in mind that the components are still under construction. The component's members are yet to be initialized.

The code fragment in listing 11.7 is executed in the constructor of Wicket's Application base class.

Listing 11.7 Instantiation check of authorization strategies

```
addComponentInstantiationListener(
    new IComponentInstantiationListener() {
    public void onInstantiation(final Component component) {
      if (!getSecuritySettings().getAuthorizationStrategy()
        .isInstantiationAuthorized(component.getClass())) {
        getSecuritySettings()
          .getUnauthorizedComponentInstantiationListener()
          .onUnauthorizedInstantiation(component);
      }
    }
  }
});
```

Note that authorizing component instantiation and taking action when it fails is abstracted in two separate interfaces. This makes it easier to write them in a generic way.

The default authorization-strategy setting allows all components to be constructed. The default implementation of the unauthorized-instantiation listener throws an exception. We need custom behavior for both. In the next section, we'll protect the page that displays the cheese discounts so that only logged-in users can access it.

11.3.2 *Protecting the discounts page*

Authorization strategies work on pages as they do on regular components. After all, pages are Wicket components like any others.

If you want to protect certain pages against unauthorized access, you first have to decide how you'll differentiate between protected and nonprotected pages. For instance, you could make it a rule that protected web pages must extend a certain base class, say ProtectedPage. And of course in that case, a sign-in page should *not* extend ProtectedPage. In figure 11.4, you can see this depicted for our example: Dis-

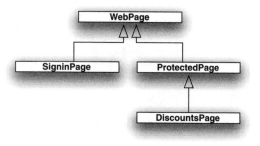

Figure 11.4 Protected and unprotected pages

countsPage extends ProtectedPage, but SigninPage, which should be accessible without authenticating, extends from WebPage directly.

The next thing we need to do is to check whether the current page is extending ProtectedPage; if it does, we have to check whether the requesting user is authenticated.

If the user isn't authenticated, and the requested page extends `ProtectedPage`, we must display the sign-in page. Otherwise, we'll let the request proceed.

To implement this, we create a class that implements both the authorization check and the action to be taken when authorization fails:

```
public final class WiaAuthorizationStrategy implements
    IAuthorizationStrategy,
    IUnauthorizedComponentInstantiationListener
```

The authorization check is implemented by providing an `isInstantiationAuthorized` method:

```
public boolean isInstantiationAuthorized(Class componentClass) {

  if (ProtectedPage.class.isAssignableFrom(componentClass)) {      ⟵─┐
    return WiaSession.get().isAuthenticated();                        │
  }                                                          Check only
  return true;      ⟵─┐ Allow all other              protected pages
}                       components
```

What we do is simple: we check whether the passed-in component extends `Protected-Page`, and when it does, we return whether the user is authenticated by querying the session object. If the check returns `false`, the other interface is called. For that interface, we provide an implementation with the same class:

```
public void onUnauthorizedInstantiation(Component component) {
  throw new RestartResponseAtInterceptPageException(
      SigninPage.class);
}
```

Here you see an interesting use of a special kind of exceptions in Wicket: *abort exceptions*. Such exceptions instruct Wicket to abort the current request, and—depending on the implementation—take an alternative action. In this case, Wicket stops what it was doing and redirects to the sign-in page. Wicket will also remember how the current request was issued, so it can reissue the request when the user successfully signs in. Remember, we did just that in the sign-in page. In figure 11.5, you can see how abort exceptions fit into Wicket's class hierarchy.

Abort exceptions are designed to prematurely break the flow of processing. Just as it's considered bad practice to use exceptions for normal application flow (because doing so produces code that is more difficult to follow, and because using exceptions is relatively expensive), you shouldn't go overboard using abort exceptions. But in this case, they're exactly what we need, because if a user isn't authorized, we want to stop constructing those objects right away. Not only is this approach more efficient, but it also does away with any risk that code will be executed (for example, performing database calls) that should never be allowed for an unauthorized user.

That's the first step in protecting the discounts page. Users who aren't authenticated are always redirected to the login page. Only authenticating successfully gives them access to the discounts page.

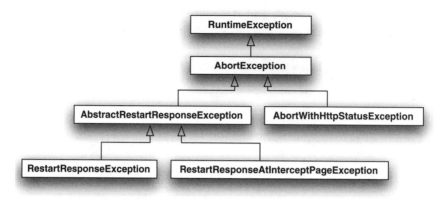

Figure 11.5 Examples of abort exceptions

To make this example complete, we need to protect the edit functionality from users who aren't administrators. Although technically we could achieve this using pages—we'd have a page that only displays discounts and another that also shows the Edit link—it's more elegant to use component-level authorization. The next section shows you how.

11.3.3 *Disabling the Edit link for unauthorized users*

Let's start with a straightforward implementation of hiding a link from users who aren't administrators. We do so by overriding isVisible and letting that method return true only when the user is authenticated and is an administrator. The code is shown in listing 11.8.

Listing 11.8 Protecting the mode link by overriding `isVisible`

```
Link modeLink = new Link("modeLink") {
  public void onClick() {
    inEditMode = !inEditMode;
    setContentPanel();
  }

  @Override
  public boolean isVisible() {
    WiaSession session = WiaSession.get();
    return session.isAuthenticated() && session.getUser().isAdmin();
  }
};
```

Not much is wrong with this implementation. But if you were working on a large project with many such components and with more complex authorization rules that differed between components, you'd soon end up with a lot of code duplication.

A declarative approach will work better here. Instead of overriding isVisble, we declare the authorization attributes on the component. And we implement an *authorization strategy*: an algorithm that decides about authorization only once. We put this in a central place.

There are many ways to support declaring authorization attributes. We'll use Java's annotation feature, which was introduced with Java 5; annotations are terse and easy to implement. Let's call the annotation AdminOnly. Listing 11.9 shows how the annotation is defined.

Listing 11.9   AdminOnly annotation

```
@Retention(RetentionPolicy.RUNTIME)
@Target(ElementType.TYPE)
@Inherited
public @interface AdminOnly { }
```

Because it doesn't have any attributes, AdminOnly is nothing more than a tagging interface. In real projects, you'd probably include more information, such as the kind of roles it applies to. But in this case, we're letting it function like an on/off switch. In case you aren't familiar with annotations, the statement that says the retention is runtime means the annotation will be available at runtime, and the target annotation declares that it's to be used on class definitions.

Annotations can't be coupled to anonymous classes, so we have to make the link a private class. Listing 11.10 shows the link annotated with AdminOnly.

Listing 11.10   Protecting the mode link using an annotation

```
@AdminOnly
private class ModeLink extends Link {

  ModeLink(String id) {
    super(id);
  }

  @Override
  public void onClick() {
    inEditMode = !inEditMode;
    setContentPanel();
  }
}
```

The functionality we're after is as follows: whenever we annotate a component with the AdminOnly annotation, the component is rendered only for users who are administrators. This is where we go back to the authorization strategy and implement the other method of the authorization-strategy interface: isActionAuthorized. Wicket calls this method to find out whether a component may be rendered and whether a component is enabled. This information is used in a variety of ways, which can be specific to individual components. For instance, some form components set the disabled="disabled" attribute on the tag they're attached to, which makes the field read-only in the user's browser. User input isn't allowed on disabled components (which is an extra check, because disabled HTML input fields normally aren't part of form submits); and, for instance, links aren't executed when disabled.

By default, Wicket ships with checks on `enabled` and `render`, but you can extend these cases if you wish. For this example, we only care about the `render` action, which is defined in `Component` as follows:

```
public static final Action RENDER = new Action(Action.RENDER);
```

The implementation of the action check is shown in listing 11.11.

Listing 11.11 Component-level checks of `isActionAuthorized`

```
public boolean isActionAuthorized(Component component, Action action) {
  if (action.equals(Component.RENDER)) {
    Class<? extends Component> c = component.getClass();
    AdminOnly adminOnly = c.getAnnotation(AdminOnly.class);
    if (adminOnly != null) {
      User user = WiaSession.get().getUser();
      return (user != null && user.isAdmin());
    }
  }
  return true;
}
```

As you can see, the implementation first checks whether the action is a `render` action, after which it checks whether the component is annotated with `AdminOnly`. If it is, the implementation checks whether the user is an administrator.

When we place the user panel on the discount page, it looks like figure 11.6 for a regular user. There is no trace of the Edit link.

Figure 11.6   Signed in as a regular user

Figure 11.7 shows the same page, but now it's rendered for a user who is an administrator.

Figure 11.7   Signed in as an administrator

Voila! The Edit link is available, and the discounts page is safe.

> ## Wicket projects that implement authorization and authentication
>
> This chapter looked at the basic mechanism for authorization and authentication. We built an authorization strategy from scratch. Although custom strategies aren't hard to build from scratch, several support projects built on top of Wicket specifically target authorization and authentication.
>
> `wicket-auth-roles`, one of Wicket's core projects, provides a simple implementation based on roles and declaring security for components using either annotations or Wicket's metadata facility. If your needs are simple, this may be the project for you. It's easy to use and extend, and you may want to look at the code just to get some inspiration.
>
> Two Wicket Stuff projects, `wicket-security-wasp` and `wicket-security-swarm`, take a slightly different approach. They provide a solution that is built around a centralized repository of authorization rules. The `wicket-security-wasp` project provides the general framework, and `wicket-security-swarm` provides an implementation that works like (and partially with) Java Authentication and Authorization Service (JAAS).

11.4 Summary

In this chapter, you learned the basics of authentication and authorization with Wicket. We made the cheese-discounts functionality secure so it's available only for logged-in users, and we made sure only administrators can access the edit functionality.

We kept the authorization example simple. For instance, we used a boolean administrator property in the user object; in real life you'd probably use groups or roles (they're more flexible). Also, we only toggled the visibility of the Edit link. This prevents users with insufficient rights from using the edit functionality, because they can't reach it. But this approach doesn't prevent other programmers from instantiating the panel without enforcing the authorization check. You could consider preventing construction of the edit panel when the current user isn't authorized. The authorization-strategy interface is simple, but you can make the implementation of your authorization model as fancy as you want.

Authorization and authentication are just a subset of security. Other security concepts, such as using Wicket with SSL and securing cookies, are beyond the scope for this book. If you need more information, you can find discussions in the mailing list archives (see for instance http://www.nabble.com/Apache-Wicket-f13974.html), and articles on security are available on Wicket's wiki.

In the next chapter, we'll keep building the discounts list example, but this time from a different angle: internationalization and localization.

Conquer the world with l10n and i18n

12

In this chapter:

- Supporting multiple languages with your web application
- Is that the second of May or the fifth of February?

As part of the previous chapter, you learned how to restrict access and optionally render or hide components depending on the user's session. In this chapter, we'll look at how you can vary what is displayed to users depending on their locale. A *locale* represents a geographical, political, and/or cultural region. In computing, it usually groups a set of parameters that represent the user's language and country. In Java, this is supported through the `Locale` object.

Localization refers to the adaptation of your application for one or more specific locales. A related term is *internationalization*, which encompasses all techniques that enable applications to be localized: being able to conveniently maintain different languages, handling different date and number formats, using the proper encoding type, and so forth. For the sake of simplicity, we'll talk only about localization in this chapter, even if it sometimes would be more precise to talk about internationalization.

NOTE Localization is commonly referred to as l10n, where 10 is the number of letters between *l* and *n*. In the same fashion, internationalization is often referred to as i18n.

Localizing components and applications can involve a large range of items. Typically, the most important are as follows:

- *Alphabets and scripts*—The ASCII character set is fine when you work with the English language; but if you need to work with Chinese, Russian, or Thai, ASCII won't cut it. Unicode is a widely supported encoding scheme that enables you to deal with a large variety of alphabets and scripts. Java standardized support for it, and we take full advantage of these built-in capabilities.
- *Formats*—Different locales typically use different formats for dates/times and numbers. For instance, the first of February is written 2/1 in the US, but in The Netherlands it's written 1-2.

In addition, you need to consider a number of issues from locale to locale, such as the patterns of bank-account numbers; government-assigned numbers like Social Security numbers and postal codes; and things like calendars (Gregorian or Buddhist), weights, measures, currencies, and so on. And we haven't even scratched the surface, when you consider cultural differences in the meaning of colors and numbers and other locally sensitive considerations and customs.

Wicket's support for localization can be summed up in the following points:

- Locale-aware support for conversions from things like numbers and dates in Java to text, and back again. You can configure converters globally or per component.
- Locale-aware markup loading. By following a simple naming pattern, Wicket automatically uses the correct locale-specific markup files. This is extended beyond locales to let you implement variations within locales.
- Extended resource-bundle support. On top of what Java supports through resource bundles, including the new XML format for property bundles, Wicket has a powerful lookup system for messages that, among other things, takes the class hierarchy and runtime component hierarchy into account. It also supports easy-to-use parameter substitutions.
- Special tags for localizing text on your pages without the need to explicitly mirror them with Wicket Java components.
- A range of components, models, and utility classes—such as the `Localizer` class—to make creating localized web applications a breeze.
- A message-replacement mechanism that fails fast when your application runs in development mode but is lenient when it runs in production mode. You'll find bugs quickly when you're developing; but if you miss any, your clients won't see error pages.

We'll touch on most of these items when we apply them in practice with our ongoing example.

NOTE   Make sure you use the multilanguage Java Development Kit (JDK) and have a browser that supports unicode if you need advanced localization features.

We'll start with how Wicket supports developing for multiple languages.

12.1   *Supporting multiple languages*

Probably the most important capability you need when localizing applications is the ability to display pages in different languages. In this section, we'll develop English, Dutch, and Thai versions of the discounts list we developed in the previous chapter. As a teaser, here are screenshots of the Dutch and Thai versions—you saw the English version in chapter 11. Figure 12.1 shows the Dutch version.

And figure 12.2 shows the Thai version.

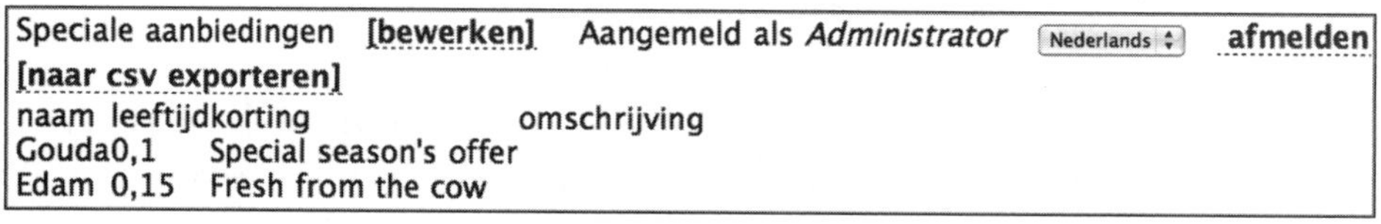

Figure 12.1   The Dutch version of the discounts list

Figure 12.2   The Thai version of the discounts list

At right on these screens is a drop-down menu that displays the current locale. It lists the available languages (English, Dutch, and Thai) in the language of the currently selected locale. Notice that this is the component we developed in chapter 8.

When a user selects a locale from that drop-down menu, that locale is set as the current one for the session. This is recognized by Wicket, and it automatically loads all the proper markup and messages automatically.

12.1.1   *Localizing the UserPanel*

Instead of putting all the text directly in HTML files, as we've done so far, we'll put the locale-dependent text in separate files. It's much easier to maintain that way (you have all the locale-dependent text together instead of scattered throughout your markup), and this approach enables you to let a third party do the translations.

We'll take the user panel as an example. Right now, the markup of the user panel is as shown in listing 12.1.

Listing 12.1   UserPanel.html without localization

```
<wicket:panel>
  Signed in as
   <i><span wicket:id="fullname">[name]</span></i>
    <select wicket:id="localeSelect" />
    <a wicket:id="signout">signout</a>
</wicket:panel>
```

The first step in localizing pages and components is to identify the locale-dependent parts. In this case, we can recognize two variable parts, which are marked in figure 12.3.

Signed in as *Administrator*   English⌄   **signout**

Figure 12.3   The user panel

The marked parts, Signed in as and signout, haven't yet been localized. We don't have to localize the user's name, and we left out the language-selection drop-down because it already includes localization. You can see how in the following code fragment:

```
public final class LocaleDropDown extends DropDownChoice {
   private final class LocaleRenderer extends ChoiceRenderer {
      public String getDisplayValue(Object locale) {
         return ((Locale) locale).getDisplayName(getLocale());    ◁─┐
      }                                              getDisplayName called
   }                                                 with current locale
   ...
```

The custom `ChoiceRenderer` used by `LocaleDropDown` uses the `getDisplayName` method of the `Locale` class to display options in the currently selected locale. The `getLocale` method is inherited from `Component`, which by default calls the `getLocale` method of the `Session` object.

We can conveniently localize the user panel by replacing the marked parts with `<wicket:message>` tags.

12.1.2 *Using <wicket:message> tags*

Wicket's message tags are somewhat of an exception to how Wicket usually works. Typically with Wicket, you explicitly instantiate Java components and add them to the component tree matching them to the markup tags. In this case, Java components are created *implicitly* when `<wicket:message>` tags are encountered, so all you need to do is define these tags in your markup.

In the code fragment in listing 12.2, we replace the locale-dependent parts of the user panel with `<wicket:message>` tags.

Listing 12.2   Localized UserPanel.html using `<wicket:message>` tags

```
<wicket:panel>
   <wicket:message key="signed_in_as">Signed in as</wicket:message>   ◁─┐
    <i><span wicket:id="fullname">[name]</span></i>
     <select wicket:id="localeSelect" />        <wicket:message> tag
     <a wicket:id="signout">
      <wicket:message key="signout">signout</wicket:message></a>   ◁─┘
</wicket:panel>
```

The `<wicket:message>` tags trigger Wicket to insert label components on the fly. These labels use the `key` attribute to look up values in resource bundles, which they then use to replace the body of the `<wicket:message>` tag pair.

NOTE   Automatically inserted components are called auto-components throughout the framework. It's unlikely you'll ever have to deal with them directly, unless you create custom tag handlers.

The resource-bundle mechanism employed by Wicket resembles Java's resource-bundle mechanism, but it's more flexible in how it can be configured and it has a more extensive search path. Resource bundles are basically a way to provide access to a collection of key/value pairs. In UserPanel.html, we have two such keys—`signed_in_as` and `signout`—and we have as many values for each as we have languages we want to support. Resource bundles in Java applications are typically implemented as `Properties` objects, often loaded from key/value pairs stored in text files (which typically use the .properties extension). These text files are ISO 8859-1 encoded (a popular eight-bit encoded character set also known as Latin 1) and consist of lines of `key=value` pairs (`key:value` and `key value` are supported as alternatives). If you have to write your application for one of the roughly 25 languages and dialects that can properly be encoded, properties files work easily. But because most of the world's population communicates in languages that aren't supported by this encoding, chances are you'll end up using escaped unicode, resulting in files full of strings like `\u8A9E\u8A00`. Fortunately, since version 5, Java supports XML files for properties. The XML format supports any encoding that Java supports, including XML's default UTF-8, at the cost of a more verbose notation. Instead of writing

```
language=\u8A9E\u8A00
```

you can write

```
<entry key="language">語言</entry>
```

which makes a lot more sense if you can read traditional Chinese. Wicket supports both formats, so you can choose what works best for you.

NOTE   You can use XML property files with Wicket 1.3 even if you use Java 1.4.

For listing 12.2, we put the messages in the file UserPanel.properties file next to the class and HTML files, so that that part of our source tree then looks like this:

```
<package>
    - UserPanel.java
    - UserPanel.html
    - UserPanel.properties
```

UserPanel.properties then has the following contents:

```
signed_in_as=Signed in as
signout=signout
```

When Wicket looks for messages, as it does in the user panel triggered by the message tag, it starts by trying to locate a properties file next to the closest component it can find. In this case, the closest component that has messages associated is the user panel; the message tags are nested in that panel, and none of the other parent components (note that the link with the identifier `signout` is a parent of a `<wicket:message>` tag) have messages.

The UserPanel.properties file is used when no better matches are found. In contrast, the bundles for Dutch and Thai are used only when that specific locale is the current one. Including the bundles for the Dutch and Thai locales, the package looks like this:

```
<package>
    - UserPanel.java
    - UserPanel.html
    - UserPanel.properties
    - UserPanel_nl.properties
    - UserPanel_th.xml
```

You can see that—as with Java's property-based resource bundles—the locale information is part of the filename. The (partial) pattern is as follows:

```
base name ["_" language["_" country] ["_variant"]] (".properties" /".xml")
```

In our case, the base filename is UserPanel (which is the name of the matching component class). Wicket tries to match the locale as specifically as possible. For instance, the Dutch locale for someone in The Netherlands is nl_NL, but the Dutch locale for someone in Belgium is nl_BE. Neither of these is found here, so Wicket tries to match on the language next, which is UserPanel_nl.

Wicket tries both the properties and xml extensions (xml first); it does so for all the language/variant/country combinations.

Let's look at the contents of the Dutch and Thai message files, where the Dutch version is maintained in a regular properties file and the Thai version in the new XML format. Here's the Dutch version:

```
signed_in_as=Aangemeld als
signout=afmelden
```

And here's the Thai version:

```
<?xml version="1.0" encoding="UTF-8"?>
<!DOCTYPE properties SYSTEM "http://java.sun.com/dtd/properties.dtd">
<properties>
    <entry key="signed_in_as">เข้าสู่ระบบ</entry>
    <entry key="signout">ออกจากระบบ</entry>
</properties>
```

Many text editors nowadays are able to recognize XML files, and most of them will switch to the appropriate encoding for editing. They do this by interpreting the declaration (the first line of the XML file, which should always contain `<?xml`). In the previous listing, the encoding is declared to be UTF-8 (unicode).

AN ALTERNATIVE TO USING MESSAGE TAGS

Instead of using `<wicket:message>` tags, we could have used normal `Label` components, like this:

```
Label signedInAs = new Label("signedIdAs", new
                    ResourceModel("signed_in_as"));
```

Although labels are great for displaying information such as the name of the current user or the result of a calculation, here we just need only a lookup following a fixed algorithm. An advantage of `<wicket:message>` tags over plain labels like those in the previous snippet is that you don't need to synchronize the Java and markup hierarchy. Having to synchronize the two is usually a minor nuisance, but with text it can become a major headache; moving pieces of text from one area on the page to another is something you'll probably do more often than, for instance, moving forms or tables.

We already hinted that Wicket's resource-bundle mechanism is similar to the one that Java provides out of the box, but more powerful. This is due to the way Wicket locates the resource bundles, which is the topic of the next section.

12.1.3   *The message-lookup algorithm*

The path Wicket uses to look up message bundles (.properties or .xml files), can be defined as follows:

```
session = The current user session
component = The component that initiated the resource lookup
name = The name of the class of the component that is currently input
    for the search, starting with the name of component
style = [component.variation""_""[session.style""_""]]
ext = (".properties" /".xml")
path = name["_"style["_" language["_" country]["_variant"]]]ext
```

First, Wicket uses the entire path. If no matches are found, Wicket traverses the path from specific to generic, ending with the shorter path, where it takes into account the case with no style and locale. For example, with the style mystyle, the language nl, the country NL, and no variant, the lookup goes like this:

1   name_mystyle_nl_NL.xml
2   name_mystyle_nl_NL.properties
3   name_nl_NL.xml
4   name_nl_NL.properties
5   name_nl.xml
6   name_nl.properties
7   name.xml
8   name.properties

The name component is variable and—as we defined—equals the name of the component that currently serves as the search input. The algorithm for trying the components works as follows:

1   Wicket determines the component that is the subject for the message. How this is determined depends on the component, model, or other variables. Typically it's the component that uses the resource model. The subjects of the Wicket message tags are the auto-components that are inserted at runtime.

2   Wicket determines the hierarchy the component resides in and creates a search stack for it. This equals the subject component plus all its parents up to the page level, but in reverse order. For the Wicket message tags used in the user panel, the search stack is as shown in figure 12.4.

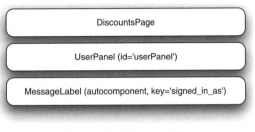

Figure 12.4   Search stack for one of the `<wicket:message>` **tags in the user panel**

3   When the search stack is determined, Wicket works from the top of the stack down to the subject component until it finds a match. For each component in the stack, Wicket performs the variation/style/locale matching described at the start of this section.

4   For the components between the page and the subject, Wickets takes the component identifiers into account as well. Declarations with the identifier of the immediate parent preceding the actual key have precedence over the plain keys.

Currently, the resources are defined in UserPanel.properties (and the language variants UserPanel_nl.properties and UserPanel_th.xml). If we add DiscountsPage.properties with the key signed_in_as, that declaration will take precedence over the ones defined on the panel. If we add userPanel.signed_in_as to that file (in the form id.key), it will take precedence.

Using message bundles like this is easy and flexible. But Wicket's support for multiple languages doesn't end here. In the next section, you'll see that the magical naming trick applies to markup files as well.

12.1.4 *Localized markup files*

The trick you just saw for resource bundles works the same for markup templates. As an alternative to separate resource bundles, you can have different markup files for each locale.

Let's change the way we implemented UserPanel as an example. The new structure looks like this:

```
<package>
    - UserPanel.java
    - UserPanel.html
    - UserPanel_nl.html
    - UserPanel_th.html
```

UserPanel.html is the English version and serves as the default. If your locale is Chinese (a locale we don't support in this example), the English version is shown.

If we didn't separate the locale-dependent parts from the rest of the markup, but instead relied on the localized loading of the templates, UserPanel's markup would be as shown in listing 12.3.

Listing 12.3   UserPanel.html without `<wicket:message>` tags

```
<wicket:panel>
  Signed in as
   <i><span wicket:id="fullname">[name]</span></i>
    <select wicket:id="localeSelect" />
    <a wicket:id="signout">
    signout
  </a>
</wicket:panel>
```

The Dutch UserPanel would look like listing 12.4.

Listing 12.4   UserPanel_nl.html

```
<wicket:panel>
  Aangemeld als
   <i><span wicket:id="fullname">[name]</span></i>
    <select wicket:id="localeSelect" />
    <a wicket:id="signout">
    afmelden
  </a>
</wicket:panel>
```

As you can see, we don't need the `<wicket:message>` tags; we use the text for the proper language directly.

But the Thai version, is shown in listing 12.5, has a catch.

Listing 12.5   UserPanel_th.html

```
<?xml version="1.0" encoding="UTF-8"?>
<wicket:panel>
    เข้าสู่ระบบ
   <i><span wicket:id="fullname">[name]</span></i>
    <select wicket:id="localeSelect" />
    <a wicket:id="signout">
    ออกจากระบบ
  </a>
</wicket:panel>
```

Note that the first line is an XML declaration. The Thai language consists of characters that can't be expressed as ASCII characters. One way to properly encode the Thai characters is to write the template in UTF-8 encoding. If you start your markup files with such a declaration, Wicket will recognize that the file should be read in as a UTF-8 stream. The declaration is optional but recommended. Because it's outside the `<wicket:panel>` tags, it's ignored for the rest of the processing, so you don't see the declaration back in your pages.

TIP   It's good practice to start your panels and borders (and possibly your pages) with an XML declaration to force Wicket to work with them using the proper encoding. It's also good practice to explicitly provide a doctype declaration so the browser doesn't have to guess how to interpret the markup.

In the last two sections, we looked at Wicket's locale matching for resource bundles and markup files. The powerful pattern that Wicket employs is used for everything that goes through Wicket's resource-lookup mechanism, like packaged CSS and Java-Script files, but also packaged images. For instance, if we wanted to display the flag of the current locale, we could include an image in the markup like this:

```
<wicket:link><img src="flag.gif" /></wicket:link>
```

In our package, we'd have flag.gif, flag_nl.gif, and flag_th.gif. Wicket would automatically load the appropriate flag for the current locale.

NOTE   Instead of adding an image component in Java and an `img` tag with a `wicket:id` attribute in our markup, we embedded the tag in `<wicket:link>` tags. You can use `<wicket:link>` tags for normal links, images, JavaScript, and stylesheet declarations.

Working with separate markup files per locale/style gives you maximum flexibility, but using resource bundles with one markup file is the better choice for most people. Message bundles can be maintained separately, and they're also more flexible in how they're located; for example, you can include the messages at the page or application level, whereas markup must always directly match the components.

You can even mix the approaches. Both have one thing in common: they use the same mechanism to load the resources, whether they're properties files or markup files (HTML). In the next section, we'll leave localization for a bit and investigate how you can customize the way Wicket searches for resources.

12.2   *Customizing resource loading*

A common question on the Wicket user list is how to deviate from Wicket's pattern of placing `Component`'s markup files next to the component's class files (this typically means you'll put them next to your Java files, relying on the build system to place copies of the markup files into the directory the class files are written to).

NOTE   Here, when we talk about resources, we mean markup and resource bundles, not the request-handling resources we discussed in chapter 10. Wicket locates resources using resource-stream locators, which are abstracted in the `IResourceStreamLocator` interface; this interface has the default implementation `ResourceStreamLocator`.

The code fragment shown in listing 12.6 is an example of a custom resource-stream locator.

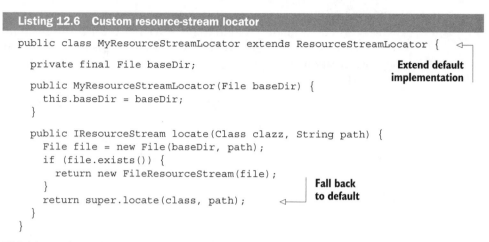

Listing 12.6   Custom resource-stream locator

```
public class MyResourceStreamLocator extends ResourceStreamLocator {      ◁─┐

  private final File baseDir;                                        Extend default
                                                                     implementation
  public MyResourceStreamLocator(File baseDir) {
    this.baseDir = baseDir;
  }

  public IResourceStream locate(Class clazz, String path) {
    File file = new File(baseDir, path);
    if (file.exists()) {
      return new FileResourceStream(file);
    }                                        Fall back
    return super.locate(class, path);   ◁──┘ to default
  }
}
```

This class takes a directory as a constructor argument and uses it as the base for looking up resources. A typical locate request has a `class` argument like `myapp.MyComponent` and a `path` argument like `myapp/MyComponent_en.html`.

If your base directory is /home/me, then the example request resolves to /home/me/myapp/MyComponent_en.html. In the example, we override `ResourceStream`'s `locate` method with two arguments. Note that this method is called by `ResourceStreamLocator`, which among other things tries to match with the most specific locale first. If the locate invocation returns `null`, it's an indication that the locator should try other combinations (for instance, myapp/MyComponent.html) before giving up.

TIP   It's highly recommended that you extend `ResourceStreamLocator` rather than implement the `IResourceStreamLocator` interface directly, and let your implementation call the appropriate superlocator method when it can't find a resource. Components you reuse may rely on the resources being packaged with the classes. `ResourceStreamLocator` will fall back to loading resources relative to classes when custom loading fails.

You register the custom resource locator in your application object's `init` method, as shown in listing 12.7.

Listing 12.7   Registering the custom resource-stream locator

```
public class MyApplication extends WebApplication {

  public MyApplication() {
  }

  public Class getHomePage() {
    return Home.class;
  }

  protected void init() {
    File baseDir = new File("/home/me");
    IResourceStreamLocator locator =
```

```
      new MyResourceStreamLocator(baseDir);
    getResourceSettings().setResourceStreamLocator(locator);
  }
}
```

That's all there is to it.

Wicket has some convenient implementations. Alternatively, we could implement the previous example like this:

```
protected void init() {
  IResourceStreamLocator locator =
    new ResourceStreamLocator(new Path(new Folder("/home/me")));
  getResourceSettings().setResourceStreamLocator(locator);
}
```

This uses a `Path` object, which in turn is an implementation of `IResourceFinder`, which is a delegation interface that is used by `ResourceStreamLocator`.

Now that you know the lookup mechanism can be customized, please heed the following warning. Wicket's default way of locating resources enables you to quickly switch between the Java files and markup files during development because they're right next to each other. Also, with this algorithm, your packaged components are immediately reusable without users having to configure where the templates are loaded from; if the components' classes can be found in the class path, so can their resources. It's a powerful default, and you may want to think twice before you implement something custom.

So far, we've primarily been looking at localized text output. In the last section of this chapter, we'll discuss localized model conversions, which you use to localize values that are stored in models.

12.3 Localized conversions

Wicket has a mechanism for handling objects that have different string representations depending on the locale. Examples of such objects are numbers and dates. The string *100,125* is interpreted as a different number depending on the locale. Americans interpret it as *one hundred thousand, one hundred and twenty-five*; Dutch people interpret it as *one hundred and one eighth.* In the same fashion, the string *10/12* in the context of dates represents the twelfth of October for Americans and the tenth of December for Dutch people. If your application is supposed to serve different nationalities in their own ways, you must format numbers, dates, and possibly other objects differently according to the user's locale.

The objects responsible for such conversions in Wicket are called converters.

12.3.1 Wicket converters

Even if you aren't interested in formatting numbers and dates for specific locales, you still need a mechanism to switch between strings (HTML/HTTP) and Java objects and back again. You can build conversions into your components or models. Listing 12.8 shows an example where a model takes care of the locale-dependent formatting.

Listing 12.8   Utility model that formats values of the nested model

```
public class NumberFormatModel implements IModel {

  private final IModel wrapped;

  public NumberFormatModel(IModel numberModel) {
    this.wrapped = numberModel;
  }

  public Object getObject() {
    Number nbr = (Number) wrapped.getObject();
    return nbr != null ? getFormat().format(nbr) : null;
  }

  public void setObject(Object object) {
    try {
      if (object != null) {
        wrapped.setObject(getFormat().parse((String) object));
      } else {
        wrapped.setObject(null);
      }
    } catch (ParseException e) {
      throw new RuntimeException(e);
    }
  }

  private NumberFormat getFormat() {
    NumberFormat fmt = NumberFormat.getNumberInstance(Session.get()
        .getLocale());
    return fmt;
  }

  public void detach() {
  }
}
```

Using this model looks like this:

```
Double number = 100.125;
new Label("number", new NumberFormatModel(new model(number)));
```

The disadvantage of using models for this purpose is that you must always be aware of this wrapping—forget it, and you'll get typing errors. In addition, there is no way to be sure conversions are executed across the board.

This is why Wicket has a separate mechanism for conversions. The main interface of this mechanism is IConverter (see figure 12.5).

To illustrate how this works, let's look at how the Label component renders its body and the process of triggering the use of a converter.

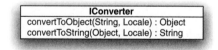

IConverter
convertToObject(String, Locale) : Object
convertToString(Object, Locale) : String

Figure 12.5   The converter interface

While rendering pages, Wicket asks components to render themselves to the output stream. That process is broken into a couple of steps, and onComponentTagBody is one of the methods a component uses to delegate a specific piece of work. Containers (components that can contain other components) delegate rendering to the components nested in them. But some components, like Label (which isn't a container), provide their own implementation of this method. Here is that implementation for the Label component:

```
protected void onComponentTagBody(final MarkupStream markupStream,
    final ComponentTag openTag) {
  replaceComponentTagBody(markupStream, openTag,
    getModelObjectAsString());
}
```

The interesting part is the call to getModelObjectAsString, which is a method of the component base class. You can see its implementation in listing 12.9 (comments are stripped).

Listing 12.9 getModelObjectAsString method of Component

```
public final String getModelObjectAsString() {
  final Object modelObject = getModelObject();
  if (modelObject != null) {
    IConverter converter = getConverter(modelObject.getClass());
    final String modelString =
      converter.convertToString(modelObject, getLocale());
    if (modelString != null) {
      if (getFlag(FLAG_ESCAPE_MODEL_STRINGS)) {
        return Strings.escapeMarkup(modelString, false, true)
          .toString();
      }
      return modelString;
    }
  }
  return "";
}
```

This method gets a converter instance, which it uses to convert the model object to a string using the convertToString method. The implementation of that method uses a NumberFormat in the same fashion as the custom model we looked at earlier.

Because converters are always used for the appropriate types, we can rewrite the previous code fragment as follows:

```
Double number = 100.125;
new Label("number", new Model(number));
```

This code fragment works for numbers, dates, and anything else for which converters are registered. Wicket's default configuration is probably good for 95% of use cases.

But the default configuration may be insufficient at times. In the next section, we'll look at how you can provide custom converters.

12.3.2 Custom converters

In this section, we'll look at how you can customize conversions for individual components or an entire application. The first step a component executes when locating a converter is to call its getConverter method—and there we have the first opportunity for customization. We discussed this customization in chapter 9, when we implemented a percentage field. Let's look at it again in a bit more detail.

CUSTOMIZING CONVERSION FOR ONE COMPONENT

You may want to use this customization when, for example, you want to deviate from the application-wide registered converter. For instance, you may want to display a date formatted with the months fully spelled out, but the converter installed on the application displays months as numbers.

Another good use case is when the conversion is an integral part of your component. An example of this is a URL text field. If you want to write a URL text field that works in all projects, you can pin down the converter (override getConverter and make it final) and return your URL converter there. That way, you guarantee that the appropriate conversion is performed, no matter how the application is configured.

The URL text field is implemented in listing 12.10.

Listing 12.10 URL text field using a custom converter

```
public class UrlTextField extends TextField {

  public UrlTextField(String id) {
    super(id, URL.class);
  }

  public UrlTextField(String id, IModel object) {
    super(id, object, URL.class);
  }

  @Override                                              Override
  public final IConverter getConverter(Class type) {   ◁┘ getConverter

    return new IConverter() {

      public Object convertToObject(String value, Locale locale) {
        try {
          return new URL(value.toString());
        } catch (MalformedURLException e) {               Throw
          throw new ConversionException("'" + value     ◁ ConversionException
            + "' is not a valid URL");
        }
      }

      public String convertToString(Object value, Locale locale) {
        return value != null ? value.toString() : null;
      }
    };
  }
}
```

This text field overrides any globally defined converter and provides its own. When it renders, convertToString is called, and the URL is returned as a string; and when values are set on the text field (typically through a user providing input), convertToObject converts the string (which comes from the HTTP request) to a proper URL object again.

There is a thin line between where it's appropriate to use a custom model and where it's best to use a custom converter. Not everyone on the Wicket team agrees, but we like the layering that custom converters enable. Converting from and to URLs is an obvious case for a converter, but formatting a mask is debatable. For instance, look at the code fragment in listing 12.11.

Listing 12.11 Using a converter to force a mask

```
add(new TextField("phoneNumberUS", UsPhoneNumber.class) {
  public IConverter getConverter(final Class type) {
    return new MaskConverter("(###) ###-####",
      UsPhoneNumber.class);
  }
});
```

In this case, because you aren't merely converting between types, but altering the user's input and the output that is rendered, you may as well use an explicit model. It's largely a matter of taste which approach you choose.

What if you want to install custom conversions for the entire application? You do so with converter locators.

USING APPLICATION-SCOPED CONVERTER LOCATORS

A *converter locator* is an object that knows where to get converter instances for the appropriate types. An application has one instance, and this instance is created by the implementation of newConverterLocator, which is an overridable method of Application that is called when the application starts up.

If you want to provide a custom converter locator and configure the existing one, you can override newConverterLocator in your application. Listing 12.12 is an example that installs a URL converter for the entire application.

Listing 12.12 Installing a converter for an application

```
protected IConverterLocator newConverterLocator() {        Default converter
  ConverterLocator locator = new ConverterLocator();   ◁── locator
  locator.set(URL.class, new IConverter() {
    public Object convertToObject(String value, Locale locale) {
      try {
        return new URL(value.toString());
      } catch (MalformedURLException e) {
        throw new ConversionException("'" + value
          + "' is not a valid URL");
      }
    }

    public String convertToString(Object value, Locale locale) {
      return value != null ? value.toString() : null;
    }
  });
  return locator;
}
```

Voila! Now we don't even need a URL text field. We can just do this

```
new TextField("url", new PropertyModel(this, "url"), URL.class);
```

or—because property models introspect the target type—this should suffice:

```
new TextField("url", new PropertyModel(this, "url"));
```

Note that in this example, we instantiate the default `ConverterLocator` rather than implement the `IConverterLocator` interface from scratch. Doing the latter is possible, but the default converter locator is designed to be easily extended.

12.4   *Summary*

We used this chapter to look at different aspects of localizing your web applications with Wicket. The two main things we discussed were how to support multiple languages with `<wicket:message>` tags and localized markup (with a detour to explain how you can customize the way markup is loaded), and how converters work and can be customized.

We've used example data in several occasions in this book, but we haven't paid much attention to where this data comes from. In the next chapter, we'll examine how you can use Wicket to build database applications.

Multitiered architectures

13

So far, we've looked at the individual nuts and bolts of Wicket through the use of simple examples. We've developed a virtual cheese store with functionality to browse through a catalogue, place orders, view discounts, and edit those discounts. The big thing missing from those examples is what you'd almost certainly have in real life: a database that stores the orders, discounts, and so on.

In this chapter, we'll look at a common pattern of organizing source code into layers. We'll use the Spring framework to manage one of these layers—the business layer—and we'll use Hibernate as a tool to access the database in a transparent (object-oriented) way. In the fashion of the last five chapters, we'll further build on the cheese discounts list.

13.1   *Introducing the three-tiered service architecture*

The architectural pattern of dividing your application into tiers (layers) with their own responsibilities as we'll describe is commonly used for creating web applications and is often called a three-tiered service architecture. Schematically, it looks like figure 13.1.

The presentation tier takes care of the UI. All the pages, components, models, and behaviors that are part of an application logically belong to this tier.

The logical (or business) tier is where the business logic resides. Components in this layer know how business processes work, how to perform business-specific calculations, how to aggregate data from multiple sources, and so forth. This layer typically consists of a number of services and can also be referred to as the service layer.

Finally, the DAO knows how to physically get data from sources like databases, web services, and file systems. This layer typically consists of a number of DAOs with which you abstract whether data is retrieved using regular JDBC or using an ORM tool such as Hibernate. The logic in this layer is typically related to the kind of resource that is accessed, whereas the logic in the business layer is typically specific to the business domain.

This architecture is useful to keep in mind as a rough sketch. In practice, the separations between layers aren't strict and unambiguous. For instance, the domain model may in one diagram be placed in the business layer, in another be in the data access layer, and in yet another may be drawn separately; after all, domain objects are typically used by all layers. Whether you let your UI layer access the data layer directly or always let it go through the business layer is largely a matter of taste.

The more strictly you keep the layers separated, the easier it will be to maintain this arrangement over time; but it comes at a cost of having to cope with more plumbing work. And all the indirections you'll encounter with this approach don't make your code prettier.

Why would you want to have a layered architecture in the first place?

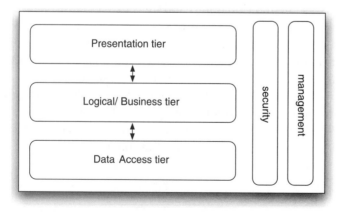

Figure 13.1   The three-tiered service architecture

13.1.1 *Advantages of utilizing a layered architecture*

Loose coupling is an important design goal when you're developing software. In a system that is loosely coupled, the different parts (like classes, components, and groups of classes) make minimal assumptions about how other parts work, so parts can be replaced without forcing changes in other parts of the system.

Layering is a common technique to achieve loose coupling. You should be able to change how (parts of) the business layer or data access layer are implemented without affecting the presentation layer and vice versa. You shouldn't have to rewrite your presentation layer when you decide to get a piece of data from a web service instead of a database.

Your application's layers likely have different characteristics for resource utilization. With the layered approach, you can put those layers on different machines (or clusters of machines) that are optimized for their particular resource-utilization characteristics.

Having several layers also makes it easier to break up work. You can have people working on the business layer while others work on the data layer or presentation layer.

Finally, the boundaries between the layers are often the right place for transaction demarcation. In the presentation layer, you typically work with volatile objects, and you use the business layer to make changes persistent or create new persistent objects.

To achieve independence of implementation between the layers, you need to let your software talk to interfaces rather than concrete classes between the layers. But who is in charge of creating the concrete classes, and how do you resolve dependencies? How do you avoid one layer knowing about the implementation details of another layer? These questions need to be answered in order to create loosely coupled systems, and a good understanding will help you create enterprise Wicket applications.

We'll search for answers in the next section.

13.1.2 *Who is in charge of the dependencies?*

One of the biggest buzzwords in software engineering in the last few years has been dependency injection (DI). The term was coined by Martin Fowler in 2004 as a special variation of inversion of control (IoC).

IoC, which is also known as the Hollywood Principle ("Don't call us, we'll call you"), is the rule of letting your software be called by a framework rather than instructing your software to call that framework. For example, you can trust Wicket to initiate the rendering of components when requests come in. This shields you from having to write a lot of plumbing code; and complicated implementation details for handling requests (when to call what, how to handle exceptions, synchronization, and so on) are abstracted away in the framework. You focus on implementing the behavior that is relevant for your particular application.

DI is a special subvariant of IoC in that it only involves resolving dependencies. Instead of letting your code resolve dependencies, you let a framework do it. To illustrate, let's first look at code that doesn't use DI.

13.1.3 *Code without dependency injection*

In the course of this chapter, we'll transform the discounts list component to use a service object to query for discounts. We'll define the interface `DiscountsService`, which is backed by a concrete implementation `DiscountsServiceImpl`. It's possible to have multiple implementations of the interface. For instance, you could have a specific implementation for testing that instead of a database uses a set of in-memory data. You want to let the discounts-list component be unaware of the actual implementation that's used. It should talk to the interface without knowledge of the concrete class backing it.

If that is our goal, then the following code isn't what we want:

```
public class DiscountsList extends Panel {
  private DiscountsService service;

  public DiscountsList(String id) {
    service = new DiscountsServiceImpl();
```

The discounts-list component instantiates a specific implementation. We can't swap the implementation for another one without having to recompile the discounts list. (We also have no central control over which instance is used and how many instances are created in the application.)

As is now in vogue in Java programming (and many other languages), we could employ a lightweight container (such containers are light in comparison to heavy EJB containers) to couple concrete implementations to interfaces. Registering an interface with an implementation could, for instance, look like this:

```
Container.getInstance()
    .install(DiscountsService.class, new DiscountsServiceImpl());
```

The discounts list could then be as follows:

```
public class DiscountsList extends Panel {
  private DiscountsService service;

  public DiscountsList(String id) {
    service = Container.getInstance().locate(DiscountsService.class);
```

In this version, the discounts list doesn't have any knowledge of the concrete implementation of the discounts service, and the container acts as a factory that takes care of all that. Now, if we replace the implementation with a test implementation, we change the configuration of the container:

```
Container.getInstance()
    .install(DiscountsService.class, new DiscountsServiceTestImpl());
```

In the constructor, we're letting the discounts list locate the instance of discounts service it needs. Using a lookup service (`Container` in this example) to resolve dependencies is often called the service locator pattern. JNDI is a famous example of this pattern.

Using a service locator is better than letting the discounts list instantiate the implementation itself, but we're not quite there yet. The discounts list now has a direct dependency on the service locator, and if we want to change the implementation of the discounts service, we'll have to adjust the container's configuration. And because the code for locating the service is hard-coded in the component, we can't directly assemble the objects ourselves.

We need a way to resolve dependencies without any special construction or lookup code in our components. We can do this using DI.

13.1.4 *Dependency injection to the rescue*

When you use DI, you ask the container to not only manage the creation and lookup of the appropriate implementations, but also set the dependencies on each of the objects it manages. For instance, the discounts service uses the discount DAO (from the data access layer) to access persistent data:

```
public class DiscountsServiceImpl implements DiscountsService {
    private DiscountDao discDao;
    public DiscountDao getDiscountDao() { return discDao; }
    public void setDiscountDao(DiscountDao dao) { this.discDao = dao; }
    public List<Cheese> findAllDiscounts() { return discDao.findAll(); }
    ...
```

For testing, we can set the discount DAO dependency ourselves:

```
DiscountsService service = new DiscountsServiceImpl();
service.setDiscountDao(new DummyDiscountDaoImpl());
List<Cheese> Cheeses = service.findAllCheeses();
```

For normal operations, we can configure the container like this:

```
Container c = Container.getInstance();
DiscountsService service = new DiscountsServiceImpl();
service.setDiscountDao(new MySQLDiscountDaoImpl());
c.install(DiscountsService.class, service);
```

When we ask the container to locate the discounts service instance, we get the instance of the discounts service with the appropriate discount DAO dependency set—with no specific code in the discounts service. We *injected* the dependencies when configuring the container; and doing that from the outside, rather than from within the container class, is the core idea of DI.

Note that during testing, the discount DAO interface is bound to a different implementation than it is when configured for normal operation. Different implementations behind interfaces is a variant of the strategy pattern, which describes the ability to swap algorithms at runtime.

Several good open source frameworks specialize in DI. The primary DI frameworks at the time of writing are Spring and Guice; other alternatives include PicoContainer and HiveMind. Guice is our favorite flavor, and Wicket has good support for it, but Spring is without a doubt the most widely used of the bunch. We'll use Spring to build the example in the rest of this chapter.

TIP   The Manning books *Dependency Injection* (Dhanji Prasanna, 2008) and *Spring in Action* (Craig Walls and Ryan Breidenbach, 2007) are excellent sources for more information about DI implementations.

In the next part of this chapter, we'll convert the cheese discounts list example to let it use the three-tiered service architecture. We'll create three layers for the example, and we'll let Spring manage those layers. The result will be a Wicket application that is loosely coupled and that has clear boundaries for things like transaction demarcation, logging, and caching.

13.2   *Layering Wicket applications using Spring*

In this section, we'll break the discounts-list example into layers. For the sake of the example, we'll stick to a strict separation of layers, even though this means the business layer isn't doing much more than sending requests to the data layer. You'll have to judge whether a stringent layer approach suits your situation or whether you want to be more lenient—or even go for a completely different approach. For example, an additional layer may give you flexibility in demarcating transaction boundaries.

Figure 13.2 illustrates what part of the discounts-list example looks like when it's built according to the three-tiered architecture.

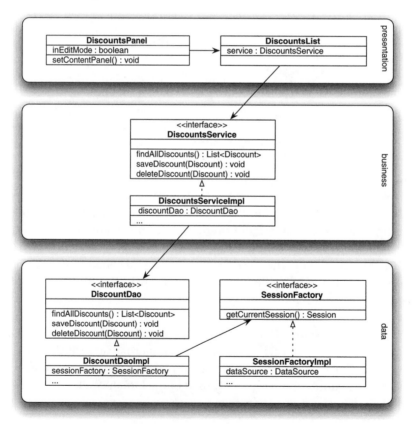

Figure 13.2   The discounts-list example in layers

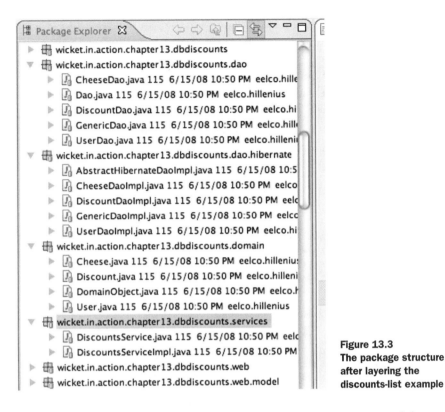

**Figure 13.3
The package structure
after layering the
discounts-list example**

As you can see from the diagram, the Wicket components are part of the presentation layer, the discounts service makes up the business layer, and the discount DAO and the Hibernate session factory (more on Hibernate later in this chapter) are part of the data access layer. We left out the domain objects (Cheese, Discount, User) because it isn't immediately clear whether they should be part of the business layer or the data access layer (or neither).

Note that these layers can exist in the same project—even in the same package if you wish, although you'd typically stress the distinction by using separate packages. See figure 13.3 for the package structure we came up with for this example.

We'll use Spring to wire up the interfaces to their appropriate implementations. The next section will introduce the Spring framework and show how we'll integrate it in the discounts-list example.

13.2.1 *Spring time!*

The Spring framework was conceived by Rod Johnson when he wrote *Expert One-on-One J2EE Design and Development* (Wrox, 2002). Johnson outlines many problems that existed with developing Java applications using the Java Enterprise Edition (J2EE) platform, and the solutions he proposed form the basis of the Spring framework.

Although the Spring framework encompasses more than just DI, its support for the strategy pattern combined with DI has arguably been one of its largest success factors.

Spring is typically configured using an XML file. In that XML file, you use <bean> tags to define the software modules (beans) you want Spring to manage for you; within these tags, you use <property> tags to identify bean properties (dependencies) that should be injected by Spring.

Listing 13.1 shows a fragment for configuring the discounts service and DAO.

Listing 13.1   Spring fragment to configure the discounts service and DAO

```
<bean id="dataSource"
    class="com.mchange.v2.c3p0.ComboPooledDataSource">
    <property name="driverClass">
        <value>${jdbc.driver}</value>
    ...
</bean>

<bean id="sessionFactory"
class="org.springframework.orm.hibernate3.annotation.
AnnotationSessionFactoryBean">
    <property name="dataSource">
        <ref bean="dataSource" />
    </property>
  ...
</bean>

<bean id="DiscountDao"
    class="dbdiscounts.dao.hibernate.DiscountDaoImpl">
 <property name="sessionFactory" ref="sessionFactory" />
</bean>

<bean id="DiscountsService"
    class="dbdiscounts.services.DiscountsServiceImpl">
    <property name="discountDao" ref="DiscountDao" />    ⟵─┐  Property references
</bean>                                                        other bean
```

The discounts service declares the property discountDao as a reference to the bean named DiscountDao. That bean is coupled to the DiscountDaoImpl class in the configuration. By default, Spring creates one instance of the class—a singleton—and shares that instance with all clients. This is typically fine for service objects, because they rarely carry state for particular clients. After Spring creates the instance, it sets the dependencies by matching the property names with setter methods of the class. The discountDao property will be matched with setDiscountDao of the Discount-DaoImpl class.

In the next section, we'll look at how to configure Wicket to use Spring.

13.2.2 *The simplest way to configure Wicket to use Spring*

The easiest way to configure Wicket to use Spring is to bootstrap Spring in your web application and expose methods to either get the Spring context directly or, if you want to avoid Spring dependencies in your components, get references to the services and DAOs. Listing 13.2 illustrates this.

Listing 13.2 Bootstrapping Spring in the Wicket application class

```
public class WicketInActionApplication extends WebApplication {

  private ApplicationContext ctx;

  @Override
  protected void init() {
    ctx = new ClassPathXmlApplicationContext("applicationContext.xml");
    ...
  }

  public DiscountsService getDiscountService() {
    return (DiscountsService) BeanFactoryUtils.beanOfType(ctx,
        DiscountsService.class);
  }
  ...
```

The discounts-list component can then use the `discounts` service like this:

```
add(new RefreshingView("discounts") {
  @Override
  protected Iterator getItemModels() {
    DiscountsService service =
      WicketInActionApplication.get().getDiscountService();
    return new DomainModelIteratorAdaptor<Discount>(
      service.findAllDiscounts().iterator()) {
      ...
```

You probably noticed that we use Spring here with the service locator pattern. There isn't much wrong with using this pattern, but there are safer and more elegant ways to use Spring, as you'll see in the next few sections.

13.2.3 *Using proxies instead of direct references*

One problem with the code from the previous section is that it can lead to memory leaks. Be careful never to hold a reference to a Spring bean in your components. Spring often creates proxies for the beans it creates (for instance, to support transactions), and when Wicket serializes your components—as it does for every request, if you use the default session store—you may end up serializing the entire Spring container with them.

The following code fragment is problematic (note the private class-level variable):

```
private DiscountsService service =
  WicketInActionApplication.get().getDiscountService();
public DiscountsList(String id) {
  super(id);
  add(new RefreshingView("discounts") {
    @Override
    protected Iterator getItemModels() {
      return new DomainModelIteratorAdaptor<Discount>(
        service.findAllDiscounts().iterator()) {
        ...
```

This can be fixed by creating proxies to the services and DAOs and returning those instead of the objects Spring provides. When implemented properly, clients can keep references without running into trouble when serialization rears its ugly head.

Note that variables declared in the scope of methods or constructor bodies are never serialized—they only exist during the execution of the methods—and are thus never problematic.

The wicket-spring project comes with a good implementation of such proxies. We'll look at these in the next section.

13.2.4 *Using proxies from the wicket-spring project*

The wicket-spring project contains a number of classes that make it easier to integrate Spring into your Wicket applications. This project builds on wicket-ioc, which is the base project for DI support in Wicket.

The project contains a factory for creating proxies. If we change the application class to create proxies using the wicket-spring project, it looks like listing 13.3.

Listing 13.3 Creating proxies for Spring-managed objects

```
public class WicketInActionApplication extends WebApplication {

  private static ISpringContextLocator CTX_LOCATOR =
      new ISpringContextLocator() {                          ❶ Static
    public ApplicationContext getSpringContext() {             context
      return WicketInActionApplication.get().ctx;              locator
    }
  };

  private ApplicationContext ctx;
  private DiscountsService discountsService;

  @Override
  protected void init() {
    ctx = new ClassPathXmlApplicationContext("applicationContext.xml");
  }

  private <T> T createProxy(Class<T> clazz) {                 ❷ Use wicket-
    return (T) LazyInitProxyFactory.createProxy(clazz,         spring's proxy
        new SpringBeanLocator(clazz, CTX_LOCATOR));            factory
  }

  public DiscountsService getDiscountService() {
    if (discountsService == null) {                          ❸ Create
      discountsService = createProxy(DiscountsService.class);  proxy
    }                                                          lazily
    return discountsService;
  }
}
```

Note that the Spring context locator (which the proxy factory uses to get a reference to the proper Spring application context object) is defined as a static member on the application ❶. That is to ensure the context locator doesn't reference the application. If the locator was a regular object member instead, the Wicket application object with all its settings would be serialized with every proxy instance.

Creating a proxy object ❷ is a relatively expensive operation, so it's created lazily, as you can see in the getDiscountsService method ❸. We don't need to synchronize the method; that would be much more expensive than creating a couple of proxies if multiple clients called the method at the same time. The proxies are created only once, whereas `getDiscountsService` will probably be called often; making it synchronized would create a performance bottleneck.

The proxy that is returned will only hold a reference to the class it was passed (DiscountsService.class in this case), and it will use that to locate the appropriate bean when needed. If you're familiar with functional programming, this may remind you of keeping a reference to a function to get an instance, rather than keeping a reference to that concrete instance. The advantage of using this proxy is that it's cheap to serialize, so you'll never have to worry about keeping references to it in your components.

Observant readers will have noticed that we're still using the service locator pattern. A problem with DI is that it's contagious. Containers can only inject dependencies they know about. This poses a problem for Wicket, because Wicket is what we call an *unmanaged framework*. With Wicket, you create your own instances rather than letting a container do it for you.

You can imagine how different Wicket would look if we put the container in charge of component instantiation. It wouldn't support the just-Java programming model we're so proud of and worked so hard on (although Wicket would have been a lot easier to implement). A declarative programming model—although useful on some occasions—would seriously limit the freedom you have when coding Wicket applications. Another way to look at this is that Wicket would be used in just one layer of your application, and you wouldn't need loose coupling for classes enclosed within the presentation tier. A declarative approach would get in the way: you're much better off using the new keyword and writing clean, object-oriented Java code.

There is an alternative that uses the service locator pattern under the covers but feels like proper DI from the perspective of end users: Spring bean annotations. We'll look at how to use them in the next section.

13.2.5 *Wicket's Spring bean annotations*

Annotations were introduced in the fifth major release of Java. They provide a way to tag your source code with metadata. Such metadata is always processed by other source code; it can't contain algorithms.

The `SpringBean` annotation is part of the wicket-spring-annot project in Wicket 1.3 and part of the main wicket-spring project in later Wicket versions. In this section, we'll look at how to use annotations and how to configure applications to be able to use them.

Listing 13.4 shows the code of the discounts-list component after it's converted to use the Spring bean annotation.

Listing 13.4 Discounts list using the Spring bean annotation

```
public class DiscountsList extends Panel {
  @SpringBean
  private DiscountsService service;

  public DiscountsList(String id) {
    super(id);
```

```
add(new RefreshingView("discounts") {
  @Override
  protected Iterator getItemModels() {
    return new DomainModelIteratorAdaptor<Discount>(service
        .findAllDiscounts().iterator()) {
    ...
```

The dependency isn't completely externalized because you have to import `org.apache.wicket.spring.injection.annot.SpringBean`; but because the annotation is only a piece of metadata that by itself does nothing, it's now safe to construct the component and set dependencies in custom ways. Using the Spring bean annotation eliminates the main problem with the service locator pattern: lack of freedom to change the way dependencies are resolved for different cases.

Using the Spring bean annotation also saves you from having to define those lookup methods in the application—and, personally, we think it looks much nicer.

TIP   Don't initialize the members you annotate as Spring beans, because the injector will run before the subclass initializes its fields. Doing `private DiscountsService service = null` would override the created proxy with `null`.

In listing 13.4, we use the Spring bean annotation as is. That results in a lookup using the class of the member declaration (`DiscountsService.class`). Alternatively, you can provide the name of the bean as it's known by Spring (the `id` attribute in the configuration file):

```
@SpringBean(name = "DiscountsService")
private DiscountsService service;
```

Using the name can be useful if you happen to have Spring manage multiple implementations of the member declaration interface; without the name, it would throw an exception because the dependency is ambiguous.

Installing the annotations processor to do something with those annotations is easy. The wicket-spring-annot project ships with a special component instantiation listener that analyzes the components you construct and injects proxies for all the Spring-bean-annotated members it finds. To install it, put the following line in your application's `init` method:

```
addComponentInstantiationListener(new SpringComponentInjector(this));
```

You also need to configure your application a bit differently. You can do so multiple ways, but we'll show you what we think is the nicest approach.

First, instead of bootstrapping Spring yourself, let's use a special servlet listener that ships with Spring. To configure the listener, put the following lines in your web.xml configuration file:

```
<listener>
  <listener-class>
    org.springframework.web.context.ContextLoaderListener
  </listener-class>
</listener>
```

This code bootstraps Spring when the servlet container starts up. By default, the context loader listener tries to load the Spring configuration from your webapp directory. It looks for a file named applicationContext.xml. We prefer to have Spring load our configuration from the classpath as we've been doing in this chapter. You can achieve this by adding these lines to your web.xml configuration:

```
<context-param>
  <param-name>contextConfigLocation</param-name>
  <param-value>classpath:applicationContext.xml</param-value>
</context-param>
```

Spring will now start up when the servlet container starts and read its configuration from the applicationContext.xml file it finds in the classpath root.

The wicket-spring project also provides a Spring-specific implementation of the web application factory interface (IWebApplicationFactory). You can use a custom web-application factory if you want more control over how Wicket creates your application object. Instead of providing a class, you provide the factory that will be in charge of creating the application. The factory in wicket-spring is called SpringWebApplicationFactory. This factory doesn't create an instance; rather, it asks Spring for one. You can let Spring manage your application object and do all the fancy stuff (like DI) with it that you might do with other Spring-managed components.

To let Spring manage the application class, you define it as a bean in the Spring configuration file:

```
<bean id="wicketApplication"
    class="wicket.in.action.WicketInActionApplication">
</bean>
```

Next, you need to tell the Wicket filter to use the Spring application factory to create an instance of the application object. You do that by defining the filter as shown in listing 13.5 (in web.xml).

Listing 13.5 Configuring Wicket filter to use the Spring application factory

```
<filter>
  <filter-name>WicketInAction</filter-name>
  <filter-class>
    org.apache.wicket.protocol.http.WicketFilter
  </filter-class>
  <init-param>
    <param-name>applicationFactoryClassName</param-name>
    <param-value>
      org.apache.wicket.spring.SpringWebApplicationFactory
    </param-value>
  </init-param>
</filter>
```

Optionally, you can provide an extra parameter that tells the Spring application factory the name of the application bean:

```
<init-param>
  <param-name>applicationBean</param-name>
```

```
<param-value>wicketApplication</param-value>
</init-param>
```

The Spring application factory is smart enough to find the application class if there is only one, so you don't need to include this parameter.

And you're done! The application object is managed by Spring, and components can use Spring-bean-annotated members.

You may wonder about your models, behaviors, and other objects you use in the UI layer that aren't components. What we described in this section works only for components. You're likely to use Spring bean annotations in other objects as well, and the next section takes a look at how to do that.

13.2.6 Using Spring bean annotations with objects that aren't Wicket components

When you use anonymous classes like we do in the discounts-list example, referring to members of components works fine. But you'll often want to create generic models and behaviors, in which case you won't want to reference specific components.

As a workaround, you could fall back to the service locator pattern. For instance, listing 13.6 shows how to properly get a handle to the Spring application context instance.

Listing 13.6 Letting Spring set the application context instance

```
public class WicketInActionApplication extends WebApplication
    implements ApplicationContextAware {

  private ApplicationContext ctx;

  public void setApplicationContext(
      ApplicationContext applicationContext) throws BeansException {
    this.ctx = applicationContext;
  }
}
```

Spring does this for you because the class implements `ApplicationContextAware` (which is a Spring interface) and the application object is managed by Spring. You could then implement the `getDiscountsService` method as before.

But wouldn't it be nice to be able to use the Spring bean annotations as you did on the components in the previous section? The answer is easy. Put this line in the constructor of any object for which you want Spring-bean-annotated members resolved:

```
InjectorHolder.getInjector().inject(this);
```

That's it!

You can create some neat classes using this pattern. For instance, listing 13.7 shows the code for a generic model that loads domain objects. This model class is a good example of how you can easily save a lot of duplication, and how to make your code more readable and more strongly typed by generalizing your problem (which in this case is the fact that you often want to load domain objects in models and detach the models afterward).

Listing 13.7   Generic model for loading domain objects

```
public class DomainObjectModel<T extends DomainObject>
    extends LoadableDetachableModel {

  @SpringBean
  private DiscountsService service;
  private final Class<T> type;
  private final Long id;

  public DomainObjectModel(Class<T> type, Long id) {
    InjectorHolder.getInjector().inject(this);
    this.type = type;
    this.id = id;
  }

  public DomainObjectModel(T domainObject) {
    super(domainObject);
    InjectorHolder.getInjector().inject(this);
    this.type = (Class<T>) domainObject.getClass();
    this.id = domainObject.getId();
  }

  @Override
  protected T load() {
    return service.load(type, id);
  }
}
```

Domain objects like `Discount` and `Cheese` need to implement the `DomainObject` interface for this to work. That interface is defined as follows:

```
public interface DomainObject extends Serializable {

  Long getId();
}
```

That concludes our Spring adventures. In this chapter so far, you've seen that layering software is a common way of keeping it manageable, and the three-tier service model is a popular way of doing this. You've read that DI is a good way to keep the layers loosely coupled. And you've worked through an example of setting up a layered application using the Spring framework. This is the responsibility of the data access layer. In the last part of this chapter, we'll take a closer look at this.

13.3   *Implementing the data tier using Hibernate*

In this section, we'll use Hibernate to implement the last tier of the multitiered application: the data access layer. At the time of writing this book, Hibernate is probably the most popular Java persistence framework, and many Wicket users (including us) use it for their projects. The next sections introduce Hibernate and show you how to use it with Wicket.

13.3.1 *Introducing Hibernate*

Hibernate tries to bridge the gap between object-oriented programming (OOP) and the relational model that is used for relational databases (much like Wicket tries to bridge the gap between OOP and the stateless HTTP protocol). Frameworks like Hibernate are commonly called Object-Relational Mapping (ORM) frameworks.

If you don't use ORM tools, you'll spend a lot of time writing code to create objects from query results and translating object relationships to relationships that fit the relational model. And to complicate things, those relationships are often each other's inversions, the relational model doesn't have the concept of inheritance, and so on.

Using Hibernate also shields you from the complexities of SQL. Although some things are easier to do with SQL, querying complex relationships often is a lot harder (even counterintuitive) with SQL than navigating through an object graph.

Hibernate also does a good job of abstracting the details of particular databases. Many databases have their own way of doing things, such as how unique keys are maintained and whether subqueries are supported. Hibernate abstracts these issues, which enables you to switch databases without any effect on your code. You can even let Hibernate generate the database schema if you want.

> **TIP** The Manning books *Hibernate Quickly* (Patrick Peak and Nick Heudecker, 2005) and *Java Persistence with Hibernate* (Christian Bauer and Gavin King, 2006) are great resources for learning Hibernate.

Before you can use Hibernate with a Wicket application, you have to configure it, as we'll explain in the next section.

13.3.2 *Configuring Hibernate*

The first thing you do when you work with Hibernate is define your domain classes and configure Hibernate to map them to database tables. Listing 13.8 shows how the `Discount` class can be mapped using Hibernate's annotation support.

Listing 13.8 Part of the `Discount` class with Hibernate annotations

```
@Entity
@Table(name = "discount")
public class Discount implements DomainObject {

    @Id
    @GeneratedValue
    private Long id;

    @ManyToOne
    private Cheese cheese;

    @Lob
    @Column(name = "description")
    private String description;

    @Column(name = "discount", nullable = false)
    private double discount;
    ...
```

The `Entity` annotation declares that the class is a persistent entity. The `Id` annotation says that the member `id` is the primary key, and `GeneratedValue` instructs Hibernate to generate unique values for every new object. `Column` annotations map regular columns (the `name` attribute is optional), `Lob` annotations map binary large objects, and `ManyToOne` annotations map relationships to other Hibernate-managed objects.

Next, you use Spring's Hibernate support to let Hibernate load and analyze these classes:

```
<bean id="sessionFactory" class="org.springframework.orm.hibernate3.
annotation.AnnotationSessionFactoryBean">
  <property name="dataSource" ref="dataSource" />
  <property name="annotatedClasses">
    <list>
      <value>dbdiscounts.domain.User</value>
      <value>dbdiscounts.domain.Cheese</value>
      <value>dbdiscounts.domain.Discount</value>
    </list>
  </property>
  <property name="hibernateProperties">
    <props>
      <prop key="hibernate.dialect">${hibernate.dialect}</prop>
    </props>
  </property>
</bean>
```

This lets Spring construct a session factory using a data source that is defined elsewhere in the configuration and a Hibernate dialect provided via a properties file or a system property. The `annotatedClasses` argument is the list of classes you want Hibernate to manage for you.

Hibernate session factories produce Hibernate sessions, which function as the main handle for users to load, save, and delete objects and create queries. These sessions also function as a first-level cache so that dependencies can be resolved efficiently and so that Hibernate can recognize which objects changed during a transaction.

In the web.xml configuration file, you configure a filter that prepares a Hibernate session for each request and cleans up that session after the request is done. Here is what we put in web.xml:

```
<filter>
  <filter-name>opensessioninview</filter-name>
  <filter-class>
    org.springframework.orm.hibernate3.support.OpenSessionInViewFilter
  </filter-class>
</filter>
<filter-mapping>
  <filter-name>opensessioninview</filter-name>
  <url-pattern>/*</url-pattern>
</filter-mapping>
```

There are alternatives to using a session per request, but for web applications, this is the recommended approach as it keeps things simple.

TIP   Always define the Hibernate session filter before the Wicket filter; doing
        so results in the session filter being executed first (so the session is
        opened before Wicket starts handling a request) and returned to after-
        ward (so the session can be closed after Wicket is done with the request).

Finally, we'll get to implementing DAOs using Hibernate in the next section.

13.3.3 Implementing data access objects using Hibernate

To avoid code duplication, you create a generified base class that handles the common things you want to do with Hibernate: loading, saving, and deleting. Listing 13.9
shows an interface that supports this.

Listing 13.9   Base DAO with common operations

```
public interface Dao<T extends DomainObject> {

  @Transactional
  void delete(T o);

  T load(long id);

  @Transactional
  void save(T o);

  List<T> findAll();

  int countAll();
}
```

The transaction annotations are a Spring construct to declare that a method should
run in the context of a transaction. For this to work, you need to configure a transaction manager like this:

```
<bean id="transactionManager"
class="org.springframework.orm.hibernate3.HibernateTransactionManager">
    <property name="sessionFactory" ref="sessionFactory" />
</bean>
 <tx:annotation-driven />
```

That's enough to let Spring (2.0 and above) pick up these annotations and *advise* (a
term from Aspect Oriented Programming [AOP]) these methods to be transactional.

To pair with the base interface, you create a base implementation, which is shown
in listing 13.10.

Listing 13.10   Hibernate DAO base class

```
public abstract class AbstractHibernateDaoImpl<T extends DomainObject>
    implements Dao<T> {

  private Class<T> domainClass;
  private SessionFactory sf;

  public AbstractHibernateDaoImpl(Class<T> domainClass) {
    this.domainClass = domainClass;
  }
```

```
public SessionFactory getSessionFactory() { return sf; }

public void setSessionFactory(SessionFactory sf) { this.sf = sf; }

public void delete(T object) { getSession().delete(object); }

public T load(long id) {
  return (T) getSession().get(domainClass, id);
}

public void save(T object) { getSession().saveOrUpdate(object); }

public List<T> findAll() {
  Criteria criteria = getSession().createCriteria(domainClass);
  return (List<T>) criteria.list();
}

public int countAll() {
  Criteria criteria = getSession().createCriteria(domainClass);
  criteria.setProjection(Projections.rowCount());
  return (Integer) criteria.uniqueResult();
}

public Session getSession() { return sf.getCurrentSession(); }
}
```

The remaining code for implementing DAO classes is tiny (although it will grow once you include more specific queries). We can define the discount DAO like this:

```
public interface DiscountDao extends Dao<Discount> { }
```

The implementation of the discount DAO is as follows:

```
public class DiscountDaoImpl extends
    AbstractHibernateDaoImpl<Discount> implements DiscountDao {

  public DiscountDaoImpl() {
    super(Discount.class);
  }
}
```

The services and DAOs are now ready to be used in the Wicket components.

To finish this chapter, we'll discuss a few common pitfalls you may encounter when working with an ORM tool like Hibernate with Wicket.

13.3.4 *Wicket/Hibernate pitfalls*

A common pitfall when working with Wicket and Hibernate comes from the fact that Hibernate sessions are designed for temporary use. Hibernate sessions use scarce resources like database connections, and they should be closed after a unit of work is done so the resources they use can be made available to other sessions.

The easiest and often safest way of making sure sessions are available when you need them—and are cleaned up properly when you're done with them—is to use a Hibernate filter, as shown in section 13.3.2. Such a filter opens a Hibernate session at the start of a request and closes it when the request is done. To understand the problem, you have to know that Hibernate creates *proxy objects* (objects that act like the objects they replace) when it returns instances of managed classes, and that those proxy objects hold a reference to the session in which they were created. Such references to the Hibernate session are used to resolve *lazy collections*, which are collections (associations) that defer querying the database until they're accessed. For example—a collection on the many side of a one-to-many relationship can defer loading from the database until accessed by client code. If you keep the objects around after a request and try to use them in a subsequent request, you may run into the problem of your objects trying to work with a closed session.

The potential problem then is that Wicket objects, such as pages and models, that can reference Hibernate managed objects can (and often do) live over multiple requests. If you keep direct references to Hibernate objects, the session objects they refer to will be stale after the first request! These sessions will be closed by the filter, but the instances of the Hibernate managed objects have no way of knowing this. And once the session is stale, Hibernate can't use these sessions to load lazy collections and will throw an exception when you tell it to do so.

Another problem is one of efficiency. You know that Wicket handles state for you and that it serializes components and all their references when saving components to second-level cache or replicating them across the cluster. But typically the only thing you need to know in order to load persistent objects is an identifier (or query) and class so you can load them when needed. You don't need to keep the complete objects around.

Yet another pitfall involves objects that come from resources like a database. These objects can be updated by other clients between requests. Most web applications don't need real-time updates, but you generally want your information to be fresh at the time the user requests the page.

You read about the solution to these problems in chapter 4 on models. The solution is to work with detachable models. After a request, you let a model deflate the object to its essence (typically the object's identifier and class); when you need the whole object again, you let the model inflate it by loading it from a Hibernate session.

A final gotcha is the fact that Hibernate and some parts of Wicket depend on a proper implementation of `hashCode` and `equals`. To illustrate a potential problem, consider the following code fragment from `DiscountsEditList`:

```
public final class DiscountsEditList extends Panel {
    @SpringBean
    private DiscountsService service;
    private List<Discount> discounts;
    ...
    public DiscountsEditList(String id) {
        super(id);
        RefreshingView discountsView = new RefreshingView("discounts") {

            @Override
            protected Iterator getItemModels() {
                discounts = service.findAllDiscounts();
                return new DomainModelIteratorAdaptor<Discount>(discounts
```

```
              .iterator()) {
          @Override
          protected IModel model(Object object) {
            return new HashcodeEnabledCompoundPropertyModel(
                (Discount) object);
        ...
      discountsView.setItemReuseStrategy(ReuseIfModelsEqualStrategy
          .getInstance());
      form.add(discountsView);
    }
```

`RefreshingView` throws away its child components at the start of each request to ensure that the rows correctly reflect the data. Between requests (possibly as a result of the last one), rows may have been swapped or deleted, and new rows may have been added.

Throwing away child components works fine for read-only lists, but when you work with forms, you don't want the repeater to throw away the rows that are still logically the same. This is particularly important for displaying errors and previous input (in case of errors); feedback messages are stored keyed on the components they're meant for, but if they're thrown away, Wicket won't be able to locate them.

The solution is to configure the repeater to follow a special item-reuse strategy: it reuses its items when the models are equal. Of course, we aren't interested in the Wicket models, but rather in the objects they produce. We created a model that implements `hashCode` and `equals` by passing calls to the objects they represent:

```
public int hashCode() {
  return Objects.hashCode(getObject());
}
public boolean equals(Object obj) {
  if (obj instanceof IModel) {
    return Objects.equal(getObject(), ((IModel) obj).getObject());
  }
  return false;
}
```

And for *that* to work well, the domain objects must have *their* `hashCode` and `equals` methods properly implemented. This can be a tricky affair, and we refer you to the Hibernate documentation to learn how to do it. Using the identifier to generate the `hashCode` and to implement `equals` often works best for us, but it's pretty much blasphemy in the eyes of the Hibernate people. Again, read all about it in their documentation.

If you want to be absolutely safe, you can consider using value objects, which are (often simplified) beans that represent (parts of) their peer domain objects. Using those enables you to keep the objects you use in the business and data access tiers separate from the ones you use in the UI tier. The disadvantage of using value objects is that you end up with quite a bit of plumbing code, especially when passing data across layers.

13.4 Summary

This chapter gave you an overview of how to set up Spring and Hibernate to create a multitiered architecture for your application. You can use Spring and Hibernate many ways with Wicket, and there are countless alternatives for both frameworks (Guice, PicoContainer, HiveMind, OSGi, JPA/EJB 3, Cayenne, iBATIS, plain JDBC, and so forth).

Various projects specialize in making Wicket work better with databases. If you're not crazy about the multitiered approach (which would be understandable, because it involves a lot of plumbing code), you can use ORM tools directly in the view layer, possibly using one of the productivity-enhancement projects that support Wicket: for example, Databinder (Hibernate-based RAD toolkit), WicketWebBeans (JavaBean editing toolkit), Quickmodels (works with ODBMS db4o), Modelibra (domain-oriented RAD environment), or Grails (Groovy-based RAD framework that has a Wicket module).

In the next and final chapter, we'll look at how to prepare your Wicket applications for production.

Putting your application into production

14

In this chapter:

- Testing your web user interface
- Providing pretty URLs for visitors and search engines
- Configuring your application for optimal performance
- Monitoring your application in production

The goal of any web application is ultimately to make a profit. Some of you may be familiar with the four-step Web 2.0 profitable business plan:

1. Build a web application.
2. Put the application into production.
3. …
4. Profit!

The previous chapters focused on the first step: how to *build* your application. You learned about using and creating components, working with databases, processing user input, securing your application, and attracting an international crowd.

    This chapter begins with step 2: preparing your application for production use by testing it and by creating a site map that is optimized for your users and search engines. With these tasks finished, you'll be ready to hand over the application to your users. Then, step 3 of the business plan starts. Most of step 3 is unknown territory, but in this chapter we'll give you several tools to keep your application healthy throughout the endless hours of the process so you can arrive at step 4.

Let's first look at testing: ensuring that your application does what it was intended for.

14.1 Testing your Wicket application

In this section, you'll learn how to create tests for your Wicket pages and components. We assume that you're familiar with unit testing, and we'll use JUnit to build our examples because it's the de facto testing framework. We'll use JUnit 4 annotation-based testing, but nothing is holding you back from using the old tried and tested JUnit 3.8.

Using the `WicketTester` class, you can test-drive your application directly in unit tests. The tester works directly on the server classes. This is in contrast to testing frameworks such as JWebUnit, HtmlUnit, and Selenium; these frameworks work on the protocol level by sending requests to a running web server. JWebUnit and Html-Unit both stub the browser, whereas Selenium runs inside the browser.

NOTE   The `WicketTester` discussed in this section will most likely be rewritten when Wicket adopts Java 5 into its core. Using Java 5 enables us to use annotations, static imports, and generics to create an API that is more natural when building unit tests. Fortunately, the ideas in this section will remain valid, although the APIs may be subject to change.

`WicketTester` is a helper class to test-drive your pages and components as if they were called during a normal request. The big advantage compared to working at the protocol level is that you get full control over the pages and components. This way, you can test a page or component in isolation and outside the servlet container, making the tests run faster and under your control. To illustrate, we'll start by unit-testing the examples from section 1.3 and then work our way through the front and checkout pages of our cheese store from chapter 3.

14.1.1 Unit-testing Hello, World

The first example in section 1.3 was Hello, World! Let's create a unit test for it. The Hello World page contains a label that displays the *Hello, World!* text. The following test shows how we can validate whether the label renders the expected text:

```
public class HelloWorldTest {
    @Test
    public void labelContainsHelloWorld() {
        WicketTester tester = new WicketTester();
        tester.startPage(HelloWorld.class);
        tester.assertLabel("message", "Hello, World!");
    }
}
```

In this test, we want to determine whether our message label contains the famous phrase. To test our page, we need to create a `WicketTester` and tell it to start the test with our `HelloWorld` page. This renders the `HelloWorld` page and makes it available for us to test with the tester. In this case, we assert that the label component with identifier `message` contains `Hello, World!`.

Navigating the component structure using compound Wicket identifiers

The first parameter to the `assertXXX` methods is the component path. The component path uniquely identifies a Wicket component in the page's component hierarchy. In our first example, we have only one level of components to navigate.

Checking the value of a nested component requires you to provide the full component path made up from each component's identifier in the tree traversal to the particular component. For example:

```
add(new ListView("cheeses", cheeses) {
    @Override
    protected void populateItems(ListItem item) {
        Cheese cheese = (Cheese)item.getModelObject();
        Link link = new Link("link") {...};
        link.add(new Label("name", cheese.getName()));
    }
});
```

To check the name of the first cheese, we have to use the following assert:

```
tester.assertLabel("cheeses:0:link:name", "edam");
```

The component identifiers are separated using colons to disambiguate component path identifiers from property expressions. For instance, would `person.name` point to a component with identifier `name` nested within a component with identifier `person`, or to a label that uses `person.name` as its component identifier?

Referencing items inside repeaters such as a `RepeatingView`, `ListView`, or `Data-View` requires the use of numbers inside the component path: these numbers are used to identify the index of an item from a repeater. In the example, we retrieve the first list item of the `ListView` named `cheeses` using the component path `cheeses:0` (like lists in Java, repeaters start their indexes at zero).

Let's modify the Hello, World! example so it can work in an international setting. Using resource bundles, we can provide translations for our label content. The next snippet shows the modified page and a French resource bundle:

```
public HelloWorld() {
    add(new Label("message",
                  new ResourceModel("greeting", "Hello, World!")));
}

# File: HelloWorld_fr.properties
greeting=Bonjour tout le monde!
```

With our new internationalized example, we can now check whether the contents of the label are correct in an international setting. The next snippet checks whether the correct message is displayed for a French visitor:

```
@Test
public void labelContainsHelloWorldInFrench() {
    WicketTester tester = new WicketTester();              ❶ Initialize
    tester.setupRequestAndResponse();                         tester        ❷ Switch to
    tester.getWicketSession().setLocale(Locale.FRENCH);                        French
    tester.startPage(HelloWorld.class);
    tester.assertLabel("message", "Bonjour tout le monde!");
}
```

To verify that our label generates the correct languages, we can switch the locale used on the session. First, we need to set up the request cycle, which binds a session to our tester ❶. This session is now valid until we invalidate it or the tester is cleaned up. Next, we set the correct locale on our session ❷.

Another technique for checking whether some text (inside components, or plain markup) is present uses `WicketTester`'s `assertContains` method. This method takes a regular expression and checks whether the contents of the page fit the expression. For instance, the next example tests for both a Dutch and an English message:

```
tester.assertContains("H[ae]llo, (were|Wor)ld!");
```

Yet another way of testing the contents of a component is to test its model value, as demonstrated in the next line of code:

```
tester.assertModelValue("message", "Hello, World!");
```

We can also test the contents of the rendered markup tags by using the `TagTester`, as shown in the next snippet:

```
assertEquals("Hello, World!",
                    tester.getTagById("message").getValue());
```

The `getTagById` method uses the DOM identifier to retrieve the tag from the rendered document (similar to JavaScript's `document.getElementById`). `getTagById` returns a `TagTester` that works on the markup tags of the provided component. Using the `TagTester`, we can check the tag's attributes and the value between the tags. For example, to test if a `Link` has a confirm script inside its `onclick` JavaScript handler, we test it with the following line:

```
assertEquals("return confirm('Are you sure?');",
            tester.getTagById("link").getAttribute("onclick"));
```

We're now able to test the contents of a page and our components. Let's look at the second example from section 1.3.2.

14.1.2 *Having fun with link tests*

Clicking a link invokes some kind of action on the server. Depending on the link, the incoming request can be an Ajax request or a normal request. The link can render a different page than the current one or perform an action in the `onClick` handler and stay on the same page. Using the `WicketTester`, you can test the actions of clicking a link using a normal or an Ajax request.

The running example from section 1.3.2 introduced you to links. The example shows a link that increases a counter on the page when clicked. A label shows the value of the counter. The following code shows how to test a link:

```
@Test
public void countingLinkClickTest() {
    WicketTester tester = new WicketTester();
    tester.startPage(LinkCounter.class);
    tester.assertModelValue("label", 0);
    tester.clickLink("link");
    tester.assertModelValue("label", 1);
}
```

We start by setting up the tester and providing it with our starting page. The first thing we check is whether the counter is zero ❶. Next, we click the link ❷ and check whether the value of the counter was increased ❸.

In chapter 1, we also modified the link-counter example to use an `AjaxFallback-Link` instead of a normal link to demonstrate Wicket's Ajax capabilities. Let's see how to create a unit test that tests the counting `AjaxFallbackLink` example. To test the fallback link thoroughly, we need to test the link using both an Ajax request and a normal fallback request. The next example tests both paths for the Ajax-enabled counting link example:

```
@Test
public void countingAjaxFallbackLinkTest() {
    WicketTester tester = new WicketTester();
    tester.startPage(LinkCounter.class);
    tester.assertModelValue("label", 0);
    tester.clickLink("link", true);
    tester.assertComponentOnAjaxResponse("label");
    tester.assertModelValue("label", 1);
    tester.clickLink("link", false);
    tester.assertModelValue("label", 2);
}
```

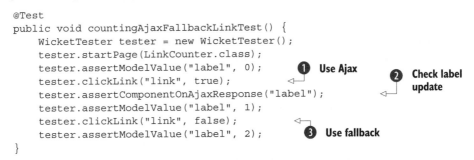

The first link click ❶ uses an Ajax request target. This mimics the scenario where a browser has JavaScript enabled and is Ajax capable. We test whether the correct components are updated in the request using `assertComponentOnAjaxResponse` ❷. To make the test complete, we click the link again using a normal, non-Ajax request, which exercises the fallback scenario ❸.

TESTING NAVIGATION

The previous examples stayed on the same page, but what happens when you click a link that navigates to a new page? The next example shows a link that navigates to a new page and an accompanying unit test to ensure the correct page was rendered:

```
public FirstPage() {
    add(new Link("link") {
        @Override
        public void onClick() {
```

```
                setResponsePage(new SecondPage());
            }
        });
    }

    @Test
    public void navigateToSecondPage() {
        WicketTester tester = new WicketTester();
        tester.startPage(new FirstPage());
        tester.clickLink("link");
        tester.assertRenderedPage(SecondPage.class);
    }
```

The example starts with the FirstPage constructor. The page has a link that navigates to SecondPage when it's clicked. We could also have used a bookmarkable page link. The test begins by creating FirstPage and then clicks the link. Finally, we assert that a SecondPage was rendered.

NOTE   If you know beforehand how the second page's markup should look, and you store it in a file, you can test the output of the request against the contents of the file. A typical way of testing your application is to manually inspect whether a page is rendered correctly and then save the markup to a master template. This template is then compared to the output of the same action in a unit test. If the output is different, the test fails. Although this type of testing can be valuable, it's brittle: the content should be static, for example displaying a date in a label invalidates the output.

We're now able to check the results of user interaction with links, but we aren't done. We haven't touched on one of the most important parts of web-application development: forms. Let's look at the Echo application from section 1.3.3.

14.1.3 Testing the Wicket Echo application

In most applications, forms and form components provide the majority of user interaction. Most of the development time goes into perfecting this part of the application using validations and type conversions, and providing feedback. Testing this part of the user interaction is usually done manually because it's hard to automate the testing. Wicket's FormTester provides the means to perform these tests automatically. The FormTester lets you set values on text fields; select values in drop-down boxes, check boxes, and radio buttons; and simulate uploading files to the form. To see the FormTester in action, we'll revisit the Echo example from section 1.3.3.

The Echo application was your first encounter with form processing. It consists of a form with a single field and a submit button. The contents of the field are echoed using a label when the form is submitted. We can test this form by setting the value of the field to some text and submitting the form. We can then check whether the label contains the right value. The following code shows how:

```
    @Test
    public void echoForm() {
        WicketTester tester = new WicketTester();
```

```
tester.startPage(EchoPage.class);
tester.assertLabel("message", "");
FormTester formTester = tester.newFormTester("form");
assertEquals("", formTester.getTextComponentValue("field"));
formTester.setValue("field", "Echo message");
formTester.submit("button");
tester.assertLabel("message", "Echo message");
assertEquals("", formTester.getTextComponentValue("field"));
}
```

We start with the EchoPage. Then, we check whether the contents of the message label and text field are empty. Using the form tester, we set the value of the text field and submit the form using the button. In the resulting page, we check whether the label echoes our submitted string and whether the field has been cleared.

NOTE In Wicket 1.3, you can use a form tester instance for only one submit. This limitation is due to be fixed in a later release.

The Echo application is simple in its form usage. Let's look at a more complicated example where we can check the functionality of validators and messages. In chapter 3, we created the online cheese store with a checkout page. Let's see how to test it.

14.1.4 Testing validators on Cheesr's checkout page

The checkout page from section 3.3 contains a form that records customers' address information. The form consists of four fields: name, street, ZIP code, and city. We made each field required to be sure we get all the necessary data from our customers.

At the start of chapter 3, we created a custom session in which to store the shopping-cart contents. The checkout page gets the shopping cart directly from the custom session, so we need to ensure that our test can create the custom session and fill it with our test values. Listing 14.1 shows a unit test for our checkout page that tests submitting empty values.

Listing 14.1 Testing the checkout page with empty values

```
@Test
public void checkoutTest() {
    WicketTester tester = new WicketTester(new CheesrApplication());    ◁─┐
    tester.startPage(Checkout.class);
                                                                    Provide
                                                                CheesrSession  ❶
    FormTester formTester = tester.newFormTester("form");
    tester.assertNoErrorMessage();
    tester.assertNoInfoMessage();           ❷ No messages yet
    formTester.submit("order");
    tester.assertRenderedPage(Checkout.class);
    tester.assertErrorMessages(new String[] {
        "Field 'name' is required.",
        "Field 'street' is required.",
        "Field 'zipcode' is required.",
        "Field 'city' is required." });
}
```

We provide the `WicketTester` with our custom `Application` object ❶, because the application is responsible for creating the session (see chapter 2). Next, we tell the tester to render the `Checkout` page. Because we haven't done anything with the form yet, we can be sure that at this moment there are no error messages ❷. When we submit the form using the Order button, we expect the checkout page to be rendered again and to contain several error messages: one for each missing input.

Because the default locale is English, the messages returned are in English. To test whether the messages are rendered correctly in a different locale, we need to change the session locale. Listing 14.2 tests the same page using the Dutch locale.

Listing 14.2   Testing the checkout page using a different locale

```
@Test
public void checkoutDutch() {
    WicketTester tester = new WicketTester(new CheesrApplication());
    tester.setupRequestAndResponse();
    tester.getWicketSession().setLocale(new Locale("nl"));    ← ❶ Bind session
    tester.startPage(Checkout.class);                         ← ❷ Switch to Dutch

    FormTester formTester = tester.newFormTester("form");
    tester.assertNoErrorMessage();
    tester.assertNoInfoMessage();
    formTester.submit("order");
    tester.assertRenderedPage(Checkout.class);
    tester.assertErrorMessages(new String[] {
        "veld 'name' is verplicht.",
        "veld 'street' is verplicht.",
        "veld 'zipcode' is verplicht.",
        "veld 'city' is verplicht." });
}
```

To make this test work, we need to bind the session first ❶ before setting the locale ❷; otherwise, Wicket will create a new session object, and the first request will negate our efforts. The rest of the test is similar to listing 14.1, but the messages have been translated.

Until now, we've tested entire pages—but what if you have a custom component and want to test it directly without creating a Christmas tree covered with bells and whistles? Let's explore testing a custom component directly by using the shopping-cart panel from chapter 3.

14.1.5   *Testing a panel directly with the ShoppingCartPanel*

One of Wicket's strengths is the ability to create custom components quickly. In chapter 7, you learned that panels provide the best way to quickly create custom components.

In chapter 3, we refactored two pages (the home page and the checkout page) and extracted the shopping-cart functionality into a panel: `ShoppingCartPanel`. The panel has a list of all selected items, and each item has a link to remove it from the cart. The panel also sports a label showing the total amount due.

The first test determines whether we can display an empty shopping cart:

```
@Test
public void emptyShoppingCartPanel() {
```

```
WicketTester tester = new WicketTester();
final Cart cart = new Cart();
tester.startPanel(new TestPanelSource(){
    public Panel getTestPanel(String panelId) {
        return new ShoppingCartPanel(panelId, cart);
    }});
```
❶ Delay panel creation

```
    tester.assertListView("panel:cart", Collections.EMPTY_LIST);
    tester.assertLabel("panel:total", "$0.00");
}
```

The test begins by creating an empty shopping cart. Next, we provide our panel for the WicketTester **❶**. We have to use a factory for the panel because the tester adds the panel to a test page internally. It must set the component identifier, and that can happen only once (at the component's construction time). The TestPanelSource factory enables us to lazily create the shopping-cart panel and pass on the provided component identifier and our shopping cart. The value of the component identifier is panel—we'll need it when testing the panel's components.

When we've set up the test, we can assert that the cart renders an empty list view and that the total amount is $0.00. Note that we prefix the component paths with panel:, because the list view and the Total label are children of the panel, and the panel is added to the test page using the component identifier value panel.

Now that we have the first test in place, let's look at testing the Remove links; see listing 14.3. To test them, we need to add items to the cart first—otherwise they aren't rendered.

Listing 14.3 Testing links inside a list view on a panel

```
@Test
public void filledShoppingCartPanel() {
    final Cart cart = new Cart();
    Cheese gouda = new Cheese("Gouda", "Gouda", 1.99);
    Cheese edam = new Cheese("Edam", "Edam", 2.99);
    cart.getCheeses().add(gouda);
    cart.getCheeses().add(edam);

    tester.startPanel(new TestPanelSource() {
        public Panel getTestPanel(String panelId) {
            return new ShoppingCartPanel(panelId, cart);
        }
    });

    tester.assertListView("panel:cart", Arrays.asList(gouda, edam));
    tester.assertLabel("panel:total", "$4.98");
    tester.assertLabel("panel:cart:0:name", "Gouda");

    tester.clickLink("panel:cart:0:remove");

    tester.assertListView("panel:cart", Arrays.asList(edam));
    tester.assertLabel("panel:total", "$2.99");
    tester.assertLabel("panel:cart:0:name", "Edam");
}
```
❶ Remove Gouda cheese

In this test, we first add two cheeses to the cart: Gouda and Edam cheese. Next, we set up the test and provide the panel under test with the shopping cart containing the cheeses. Now we're ready to test the panel: we determine the current contents by checking the list view and the total value of the cart, and then we remove the Gouda cheese from the cart by clicking its Remove link ❶. Finally, we can check whether the only remaining cheese is Edam and that the total amount is $2.99.

With all this testing, we're confident that our application works as advertised. This implies that we're ready to go into production. But we need to consider one more thing: a site map with a good URL layout, so search engines and visitors can navigate your website with ease.

14.2 Optimizing URLs for search engines and visitors

When you have a public website, you probably want to ensure that it's search-engine friendly and that the URLs used on the public pages are easy for visitors to remember. The default URL-generation strategy may not be to your liking, so Wicket provides several approaches that will keep search engines and visitors happy.

14.2.1 Bookmarkable requests vs. session-relative requests

One of the great inventions of the last millennium was the search engine. It's never been easier to get access to ~~naughty pictures~~ interesting information than it has been since the invention of the search engine. Search engines drive traffic to websites, and our cheese store needs visitors in order to return a profit.

The front page of the cheese store shows short descriptions of the cheeses in our inventory. We want to show more information on a detail page for each cheese, such as the region of origin, how it's made, which wine goes well with it, and more about the ingredients. On the front page, we'll add a link to this details page with each displayed cheese.

SESSION-RELATIVE REQUESTS

Armed with our knowledge of links, we add the following snippet to each of our front-page items:

```
item.add(new Link("details", item.getModel()) {
    @Override
    public void onClick() {
        Cheese cheese = (Cheese)getModelObject();
        setResponsePage(new CheeseDetailsPage(cheese));
    }
});
```

This example adds a link to the list item and uses the item's model to gain access to the selected cheese in the `onClick` event handler. This cheese is passed to the `CheeseDetailsPage`, which is rendered to the browser. To see the effect of this implementation, we need to look at the generated URL:

```
http://cheesr.com/shop?wicket:interface=:0:details1::ILinkListener::
```

When visitors share the URL with their friends, they'll receive a page-expired error because they're trying to directly access the page instead of coming through the shop front. The problem with this URL is that it relies on a previous request to the server:

the request that generated the list of cheeses. Search engines could store this link information—but then search results would be useless.

To make this work, the server needs to know which link points to which cheese. The URL doesn't provide enough information to make it work without any prior knowledge. Using this way of linking is known as using *session-relative URLs*. The URL depends on the history of the session, which makes it relative for the session.

These URLs provide some resilience against *cross-site-request-forgery* attacks. When all navigation in your application is done through session-relative requests, it's difficult (although not impossible!) to forge a request to trigger a specific action in your application.

Encrypting your URLs

If you're concerned about cross-site-request forgery, you may want to encrypt each URL that Wicket generates. `CryptedUrlWebRequestCodingStrategy` provides the means: it uses a two-way encryption facility to obscure each generated URL. You can configure this strategy by overriding the `newRequestCycleProcessor` on your Application class, as shown in the following example:

```
@Override
protected IRequestCycleProcessor newRequestCycleProcessor() {
    return new WebRequestCycleProcessor() {
        @Override
        protected IRequestCodingStrategy newRequestCodingStrategy() {
            return new CryptedUrlWebRequestCodingStrategy(      encrypt
                new WebRequestCodingStrategy());                URLs
        }
    };
}
```

Using this code, Wicket will encrypt all your URLs—including bookmarkable URLs. This strategy uses the encryption facility that is configured in the security settings—see `ISecuritySettings`' `getCryptFactory` and `setCryptFactory` methods. By default, Wicket uses the Sun JCE encryption facilities. When these aren't available (for example, if you deploy on a JVM that doesn't ship with the Sun JCE classes), Wicket defaults to *no encryption*. In this case, you must provide your own crypt factory.

Note that you should modify the default encryption key that is stored in the `ISecuritySettings` to prevent malicious hackers from using the default publicly available key as an attack vector.

BOOKMARKABLE REQUESTS

We can also create links to the details pages by using the bookmarkable links and encoding everything we need into the request's URL. The advantage is clear: you can bookmark this item in your browser and go directly to that specific place in your application. The following snippet shows how to add such a link:

```
PageParameters pars = new PageParameters();
pars.add("cheese", cheese.getName());

add(new BookmarkablePageLink("show", CheeseDetailsPage.class, pars));
```

In this example, we externalize all necessary information by putting it in the page parameters, and give that information (here, the name of the cheese) to the link. Wicket generates the appropriate URL that targets the correct page and encodes the parameters. The resulting URL becomes

```
http://cheesr.com/shop?wicket:bookmarkablePage=
            %3Acom.cheesr.shop.CheeseDetailsPage&cheese=edam
```

This URL provides our application with the essential data: the target page and the name of the cheese. These types of URLs can be shared among users and used in promotional emails; and when search engines store them, they work instead of showing users an expiration error.

But this bookmarkable URL isn't something people will remember easily. It's also likely to result in error messages when we rename the page class or move it to another package (because the fully qualified classname is encoded in the URL). Let's look at how to make this URL prettier.

14.2.2 *Extreme URL makeover: mounting and URL encodings*

In the previous section, we showed you a Wicket URL for a bookmarkable page, as it's generated by default. The default URL looks ugly, even to someone who normally doesn't care about URLs. Although few users look at the address field in the browser to see where they are, creating nice-looking URLs has merit. They give structure to your site, and they make linking to your website easier. Even search engines favor URLs with paths instead of query parameters. So, having clean URLs for your website will attract more users.

You can change the way Wicket generates these URLs for you with *mounting* and *URL encoding*. Let's first look at mounting.

MOUNTING YOUR PAGES

In the previous section, you saw that the default URL for bookmarkable pages contains the fully qualified classname for the page. This is less than ideal, because bookmarkable pages are a public API to your application. When you move the page to another package or rename the class, newly generated URLs will be modified—but all those URLs stored in marketing emails, bookmarks from visitors, and (probably most important) search-engine indexes will remain unchanged. When someone tries to visit your site through one of those stored URLs, they will see a page-not-found error (also known as the 404 HTTP status code).

Wicket allows you to *mount* your bookmarkable pages to a specific path in your application. Let's look at an example that mounts the CheeseDetailsPage. Mounting a page is typically done in the init method of the application object, as follows:

```
public class CheesrApplication extends WebApplication {
    @Override
```

```
    protected void init() {
        mountBookmarkablePage("cheeses", CheeseDetailsPage.class));
    }
}
```

This example mounts our cheese details page to the path cheeses. When we generate the bookmarkable URL to the page, it now looks like this:

```
http://cheesr.com/cheeses/cheese/edam/
```

As you can see, this clears up the URL considerably. The *cheeses* part of the URL points to the mount path for the details page. This way, Wicket will map the two. The *cheese* part of the URL is the name of the parameter, and the *edam* part is the value of the parameter.

Even though this new URL looks a lot better than the previous incarnation, we can alter it even further. For instance, the parameter name seems superfluous; removing it gives us the following, more concise URL:

```
http://cheesr.com/cheeses/edam
```

Being able to generate such a tidy URL is great for both users and search engines. Let's look at options to modify URLs into a format you like.

THE PLASTIC SURGEON FOR URLs: URL ENCODING STRATEGIES

The default URL encoding used to generate our details URL uses the mount path and encodes both the keys and values of parameters into the ultimate URL. But there are many more ways to encode the same information by specifying a different URL encoder for your mounted pages.

Let's look at the ways we can encode the URL for our details page. The next example shows three URLs that point to the same page but are encoded using different strategies:

```
http://cheesr.com/cheeses?cheese=edam
http://cheesr.com/cheeses/cheese/edam
http://cheesr.com/cheeses/edam
```

The encoding is specified when we mount the page in the init method. The following snippet generates the first URL:

```
mount(new QueryStringUrlEncodingStrategy("cheeses",
                                          CheeseDetailPage.class));
```

Table 14.1 shows a list of the standard URL formats with their respective encoding strategies provided by Wicket.

Table 14.1 URL encodings provided by Wicket

URL	Name
/cheeses?cheese=edam	QueryStringUrlEncodingStrategy
/cheeses/cheese/edam	BookmarkablePageRequestTargetUrlCodingStrategy
/cheeses/edam	IndexedParamUrlCodingStrategy

Table 14.1 URL encodings provided by Wicket (continued)

URL	Name
/cheeses/edam/?age=33	MixedParamUrlCodingStrategy
/cheeses/name/edam	HybridUrlCodingStrategy
/cheeses/edam	IndexedHybridUrlCodingStrategy

Let's see what each encoding strategy can do for you.

QUERYSTRINGURLENCODINGSTRATEGY

This URL encoding is common in get requests where a query is sent to the server—for instance, a Google search. The parameters are encoded in a key/value pair and appended to the URL after a question mark. Multiple parameters are separated by ampersands.

TIP Rumor has it that even though this is the "official" way of encoding your URLs, search engines tend to like the other encoding strategies better.

Here's an example of using this encoding strategy and the resulting URL:

```
mount(new QueryStringUrlCodingStrategy("cheeses",
                                    CheeseDetailsPage.class));

http://cheesr.com/cheeses?cheese=edam
```

When the CheeseDetailPage is created, Wicket invokes the constructor with PageParameters. We can retrieve the values of the parameters by asking for the right key, as shown in the next example:

```
public CheeseDetailPage(PageParameters pars) {
    String name = pars.getString("cheese", "");
    ...
}
```

When we retrieve the value of the name parameter, we supply a default value. When working with request parameters, you should always assume something is wrong—people often modify parameters by hand and make (intentional) mistakes.

BOOKMARKABLEPAGEREQUESTTARGETURLCODINGSTRATEGY

Wicket uses this strategy as the default encoding for mounted pages. The parameters are encoded as key/value pairs separated by forward slashes. This type of encoding is currently popular for public-facing sites, probably because search engines seem to prefer it. The previous section shows an example and the result of using this strategy.

INDEXEDPARAMURLCODINGSTRATEGY

The IndexedParamUrlCodingStrategy strategy encodes parameter values based on index. You must put and retrieve the parameters by index. This strategy is currently the most popular for encoding URLs in web applications. Encoding your URLs in this way is also known as *RESTful encoding*.

The following example shows how to mount a page and how to create a bookmarkable link for our details page:

```
mount(new IndexedParamUrlCodingStrategy("cheeses",
                                        CheeseDetailsPage.class));

add(new BookmarkablePage("details",
            CheeseDetailsPage.class, new PageParameters("0=edam")));
```

Using this strategy has an influence on how you put and get the values for page parameters. When you build your pages using the default strategy, all your bookmarkable pages retrieve their values based on a name/value pair. When you switch to the indexed strategy, you must change all affected pages to retrieve the values based on their index. Fortunately, Wicket provides has a mixed encoding strategy that solves this problem.

MixedParamUrlCodingStrategy

`MixedParamUrlCodingStrategy` encodes parameters in a combination of indexed-based and *query=string* encoding. Any parameter key that isn't specified at mount time is encoded as a query string in the final URL. Applying this strategy to a page mount is shown here:

```
mount(new MixedParamUrlCodingStrategy("cheeses",
                CheeseDetailsPage.class, new String[]{"name"}));
```

The string array tells the strategy which parameter key needs to be mapped to which index. Any parameter key that isn't listed in this array is encoded using the query-string encoding. For example, this could lead to the following URL:

```
http://cheesr.com/cheeses/edam?color=blue&age=34
```

In this example, the `color` and `age` parameters are query-string encoded.

The hybrid URL-encoding strategies

The hybrid URL-encoding strategies from table 14.1 are the same as their nonhybrid variants, but they provide one additional feature. We'll discuss this shortly and use `HybridUrlCodingStrategy` as an example (`IndexedHybridUrlCodingStrategy` is similar in this respect).

When a bookmarkable URL is sent to the server, Wicket creates a new page instance for the requested page. When the page contains Ajax components, they update the page state by adding, replacing, or removing components. This works flawlessly until the user decides to refresh the page in the browser. Doing so sends the original, bookmarkable URL to the server, causing Wicket to create a new instance of the page and losing the component modifications.

The hybrid strategy redirects the browser after the first request to a URL that contains the page number (and Ajax version when necessary), as follows:

```
http://cheesr.com/shop/cheeses.4
```

This link is the shop's front page after the user has added items to the cart or browsed the catalogue using an Ajax navigator. The URL consists of two parts: the bookmarkable part (http://cheesr.com/shop/cheeses) and a state part (.4). When the user refreshes the page, Wicket notices the state part and returns the page instance that is already available instead of creating a new instance. When the user shares this link with someone else, Wicket ignores the state part and creates a new instance of the page.

Pretty URLs clearly make it easier for users to navigate your site. They also provide search engines with crawlable URLs that can be stored in their indexes and shown in search-result pages, driving new customers to your site. As search engines deliver more visitors, it's important to have your site running with optimal performance. Using the right configuration can save precious milliseconds for each request and make the user experience snappier. You'll learn how to tune Wicket for production in the next section.

14.3 Configuring your application for production

When you're building an application, Wicket provides useful tools for discovering and troubleshooting errors. One example is the detailed exception-reporting page, which is helpful for developers—but that would scare the living daylights out of your end users. There are other developer-friendly features that you may want to switch off when your application goes live, as we'll discuss later in this section.

14.3.1 Switching to deployment mode for optimal performance

While you're developing your application, you can use Wicket's tools to discover potential problems early on. This helps you diagnose and solve those problems before they become an issue for users. But the diagnostic tools come at a price: each check takes resources (time, memory, and CPU power).

Wicket applications can run in two modes:

1 *Development*—Maximum developer support
2 *Deployment*—Maximum performance and security for production

By default, Wicket starts in *development* mode. You're advised to switch to deployment mode for all production systems. You can see in the logs whether Wicket was started in development or deployment mode, as shown in the following snippet from a log file (the format may be different depending on your logging configuration):

```
INFO - WebApplication - [WicketInActionApplication] Started Wicket
                                  version 1.3.0 in development mode
**********************************************************************
*** WARNING: Wicket is running in DEVELOPMENT mode.            ***
***                    ^^^^^^^^^^^                             ***
*** Do NOT deploy to your live server(s) without changing this. ***
*** See Application#getConfigurationType() for more information. ***
**********************************************************************
```

As you can see, Wicket clearly warns against using development mode in live systems. If you start the server in deployment mode, Wicket logs the following lines (you'll learn how to switch to deployment mode in a minute):

```
INFO - WebApplication - [WicketInActionApplication] Started Wicket
                                  version 1.3.0 in deployment mode
```

Note that the big warning is missing and the info line shows *deployment* mode. How you can switch between these two modes?

SWITCHING WICKET BETWEEN DEVELOPMENT AND DEPLOYMENT MODE

There are three levels at which you can configure the mode in which an application is started. The following list shows them in order of priority:

1 Through a system property
2 Through a servlet/filter-initialization parameter
3 Through a context-initialization parameter

The system property is provided on the command line to the JVM. For production servers, this is probably the best way to ensure that your application is always started in deployment mode. Depending on your server, you need to configure this in the startup script or in an administration console that controls your server's startup parameters. The other two options are available in the web.xml deployment descriptor for your web application. Table 14.2 lists the configuration parameters and how you can set them.

Table 14.2   Configuring Wicket for development or production use

Method	Example
System property	`java -Dwicket.configuration=deployment`

Servlet/filter init	```<filter>```
	``` ... filter-name and filter-class ...```
	``` <init-param>```
	``` <param-name>configuration</param-name>```
	``` <param-value>deployment</param-value>```
	``` </init-param>```
	```</filter>```

Context init	```<context-param>```
	``` <param-name>configuration</param-name>```
	``` <param-value>deployment</param-value>```
	```</context-param>```

You now know how to switch applications to a different mode, but let's take a closer look at *why* you want to perform the switch. First we'll discuss configuration of development mode, and then deployment mode.

CONFIGURATION FOR DEVELOPMENT MODE

When your application runs in development mode, it's configured for optimum developer support. The following list describes what is done to help developers solve problems and to make development a lot easier:

- All resources are monitored for modifications and reloaded when modified.
- Wicket checks whether all components added to the Java component hierarchy are rendered.

- Wicket leaves all Wicket tags in the rendered markup that is sent to the client.
- Unexpected exceptions are shown in a page showing the full stack trace.
- Pages containing Ajax components show the Wicket Ajax Debugger (shown in figure 14.1).
- Wicket doesn't strip comments and whitespace from JavaScript files (also known as *minifying*).
- Wicket doesn't compress static text resources such as JavaScript and CSS files.

For example, reloading resources when they're modified means that developers have to restart applications less often, saving valuable time. Leaving the Wicket tags in the markup makes it easier to determine what markup comes from which component.

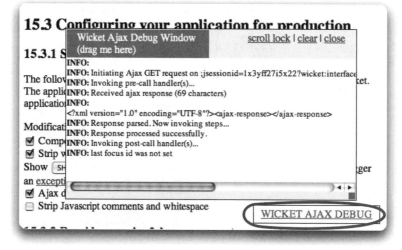

Figure 14.1   Wicket's Ajax Debugger is available in development mode and shows requests going from browser to server.

These developer-friendly options come at a price: they take time during request processing, use more bandwidth than necessary, and expose the nitty-gritty details of your application to your users.

CONFIGURATION FOR DEPLOYMENT MODE

Running your application in deployment mode does the opposite of the configuration settings used in development mode, as evidenced in the following list:

- The resource-modification watcher is turned off.
- Wicket ignores components added to the component hierarchy but not in the markup.
- All Wicket tags are stripped from the rendered markup that is sent to the client.
- An unexpected exception results in an error page with only a link to the home page (see figure 14.2).

- The Ajax debugger is turned off.
- Whitespace and comments are stripped from JavaScript files
- Static text resources (such as JavaScript and CSS files located on the classpath) are also compressed using gzip when supported by the client browser.

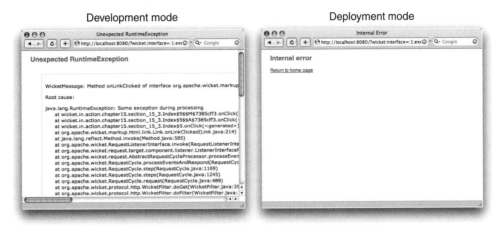

Figure 14.2   Development mode shows stack traces; deployment mode shows only a link to the home page.

These settings tune Wicket for better performance and save some bandwidth by minimizing JavaScript and sending it compressed. When your users visit a page with Ajax components, they aren't presented with the Ajax Debugger.

MODIFYING THE DEFAULT CONFIGURATION

The defaults presented by Wicket are sane. But sometimes you *want* to be able to modify markup and other resources at runtime on your production box. You have to modify Wicket's configuration to achieve this.

TIP   If you're modifying your application's configuration for use in production, *always* start tweaking the *deployment* mode. This way, you'll begin with the best settings for a production environment.

You can modify the configuration in the `Application`'s init method. Don't do this in the `Application`'s constructor, because the `Application` object hasn't been completely constructed and configured yet. If you modify the settings in the constructor, Wicket will override them with the defaults when it configures your `Application` object using the configuration parameter.

The next example shows how to configure Wicket to scan for changes in markup files in development mode:

```
public CheesrApplication extends WebApplication {
    @Override
    public void init() {
        if(DEPLOYMENT.equalsIgnoreCase(getConfigurationType())) {
```

```
                        IResourceSettings resourceSettings = getResourceSettings();
                        resourceSettings.setResourcePollFrequency(Duration.ONE_MINUTE);
                }
        }
}
```

This example checks the configuration type before tinkering with the resource settings. The resource-poll frequency tells Wicket to scan for changes in each resource (properties, JavaScript, or HTML files, for example) that is cached. If the underlying file is modified, Wicket discards the cached copy and reads the new version.

Wicket has many settings—too many to discuss in this book. To make modifying and understanding the settings easier, they've been grouped into categories. Table 14.3 lists the interface of each category. You can obtain the settings for each category by stripping the *I* from the interface name and using the remaining name for the getter. For example, to get at IRequestCycleSettings, you should use the getRequestCycle-Settings method.

In deployment mode, Wicket shows users a Spartan error page instead of a page with a cryptic error message containing a stack trace. Even though some of your users may enjoy puzzling over a Java stack trace, it's not customary to show users the guts of

Table 14.3 Configuration settings

Category	Description
IApplicationSettings	Specifies error pages, the class resolver, and the default maximum upload size.
IDebugSettings	Enables the Ajax Debugger, line-precise error reporting, and a component-use check.
IExceptionSettings	Specifies what to do with an unexpected exception (see section 14.3.2).
IFrameworkSettings	Stores the Wicket version.
IMarkupSettings	Specifies before/after disabled links, autolinking, markup encoding, markup stripping, and XML declaration checking.
IPageSettings	Specifies the component resolver, automatic multiwindow detection, and default page versioning.
IRequestCycleSettings	Specifies the render strategy, timeout, response filters, response buffering, and extended client info.
IRequestLoggerSettings	Enables requestlogger, records session sizes, and keeps the last *N* requests (see section 14.4.1).
IResourceSettings	Specifies gzip compression, resource filters, folders, the watcher, and the localizer.
ISecuritySettings	Specifies the authorization strategy, unauthorized component instantiation listener, cookie persister, and encryption for URLs.
ISessionSettings	Contains settings specific to the HttpSessionStore.

an application. The default deployment error page (right screenshot in figure 14.1) probably doesn't fit with the overall design of your application—there is no feedback about what went wrong and no information that might help users solve the problem. Let's look at improving your image and providing visitors with better error pages.

14.3.2 *Providing meaningful error pages*

An error page is shown when something unexpected occurs—for instance, when a database connection is lost, or a web service that always works starts returning unforeseen messages, or a coworker forgot to check for `null` when they called your function. These are exceptional occurrences; no matter how comprehensively you test, such things will occur at one time or another in production use. A helpful and friendly error page keeps users informed and may help you solve the problem.

Figure 14.2 showed two screenshots of different error pages: one with a formatted stack trace aimed at developers, and one generic error page aimed at end users. Although the end-user page looks nice (ahem), you may want to provide your own styling or add some functionality. Figure 14.3 shows an alternative error page for our cheese store; it looks much better than the standard page from figure 14.2.

Figure 14.3   An alternative error page for the Cheesr store. It provides a link back to the cheese store and an optional form to receive feedback from the user who encountered the problem.

There are various ways to implement your own error page. For example, you can generate a support ticket automatically in your bug-tracker system, ask the user for additional feedback, and provide avenues to let users return to work. Note that the bug-tracking system can go down and not all users are capable of providing meaningful feedback, which we learned the hard way.

User comments: You get what you ask for

In one of our systems, we provided a special error page asking users for comments about what they were doing before the error occurred. This system was relatively new and was experiencing growth while we added more functionality. Our application was going through growing pains, which triggered serious stability problems and resulted in users seeing the error page quite often. During this period we learned that having a fax number on your support page, and locating the fax machine directly under our alarm system's motion sensor, is not recommended. We also learned having a feedback form on your error page is a great way to enlarge your cursing vocabulary.

The error page isn't the only page you can customize. Here's a list of all the pages for which you can (and should) provide custom implementations:

- *Access-denied page*—Shown when a request is denied due to a security constraint
- *Internal-error page*—Shown when an unexpected error occurs
- *Page-expired error page*—Shown for a request in an expired session

We discussed creating pages earlier in this book, and creating an error page is no different from creating a normal page. We therefore leave building error pages as an exercise for you.

Setting an HTTP status code

If you want to set an HTTP status code for your page, such as 404 (not found), you can do so by overriding the page's `setHeaders` method:

```
@Override
protected void setHeaders(WebResponse response) {
    response.getHttpServletResponse().setStatus(
        HttpServletResponse.SC_NOT_FOUND);
    super.setHeaders(response);
}
```

Alternatively, you can throw an `AbortWithWebErrorCodeException` and provide it with the appropriate error code and an optional message.

Instead, you'll learn how to configure Wicket to use your custom page instead of the default one.

SETTING CUSTOM ERROR PAGES

The three custom error pages can be set in the init method of your Application using the application settings. Here's an example:

```
@Override
protected void init() {
    IApplicationSettings settings = getApplicationSettings();
    settings.setAccessDeniedPage(CheesrAccessDeniedPage.class);
    settings.setPageExpiredErrorPage(CheesrPageExpiredErrorPage.class);
    settings.setInternalErrorPage(CheesrInternalErrorPage.class);
}
```

In our Cheesr application, we set the three error pages to our custom pages in the init method. These settings tell Wicket to show users our customized, friendlier error pages.

The internal error page is mostly meant for exceptions you don't expect; it's a one-size-fits-all solution. But sometimes you can expect exceptions—for instance, a remote service that is temporarily unavailable. Normally, you should handle such exceptions locally by retrying, redirecting to another page, or using Wicket's feedback mechanism to notify the user of the failure. You can also let the request cycle catch the exception and respond with a different error page for a specific error.

RESPONDING WITH DIFFERENT ERROR PAGES FOR SPECIFIC ERRORS

The settings we described don't provide a way to act on a particular exception. Fortunately, the request cycle gives you that ability. The next example shows a custom request cycle that acts on a particular exception and uses the defaults for all other exceptions:

```
public class CheesrRequestCycle extends WebRequestCycle {
    public CheesrRequestCycle(WebApplication application,
                              WebRequest request, Response response) {
        super(application, request, response);
    }

    @Override
    public Page onRuntimeException(Page page, RuntimeException e) {
        Throwable cause = e;
        if(cause instanceof WicketRuntimeException)
            cause = cause.getCause();                          Get
        if(cause instanceof InvocationTargetException)         cause
            cause = cause.getCause();

        if (cause instanceof OutOfCheeseException) {
            return new CheesrErrorPage();
        }
        return super.onRuntimeException(page, e);
    }
}
```

This request cycle's onRuntimeException is called when an uncaught exception occurs during request processing. The request cycle provides the page on which the error occurred and the caught exception. The caught exception is wrapped in a WicketRuntimeException, and its cause is the exception that occurred. If the exception occurs in an event handler (for example, onClick or onSubmit), the exception is wrapped in an

`InvocationTargetException`. To get at the root exception, we need to traverse that tree before we can decide how to handle the exception. Our example defaults to the usual behavior when the exception isn't `OutOfCheeseException`.

In this section, you've learned how to configure your application so it runs optimally for production. You learned how to provide users with meaningful error pages and possibly get valuable comments from them. Now it's time to take the plunge and start making a profit. Before you fire up your servers and harvest your fortune, we'll look at how you can ensure your servers are healthy.

14.4   Knowing what is happening in your application

Once your application is running on your server and delivering pages to visitors, you need to ensure that the application keeps running. This means monitoring the application and, when things go wrong, figuring out what happened and how to fix it.

Being able to retrace a user's session and follow the requests until the point of failure is invaluable. The request logger provides this information. But you don't just want to react to failures—if possible, you want to prevent them by tuning or modifying parameters. Wicket's JMX support allows you to monitor and tweak runtime settings. Let's start with the logger.

14.4.1   Logging requests with RequestLogger

A user just called: the application showed our carefully crafted custom error page, and the user dialed our support number. We wrote down the time the error page was shown, what the user tried to achieve, and the user's email address to get back in touch when the problem is solved or if we need more information.

We fire up a terminal window, log on to the production server, and go to the directory where the log files are written. We open the application's log file and go to the time of the error. Sure enough: a `null` pointer exception occurred. We open the offending line in our IDE and see the problem: there is no `null` check in place. Before we adjust the code, we need to make sure we can reproduce the problem in our development environment. We can then apply a fix and see if that solves the problem.

To trace the user's steps, we open the HTTP logs on our server and try to find out what the user clicked. This is what the logs shows:

```
14:00:18 192.0.2.10 "POST /vocus/app?wicket:interface=:4:lijst::IBehavi
14:00:19 192.0.2.50 "GET /vocus/app/resources/wicket.ajax.AbstractDefau
14:00:19 192.0.2.120 "GET /vocus/app?wicket:interface=:12:medewerkers:1
14:00:20 192.0.2.126 "POST /vocus/app?wicket:interface=:1084:filterform
```

The log includes a lot of information but not much that is particularly useful. We don't know which request belongs to the user (the HTTP server is oblivious to the session); even if we logged the session identifier, we wouldn't know which one was the user's. And the URLs in the log are mostly like the following:

```
POST /vocus/app?wicket:interface=:1084:filterform::IFormSubmitListener
GET /vocus/app?wicket:interface=:1084::
```

With this information, we can't determine which page is involved in the request, and it's hard to find out what went on. Fortunately, Wicket provides a special logging facility that enables us to log the information we need: the request logger. Let's first look at what the request logger provides. The following log line (it's all logged in one line) comes from the same production system:

```
14:00:19 time=101,
    event=Interface[
        target:DefaultMenuLink(menu:personalia:dropitems:relatiesLink),
        page: nl.topicus.vocus.web.gui.student.ToonPersonaliaPage(4),
        interface: ILinkListener.onLinkClicked],
    response=PageRequest[
        nl.topicus.vocus.web.gui.student.ToonLeerlingRelatiesPage(6)],
    sessioninfo=[
        sessionId=D574D35FF49C047EF4F290FE59EB7DA4,
        clientInfo=ClientProperties: {
            remoteAddress=192.0.2.50,
            browserVersionMajor=7,
            browserInternetExplorer=true},
        organization=Vocus Demo School,
        username=Demo User],
    sessionsize=-1,
    sessionstart=Fri Dec 14 13:59:14 CET 2007,
    requests=14,
    totaltime=3314,
    activerequests=2,
    maxmem=2390M,
    total=2390M,
    used=1760M
```

This log also contains a lot of information: the time of the request, the duration of the request (101 milliseconds), and what triggered the request. Apparently, this request was a click on a link in a menu with the component path `menu:personalia:dropitems:relatiesLink`; the menu is part of `ToonPersonaliaPage`. The response target is also logged (fortunately, because exceptions also occur during rendering!); in this case, the application renders `ToonLeerlingRelatiesPage`.

The request logger also keeps track of the active sessions and keeps information about the session in a special store. The logger records the session ID, the start time of the session, the number of requests for this particular user, and the total amount of server time used in processing. Recording the session size is optional: it uses serialization to calculate the size of the session, so it can be an expensive metric to track. In our example, the user has fired 14 requests to our server, which took a total of 3.3 seconds on the server.

The request logger provides a way to add application-specific information to the log: in this example, we added client info and the organization and username. This lets us track the requests performed during a session and play back the events in our development environment.

ENABLING THE REQUEST LOGGER IN YOUR APPLICATION

Now that you know what the request logger can do for you, let's discuss how to enable it. The next snippet shows how to do so:

```
Application.get().getRequestLoggerSettings()
                        .setRequestLoggerEnabled(true)
```

You can enable it during application startup or toggle it using a link or check-box component in an administration page.

The next step is to configure the logger. By default, it keeps track of the last 2,000 requests for programmatic access. You can show the last X requests in an admin interface, or calculate the throughput of your server based on this information. You can change the number of stored requests in the `RequestLogger` settings:

```
Application.get().getRequestLoggerSettings().setRequestsWindowSize(10);
```

Next, you need to ensure that the request logger is able to write its information to a log file. This is done through your application's log configuration—which is specific to the logging facility you use. Because log4j is popular, we'll show an example configuration from our log4j.properties file to enable the request logger:

```
log4j.rootLogger=INFO,Stdout
log4j.category.org.apache.wicket.protocol.http.RequestLogger=INFO
log4j.appender.Stdout=org.apache.log4j.ConsoleAppender
log4j.appender.Stdout.layout=org.apache.log4j.PatternLayout
log4j.appender.Stdout.layout.conversionPattern=%d %-5p - %-26.26c{1} - %m\n
```

Typically, you'll log the request-logger information to a separate daily log file and process it offline. Consult your logging facility's manual for the specific configuration.

If you want to log specific information pertaining to your application, you need to let your session implement the `ISessionLogInfo` interface. This interface requires the one to be implemented: `getSessionInfo`. This method can return any object. The request logger logs the `toString` value of this object. The following example shows how to return the name of the user associated with the session:

```
public class MySession extends WebSession implements ISessionLogInfo {
    private User user;

    public MySession(Request request) {
    }

    public Object getSessionInfo() {
        return "user=" + (user == null ? "n/a" : user.getFullname());
    }
    public void setUser(User user) {
        this.user = user;
    }
    public User getUser() {
        return user;
    }
}
```

Finally, you can get programmatic access to the request logger to show this data in an administration console for your application. The following example shows how to gain access to the live sessions recorded by the request logger:

```
IRequestLogger requestLogger = Application.get().getRequestLogger();
List<SessionData> sessions = requestLogger == null ?
            Collections.EMPTY_LIST
            : Arrays.asList(requestLogger.getLiveSessions());
for(Session session : sessions) {
    System.out.println("Session id: " + session.getSessionId());
}
```

This example lists the currently active session IDs. Much more information is at your disposal, and we encourage you to investigate the API.

The request logger has given us valuable insight into the workings of our applications and is an invaluable debugging tool when a nasty bug needs solving. Although having log files helps you go back in history, you may need to take more immediate action and modify a parameter in a running application.

14.4.2 *Using JMX to work under the hood while driving*

We've run our application in deployment mode, enabled the request logger, had all our unit tests pass, and implemented a nice URL scheme for search engines to explore. The server is humming in the rack, and our users are being served. Then, someone from the marketing department calls and tells us about a few spelling errors on the pages. We don't panic; we fire up a terminal, log on to the production server, and fix the markup files. We refresh the offending page in our browser and … nothing changes.

Running an application in deployment mode has some advantages, and one of them is that the markup files are cached and Wicket doesn't scan for changes to save precious CPU cycles and IO bandwidth. But now this feature is getting in the way of us updating our site. One way of forcing Wicket to reload the markup is to restart the application. This is usually a bad idea for production servers. Keeping a minor change until the next service window is just as bad. If only there were a way to clear the markup cache.

Java Management Extensions (JMX) provide a way to look inside a running server and adjust parameters on the fly. Wicket provides a special module that you can include in your project and that exposes some of Wicket's internals using *Managed Beans* (MBeans). Using Java's JConsole or your application server's management console, you can peek at Wicket's settings and modify the values. In this section, we'll look at configuring your application to expose the application's configuration through JMX and using JConsole to clear the cache, forcing Wicket to reload the markup once and fix the spelling errors.

ENABLING JMX IN YOUR APPLICATION

The first step is to add the wicket-jmx jar to your project's classpath and have it packaged in the war file. If you're running Jetty as your servlet container, you'll need to enable the management facilities by adding the `jetty-management` dependency to the project. Instructions for other containers and application servers should be available in their respective documentation.

When you're running the embedded Jetty server, you still need to perform two steps before you can fire up JConsole. First, add the lines in listing 14.4 to the `Start` class's `main` method before starting the servlet container.

Listing 14.4   Enabling JMX in an embedded Jetty container

```
public static void main(String[] args) throws Exception {
    Server server = new Server();
    SocketConnector connector = new SocketConnector();

    connector.setMaxIdleTime(1000 * 60 * 60);      Set timeout options to
    connector.setSoLingerTime(-1);                 make debugging easier
    connector.setPort(8080);
    server.setConnectors(new Connector[] { connector });

    WebAppContext bb = new WebAppContext();
    bb.setServer(server);
    bb.setContextPath("/");
    bb.setWar("src/main/webapp");

    MBeanServer mBeanServer=ManagementFactory.getPlatformMBeanServer();
    MBeanContainer mBeanContainer = new MBeanContainer(mBeanServer);
    server.getContainer().addEventListener(mBeanContainer);
    mBeanContainer.start();                                      Start JMX
                                                                 server  ❶
    server.addHandler(bb);

    try {
        System.out.println(
                    "STARTING JETTY SERVER, PRESS ANY KEY TO STOP");
        server.start();
        while (System.in.available() == 0) {
            Thread.sleep(5000);
        }
        server.stop();
        server.join();
    } catch (Exception e) {
        e.printStackTrace();
        System.exit(100);
    }
}
```

If you use Wicket's quickstart project, all you need to do is uncomment these four lines ❶ because they're already available. These lines register Jetty's management bean container with Java's bean server. The remainder of the example starts the servlet container and waits for a keypress to stop the server.

As a final step before you can connect JConsole, add the following system property to the Java command line used to start your server (see your IDE or server startup script for more information about how to achieve this):

```
-Dcom.sun.management.jmxremote
```

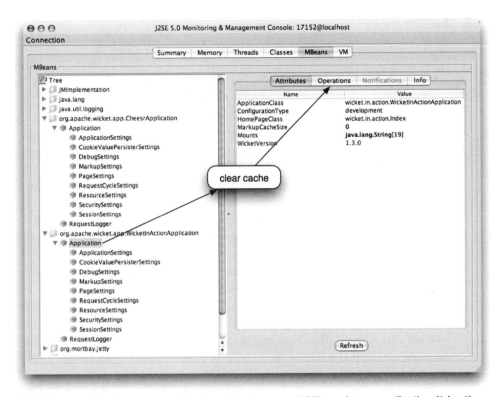

Figure 14.4 Java's JConsole provides access to the exposed MBeans in your application. Using these MBeans, you can modify the application and request logger settings. The MBeans also provide the ability to stop and start the request logger and to clear the markup cache.

This property configures Java to expose all the registered management beans to a console. Firing up JConsole gives you access to the Wicket management beans. Figure 14.4 shows the beans that are available for the examples.

Now, if you want to clear the markup cache, you need to navigate in your management console to the `Application` MBean and go to the Operations tab. There you'll find a button to clear the markup cache, forcing Wicket to reload its markup files.

EXPOSING YOUR OWN CONFIGURATION AND PARAMETERS THROUGH JMX

Creating your own MBeans isn't difficult. It can be beneficial from an operations point of view to expose settings such as MBeans and have the application's and all other services' information available in one management console. Creating MBeans is beyond the scope of this book, but fortunately the excellent book *JMX in Action* (Manning: Benjamin Sullins and Mark Whipple, 2002) is at your disposal to learn more about this topic.

Getting a view of the internals of your application while it's running is helpful. Wicket isn't the only product that provides the ability to view and modify settings using JMX. For example, Hibernate and Ehcache provide MBeans to peek under the hood, so enabling JMX will allow you to control much of your application while driving.

14.5   *Summary*

All the tools and methods we described in this chapter will help you launch a successful product. Using the Wicket tester, you can ensure that your code works correctly before you show it to customers. By mounting your pages using the right URL encoding, you'll help visitors navigate quickly to the page they need. Having the correct URL encoding also enables search engines to index your site and provide meaningful links to your products. We looked at configuring applications to optimize developer productivity and with a flick of a switch make the application run in production mode.

Custom error pages ensure that the inevitable errors fit into your site's design and don't stand out like the default Wicket error page. When errors occur, having diagnostic tools at your disposal is indispensable. The request logger provides a way to keep track of what users do with your application and lets you play back what a user did to trigger a bug. With Wicket's JMX support, you can look at and modify operational parameters to ensure a healthy running application.

With this chapter, we've reached the end of this book. Over the course of these pages, you've learned how to build applications using Wicket components, validate user input, create custom components, and build secure applications for a global audience.

The most important advice we want to give you is the following: when you find yourself lost while building an application, remember that you're working with *just Java and HTML*. If you find something that Wicket doesn't provide out of the box, it's not hard to extend a component, behavior, or model that provides a good starting point on which to build your customization. If you still have problems, consult this book and the accompanying examples project, or other online resources such as the Wicket examples, the wiki, or the user mailing list. You'll find a welcoming community eager to provide help and support.

Now, put down this book and start working on your killer Wicket application: this is the final item we leave as an exercise for you.

index

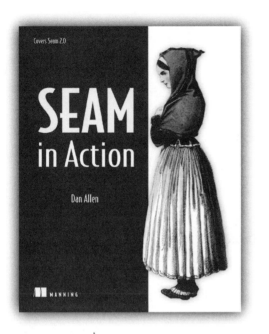

Seam in Action

by Dan Allen

ISBN: 1-933988-40-1
550 pages
$44.99
September 2008

Struts 2 in Action

by Donald Brown, Chad Michael Davis,
   and Scott Stanlick

ISBN: 1-933988-07-X
424 pages
$44.99
May 2008

For ordering information go to www.manning.com

MORE TITLES FROM MANNING

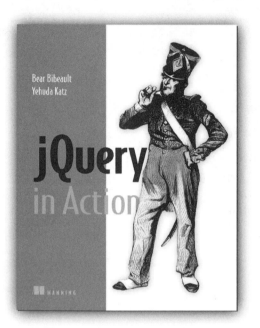

JQuery in Action
by Bear Bibeault and Yehuda Katz

> ISBN: 1-933988-35-5
> 376 pages
> $39.99
> February 2008

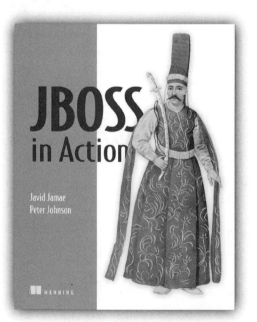

JBoss in Action
Configuring the JBoss Application Server
by Javid Jamae and Peter Johnson

> ISBN: 1-933988-02-9
> 476 pages
> $49.99
> September 2008

For ordering information go to www.manning.com